TEXTS AND STUDIES

CONTRIBUTIONS TO

BIBLICAL AND PATRISTIC LITERATURE

EDITED BY

J. ARMITAGE ROBINSON D.D.

HON. PH.D. GÖTTINGEN HON. D.D. HALLE

HON. FELLOW OF CHRIST'S COLLEGE

DEAN OF WESTMINSTER

VOL. VII.

No. 4. A STUDY OF AMBROSIASTER

A STUDY OF AMBROSIASTER

BY

ALEXANDER SOUTER B.A.

YATES PROFESSOR OF NEW TESTAMENT GREEK AND EXEGESIS
MANSFIELD COLLEGE OXFORD
FORMERLY SCHOLAR OF GONVILLE AND CAIUS COLLEGE CAMBRIDGE
LATE LECTURER IN LATIN AND LECTURER IN PALAEOGRAPHY
UNIVERSITY OF ABERDEEN

Wipf & Stock
PUBLISHERS
Eugene, Oregon

Wipf and Stock Publishers
199 W 8th Ave, Suite 3
Eugene, OR 97401

A Study of Ambrosiaster
By Souter, Alexander
ISBN: 1-59244-900-X
Publication date 9/29/2004
Previously published by Cambridge, 1905

VIRO · REVERENDO

HENRICO · BREWER · S · I ·

CVIVS · LIBERALITATI · BENEFICIIS · QVE
PLVRIMVM · DEBET
HIC · LIBELLVS
GRATO · ANIMO
D · D · D
SCRIPTOR

PREFACE.

THE present work was undertaken in a rash moment, when the completion of a year's study of the language of Ambrosiaster's commentaries on St Paul's Epistles coincided with the publication by Dom Morin of the earlier of his two suggestions as to the author's identity. It has since been finished amid interruptions of various kinds. During nearly the whole of the period of composition the author's leisure has been scanty. He was, besides, resident in Scotland, where no scholar's library exists and private libraries rarely contain anything patristic: the kindness of friends, which he tried not to abuse, and occasional brief visits to Cambridge, had to make up for this.

Thanks to the liberality of the Managers of the Craven and Hort Funds at Cambridge, the Imperial Vienna Academy of Sciences, and Father Brewer, his knowledge of manuscript sources has been greatly increased during the progress of the work.

The shortcomings, for which those difficulties, joined to inexperience, are responsible, may be forgiven for the sake of such contributions to knowledge as the book contains: the lists of manuscripts and the use made of them, the study of the Biblical text, now for the first time really attempted, the study of the author's language, and new arguments as to his date.

The work was decidedly worth attempting. The value of our author's writings is recognised by the highest authorities. It may suffice to quote the opinion of Harnack: 'We ought to call him the great unknown; for what Western expositor of the early period or the Middle Ages is his equal?' Again: 'The "Quaestiones" pass under the name of Augustine, the commentary under that of Ambrose. Both works are admirable in their kind, and perhaps the most distinguished product of the Latin Church in the period between Cyprian and Jerome.'

The real reason why the author has been neglected is the uncertainty as to his identity. I trust the present attempt to make the study of his works easier will cause more attention to be paid to them in future.

The book, such as it is, the work of a philologist, not a theologian, could never have appeared but for the kindness of various friends at home and abroad. Other contributors to the series in which it has the honour to appear, have given me ungrudging help; the Editor, who has tended it carefully from the beginning; Dr A. E. Burn, the reading of whose article in the *Expositor* first gave me the resolution to attempt the task; Mr F. C. Burkitt, and Dr M. R. James. The librarians and officials of all libraries I have visited have earned my gratitude: they are named in a more fitting place. How much the book owes to the inspiration of Professors W. M. Ramsay, John E. B. Mayor, and Eduard von Wölfflin, and in its later stages to the Oxford patristic school, with its *doyen* Dr Sanday, and contact with the priceless treasures of the Bodleian Library, it would be impossible to estimate. But perhaps the brightest memories of the progress of the work are those associated with Father Brewer, to whose unspeakable kindness the book owes so much, memories of converse in the Bollandist Library in Brussels and by the banks of the Bacchiglione, as the sun was setting behind the Euganean hills.

It is a pleasure to acknowledge help given me by Mr W. B. Anderson, of the University of Manchester, and in the reading of the proofs by my wife. Other obligations are acknowledged in detail throughout the book[1].

THE AUTHOR.

OXFORD.
January 15*th*, 1905.

[1] Chapter III. of the present work, along with the last three articles mentioned on p. xi, has just been awarded the degree of D.Litt. of the University of Aberdeen.

CONTENTS.

BIBLIOGRAPHY OF RECENT LITERATURE[1].

A. Harnack, *Der pseudoaugustinische Traktat Contra Novatianum*, in *Abhandlungen Alexander von Oettingen zum siebenzigsten Geburtstag gewidmet von Freunden und Schülern* (Munchen: Beck, 1898), pp. 54–93.

G. Morin, *L'Ambrosiaster et le Juif Converti Isaac, Contemporain du Pape Damase* (*Revue d'Histoire et de Littérature Religieuses*, IV (1899) pp. 97–121 (=1–25)).

Th. Zahn, *Der "Ambrosiaster" und der Proselyt Isaak* (*Theologisches Literaturblatt*, XX (1899) pp. 313–317).

A. E. Burn, *The Ambrosiaster and Isaac the Converted Jew* (*Expositor*, 1899 II pp. 368–375).

H. Zimmer, *Pelagius in Irland: Texte und Untersuchungen zur patristischen Litteratur* (Berlin: Weidmann, 1901), pp. 117–120.

A. Souter, *An Interpolation in 'Ambrosiaster'* (*The Expository Times*, XIII (1901—1902) pp. 380–381).

A. Souter, *'Emmaus' mistaken for a Person* (*The Expository Times*, XIII (1901—1902) pp. 429–430).

A. Souter, *The Genuine Prologue to Ambrosiaster on 2 Corinthians* (*The Journal of Theological Studies*, IV (1902—1903) pp. 89–92).

C. H. Turner, *Pelagius' Commentary on the Pauline Epistles and its History* (ibid., pp. 132–141).

H. S. Sedlmayer, *Der Tractatus Contra Arianos in der Wiener Hilarius-Handschrift, mit einem Nachwort von Dom Germain Morin* (*Sitzungsberichte der Kais. Akademie der Wissenschaften in Wien*, Phil.-Hist. Kl. Band CXLVI (ii), Wien, 1903, 21 pp.).

G. Morin, *Hilarius L'Ambrosiaster* (*Revue Bénédictine*, XX (1903) pp. 113–131).

A. Souter, *A New View about Ambrosiaster* (*Expositor*, 1903 I pp. 442–455).

F. Cumont, *La Polemique de l'Ambrosiaster contre les Paiens* (*Revue d'Histoire et de Littérature Religieuses*, VIII (1903) pp. 417–440).

A. Souter, *Reasons for Regarding Hilarius (Ambrosiaster) as the Author of the Mercati-Turner Anecdoton* (*The Journal of Theological Studies*, V (1903—1904) pp. 608–621).

A. Souter, *An Unknown Fragment of the Pseudo-Augustinian Quaestiones Veteris et Novi Testamenti* (*The Journal of Theological Studies*, VI (1904—1905) pp. 61–66).

A. Souter, *De codicibus manuscriptis Augustini quae feruntur quaestionum Veteris et Novi Testamenti* CXXVII (*Sitzungsberichte der Kais. Akademie der Wissenschaften in Wien*, Phil.-Hist. Kl. Band CXLIX (i), Wien, 1905, 24 pp.).

[1] For older work on Ambrosiaster, see Arnold's article *Ambrosiaster* in Herzog-Hauck's *Real-Encyclopädie*, and Schanz's *Geschichte der römischen Litteratur* IV (1904) p. 324 ff.

ABBREVIATIONS.

pr =prohoemium.	pm=post medium.
ppr=post prohoemium.	aex=ante exitum.
am =ante medium.	ex =exitus.
m =medium.	

ADDENDA.

p. 16, add, after no. 36,

37. Verona, Capitular Library LXXV, s. IX (Gal. Eph. Phil., 1, 2 Thess., Col., Tit. 1, 2 Tim. Philem.)

38. Paris, Bibliothèque Nationale, lat. 1761, s. IX (Rom.)

39. Salzburg, Monastery of St Peter. Of this MS I know neither the number, date, nor contents.

p. 19, add, after no. 15,

15*. Madrid, Biblioteca Nacional, A 61, s. XIV.

p. 71, *porro autem* occurs also in Aug. ep. 200, 3.

p. 72, n. 2, *itaque ergo* occurs also in Rom. xiv 18 (D).

p. 73, l. 9. I find the suggested alteration in the Padua MS.

p. 105. Add to the examples of *emorior* qu. 114 § 17.

p. 124. On *Paulianus* and other terms meaning 'a follower of Paul *of Samosata*,' see C. H. Turner, *Ecclesiae Occidentalis Monumenta Iuris Antiquissima*, Fasc. i, p. 248.

p. 148, l. 19. Other words which might have been added are *incommutabilis*, *adflictio*, *auersio*, *uerax*, *tumesco*, *uentilatio*, *uentilo*, *congratulor*, *congruenter*, *coniugalis*, *consequens*, *consideratio*, *aduersitas*. These are all favourites with Aug.

p. 154. Ps. xxiii 7 was thus read by Firmicus Maternus and the *Altercatio Simonis Iudaei et Theophili Christiani* also. Halm ought to have followed the sole MS in c. 24 § 4 (p. 115, 13) of Firmicus, and Bratke ought to have put the reading of two of his MSS in the text of the *Altercatio* (p. 41, 7 of his edition). So also in Cypr. *Test.*

p. 178, l. 13. Compare also 403 D (in Eph. iii 8).

p. 189, last line. The quotation in the Irish *Liber Hymnorum* (cf. p. 164) is from the earlier edition of the *Quaestiones*, and proves that that edition was known in Ireland in the eleventh century. This quotation also has *corripitur*.

p. 197. Since I wrote the above, it has become clear to me that the order in which the Pauline epistles appear in Ambrosiaster's MSS was a widespread Old-Latin order. Mr C. H. Turner has shown (*Journal of Theological Studies* VI (1905) p. 262) that Titus followed Colossians in Cyprian's *codex* of the epistles. The true significance of the appearance of this order in Primasius and Sedulius Scottus is that it was the order in their common source, Pelagius. No doubt this is also the explanation of the order in the Book of Armagh and the *codex Paulinus Wirziburgensis* (*cf.* Zimmer, *Pelagius in Ireland* p. 10).

INTRODUCTION.

§ 1. *The scope of the Present Work and the History of the Controversy.*

The present work is concerned with a series of commentaries (called in most MSS *tractatus*) on thirteen epistles of Saint Paul, which were wrongly attributed to S. Ambrose[1] until about the year 1600, and, since that time, have passed under the rather fanciful name of 'Ambrosiaster.' The commentary is clear and generally brief; it shows considerable mental acuteness and even historical insight. Its praises have been sung by the late Bishop Lightfoot[2], by Dr Jülicher[3], who styles it the best commentary on S. Paul's epistles previous to the 16th century, and by others. The commentary has a further value from the fact that the writer comments, not on the Vulgate, but on a pre-Hieronymian version, which is cited throughout the work. A new interest has been given to this commentary by suggestions as to its authorship which have been recently propounded by Dom G. Morin[4].

The present study consists of two parts. The first is a new and elaborate argument in behalf of the view that the author of the commentaries is also the author of the Pseudo-Augustinian 'Quaestiones Veteris et Noui Testamenti,' a series of short essays

[1] But see chap. v.

[2] *Comm. on Ep. Gal.* p. 232.

[3] Pauly-Wissowa's *Real-Encyclopädie* i³ (1894) *s.v.* Ambrosiaster.

[4] 'L'Ambrosiaster et Le Juif Converti Isaac,' in *Rev. d'Hist. et de Litt. Religieuses*, t. iv (1899) no. 2, pp. 97–121; see also Zahn, *Theologisches Literaturbl.*, Juli 7, 1899 (col. 313–317), and Rev. A. E. Burn, *Expositor* 1899 ii 368 ff. For Morin's second view, see *Revue Bénédictine*, xx (1903) 113–131.

on difficult passages of the Old and New Testaments and longer tracts on other subjects, some of which are addresses or sermons. The view that the commentaries and *Quaestiones* are from the same hand is no new one. It is suggested and reasons are given in support of it in the old editions[1]. Langen has supported it at some length, and Harnack[2], Jülicher[3] and others state it as a fact categorically. Marold[4], however, unconvinced by Langen[5], wrote against the common authorship; and, though Dom Morin[6] has proved the falsity of some of his statements, it is desirable to give a proof which may suffice to settle the question. Recent collations of old MSS of both works have revealed many instances of identity in language which could not be learned from the printed texts, a testimony which is all the more valuable, as the common authorship was quite unsuspected till after the invention of printing. The Vienna Academy has undertaken to publish a new edition of both works in the *Corpus Scriptorum Ecclesiasticorum Latinorum*, the commentaries to be edited by Father Brewer[7], S.J., the *Quaestiones* by the present writer.

The second part of this study is an answer to the question: Who is the author of these works? The answer adopted is the later view of Dom Morin, which entirely satisfies the conditions of the problem; in this his former suggestion, widely supported as it was[8], failed. A chapter is added on the biblical text of 'Ambrosiaster.'

First, however, in a study of this kind it is desirable to gather together the names of the various men to whom these works have been credited, and here I am indebted to Dr Joseph Langen, Old Catholic Professor of Bonn, who in a dissertation[9] published at

[1] See e.g. the Benedictine *Augustine*, t. III 2 Append. 35 36 (or Migne *P.L.* XXXV 2207 2208).

[2] *History of Dogma* (Eng. trans.) V 38, n. 4.

[3] Pauly-Wissowa, *s.v.* Ambrosiaster.

[4] *Zeitschr. f. wissenschaftl. Theol.* XXVII (1883) 441 ff.

[5] Diss. Bonn. 1880, p. 20 ff.

[6] Especially p. 98 n. 3 of first article.

[7] Of the Stella Matutina, Feldkirch.

[8] *Theol. Jahresb.* XIX (1900) 217: *Journ. of Theol. Studies* I (1899) pp. 154–156.

[9] Entitled 'De Commentariorum in epistulas Paulinas qui Ambrosii et Quaestionum biblicarum quae Augustini nomine feruntur scriptore dissertatio.' His views are epitomised in his later 'Geschichte der Römischen Kirche bis zum Pontifikate Leo's I' (Bonn 1881) p. 599 ff.

Bonn in 1880 collected various conjectures as to the authorship. The commentaries are first quoted by S. Augustine about the year 420, who writes (*c. duas epist. Pelag.* 4. 4. 7): 'nam et sic sanctus Hilarius intellexit quod scriptum est, *in quo omnes peccauerunt*[1]: ait enim: "*in quo*, id est in Adam, *omnes peccauerunt.*" Deinde addidit: "manifestum in Adam omnes peccasse quasi in massa: ipse enim per peccatum corruptus, omnes quos genuit nati sunt sub peccato." Haec scribens Hilarius sine ambiguitate commonuit quo modo intellegendum esset *in quo omnes peccauerunt.*' The words here quoted appear in the commentaries of 'Ambrosiaster' at Rom. v 12. Marold[2], with astonishing recklessness, denies that S. Augustine ever takes anything else from the commentaries. About no author is it more dangerous to make general statements than about S. Augustine. The following instance ought to have been mentioned by Marold, though the borrowing is certainly on the part of 'Ambrosiaster,' or rather of his editors[3], as the passage is wanting in all MSS of which I have any knowledge[4].

Ambrst., 1 Cor. vi 18.	Aug. serm. 162. 2 in Eugippius (on the same words).
Omne peccatum quodcumque fecerit homo, extra corpus est. Quia cetera peccata etsi per corpus generantur, non tamen animam ita carnali concupiscentia faciunt obstrictam et obnoxiam, quemadmodum commisceri facit animam cum ipso corpore usus libidinis, agens in opere carnalis fornicationis; quia in tantum agglutinatur anima corpori, ut in ipso momento nihil aliud cogitare homini liceat aut intendere, quia ipsam mentem captivam subdit ipsa submersio et absorbitio libidinis et concupis-	Videtur enim beatus apostolus, in quo loquebatur Christus, aut exaggerare voluisse fornicationis malum super cetera omnia peccata, quae etsi per corpus committantur, non tamen animum humanum concupiscentiae carnali ita efficiunt obstrictum et obnoxium, quemadmodum in solo opere fornicationis corporalis commisceri facit animum vis ingens libidinis cum ipso corpore, et unum cum ipso quodam modo adglutinari et deuinctum esse; in tantum ut nihil aliud ipso momento et experi-

[1] Scriptural quotations are italicised.

[2] Marold, *op. cit.* p. 459: 'das Citat selbst bleibt darum höchst auffallend, da Augustin sonst nichts aus dem Commentar verwendet.'

[3] See *Expository Times* XIII (1902) 380 f.

[4] Or the Benedictines; see their note.

Ambrst., 1 Cor. vi. 18.	Aug. serm. 162. 2. in Eugippius (on the same words).
centiae carnalis. Unde subditur: *Qui autem fornicatur* cet.	mento huius tam magni flagitii cogitare homini liceat aut intendere, nisi quod sibimet addicit mentem, quam captivam subdit ipsa submersio et quodam modo absorbitio libidinis et concupiscentiae carnalis, ut hoc esse uideatur quod dictum est: *Qui autem fornicatur* cet.

It is possible, or rather probable, that Cassiodorus, about a century and a half later, alludes to our commentaries as a work which he had not been able to find, in his *De Instit. Diuin. Litter.* c. 8 (Migne *P.L.* LXX 1120 C D). His words are: 'dicitur etiam et beatum Ambrosium subnotatum codicem epistularum omnium sancti Pauli reliquisse, suauissima expositione completum; quem tamen adhuc inuenire non potui, sed diligenti cura perquiro.' Amalarius (c. 820—Migne, *P.L.* XCIX), Haymo (†853—Migne CXIII—CXVIII), Prudentius (†861—Migne CXV), Hincmar (†882—Migne CXXV—CXXVI)[1] used the commentaries as the work of Ambrose. So do the medieval 'doctors,' including Lanfranc, Ivo Carnutensis, Gratian, and Peter Lombard. Erasmus, in the year 1527, was the first to suspect the accuracy of this ascription; and thereafter speculation became rife as to the real author. At the dawning of modern scholarship, as it is still more clearly at the present time, Ambrosian authorship was seen to be an impossibility. Some guessed that the work was a cento made from S. Jerome and S. Chrysostom[2] by some unknown person; others believed it to be by Julian of Aeclanum or some other Pelagian[3]; others by Remigius[4], others by Tyconius[5], the author of the 'Rules,' others by S. Hilary of Poitiers, others by Hilary of

[1] Langen, Diss. p. 4. I add the numbers of Migne's volumes, in which the works of each are contained.

[2] Cf. the 'admonitio' in Migne XVII 41 42. This view was refuted by the Benedictines. One can only wonder at its impertinence.

[3] This view is confuted by Petavius, Garnerius, and Natalis Alexander.

[4] Maldonatus' view. How could the passage of Aug. escape him? asks Langen.

[5] But Tyconius is African, while Ambrst. is Italian, to say nothing of difference of style.

Pavia[1], others by Hilary of Syracuse[2]; very many have attributed the work to Hilarius[3], a deacon of Rome. The statement of S. Augustine, who undoubtedly meant S. Hilary of Poitiers as the author of the quotation he makes, is responsible for the last four views. S. Hilary of Poitiers is unhesitatingly to be rejected owing to known differences of style[4]. Most of the other names are idle conjectures, carelessly thrown out before the days of exact method in the study of literature and history. Langen himself put forward a view that Faustinus, a Roman presbyter, is the author. His proof[5], built up chiefly from a comparison of the language of both works with that of the *De Trinitate* and other writings of Faustinus[6], is so far from being convincing that it certainly shows Faustinian authorship to be impossible. This conjecture has had the fate of the others. Dr Marold[7] and Dom Morin[8], for example, explicitly reject it. The recent view, that Isaac, a converted Jew, who was concerned in the disturbances at the election of Pope Damasus and afterwards relapsed to Judaism, wrote the commentaries and the *Quaestiones V. et N. Testamenti*, is due to Dom Germain Morin, O.S.B., of the Abbaye, Maredsous, who by his successful researches and independent criticism has shown himself a worthy follower of his Benedictine predecessors. Dr Zahn[9] and Mr A. E. Burn[10] both called for a fuller treatment of the subject. This I have endeavoured to supply, as the special study I had devoted to the language of the commentary[11] seemed to invite me to the task. I can heartily support Dom Morin's second suggestion, that Hilary, the Layman, was the author.

1 So thought Petavius and Ceillier.

2 Not mentioned by Langen, but in Morin, p. 4.

3 See Benedictine Pref. to Ps.-Aug. *Quaest.* (M. xxxv 2207 2208), or that to the commentaries (M. xvii 43). Langen refutes (p. 5).

4 See e.g. *Tract. s. Psalmos*, in Vienna *Corpus*, xxii.

5 Diss. pp. 33–41. He says (p. 41) that his view 'nullis argumentis refutari potest.'

6 Printed, e.g. in Migne, *P.L.* xiii.

7 *Zeitschr. f. wissensch. Theol.* xxvii 462–3, especially 464 ff.

8 *Op. cit.* p. 4.

9 *Theol. Literaturbl.*, xx nr. 27 (7 Juli, 1899) 316: 'ein Anderer würde aus dem, was Morin kurz und schlagend ausführt, ein dickes Buch machen, und das könnte ein interessantes Buch werden.'

10 *Expositor* 1899 ii (Nov.)

11 For the new *Thesaurus Linguae Latinae* (Lipsiae 1900 ff.)

§ 2. *General Character of the Commentary.*

As the commentary[1] of 'Ambrosiaster' has received in modern times much less attention than its excellence deserves, a few words with reference to its general character may be in place here. Even the difficulties of the current text, many of which will have disappeared in the Vienna edition, need not deter readers from giving careful attention to it. The work is in its tone wonderfully in harmony with the critical and objective attitude of present day investigation, and will certainly reward close study.

The commentary (*tractatus*) on each epistle is prefaced by a short argument (*argumentum, prologus*), giving some account of the community or person addressed in it, and of its purpose. The comments are as a rule brief and pointed, and follow immediately on the verse or clause to which they refer. The treatment of the longer epistles is relatively more extended than that of the shorter. There is an exception to this rule, however, in the discussion, for example, of matters connected with church government. The historical importance of such comments as those on Eph. iv 11—12, 1 Tim. iii 12—13, &c., has been fully recognised in Bishop Lightfoot's classical essay on 'The Christian Ministry.'

The work is throughout Roman and practical in tone. Common-sense explanations are the rule. The tone is rather that of the calm dispassionate searcher for truth than of the mystic visionary who seeks to soar to the heights of the Apostle's thought. We have here none of the spiritual insight of an Augustine or a Bengel, but the work of a conscientious writer who seeks in Scripture for plain useful lessons which may serve to elevate the daily lives of his Roman fellow citizens. The author never loses his hold on the ordinary life of the day. The emperor, the magistrates, the laws, etc., ever present to the eyes and minds of his readers, are constantly mentioned in illustration. Yet the work is intended for Christians, and indeed for orthodox Christians.

[1] The MSS call the commentary on each epistle a *tractatus*, or simply *in epist. cet.* As far as I can learn, there is no title in the MSS to cover the entire commentary. The MS of Monte Cassino, in its subscriptions, does not mention the name of Ambrose: thus we find simply 'expl. ad Thess.'

The current heretical errors are from time to time pointed out and stigmatised. Everything written springs from a desire, first, to interpret the Apostle's meaning plainly and naturally, and, secondly, to enforce the lessons he sought to teach. The allegorical method of interpretation, introduced by the Alexandrians and extensively adopted by S. Augustine and others, is almost entirely absent.

The author had pondered much on the historical background of the epistles, and some of his conclusions agree with the latest results of historical criticism. For example, he affirms the original identity of bishop and presbyter[1]. He has a historical mind and recognises the differences of organisation in apostolic times and his own. In speaking of bishops in the early period he says 'adhuc rectores ecclesiis paucis erant in locis' (in Rom. xvi 22). Another indication of his insight is his mentioning from time to time that Jews are referred to, where they do not appear by name in the sacred text. Other examples of this quality in our author may be seen in Arnold's excellent article *Ambrosiaster* in Herzog-Hauck's *Realencyclopädie*.

The commentary seems to be for the most part, if not entirely, original. It would be unsafe to draw this conclusion from the fact that no previous commentators are referred to by name, or even in general terms. Ancient authors, as a rule, were so skilful in interweaving the work of their predecessors with their own, that the 'sutures' are difficult to detect. Moreover, with them the matter was the important thing, the ascription of particular opinions to their authors quite a secondary consideration. But there is an independence and a uniformity about the comments which convey the impression of originality. The author's antagonism to Greek[2] authorities makes it improbable that he used any. Of Latin authorities the only extant commentator on the Pauline epistles prior to 'Ambrosiaster' is C. Marius Victorinus[3],

[1] In Eph. iv 11: See Lightfoot's *Philippians* (ed. 1) p. 97, n. 2; Rainy's *Ancient Catholic Church* (Edinb. 1902) p. 34 ff.

[2] In Rom. v 14 cet.

[3] The Victorinus referred to along with Tertullian and Cyprian (In Rom. v 14) must be the other Victorinus, of Petabio (Pettau). C. Marius Victorinus, since he was flourishing in 353 (Hieron. chron. ad ann. 2370), could not be referred to as one of the 'veteres.'

whose expositions are so different in character that it is unlikely that they were much used by him. We shall probably be right in thinking that the commentary drew but little directly from earlier authors[1].

§ 3. *General Character of the* Quaestiones.

The *Quaestiones Veteris et Noui Testamenti*[2] is in all the older and most of the later MSS a collection of one hundred and twenty-seven documents, varying in length[3] and character, and purporting to be the work of S. Augustine. Several recent MSS offer a larger collection[4], but the additional documents, though certainly by the same author, are relatively unimportant. Five late MSS contain a smaller collection[5]. In the MSS of the first class, called (a) by the Benedictine editor[6], there is a division between XLVII and XLVIII, which are separated from one another by the title '*Questiones Noui Testamenti.*'

Quaestio, in this connexion, means an enquiry[7] or investigation into passages of Scripture which are difficult to understand. The title is a correct description of the majority of the documents, but is not fitly applied to many of the longer tracts which find a place at the end of the collection. The title *Quaestiones* became a common one in religious literature, and the fact that there are among the genuine works of Augustine several containing the word in their title (*De Diversis Quaestionibus LXXXIII liber unus,*

1 It would be an interesting study to compare the comm. of Victorinus, Ambrosiaster, and Jerome. The last speaks contemptuously of Victorinus (Praef. in comm. ad Galat.) and entirely ignores Ambrst. Has he used either, in spite of this? Marold (*op. cit.* p. 439) thinks that Jerome on Gal. i 2 and iii 1 shows acquaintance with our author's notes.

2 The full title in the MSS is :—*Liber Quaestionum Sancti Augustini Veteris et Noui Testamenti numero CXXVII.*

3 The difference in length is best shown by the fact that in the splendid MS of Reichenau the first half ends with the title of qu. 99.

4 See § 5 *infra* for details.

5 In one of these part of the work is attributed to S. Ambrose. See § 5.

6 Pierre Coustant, as Kukula shows (*Sitzungsb. d. Wiener Akad.* CXXI, 5, p. 56, n. 2).

7 Cf. e.g. qu. 97 (col. 2294 42) *solent etiam ipsi de deo patre aliam facere* quaestionem, qu. 95 (col. 2290 26) quaestionis *singula membra curiose inspicere*; more examples in Langen, diss. p. 29.

De Diversis Quaestionibus ad Simplicianum libri duo, De octo Dulcitii Quaestionibus liber unus) may have led to the mistaken ascription, if it was innocent, or may have been expected to hide the fraud, if it was intentional. There is, of course, no mention of our work in the Retractations. Examination of old MSS has already revealed some important facts about still earlier copies, and it is possible that further study will lead to the dating and localisation of the archetype, and help to explain the origin of the title of the work as we have it.

In the case of a work so little read as the *Quaestiones*, some account of the contents is necessary. The manuscripts provide a table of contents at the beginning, which is very different in language from that given in the Benedictine edition, but I do not propose to occupy valuable space by printing it here: the printed list is sufficient for practical purposes. I merely wish to select a few of the titles. The complete table of contents shows in a very striking manner how each age finds its own difficulties in Scripture. Some of the more important *quaestiones* are:—I Quid est deus? II Cur deus mundum fecerit. IIII Quare legem non in primordio dedit? XIII Si iudicium dei iustum est, quare infantes in Sodomis cremati sunt? XIIII Quid est ut deus peccata patrum filiis dicat reddi? XVIIII Quaerendum est si factus Adam corpus inmortale habuit. XXI Quid sit ad imaginem et similitudinem dei fecisse hominem. XXIII An ex traduce sint animae sicut corpora. XLVIIII Cur saluator baptizatus sit. Some tracts are polemics against the well known enemies of the Catholic Church:—XLIIII Aduersum Iudaeos, LXXXXI Aduersus Fotinum, LXXXXVII Aduersus Arrium, CII Contra Nouatianum, CXIIII Aduersus paganos. The last is of great historical value, as are also CXV De fato (against astrology), and CI De iactantia Romanorum leuitarum. Some are running commentaries on psalms[1], others are discussions of passages in the Gospels[2]. Others are on Old Testament heroes, CVIIII on Melchisedech, CXVII on Abraham, CXVIII on Job, CXVIIII on Tobit. This may suffice as an indication of the contents and the interest of the collection.

[1] CX on Ps. i, CXI on Ps. xxiii, CXII on Ps. l.

[2] LXXXXVIII on Ioh., C on Matth., CIIII on Luc.

Even from this slight account it will readily be seen that the contents of the collection are by no means the same in character throughout. Further, while most of the tractates are addressed to a reader, a few are evidently sermons or homilies. The frequent use of the second person singular[1], and such expressions as *ne* legendi *fastidium patiaris* (qu. LXXXXV col. 2290 25), *de re quae nulli aliquando in dubium uenit* scribimus (qu. CI pr), show that the work is intended for readers; but such phrases as *audistis quae contestetur sacrosanctum euangelium* (qu. LXXXXVIII pr), *audistis, fratres carissimi* (qu. C pr), *pascha, dilectissimi fratres* (qu. CXVI pr), *magna dilectio est, fratres dilectissimi* (qu. CXVIII pr), *congruum est, fratres carissimi* (qu. CXX pr) show unmistakeably that the documents in which they occur are spoken sermons. Quu. CX, CXI, and CXII, on the three psalms above mentioned, have also the appearance of sermons: possibly some others of the later tractates are sermons too.

A few words must be said on the question whether all the tractates proceed from one author or not. In favour of common authorship is the fact that six ninth-century and two tenth-century MSS contain them, each with the full table of contents. The style and language are practically the same throughout. I could fill many pages with proofs of this, but I hope that the later chapter on language will serve to show it. I am of opinion that the collection of one hundred and twenty-seven proceeds from

[1] The following list does not profess to be quite exhaustive:—*uides* (qu. 9 col. 2222 71 qu. 46 col. 2246 56 qu. 80 col. 2273 56 qu. 91 col. 2282 77 qu. 97 col. 2291 52, 2293 1 qu. 101 col. 2302 49 qu. 102 col. 2310 14) *uide* (qu. 10 col. 2223 47 qu. 12 col. 2224 37 qu. 13 col. 2225 7) *confer* (qu. 13 col. 2224 71) *uelis* (qu. 12 col. 2224 10) *adde* (qu. 13 col. 2225 4) *superadde* (qu. 95 col. 2290 19) *putas* (qu. 44 col. 2242 4) *occultas* (qu. 78 col. 2271 73) *uocas* (qu. 78 col. 2272 1) *obtendis* (qu. 79 col. 2272 31) *redegisti* (qu. 79 col. 2272 54) *dicis* (qu. 91 col. 2283 3 qu. 97 col. 2294 3) *incurris* (qu. 91 col. 2283 4) *times* (qu. 91 col. 2283 4) *negas* (qu. 91 col. 2284 70–71) *ignoras* (qu. 91 col. 2284 71) *quaere* (qu. 95 col. 2290 8) *inuenies* (qu. 95 col. 2290 8 18 24 38) *tene* (qu. 95 col. 2290 12) *redi* (qu. 95 col. 2290 13) *perueni* (qu. 95 col. 2290 15) *habebis* (qu. 95 col. 2290 16) *patiaris* (qu. 95 col. 2290 25) *sis* (qu. 95 col. 2290 28) *discas* (qu. 95 col. 2290 29) *retrahe* (qu. 95 col. 2290 31) *computes* (qu. 95 col. 2290 39) *praedicas, ais* (qu. 97 col. 2294 1) *facis* (qu. 97 col. 2294 3) *aduertas* (qu. 103 col. 2313 13). The plu., however, occurs: *dicitis* (qu. 97 col. 2293 61). I owe one or two of these exx. to Langen (diss. p. 30), who collects them for a different purpose.

one author; also that all (with one exception[1]) of the additional *quaestiones* supplied by three late MSS are by the same author. At first sight the difference in character of the first and last documents, which has been already alluded to, suggests different authorship. But a close study of the language, aided by examination of the lections of the early MSS, which preserve many lost readings of importance[2], shows much in expression that is common to all. We must also remember that there is necessarily a considerable difference between the *quaestio* proper, which is meant to be read, and a spoken homily. There are, however, one or two passages which are certainly interpolated. In qu. LXXV the words *quod nunc pannosum*[3] *aurum appellatur, quia et pauperes exiguntur* appear, wrongly, in most printed editions: they are inserted from MSS of the second class. The greater part of qu. CVIIII is wanting in the early MSS and in the *editio princeps*. It is not, however, interpolated. Its absence from all but the Padua MS is due to an accidental loss of leaves.

It is extremely likely that the longer *quaestiones* were circulated separately at first, and perhaps anonymously. It is probable, for instance, that qu. CI, on the boastfulness of the Roman deacons, was issued anonymously. It is almost too bitter for a man to own it at the time of publication. Again qu. CVIIII, on Melchisedech, if, as is almost certain, it is the same tract as was sent to S. Jerome[4], was certainly issued anonymously. The whole collection was probably afterwards issued, still anonymously, by its author, or by some friend of the author anonymously or under the name of S. Augustine. It may be that the entire work, as an anonymous production, was found among the books of S. Augustine at his death and thus became attributed to him. It is easy to

[1] Viz. Quaest. V. T., pars secunda, I (col. 2385 ff.), which looks like genuine Augustine. Langen (diss. p. 10) thinks this document is by Minucius Felix.

[2] As I hope to show in my edition.

[3] I have been unable to find any other example of this interesting expression. The passage is bracketed in Lugd. ed. of 1561 as in Bened., but appears without brackets in Basel ed. (1569) and Lovan. ed. (Colon. 1616).

[4] Ep. 73 (to Euangelus, date 398) *misisti mihi uolumen ἀνώνυμον ἀδέσποτον, et nescio utrum tu de titulo nomen subtraxeris an ille qui scripsit, ut periculum fugeret disputandi, auctorem noluerit confiteri*: Langen, diss. p. 14, Morin *op. cit.* p. 120. See also Zahn *op. cit.* for a passage which will be discussed later.

speculate on the subject: but discussion as to the authorship is properly referred to the second part of this study.

§ 4. *Notes on the Manuscripts of the Commentaries.*

It is necessary to await Father Brewer's[1] account of the MSS before the history of the textual tradition of the commentaries can be understood. My notes, laboriously gathered and meagre as they are, indicate one or two landmarks only in that history. Considerable portions of the work were thought to have been lost, as authors like Rabanus Maurus and Lanfranc quote as parts of it passages found in none or few of our MSS as at present known[2]. Yet, as I am convinced from a minute study of the language, the text printed in Migne proceeds in the main from one author[3]; and I cannot but think that the work, as we have it there given, is complete. Fortunately, the researches of Cardinal (then Dom) Pitra[4], O.S.B., and others in the last century have shown that at some period in the early Middle Ages a Latin translation of Theodore of Mopsuestia's[5] commentaries on S. Paul's epistles, from Galatians onwards, became attached to certain MSS of 'Ambrosiaster' after the Second Epistle to the Corinthians, displacing the remainder of the original work. The oldest known MS of the commentaries, that of Monte Cassino (*Casinensis*), belonging to the 6th century[6], shows the real 'Ambrosiaster' throughout, except

[1] Scholars are agreed that the gorgeous form of Ballerini's edition (*Ambrosii opp.* t. III 1877) constitutes its chief merit.

[2] Cf. Langen, diss., p. 6.

[3] So Langen, p. 6, who shows that Gal. iii 22 refers to Rom., 2 Cor. ii 5 to 1 Cor., 1 Th. iv 12 to Ph. ii 27, and gives other proofs, such as unity of thought and expression. Marold, p. 470, and G. Krüger, *Lucifer, Bischof von Calaris*, p. 89, n. 4, are of the same opinion. For one interpolation, see above, p. 3.

[4] *Spicilegium Solesmense* I (Paris, 1852), pp. XXVI—XXXIV, 49–159.

[5] Mopsuhestia is a more exact spelling (Μόψου ἑστία). The town was in Cilicia, and was called also Mopsus, Mompsuestia.

[6] The MS was written perhaps as early as 522, but at latest in 568 (Marold, in *Ztft f. wissensch. Th.* 1883, p. 49). A facsimile of part of it is in Thompson's *Palaeography*, p. 202. An imperfect collation of it is in *Bibliotheca Casinensis* (fol.) III.

for a part of the commentary on the Epistle to the Romans, which is a translation of Origen[1]. The other recension is represented by the ninth-century codex *Harleianus* 3063, the later codex *Corbeiensis*[2], now in Amiens (of the 10th century, probably), and an inferior MS in an unknown private library. The Harley MS had originally, just as the Corbie MS has, the commentaries of 'Ambrosiaster' on Romans, 1 and 2 Corinthians, in its first eight quires, some of which are now lost[3]. The discovery that the remaining part in this class of MSS is really a Latin translation of Theodore was made independently by Jacobi[4] and Hort[5]. The division at the end of Second Corinthians is seen also in codices 101 and 100 (saec. IX s. X) of the Stifts-bibliothek at S. Gall, which form respectively volumes I and II of a single copy[6]. Cod. 101 contains Rom. 1 and 2 Cor.: cod. 100 contains Gal. Eph. Phil. 1 and 2 Thess. Col. (in this order) Tit. 1 and 2 Tim. Philem. Cod. 330 (saec. IX) of the same library contains the same epistles as cod. 100, and in the same order. The contents of *Parisiacus* 13339, *Palatinus* 169, *Ashburnham.* 60, *Patavinus* (scaff. V N. 94), and *Augiensis* CVIII (now *Caroloruhensis*) also go to show that complete copies of 'Ambrosiaster's' commentary were often in two volumes, the first containing the longer epistles, the second the shorter. It is thus seen that at some period between the sixth and ninth centuries, perhaps, the two parts of a copy of 'Ambrosiaster' got separated from one another, the division being between 2 Cor. and Gal.[7], and a possessor of the first part had the

[1] Nirschl *Lehrbuch d. Patrologie* II (1883) 383.

[2] The readings of Harl. and Corb. for the later epp. are given in Prof. Swete's edition of Theod. Mops., from which (I p. xiv) I gain these particulars about them. Corb. had been published in part by Pitra (*op. cit.*), as the genuine work of S. Hilary of Poitiers (!), and the view even found supporters (Swete I p. xiv, for reff.). Pitra afterwards adopted the correct view (Jacobi in *Gött. Gel. Anz.* 1881 1186). Pitra alone among *savants* had seen the third MS, but he was pledged to secrecy about it.

[3] See below, p. 16.

[4] *Deutsche Zeitschr. f. christl. Wissensch. u. christl. Leben*, Aug. 5–12, 1854.

[5] *Camb. Journ. of Class. and Sacred Philol.* IV 302–308.

[6] I owe my first knowledge of S. Gall MSS to a kind letter of Professor Zahn. He examined them in 1893.

[7] The disturbed state of the text at the end of 1 Cor. and the beginning of 2 Cor. in many MSS suggests that they ultimately derive from a mutilated copy, the gaps in which were supplied in various ways.

Latin Theodore on the remaining epistles copied, believing it to be a continuation of the part which he already possessed.

The Epistle to the Hebrews. The author of the commentary did not regard the Epistle to the Hebrews as Pauline. The reference to this epistle at 2 Tim. i 3—5 is in the following terms: *nam simili modo et in epistula ad Hebraeos scriptum est* (cf. qu. 109). Passages in the undoubted epistles are introduced by such words as: *sicut dicit, ait, alio loco dicit*[1]. It does not therefore surprise us to find that the oldest MSS[2] of 'Ambrosiaster' are without a commentary on this epistle, and that it has been excluded by Amerbachius, Erasmus, and the Benedictines. For example, S. Gall codex 100 was originally without the Epistle to the Hebrews[3]. It has on page 244 in large red characters the subscription EXPLICIT · EPISTOLA · AD · PHILEMONEM, and the rest of the page remains blank. The exposition of the Epistle to the Hebrews begins on page 245 with a new quaternion (no. 17). Quaternions 17—21 were bound up with the others afterwards, as is seen from the fact that the preceding quaternion (no. 16) contains only four folia, not, like the extra five, eight folia each. Codex *Sangallensis*, n. 330, remains even to the present day without the Epistle to the Hebrews, as do the Toulouse and Le Mans MSS, &c. But Hebrews is found, e.g. in the Monza MS, and *Vindobonensis* 4600. The epistle was introduced later by some person or persons who believed in its Pauline origin, and considered it indispensable to the collection of commentaries.

LIST OF MSS OF THE COMMENTARIES.

An asterisk is appended to those MSS of which complete or partial collations are in my possession.

(*a*) Complete MSS :—

*1. Monte Cassino (*Casinensis*) 150 (346—242) s. VI, containing Rom. (from iii 9), 1, 2 Cor. Gal. Phil. Eph. 1, 2 Thess. Tit. Col. 1, 2 Tim. Philem. (*minus* 17 to end[4]). It is by no means certain that this is the best MS, though it is the oldest. I agree with the opinion of Dom Morin (p. 121) that

[1] Marold, p. 419.

[2] See the 'admonitio' in Migne (col. 47 48).

[3] Here I am indebted to a communication of Dr Zahn.

[4] It ends at the word *superius*.

'l'exemplaire cassinien ne contient qu'un texte fortement retouché, dont on a éliminé la plupart des traits vraiment intéressants.' There is an imperfect collation of it in *Bibliotheca Casinensis* III pp. 316–362. Ballerini used it, and records some of its readings (v. also Reifferscheid, *Biblioth. Patr. Ital.* II 416 ff.).

*2. St Gallen Stifts-bibliothek (*Sangallensis*) 101 and 100, s. IX or X, are vols. I and II of one MS, containing Rom. 1, 2 Cor. Gal. Eph. Phil. 1, 2 Thess. Col. Tit. 1, 2 Tim. Philem. (from *v.* 22 onward in another hand, cf. MSS 35 and 36).

*3. Köln (*Coloniensis*) XXXIV, s. X, containing Rom. 1, 2 Cor. Phil. 1, 2 Thess. Col. Tit. 1, 2 Tim. Philem. (ending *v.* 22 solo Christo).

4. Chartres (*Carnutensis*) s. X ex., formerly of the monastery of S. Peter (*cf.* Montfaucon's *Biblioth. Bibliothecarum* II 1243 A).

5. Toulouse (*Tolosanus*) 154 (I 7) s. XIII ex.

6. München (*Monacensis*) (*olim Frisingensis* 65) 6262, s. XII.

7. München (*Monacensis*) 27031, s. XV.

8. Monza (*Modoetianus*), the cathedral library, $\frac{c-2}{62}$, s. IX–X, includes Hebrews (see Ballerini's edition, and Burkitt's *The Book of Rules of Tyconius*, p. xxvii f, for a description of the MS).

*9. Oxford, *Bodl.* 689 (2530) s. XII, including Hebrews.

*10. Oxford, *Bodl.* 756 (2526) (*olim Saresberiensis*) s. XI.

11. Zwettl (Austria), the monastery library, 33 s. XII.

12. Bramshill House, IV, s. XII[1].

(*b*) MSS of Portions :—

*13. Paris, Bibl. Nat. (*Parisiacus*) 13339 s. IX (Rom. 1 Cor. 2 Cor. to xi 21). I saw this MS in August 1902.

*14. Trier (*Treuericus*) 122 s. VIII ex. or IX in. (Rom.).

*15. Corbie, now at Amiens (*Ambianensis, olim Corbeiensis*) 87 s. IX or X (Rom. 1, 2 Cor.), (*vide* Bened. edition, wh. reports readings with fair exactness, Montfaucon *Bibl. Bibl.* II 1406, Pitra *Spicileg. Solesm.* I p. xxvi ff. 49 ff., Swete's Introd. to *Theod. Mops.* I p. xxiii ff.).

16. St Mihiel 16 s. X (Rom.) (Montfaucon, II 1179).

*17. Köln XXXIX, s. IX (Rom.).

*18. Vatic. 283, s. XI–XII (Rom.).

19. Vendôme (*Vindocinensis*) s. XIII (Rom. to xvi 11).

20. Orléans (*prob. olim Floriacensis*) 85 (82) s. XI (Rom.).

21. Laon (*Laudunensis*) 107 s. IX (Rom.) (Montfaucon, II 1296 B).

22. Avranches (*Abrincensis*) 241 s. XII (Rom. incomplete).

23. München (*Monacensis*) 17043 (Scheftl. 43) s. X (Rom.).

[1] The Florence catalogue, Tom. I (Flor. 1774), mentions a complete MS (with Hebr.), of saec. XI, in plut. XIV cod. 6. This MS is mentioned also in Montfaucon, *Bibl. Bibl.* I 272 A. There are also others in Florence, which I have seen.

24. Wien (*Vindobonensis*) 4600 s. xv (Rom. Hebr.)

25. Karlsruhe (*Augiensis* cviii) s. x ex. or xi in. (Rom. 1, 2 Cor.). I saw this MS in August, 1901.

26. Wien (*Vindobonensis*) 743, s. ix (Rom.) (v. Berger, *Histoire de la Vulgate*, p. 118).

*27. Vatic. (*Palat. lat.*) 169 s. ix–x (1, 2 Cor.). This MS once belonged to Lorsch (*Laureshamensis*), v. Reifferscheid, *Biblioth. Patr. Ital.* i 198 ff.

*28. *Harl.* 3063 s. ix (2 Cor. from i 17 [adpa]ratibus). This MS is described in Swete's edition of Theodore of Mopsuestia's *Comm. on S. Paul's epp.* i p. xxv ff., and *Catalogue of Anc. MSS in the British Museum, Part II, Latin* (London 1884) pp. 50, 51. I collated it in July 1901.

*29. Gand (*Gandavensis*) 455, no. 129 (159) s. x (1, 2 Cor. Gal. Eph. Phil. 1 Thess. Col. 2 Thess. 1, 2 Tim. Tit. Philem.), (formerly of S. Maximin in Trier).

*30. Troyes 432 s. ix–x (1, 2 Cor. [Col. was before Tit.] Tit. Philem.).

31. Wien (*Vindobonensis*) 550 s. x (extracts of 1 Cor.).

32. Bruxelles (*Biblioth. Reg. Belg.*) 282 (ii 953) s. xiii (1, 2 Cor.). This is not a MS of Ambrst., but contains portions of Ambrst. *Comm.* mingled with external matter. I saw it in Aug. 1901. Brussels has genuine MSS.

*33. St Gallen (*Sangallensis*) 330 s. ix (Gal. Eph. Phil. 1, 2 Thess. Col. Tit. 1, 2 Tim. Philem.).

*34. *Ashburnham.* 60 saec. viii–ix (Gal. Phil. Eph. 1, 2 Thess. Col. 1, 2 Tim. Philem. Tit.), now in Laur. library at Florence (cf. Delisle in *Notices et Extraits*, &c. xxxii p. 1 (Paris, 1886), p. 35 f.).

35. Le Mans 229 s. xi (Gal. Eph. Phil. etc., 1, 2 Tim. Philem. (ending *v.* 22 *requies non erat nisi in solo Christo*)).

36. Padova (*Patavinus*) (Scaff. v N. 94) s. ix (Gal. Eph. Phil. 1, 2 Thess. Col. Tit. 1, 2 Tim. Philem. (ending *v.* 22, as no. 35)).

This list could easily be extended, but I do not think that any valuable MS has been omitted. My original knowledge of most of the MSS I owe to Father Brewer: to his rare kindness, also, I owe the collations of all those marked with an asterisk except 9, 10, 28. The classification of MSS must be left to him; but I should like to call attention to the fact that the order of the epistles varies in MSS, and that, while this is a means of classification, it is also an indication that originally the commentaries were issued singly, which is *a priori* probable. Again nos. 2 (originally), 3, 9, 10, 35, 36 end with verse 22 of the epistle to Philemon (at the words *requies non erat nisi in solo Christo*)[1].

[1] The biblical MSS F and G omit *v.* 21 to end (Bernard, *Philemon, Epistle to*, in Hastings' *Dictionary of the Bible*).

This is another help to classification, as nos. 1 and 30, for example, end at a different point. Photography may show that two parts of the same MS are here under separate entries. Finally, I have tried to make the above reports of MSS as accurate as possible, but not even an examination of good catalogues can altogether take the place of personal inspection.

§ 5. *Notes on the Manuscripts of the* Quaestiones.

The manuscripts of the *Quaestiones Veteris et Noui Testamenti*, as has already been mentioned, readily divide themselves into three classes. The first class contains one hundred and twenty-seven Quaestiones, of which the first forty-seven are separated from the remainder by the title *Quaestiones Noui Testamenti*. These alone are extant in old MSS and are all that were published at first. The last thirty were constituted by the printers a separate section, inscribed 'Ex Utroque Mixtim.' Of this class the Benedictine editor knew five examples, a *Colbertinus*[1] which he dates about 990 A.D., but which is still extant and is of the ninth century; two MSS in the library of the Sorbonne, and two in the library of S. Victor. Had he followed Colbertinus more closely instead of looking at it only occasionally, and had he made some search for MSS in Benedictine monasteries elsewhere in Europe than Paris, he would have anticipated the gratifying result of my own investigations. A study of many catalogues in the Bollandist library in Brussels[2], made possible for me by the courtesy of Father Van den Gheyn, S.J., Conservateur à Manuscrits in the Bibliothèque Royale there[3], has led to the discovery of six ninth-century and two tenth-century MSS, besides some later copies.

Of the second class only three examples were known to the Benedictine editor, one in the Sorbonne[4], one in the Abbey of

[1] On the Colbertine library, see L. Delisle *Le Cabinet des Manuscrits* I (Paris, 1868), pp. 439–486.

[2] The Vienna Academy has now (1902) published a *Catalogus Catalogorum* (ed. W. Weinberger) for the use of contributors to the *Corp. Scr. Eccl. Lat.*

[3] He kindly introduced me to the library, and put the services of the obliging assistant-librarian at my disposal.

[4] On this library, see *Literatur früh. und noch bestehend. europ. öffentl. u. Corporations-Biblioth.*, von E. G. Vogel (Lpz. 1840), p. 281.

S. Victor[1], and one of the Abbey of S. Germain-des-Prés[2]. I am unaware whether the two former MSS still exist, but have discovered two others of this class. This class contains one hundred and fifty-one Quaestiones, fifty-six being 'Ex Veteri Testamento,' and ninety-five being 'Ex Nouo Testamento.' This larger collection shows sixty-one (the last giving a title only, not the text), which are absent from the first, but wants thirty-seven which are found in the first[3]. In the case of some Quaestiones the texts of the two collections differ more or less; and the same Quaestio is sometimes treated more than once in the same collection.

There are at least five examples of a third class, unknown to the editors. This third class contains ninety-four Quaestiones, with a set of twenty-one added as a separate book, and is not entirely derived from either the first or second class.

LIST OF MSS OF THE QUAESTIONES.

An asterisk appended indicates that I have collated the MS.

CLASS I.

*1. Karlsruhe, *Augiensis* IX, s. IX ("before 830," Holder).

*2. München (*Monacensis lat.*) 6312, *olim Frisingensis* 112, s. IX.

*3. München (*Monacensis lat.*) 14537, *olim S. Emmerami* F. 40, at Ratisbon (Regensburg) s. IX. This MS is a copy of 2.

*4. Bruxelles (*Biblioth. Reg. Belg.*) II 972 *antea Phillippsii Cheltenhamensis* 363, *olim S. Ghisleni in Hannonia* zzz, s. IX.

*5. Colbertinus (*Parisiacus, Bibl. Nat. Lat.* 2709) s. IX (cf. *Catal. Bibl. Regiae* (Par. 1744) P. III, T. 3 p. 318).

*6. Gand (*Gandavensis*) 95 (156, St Genois 529, old no. 60), formerly of the Abbey S. Maximin near Trier, s. X. ex.

*7. Metz (*Met(t)ensis*) 322, formerly of the Cathedral of S. Arnulfus, s. X.

*8. Nostradamensis (*Parisiacus, B. N. Lat.* 17385), formerly of the Chapter of Notre Dame, s. IX.

9. Utrecht (*Rheno-Traiectinus*), 46 (Eccl. 253, antea 282) s. XV ("Pertinet Regularibus in Traiecto").

*10. Padova (*Patavinus*) (Scaff. X, N. 191), s. XIII. It wants quaest. 47 to 101, and the end of 127.

11. Leipzig (*Lipsiensis*) 231, s. XII.

12. Paris (*Bibl. d'Arsenal* 473) s. XIV.

[1] Vogel, p. 279. [2] Vogel, p. 278.

[3] Cf. Langen, p. 5.

13. Cambridge University Library, Ee. 1. 25, s. XV (date 1442).
14. Salisbury (*Sarisberiensis*) 129, s. XII.
15. Durham (*Dunelmensis*) B. 2. 12, s. XIV in.

The *editio princeps* was edited by Augustinus Ratisponensis and published at Lyons by J. Trechsel (1497).

The inter-relation of MSS of the 1st class is discussed in the *Sitzungsberichte* of the Vienna Academy for 1904.

CLASS II.

*16. Bruxellensis 1125 (625–636), s. XV.
17. Padova, University Library, 1444, s. XV.
*18. Germanensis (now *Parisiacus, B. N. Lat.* 12,223) s. XII.

CLASS III.

19. Heiligenkreuz, *Stift*, no. 229, s. XII.
20. Wien (*Vindobonensis*), no. 753, s. XIV.
21. Wien (*Vindobonensis*), no. 1044, s. XI–XII.
22. Görres no. 31, on sale in München in 1902[1], s. XIII–XIV.
23. Leipzig (*Lipsiensis*), no. 267, s. XIII.

[1] I owe my information about this MS to Dr A. Engelbrecht. This is the MS which attributes a section of the *Quaestiones* to S. Ambrose.

PART I

COMPARISON OF THE COMMENTARIES AND THE *QUAESTIONES.*

CHAPTER I.

COMMUNITY OF ILLUSTRATIONS AND ALLUSIONS.

It will be allowed that illustrations and allusions provide a very strong indication of a writer's individuality, and that, when we find in those of the commentaries and the Quaestiones a close likeness, we have a powerful argument for common authorship. The scope of the illustrations in these works is not a very wide one, but this fact serves only to strengthen the proof. A prominent feature is the large number of them which are derived from Government and Law. At first sight, it might seem that such as these, being, to an inhabitant of the Roman empire, obvious and easily drawn, do not form a sound criterion. But it is remarkable that S. Augustine, to take a writer very nearly contemporary, is hardly, if at all, given to drawing illustrations from this source. An examination of other writers of the time would probably show the same result. At any rate, such illustrations are a prominent feature of the two works under consideration. Besides illustrations, allusions to definite statutes and edicts also appear. References to the Jews, another marked characteristic, are reserved for a later chapter.

Among terms connected with government, the *Imperator* and his subordinates, often coupled with him, may conveniently come first. As an alternative expression, *Rex*[1] sometimes occurs, and *regnum Romanum*[2]. 'Astrologers and physical philosophers excuse

[1] E.g. 'apud Romanos *reges* Augusti appellantur' (144 A); cum stella indice temporalis *rex* soleat designari (qu. 63). The name, as obnoxious to all Romans, was scrupulously avoided by the founder of the Empire. (Glover, *Life and Letters in the Fourth Century*, p. 325, has exx. from Symmachus and Claudian.)

[2] 479 B; 482 B, C; qu. 55; 107 m; 115 pr. The phrase is probably very rare in Latin: indeed it is *incorrect*.

themselves for neglect of God by saying that they use the stars and elements as stepping-stones to Him, just as people obtain an audience of the *rex* through the *comites*. Come! no one is so senseless as to claim that the *comes* should receive the honour due to the *rex*: any who attempted to confer it *iure ut rei damnantur maiestatis*.' 'People have to see the *tribuni* and *comites* first, because the king is a mere man, and does not know to whom he ought to entrust state business. To win God's favour, one has no need of a canvasser (*suffragator*),' etc. (60 C). 'God appears to have addressed His angels as the commander-in-chief or emperor (*Imperator*) his army' (qu. 45 ppr). 'The rule of the *Imperator* depends on the obedience of his soldiers, but the army is not better than, or equal to, the *Imperator*' (qu. 101 ex). 'We cannot speak of a common likeness between God and His angels, such as exists between the *Imperator* and his *comites*' (qu. 45 ppr). 'It is an insult to the Creator that His bondservants are courted, while He Himself is slighted; just as it is, when the *Imperator* is contemned, while his *comites* receive worship' (qu. 114 pr). 'No *Imperator* allows his *tribuni* and *comites* to be worshipped in his own name' (qu. 114 am). 'The bust of the *Imperator* has authority in his absence, not in his presence' (456 A). 'God can be said to be seen, only by the understanding....Similarly, when we do not know the *Imperator*, we see him *in figura, non in ueritate*' (qu. 71). The mistakes that are made in years, months, and the 'days'[1] (*dies*) of the *Imperatores* are referred to in qu. 44 ex. 'Some things are allowable in the company of other people, which are not permitted before the *Imperator*' (qu. 127 ex). 'The tunic of an ordinary man, however neat and clean, is yet mean, and not to be worn by the *Imperator*' (qu. 127 ex). 'Those who wait at the table of the *Imperator* must be clothed brightly and neatly' (qu. 127 ex). 'The fifth (of the elements) is the spirit of man, which is a kind of charioteer to drive the body when formed, being a sort of *Imperator* (or commander-in-chief) for it' (qu. 108 pr). 'The authority of the earthly *Imperator* runs through all in order that, in all, respect should be paid to him; so God arranged,' etc.

[1] The birthday (*dies natalis*) and the anniversary of the first day of his rule are meant. Cf. Plin. *ep. Trai.* 62, with Hardy's note.

(qu. 110 ppr). 'The spirit is the *Imperator* of the body, to direct the man by the tiller-ropes of the divine law' (qu. 115 am). 'Men, when oppressed by the governors (*rectores*) of provinces, have recourse to the *Imperatores* to have their wrongs set right. So men, if they fall on evil days, commit themselves in prayer to God' (qu. 115 am). 'The *Imperator* alone can repeal a sentence, and pardon one condemned to death: *iudices* cannot recall a verdict once passed. If the *Imperator* can do this, how much more God?' (qu. 115 am). 'Christ is the *Imperator*, whose battles are being fought by those who serve in His armour' (qu. 126 aex). 'The armour of the Christian bears the devices of his *Imperator*' (334 B). Imperial edicts are referred to from time to time: those which are specially named will be found in the paragraph about Law[1].

'Those who are consuls, or those who are honoured by statues, delight in vanity' (qu. 81 m). 'That consul is named first who is elected first' (qu. 107 pm). 'A *praefectus* can take the duty of a *praefectus*, and a *praetor* of a *praetor*: but a person not in office cannot carry out the duty of any official position' (qu. 46 m). The *vicarius*, or substitute of the Emperor, appears occasionally. 'This is, therefore, the image of God in man, that one has been made a sort of *dominus*, from whom the rest were to spring, he having the *imperium* of God, as His *vicarius*; because every king has the image of God' (qu. 106 aex). 'Christ is the *vicarius* of the Father, and the *antistes*, and thus He is called also the *sacerdos*,' etc. (qu. 109 ex, col. 2329, 68 f.). 'The *antistes* of God must be purer than others: for he is seen to have His rôle; he is His *vicarius*: so that what is allowable to others is not allowable to him,' etc. (qu. 127 ex). 'The apostles are the *vicarii* of Christ' (210 B; so also 328 C; 334 A): 'a bishop is *vicarius* of the Lord' (254 A)[2]. This is the place to exemplify *legatus*, the older equivalent of *vicarius*. Besides *legatus*, the title of the office, *legatio*, also appears[3]. 'God then was in Christ. In what way? *Quasi in vicario aut legato?*' he asks (314 B).

[1] The emperor is often introduced in the Clementine Homilies also.

[2] Cf. Langen, *diss. Bonn.*, p. 6.

[3] The image was partly derived from 2 Cor. v 20 and Eph. vi 20, passages in the writer's mind in 53 A, 219 C, 263 A, 298 C, 299 C, 402 C.

'*Sacerdotes* or *legati* are so named, because they show forth in their own person him whose *legati* they are; for they are his likeness: and thus Christ and the Holy Spirit, having by nature the image of God, are named His *sacerdotes*' (qu. 109 ex). 'The apostles are the *legati* of Christ' (263 A). 'The man (in relation to the woman) is the *legatus* of Christ' (273 B). 'Consuetudo et lex est *legatis* hominum non inferre exitia: qua praesumptione et audacia *legatis* Dei non solum exitia, sed et mors inrogatur?' (425 A). 'Seeing we cannot reciprocate all God's kindnesses, let us at least faithfully and earnestly carry out the duty of His representatives (*legationem* eius agamus)' (513 D). '*Iurisconsulti* or *pontifices, quos vocant sacerdotes,* have decreed fixed days on which cases are to be tried' (214 A). The title *praefectus,* so frequent in its various applications in Imperial times, is also found. One example has already been given (with *praetor*). 'If, in a proclamation (*programma*) by one *praefectus praetorio,* the rest of the prefects also are said to issue a command, on account of the authority of the one power (*potestas*): how much more suitably in the case of the power (*imperium*) of one God, if One of Three have spoken, will Three be said to have spoken?' (qu. 97 pm). 'To compare the priests with the bearers of the tabernacle and all its vessels, the hewers of wood and the carriers of water, is like putting *praefecti* on a level with their *officiales*[1], or slaves on a level with their owners and masters' (qu. 101 ppr). 'To say that the Sabbath had already lapsed, because the Saviour worked on that day, is like saying, if a man be an *ex-praefectus,* and have experienced an injury, that the office of praefect (*praefectura*) has experienced an injury' (2 qu. N. T. 31). The *officiales* are met with again[2] in qu. 101 am: 'whatever honour is conferred upon the *officiales* results in increase to the constituted authority: as an honour to a slave works towards the praise of his master.' The senatorial class—for time had served only to make this order in society more distinctive than ever[3]—is alluded

[1] These underlings are called also *officiarii.* They wore a special uniform (qu. 47, quoted p. 27).

[2] See also *senatores* (1st example).

[3] See Dill, *Roman Society in the Western Empire* (ed. 1), pp. 176—178, 207—208, and index.

to several times. '*Senatores* and *officiales* are recognised to be such by their dress' (qu. 47 pm). 'It is disgraceful in a man of rank to engage in business, and a crime to enter an eating-house. It is *infamia* for senators even to exact interest for money lent' (qu. 102 ppr)[1]. '*Senatores* generant *senatores*' (qu. 81 m). 'All senators, then, have one destiny: for no senator is unlettered; and people who are unlettered have one, and all slaves have one fate: for no slave is a senator' (qu. 115 aex, in an argument against astrologers, etc.). *Fiscalia*[2] are mentioned on Rom. xiii 6 (172 A): 'ideo dicit "tributa" praestari, uel quae dicuntur *fiscalia* (imperial dues), ut subiectionem praestent,' etc.

The references to Law in general or to particular statutes are unusually frequent. Were the works to any extent apologetic, we could understand this frequency: as this is not so, the presence of such references must be due to special knowledge and interest in law on the part of the writer. In Tertullian the influence of juristic training shows itself more in his vocabulary, which is well known to be permeated with recondite legal terminology, than in the quotation of special statutes. The language of 'Ambrosiaster,' on the contrary, shows less of a legal nature[3], and his knowledge of law is evidenced mainly by his references[4]. I may begin by quoting his derivation of the word 'lex,' which is interesting: '*lex* a lectione[5] dicta est, ut de multis quid eligas scias' (2 qu. N.T. 15). The writer's feeling for Roman law appears in the following sentences (366 A B): 'nam quomodo fieri poterat ut Romanis legibus imbuti, quorum tanta auctoritas in seruandis mandatis est, nescirent homicidium non esse faciendum: quippe cum adulteros, et homicidas, et falsos testes, et fures, et maleficos,

[1] Senatorial order forbidden to trade (*Cod. Theodos.* 5, p. 11, Ritter's ed. and 13, 1, 21). *Cod. Theod.* 2, 33, 4 allows them to lend at 6 °/₀ and 2, 33, 3 allows senators who are minors to lend money at interest (Dill, *op. cit.* p. 220, n. 1, *q.v.*).

[2] The word occurs also in Theodos. *de situ terrae sanctae* 32 (Geyer, p. 150).

[3] There is plenty of legal language, as in all Latin Christian writers, but little of a highly technical character.

[4] Cf. Dom Morin, pp. 20, 21.

[5] Modern philologists, too, connect with *lĕgo*, but in the sense of "read" (Bréal et Bailly, *Dict. Étymol. Lat.* (Paris, 1886) s.v. *lex*: Lindsay, *Latin Language* (Oxf. 1894), p. 260).

et ceterorum malorum admissores puniant leges Romanae? Denique tria haec mandata ab apostolis et senioribus data reperiuntur, quae ignorant leges Romanae, id est, "ut abstineant se ab idolatria, et sanguine, sicut Noe, et fornicatione."' The 'leges Romanae' excuse fornication (64 c). An edict of Diocletian against the Manichaeans is cited[1], 521 B; 'Quippe cum Diocletianus imperator constitutione sua designet, dicens: *sordidam hanc et impuram haeresim, quae nuper*, inquit, *egressa est de Persida*[2]. In qu. 127 m. the plural, *edictis*, is used, also with reference to the Manichaeans. Addressing them, the author says: 'sanctimonium enim profitentes, latenter inmunditiae studetis, quod non solum privatim sed et *edictis* prodictum est *Imperatorum*.' If these be not rhetorical plurals, and there is no special reason to take them as such, the edict of Valentinian I, and those of Gratian, against the Manichaeans, Eunomians, and Photinians are probably included[3]. If Langen's date[4] for this quaestio—after 385—be right, room is provided for yet more edicts[5]. An edict of Julian, permitting, for the first time in history, the divorce of husbands by their wives, is mentioned in qu. 115 pr. The author tells us that this permission was abused: 'coeperunt enim cottidie licenter uiros suos dimittere.' In the same passage another law is mentioned: 'eunuchos[6] in regno Romano fieri non licet, apud alios licet.' The oft-repeated expulsion of the *mathematici*, or astrologers, from Rome during the Empire[7] is referred to with a touch of humour in an argument against them. 'In what way,' asks our author, 'will they be said to have been born,

[1] This edict is otherwise known only from the *Lex Dei* or *Mosaicarum et Romanarum legum collatio*, xv 3, a work once wrongly attributed to S. Ambrose (see Mommsen's edition, Berl. 1890).

[2] The punishment was death and confiscation of property: the edict referred to Africa. Cf. Baron. *Annal.* a. 287, n. 2. For the form *Persida* see Ihm (*Rh. Mus.* XLIX (1894) 316 f.), and Marx's index to Filastrius.

[3] Socr. *H. E.* 5, 2; Sozom. *H. E.* 7, 1: see, too, *Cod. Theod.* 16, 5, 4–5, for a later edict of Gratian.

[4] *Diss.* p. 19.

[5] Of Valentinian II and Theodosius; cf. *s.* Manichaei in Wetzer und Welte's *Kirchenlexikon*, VIII² (Freib. 1893).

[6] For references to the statutes, see Rein, *Criminalrecht der Römer*, pp. 422–424.

[7] Cf. Tac. *ann.* II 32, *hist.* I 22, and the exhaustive note of Prof. Mayor on Juv. *Sat.* 14, 248.

who excluded the astrologers from the city of Rome?' (qu. 115 pm). The punishment of the thief is said to be restoration fourfold according to the law (*iuxta legem*), exactly as it is laid down in Gaius[1]. Ambrosiaster's words are: 'numquid fur deprehensus, et iuxta legem in quadruplum condemnatus, ausus est queri?' (qu. 83 aex). The edict (of Constantine) abolishing crucifixion[2] is alluded to (qu. 115 aex): 'et antea cruci homines figebantur, quod postea edicto prohibitum manet.' The story of the origin of Roman Law, derived, no doubt, from Livy, or one of the epitomes of Livy[3], is given in similar terms in both works: 'sciunt ergo legem Romani, quia non sunt barbari; sed comprehenderunt naturalem iustitiam partim ex se, partim ex Graecis: nam leges Romanis ex Athenis perlatae sunt: sicut et Graecis ex Hebraeis[4]' (110 D): 'nam utique in legem erant Romani (inducti), quam de Athenis decem uiri missi et post alii duo attulerunt, quae in duabus tabulis scripta est, quae in Capitolio obrutae sunt' (2 qu. N.T. 46). With the thought and mode of expression in the second extract, compare 'Romani in lege inducti erant' (180 C), and 'in legem [some MSS 'lege'] (Romani) inducti fuerant' (185 D). The principle of adoption is mentioned in qu. 125 pm in the following terms: 'in filiis enim, quamuis adoptiui sint, patris tamen ex aliqua parte debet uideri substantia. In mundo enim, quia res imperfectae sunt, adoptati ab hominibus filii nullum pignus sed solum nomen accipiunt.' The contrast is between the adopted sons of God, who receive the Holy Spirit, and the sons adopted by earthly fathers, who receive no pledge. A story is quoted (qu. 115 aex) from *quidam iuris libellus*, to the effect that 'aliquando mulierem quinque peperisse.' There are one or two references also to the law-courts, judges, etc. 'Aduocatorum

[1] Gai. 3, 189: cf. Quint. decl. 361.

[2] See the article *crux* in Daremberg and Saglio's *Dict. Antiq.* (a reference for which I have to thank Prof. J. S. Reid).

[3] Recent research has revealed something of ancient epitomes of Livy, of various size; cf. H. A. Sandars, *Die Quellenkontamination im* 21. *und* 22. *Buche des Livius* (Berl. 1897); v. Wölfflin in *Arch. f. lat. Lex.* 11, 1 ff; Oxyrhynchus Papyri, vol. IV; Reid in *Classical Review*, July, 1904, etc.

[4] There is, of course, nothing of this in Livy, but the statement is current in Christian books. Plato, according to some, borrowed from Moses. (The MSS vary greatly here.)

enim more accipe antistites: numquid, si malae uitae sit aduocatus, contra susceptum ('client') eius pronuntiabitur? Hoc est officium aduocati, ut secundum iuris ordinem suscepti sui causam peroret: numquid poterit uita eius, si turpis est, obesse causae suscepti? Persona enim aduocati nec obesse nec prodesse poterit: qualis enim fuerit causa, sic et respondebitur ei' (qu. 102 ex). In qu. 115 m. we are told that '*iudices* cannot recall a sentence passed on an accused person. Only the emperor can do this; he can even commute a death sentence' (see p. 25). Qu. 101 m. says: 'et turpe est iudici dicere primiscrinium[1]' (i.e. because the latter is much inferior). In qu. 124 the author makes a statement about the venality of the courts, true, no doubt, but requiring some courage, probably, to utter it: '(diuites) securi sunt de impunitate, scientes uenalia esse iudicia, et nec redargui se ab aliquo' (cf. qu. 4). The courts are alluded to also in 223 C; qu. 2, 112, 115, 127. He refers once in each work to the ancient Roman statute forbidding wine to women[2]: (461 A) '*nam et mulieribus* eorum (*Romanorum*) castitatis causa *uini usus incognitus fuit,* sicut nunc aquae; in tantum *enim* uigebat *disciplinae* auctoritas cet.'; (qu. 115 ppr) '*mulieribus etenim Romanorum* multis temporibus *uini usus incognitus fuit. Disciplina enim,* facta consuetudine, confirmauit sensum suum, cet.' The autopsy on the body of a condemned person in the olden times is mentioned[3] (144 C). Qu. 79 (75) explains that the 'didragma' of Matt. xvii 27 is a poll-tax, not a land-tax[4]. Qu. 102 refers to the 'professio' (returns made at the census). A principle of Roman law is stated in 392 A: 'ubi holographa manus est, falsum dici non potest[5].' Judges cannot be prosecutors. 'Quasi possint ipsi accusatores esse, qui sunt iudices...Nam quis iudex accusatoris sumat personam?' (qu. 102 aex). There are several places where *ius*

[1] *Migne* primicerium. It is difficult to say exactly what a *primiscrinius* was. Other exx. are in Cassiod. *Variae* (see Traube's index in Mommsen's ed.).

[2] Attributed to Romulus by Dion. Hal. 2, 25 *εἴ τις οἶνον εὑρεθείη πιοῦσα γυνή,... θανάτῳ ζημιοῦν συνεχώρησεν ὁ Ῥωμύλος* (cf. Bruns, *Fontes Iuris Romani* (ed. 6), p. 6).

[3] Antiqui medici in hominibus morte dignis uel mortis sententiam consecutis requirebant quo modo prodessent uiuis, quae in homine latebant apertis, ut his cognoscerent causas aegritudinis, et poena morientis proficeret ad salutem uiuentis.

[4] What follows in the printed text is not in the MSS of cl. I: see above, p. 11.

[5] This principle holds still in the law of Scotland; a holograph will is legal.

ecclesiasticum is mentioned: 'hoc concessum est iuri ecclesiastico ab auctore, ut et paenitentiam det, et post paenitentiam recipiat (qu. 102 aex); 'sic sunt ei qui uolunt fieri Christiani: accedunt ad antistitem; dicunt ei uota sua; ille facit uerba iuris ecclesiastici. Si uera uota sunt, suscipiuntur a iudice, cet.' (qu. 102 ex); 'dicitur eis "accipite Spiritum Sanctum": et quia uere ad ius ecclesiasticum pertinet, statim subiecit, dicens: "Cuius tenueritis peccata, cet." (Iohann. 20, 23) (qu. 93); '(forma) ad ius ecclesiasticum pertinet in regenerandis uel ceteris officiis' (qu. 93). Finally there is an interesting and important passage near the end of qu. 127 (col. 2385) about what is allowed and forbidden to ecclesiastics. With it compare the note on 1 Tim. iii 12–13.

I now turn from illustrations and allusions connected with Government and Law to those taken from Astrology, and other subjects.

No Christian writer is more emphatic against astrology than 'Ambrosiaster.' Among Christian writers we find varying degrees of antagonism to the art, and it is much to be desired that some one should write the history of the Church's attitude towards it. It is now satisfactorily proved[1] that Iulius Firmicus Maternus, who published his *Mathesis*, or 'Handbook of Astrology,' between 335 and 337[2], is the same as the author of the *De Errore Profanarum Religionum*. S. Augustine, too, tells that he dallied with astrology in his youth[3]. The astrologers, spoken of usually as *scrutatores siderum* (though the technical term *mathematici* is also used once or twice, and is coupled occasionally with the *sophistae Graecorum*, the physical philosophers, scientists, or rather pseudo-scientists, of the day), are the subject of a considerable attack in qu. 115, which has the heading 'De Fato.' The attack is well delivered; the weapon of humour is employed: and the

[1] By Prof. Clifford H. Moore, of Chicago, *Iul. Firmicus Maternus, der Heide und der Christ* (Leipz. 1897); see also v. Wölfflin in *Archiv f. lat. Lex.* x 428 ff.

[2] The date was discovered by Th. Mommsen (*Hermes* xxix (1894) p. 468 ff.) to be between 30 Dec. 335 and 22 May 337. The first half of this interesting work can now be read in the edition of Kroll and Skutsch (Leipz., Teubn. 1897).

[3] *Conf.* 4, 3, 4: see Prof. Mayor's note (Iuu. xiv 248) for more passages from Aug. on this subject.

tract is altogether a valuable historical document. Resourc of learning, very considerable for those days, are drawn upon; anc if each statement were traced to the source from which it came, we should have some valuable data as to the reading of an educated man of the period[1]. On 1 Cor. i 20 the commentator writes: Gentiles say 'nihil posse fieri sine commixtione, et stultum iudicant (that God should have a Son). *Conquisitor* tamen *saeculi* hic est, qui constellationibus agi mundum et duodecim signis ortus et occasus fieri decernit calculis, nihil omnino sine horum motu putans posse fieri' (199 A). 'Naturalis lex' is a better teacher than 'cursus siderum' and 'calculi signorum' (207 A). Again, on Col. ii 18: '*inflantur* enim motum peruidentes stellarum, quas *angelos* uocat cet.' (456 B). On 1 Cor. i 26 appear those, 'qui stellarum motus inspiciunt et discernunt' (200 D). The best exposition of his view to be found in the commentaries is that on Col. ii 8, 9 (cf. prol. to Col.), but it is too long to quote. One clause is: 'omnem uim astris adsignantes, carnali rationi obnoxii' (452 D). The whole of qu. 84 is on the observation of the moon's course, with which compare 381 B: 'qui cursus lunae perscrutantur.' The long and important qu. 115, as has been said above, is occupied with astrology. It begins with the statement that nothing is so detrimental to the Christian as to pay attention to the art of astrology (mathesis): other statements are: 'ars matheseos euitanda et fugienda est'; 'things are not as the "stellarum speculatores" consider them to be.' 'Astrologi' are the enemies of the truth (qu. 63). 'Abraham, by nature an astrologer (Chaldaeus), showed himself a master of faith; although skilled in *astrologia*, he yet preferred God to human wisdom,' etc.[2] (qu. 117 m). The enactments expelling astrologers from Rome are referred to above. The *sapientia carnis* of Rom. viii 7 is defined as 'primo in loco, astrorum ab hominibus inuenta disputatio, deinde, uisibilium oblectatio' (125 B). Unbelievers are

[1] Not that such data are wanting: we find them in Ausonius and Symmachus; but while these authors throw light mainly on poetical reading, our author gives evidence as to prose reading. In this connexion references in Augustine's *confessions* and *civitas Dei* (see Teuffel-Schwabe, *Röm. Lit.* § 440, 10) are interesting.

[2] Here there is a very natural confusion between the two senses of Chaldaeus, both of which occur in O. T.

blind to the fact that all 'sapientia et scientia' is in Christ; because they do not read of 'astrologia' in the Gospels, 'geometria' in S. Paul, or 'arithmetica' and 'musica' in the prophets (451 C). Our author thinks of the physical philosophers or materialists and the astrologers together. Compare: 'sophistae mundi et scrutatores[1] siderum' (282 C); 'sapientes mundi' and 'scrutatores siderum' (qu. 100 am); 'dicant sophistae Graecorum cet.' (366 AB); 'sophistae et nobiles mundi' (qu. 114 ex): compare, too, on 1 Cor. xv 36: 'cum animali homine...agit...*physica* ratione, *de qua sibi blanditur*, ut non credat resurgere resoluta et emortua corpora cet.' Enough has been written to prove that there is an especial antipathy to astrology in both works, finding vent in the same terms.

A kindred subject, pagan religion and ritual, comes in for occasional mention. Qu. 114 is entitled 'Aduersus Paganos,' and, in a list of pagan gods, brings forward, quite unobtrusively, one Fruxilla, unknown even to Roscher[2]. The list is: 'Ianus enim et Saturnus et Iouis (*nomin.*)[3] et Mercurius, et Apollo et ceteri, item Minerua, et Isis, et Fruxilla[4], et Venus, et Flora meretrix[5] cum ceteris, dii deaeque sunt.' The order shows a fine disregard of the relative dignity of the different divinities; and where are Juno, Mars, Diana, Vulcan, etc.? The selection is intentionally random, perhaps, and meant in itself to convey contempt; or, may the list be considered as indicating the most popular worships of the time? The whole tract is important and seems virgin soil for the historian. There is a briefer list of gods in the commentaries (239 B): 'a paganis et sol et luna et cetera sidera di caelestes dicuntur: in terra Apollinem Aesculapium Herculem Mineruam deos dicunt et dominos.' The veiling of the

[1] The words *scrutor*, *scrutator* express close and searching examination (cf. *scrutari* occulta significat penetrare qu. 125 m): for the verb, in the present connexion, cf. scrutantes cursus siderum (60 c); scrutatis igitur stellarum motibus [Prosper] *De Rev. Div.* 75.

[2] *Lexikon der Mythologie.*

[3] For other exx. of this form, see Georges, s.v.

[4] Perhaps one ought to read *Phryx illa*, and consider the reference to be to the *Mater Magna*.

[5] The same epithet is applied to *Flora* in Minucius Felix, c. 25, and in Riese *anthol.* I², p. 24 carm. c. paganos, v. 112, of date about 390. This poem may have been written by or known to our author.

eyes in the presence of the pagan mysteries is attacked (271 B): 'religionem in qua nihil fucatum, nihil *in tenebris* uidet geri, sicut apud *paganos, quibus uelantur oculi,* ne, quae "sacra" uocant perspicientes, uariis se uanitatibus cernant *inludi*'; (418 B) *pagani in tenebris* mystica sua celebrantes *in spelaeo uelatis oculis inluduntur*: and in qu. 114: 'Illud autem quale est quod *in speleo uelatis oculis inluduntur*? Ne enim horreant turpiter dehonestari se, *oculi illis uelantur*' etc. (again: p. 2346 15). Again, compare: 'sententia paganorum turpis et foeda est, maxime quae in Phrygia inuenta est, in qua nisi spurcus intersit, sacramentum mutum est et torpescit religio' (110 A) with a passage of quaestio 114 (col. 2343 44 ff.): 'e contra autem paganorum traditio antestites et ministros idoneos sibi esse non posse nisi ex uiris transfigurentur in feminas, ut licenter et publice muliebria patiantur et discussis in aqua inhoneste crinibus mollem quassatamque uocem et turpem emittant. Quod si publice facerent, ab omni populo lapidarentur. Et cynocefalus ille qui nutabundus per omnia se circumfert loca quaerens membra adulteri Osiris uiri Isidis!'

Certain Roman festivals are named in 381 B, on Gal. iv 10: "*Dies obseruatis et menses et tempora et annos.*" The passage is worth transcribing, though it mentions Roman rather than Galatian practices. "*Dies* ergo *obseruant,* qui dicunt, ut puta: 'crastino proficiscendum non est; post crastinum enim non debet aliquid inchoari': et sic solent magis decipi. Hi autem *colunt menses,* qui cursus lunae perscrutantur, dicentes, ut puta: 'septima luna instrumenta confici non debent'; 'nona iterum luna seruum emptum, ut puta, domum duci non oportet': et per haec facilius solent aduersa prouenire. *Tempora* uero sic *obseruant,* cum dicunt: 'hodie ueris initium est, festiuitas est, post cras Vulcanalia sunt.' Et talia iterum aiunt: 'posterum est, domum egredi non licet.' *Annos* sic *colunt,* cum dicunt: 'Kalendis Ianuariis nouus est annus,' quasi non cottidie anni impleantur: sed ut Iani illius recolant memoriam bifrontis[1], hac superstitione utuntur, quae longe debet esse a seruis Dei." 'Coracina sacra' are mentioned on page 61 C (see below for context), and in qu. 114 (col. 2343 58, 59): 'alii autem sicut ales alas percutiunt uocem *coracis* imitantes.'

[1] Cf. 'Ianique bifrontis' carm. adu. paganos v. 93.

The Amazons are mentioned in both works. 'Postquam enim mulieres eorum (Scytharum) lege uiri uti coeperunt, quas Amazonas primitus adserunt appellatas, totam Asiam contra naturam subicientes, sic contigit ut et uiri canum more rabidi efficerentur, inmanes siluestres, inculti, plus quam barbari, in tantum inmutati, ut carne humana uescenda imbuerentur' (461 A): 'traduntur enim mulieres Scytharum, quae Amazonae dictae sunt, quia cum uiri earum occupati bello longinquo diu abessent, propter subolem seruis se miscuisse, et omnem marem natum necauisse, relictis feminis ita, ut nulla lanificio operam daret, sed ab ineunte aetate palaestra et armis inbuerentur. Harum tanta uirtus et industria in rebus gestis fuit, ut per multam annorum seriem regnantes non nullas gentes subigerent, Asiam omnem sub tributo ponentes' (qu. 115 aex). The two passages, by their differences as well as their resemblances, constitute in themselves an undoubted proof of common authorship.

The Babylonians and the Egyptians are mentioned in both works. On Rom. i 23 the Babylonians are said to have been the first to call by the name of a 'god' the representation of a certain dead Belus, once a man, who is said 'principatum in eos egisse.' They also worshipped a 'serpens draco,' which Daniel, the man of God, killed, and whose likeness they possess (61 B)[1]. The author asserts (2 qu. N. T. 17) that the Samaritans are well known to have sprung from the Babylonians ('erat enim Samaritanus, quos *constat* ex origine esse Babyloniorum')[2]. His interest in the customs of nations is considerable. 'The Persians wear ear-rings like women, a thing which here (in Rome) is dishonourable and illegal: but that it can be done here also, the priests of Mater Magna show'; etc. (qu. 115 ppr). 'It is a custom of Moorish women to wear rings even in their noses (*ibid.*).' In the same passage there is a comparison of the several riding customs among the Jews, the Romans, the Garamantes, the Persians, the Midianites, and the Africans, with respect to the animals used.

The references to Egypt are rather frequent, and must be mentioned in detail here, their significance being reserved for

[1] This is from the apocryphal book 'Bel and the Dragon' (Swete, *Introd. to the Study of the LXX*, pp. 260 ff.).

[2] This fact was got from 2 Reg. xvii 6, 23, especially *v.* 24; xviii 34.

discussion in a later chapter. The most remarkable, perhaps, is that to the Alexandrian Library founded by Ptolemy, and the proofs there existing as to the signs wrought in Egypt for the deliverance of the children of Israel. The passage is as follows (qu. 114 aex): 'In monte enim apparuit maiestas Dei ad dandam legem hominibus. Et ut huic fides possit haberi, praemisit signa multa et prodigia facta in Aegypto, quod *hodieque libri testantur a Ptolomaeo reconditi in bybliothecam Alexandriae.*' This 'testimonium' has been overlooked by Susemihl[1], who mentions that Justin Martyr (Apol. 2), Pseudo-Justin (Coh.), Augustine (C. D. 18, 42), and Jerome speak inaccurately of the library (singular) founded by Ptolemy. The present passage does not commit itself to a statement of the number of libraries founded by the king (apart from the possibility that one collection may have been stored in two buildings[2]), and has a certain value as evidence. The reference is evidently not to a Greek Old Testament, unless we suppose that the author is giving the statement on hearsay, or at random, for controversial purposes, knowing that it would not be verified. We know from Orosius, who had seen the empty shelves[3], that they were rifled by Theodosius the First in the year 389: so the date of qu. 114 is fixed as previous to that year. The following quotations will show that the author had some connexion with or special interest in Egypt. The worship of Apis and of birds is referred to (61 c): 'Aegyptii autem colebant quadrupedem, quam[4] (*v. l.* quem) dicebant Apem, in similitudinem uaccae, quod malum imitatus est Hieroboam, uaccas[5] instruens in Samaria, quibus sacrificarent Iudaei, et uolucres, quia coracina[6] sacra habebant pagani. Harum tamen

[1] *Gesch. der griech. Litt. in der Alex. Zeit* I (Leipz. 1891), p. 337, n. 39, a convenient book for information about the Alexandrian Library (or Libraries) of Ptolemy. It is possible that our passage may be from Tert. *apol.* 18.

[2] This is the view of the writer of 'Alexandria' in Hastings' *Dict. Bibl.*

[3] Oros. *Hist. adu. Pag.* 6, 15, 32.

[4] The feminine is curious, as Apis, elsewhere (e.g. Plin. *h. n.* VIII 184—186), is a 'bos.' It is possibly meant to express contempt. So the Spaniards in the present time, call out 'vaca' to a cowardly bull in the ring.

[5] The LXX has δαμάλεις, the Vulg. uituli (3 Reg. xii 28, 32). Modern criticism, too, attributes Israel's idolatry greatly to Egyptian influence.

[6] See qu. 114 also, cited supra, p. 34. We should expect 'coracica' (cf. ἱεροκορακικός) of the mysteries of Mithras; 'coracina' has a different meaning

rerum, quas memoraui, simulacra coluerunt Aegyptii, et alia[1] quae nunc dicere non est necesse.' Compare (qu. 3 pr): 'Adubi autem creuit error generi humano, ita ut etiam filii Israhel contra hanc expositionem (i.e. the Biblical account of the creation) in Aegypto tradi audirent a philosophis Aegyptiorum, a quibus etiam *Moyses fuerat instructus omnem peritiam Aegyptiacam* (Act. vii 22), quae Apim (*v. ll.* Saclam, Salam) quendam mundum istum adserit per malos angelos condidisse; hunc quoque *principem mundi* (Io. xii 31) uideri, id est, satanan. Quam sententiam Marcion secutus ruit in mortem. Nam et Manichei ab eodem satana (*v. l.* Sacla)[2] hominem dicunt factum, non mundum istum, stultiores ceteris.' The history of the belief in an angel Saclas is a somewhat obscure one. Seemingly, it was adopted by the Manichaeans from the Ophites. In qu. 106, where the creation of the world is again the subject, the mysterious Saclas recurs[3]: 'quibusdam enim uidebatur (mundus) initium non habere, aliis initium quidem habere, sed ab angelis quibusdam fabricatus esse; non nullis uero factus similiter, sed a Sacla (*v. ll.* spiritu, Secla) quodam, qui esset deus potestatis aduersae: pauci autem de origine, cet.' A knowledge of Church government in Egypt is also evidenced (410 C); 'apud Aegyptum presbyteri consignant[4], si praesens non sit episcopus. Sed quia coeperunt sequentes presbyteri indigni inueniri ad primatus tenendos, immutata est ratio, prospiciente concilio[5], ut non ordo sed meritum crearet episcopum, multorum sacerdotum iudicio constitutum, ne indignus

(*raven-coloured*). We have here, perhaps, a slip of the author himself, who had the Nile delicacy, the coracīnus (*κορακῖνος—a fish*), running in his mind. Some MSS have *coruina*.

[1] E.g. the cat.

[2] Read 'Saclam' in the first place and 'Sacla' in the second.

[3] Saclas is mentioned also in Aug. *haer.* 46, and in Theodoret, *haer. fab.* 5, 9 οὐ τὸν Θεὸν τοῦτο διαπλᾶσαι φασὶν (οἱ τοῦ Μάνεντος διάδοχοι), ἀλλὰ τὸν Σακλᾶν, τῆς ὕλης τὸν ἄρχοντα. The most important passages are three in Priscillian, kindly pointed out to me by Dr M. R. James.

[4] This is the correct reading; the meaning is perhaps *to confirm* (by making the sign of the cross on the brow with holy chrism). V. Bartlet (*Contemporary Review*, April 1902, p. 541) takes it to mean 'consecrates (or seals).' The word occurs elsewhere in this connexion only in Hauler's Latin *Didasc. Veron.* App., as far as I know.

[5] *Concilio* according to Lightfoot (*Philippians*[4], p. 203) refers to *Apost. Const.* Some MSS read *consilio* here.

temere usurparet, et esset multis scandalum': so in qu. 101 'in Alexandria et per totam Aegyptum, si desit episcopus, consignat presbyter[1].' The following analogy has an interest of its own, apart from its connexion with the present paragraph:—'*Pharaoh* was the name of the kings among the Egyptians, just as among the Romans *reges* are called *Augusti*' (144 A).

Another point of contact between the two writings is found in the names of heretics. Hardly any heretic is mentioned in the one that does not appear in the other also. Some references to heretics in general will be found in Migne's index to the volume containing the commentaries[2]: Langen, too (on page 20), gives a list of references. The words used are *haeretici* and *schismatici*, *haereses* and *schismata*. A good enumeration occurs in the note on 1 Cor. i 13 *diuisus est Christus*: Fotiniani, Arriani[3], Cataphrygae, Nouatiani, Donatiani[4], Manichei (197 A; cf. 72 B). In qu. 72 there is another: 'Fotinus[5], Sabellius[6], Arrius[7], Marcion[8], Manicheus[9].' The whole of tract 102 is directed against Novatian, as is qu. 91 against Fotinus and qu. 97 against Arius. The tract against Arius is perhaps referred to in qu. 125 ex: 'hic finis sit: iam enim in libello aduersus Arriam impietatem digesto reliqua plene tractata sunt, quae trinitatis conplexa sunt indiscretam unitatem.' It may be remarked that dead heretics, for example Novatian, are addressed as if alive in the persons of their followers.

The previous authors referred to or quoted are Tertullian,

[1] For other occasions on which a *presbyter* could act only in the absence of an *episcopus*, cf. Synod of Elvira (305 or 306 A.D.) can. 32, Synod of Carthage (387 or 390 A.D.) can. 4.

[2] The index to the commentaries in Migne is not complete, and there is none to the *Quaestiones*.

[3] This form is far commoner in the best MSS and in inscriptions than the form with one *r* (see s. v. *Arrius* in the *Thes. Ling. Lat.*).

[4] Filastrius has the form *Donatiani* once, never *Donatistae*. Does Augustine know the former? *Donatistae* seems the only form in Aug., and is the only form in Optatus Mileuitanus. Is the latter form, then, African, and the former Italian?

[5] Cf. 216 C; qu. 23; qu. 56; 2 qu. N.T. 53; 57.

[6] Cf. in 2 Cor. i 3 (some MSS); 2 qu. V.T. 3.

[7] Cf. qu. 23.

[8] Cf. 194 B; 203 A: 216 B; 2 qu. N.T. 53.

[9] Cf. 194 B; 2 qu. N.T. 53.

Victorinus[1], Novatian[2], Cyprian, and Eusebius. Tertullian, Victorinus and Cyprian are joined together as 'ueteres,' whose readings of scripture passages are now impugned (101 A). 'Tertullian and Novatian possessed no small *scientia*; *sed quia per zelum caritatis foedera perdiderunt, in schisma uersi ad perditionem sui haereses creauerunt*' (266 A). The *liber aduersus Iudaeos* of Tertullian is mentioned (qu. 44 ex) as showing that 490 years intervened between the accession of Darius, king of the Persians, and the birth and passion of our Lord and the destruction of Jerusalem[3]. This is misleading. The book does indeed say that 490 years elapsed between the first year of Darius and the destruction of Jerusalem, but Tertullian gives 437½ years after Darius' accession as the date of the birth of Christ. The quotation from Eusebius, on which qu. 125 is an attack, is introduced thus:—'memini me in quodam[4] libello Eusebii quondam, egregii in reliquis (*in other respects*)[5] uiri, legisse quia nec spiritus sanctus sciat mysterium natiuitatis domini nostri Iesu Christi, et admiror tantae doctrinae uirum hanc maculam sancto spiritui inflixisse.' Who the Eusebius referred to is, the biographical dictionaries do not attempt to say. There can be little doubt that Eusebius of Vercellae[6] is meant. I have gathered together here the names of all authors expressly mentioned, though Tertullian and Novatian alone appear in both works.

The writer possessed acquaintance with apocryphal literature. He attributes the sentence 'quod oculus non uidit, nec auris audiuit, nec in cor hominis ascendit, quae praeparauit deus diligentibus eum' (1 Cor. ii 9) to the 'Apocalypsis Heliae in apocryphis[7].' In this he may have made a mistake, as in qu. 112 (col.

[1] See above, p. 7, n. 3.

[2] In 2 Tim. ii 20 *bis*; 2 Cor. xii 21; 1 Cor. vi 18; qu. 102 (where col. 2307, 3—4; col. 2310, 22—25; 67—68 may be quotations from Novatian's works). A list of N.'s works may be found in Bardenhewer's *Patrologie*[2], § 55.

[3] *adu. Iud.* 8.

[4] For the vagueness of quotation in ancient authors, irritating to us, cf. *quidam iuris libellus* (qu. 115 aex).

[5] This is what is meant by the expression, cf. qu. 97 *in reliquis* sunt conuicti (col. 2293, 44), the only other passage in the *Quaestiones* where the phrase occurs.

[6] Mr A. E. Burn (*Journ. Theol. Stud.* I p. 594) and Dom G. Morin (*Revue Bénédictine* xx (1903) p. 115, n. 2) have also come to the same conclusion.

[7] This is a 'testimonium' to the apocalypse unknown either to Harnack *Altchr. Litt.* I 853 ff. or Steindorff, as Dom Morin (p. 112) points out.

2338, 27) he cites *quis gloriabitur mundum se habere cor aut inmunem esse a peccatis?* from 'alius psalmus[1],' whereas it comes from Prov. xx 9. But it is more probable that the words really occurred in that apocalypse, having been adopted by its author from Is. lxiv 4. The statement 'Simone mago, qui dicitur in aera sursum, ut populum Christi scandalizaret, uolasse' (in Rom. viii 38, 39) is doubtless derived from one of the 'Clementine' writings[2], like the other statement (qu. 127, col. 2384, 64), 'sanctus Petrus uxorem et filios[3] habuisse cognoscitur[4].' Of Iannes and Mambres, mentioned in 2 Tim. iii 8, he says 'exemplum hoc de apocryphis est: Iamnes enim et Mambres fratres erant magi uel uenefici Aegyptiorum qui arte magiae suae uirtutibus dei, quae per Moysen agebantur, aemulatione commenticia resistere se putabant. Sed cum Moysi uirtus in operibus cresceret, humiles facti, confessi sunt cum dolore ulcerum deum in Moyse operatum' (521 c).

[1] So the MSS. Cyprian, in the *Testimonia*, makes the same kind of mistake sometimes.

[2] Cf. Headlam on *Simon Magus* in Hastings' *D. B.* IV 522 (second column).

[3] The editors have carefully eliminated the children.

[4] Add this reference to those in Hort's *Notes Introductory to the Study of the Clementine Recognitions* p. 51 ff. If I mistake not, the above references, if they should be held to come from the 'Clementine' writings, have some bearing on their history.

CHAPTER II.

COMPARISON OF SCRIPTURE QUOTATIONS.

In this chapter I shall consider the text of those quotations from the third and fourth Gospels and the Pauline epistles[1], which are found both in the commentaries and in the one hundred and twenty-seven *Quaestiones*[2]. It is unfortunate for this investigation that there are hardly any long quotations. For the longer quotations of an author are generally copied directly from the Bible, while he trusts to his memory for the shorter quotations. Accordingly we cannot be quite sure that we have the *ipsissima uerba* of our writer's bible. Again, as may be seen from the Introduction, there are many ancient MSS of the commentaries of which I do not possess collations, and these may be of importance in finally constituting the text. I have, however, decided to write this chapter, as I believe that the text of Scripture, as it appears in the old MSS of the *Quaestiones*, will form a test of the comparative value of the numerous MSS of the commentaries, and simplify the task of editing that work. Allowance must be made in this, as in every other investigation of the kind, for the alterations, conscious and unconscious, which were made in scriptural quotations by scribes.

For obvious reasons I have confined my attention to the Gospels and the Pauline epistles. Copies of the Old Testament in Latin differed comparatively little in text, but in the Epistles, and even more in the Gospels, there is an abundance of variants. So many are they, that if, given a sound edition of both our

[1] I have confined the enquiry to two Gospels, as being sufficient for the present purpose.

[2] I had not at the time of writing collated the MSS of the extra *Quaestiones*, and therefore leave them out of account.

works, the Gospel quotations were found to be almost identical in text, a very strong presumption of common authorship would be established, even in the absence of any other evidence. Parallel quotations from the Pauline epistles have been selected because in the commentaries the text commented upon is quoted *in extenso.* It must be remembered, however, that the very acquaintance with the Epistles which the writer acquired in the course of commenting on them might cause him to quote them more readily from memory in a later work.

In giving the quotations I follow this method. Those quotations which occur in the commentaries I give in the left-hand column according to the Benedictine text, appending all manuscript variants known to me. The MSS I have used are indicated in the Introduction (§ 4) by asterisks, but are not named here, as I am not editing the quotations, or seeking to forestall the work of Father Brewer. But I have edited the quotations in the *Quaestiones* from my MSS, having come to recognise that the Benedictine text is no less worthless in the scriptural quotations than in the rest of the work.

Finally, I have asterisked all quotations where the text in the *Quaestiones* differs from the Vulgate.

Quotations from the Third and Fourth Gospels.

*Luc. i 32—33.

(Comm. in 1 Cor. xv 24—26)	(Qu. 86, col. 2280, 17)
et dabit illi dominus deus sedem Dauid patris sui, et regnabit in domo Iacob in aeternum, et regni eius non erit finis	et dabit illi dominus deus sedem Dauid patris sui, et regnabit in domo Iacob in aeternum, et regni eius non erit finis

*Luc. ii 29.

(Comm. in Rom. x 15)	(Qu. 127, col. 2382, 8)
nunc (ait) *domine dimitte* seruum tuum in pace domine dimittis (dimittis domine) (dimitte domine | *add.* domine *post* tuum	domine nunc dimitte seruum tuum secundum uerbum tuum in pace

*Luc. ii 48.

(Comm. in Gal. i 19)	(Qu. 56, col. 2253, 56)
quid fecisti nobis, fili? ego et pater tuus maesti et tristes quaerebamus te	fili, quid fecisti *nobis*? etenim ego et pater tuus maesti et tristes ambulantes quaerebamus te
ins. etenim (et) *ante* ego	nobis sic *aliquot codd.*

*Luc. xi 52.

(Comm. in Rom. xi 8—10; in 1 Cor. xiii 2)	(Qu. 102, col. 2307, 37)
uos habetis *clauem* scientiae et neque uos intratis neque alios sinitis introire	uos habetis clauem scientiae et neque uos intratis neque alios sinitis introire
claues	

*Luc. xxii 31—32.

(Comm. in Rom. viii 34)	(Qu. 79 (75), col. 2270, 16)
ecce *expostulauit* satanas ut uos uentilet *sicut* triticum; ego autem rogaui pro te ne deficiat fides tua	ecce satanas expostulauit ut uos uentilet uelut triticum; ego autem rogaui pro te ne deficiat fides tua
(et) postulauit | uelut	

*Luc. xxiv 21[1].

(Comm. in Rom. i 4 cf. in 1 Cor. xv 5)	(Qu. 77 (73), col. 2268, 16)
(nam et discipuli in morte eius dubitauerunt dicente Cleopha *in Emmaus*): nos putabamus quia ipse *erat* qui incipiebat liberare Israhel	(denique Cleopas et *Emmaus* euntes in uia tristes dicunt inter cetera ipsi domino nescientes quia dominus est): nos putabamus quia ipse erat qui incipiebat liberare Israhel
et emmau | esset | nos autem putabamus quia ipse esset redempturus Israhel	amaus (emaus)

*Io. i 3—4.

(Comm. in Gal. iv 26; in Phil. i 18—21)	(Qu. 122, col. 2368, 4)
quod factum est in *ipso* uita *est*...et uita erat lux hominum	quod factum est in ipso uita est
illo...erat *Migne in Phil. codd. Gal.* (*contra codd. Phil.* est)	

[1] See *Expository Times*, XIII (1902), 429, 430.

Io. i 5.

(Comm. in Rom. x 16)

lux in tenebris lucet et tenebrae eam non comprehenderunt

(Qu. 64, col. 2259, 41)

lux in tenebris...et tenebrae eam non conprehenderunt (an allusion, not a quotation)

Io. i 14.

(In 2 Cor. vi 17—18)

uerbum caro factum est cet.

(Qu. 91, col. 2284, 65)

uerbum caro factum est

*Io. iii 13.

(Comm. in Eph. iv 10)

nemo ascendit in caelum nisi qui descendit de caelo filius hominis *qui est* in caelo

qui et est

(Qu. 89, col. 2281, 51)

nemo ascendit ad deum nisi qui descendit a deo

*Io. iii 16.

(Comm. in 1 Cor. vi 2, cf. in 2 Thess. ii 15—16)

sic *dilexit deus mnndum* et cetera

deus dilexit | hunc m. (m. hunc)

(Qu. 91, col. 2283, 18)

sic enim dilexit deus mundum hunc...

*Io. iii 18.

(Comm. in Rom. ii 16)

qui non crediderit iam iudicatus est

(Qu. 126, col. 2376, 30)

qui non crediderit iam iudicatus est

*Io. v 18.

(Comm. in Phil. ii 5—6)

propter ea persequebantur Iudaei Iesum quia non solum soluebat sabbatum sed et patrem sibi proprium dicebat deum aequalem se faciens deo

(Qu. 91, col. 2283, 71; qu. 97, col. 2291, 19, cf. qu. 91, col. 2283, 48)

non solum enim soluebat sabbatum sed et patrem proprium sibi dicebat deum aequalem se faciens deo

Qu. 91 *breuior est et habet* patrem *inter* sibi *et* dicebat

*Io. v 26.

(Comm. in Gal. iv 26)

sicut enim pater habet uitam...ita dedit et filio uitam

(Qu. 40, col. 2237, 17)

sicut habet pater uitam...ita dedit filio uitam

*Io. v 26.

(In Col. i 19)	(Qu. 97, col. 2291, 27; qu. 122, col. 2368, 6)
sicut habet pater uitam in semet ipso ita dedit *et* filio uitam habere in semet ipso	sicut (enim) habet pater uitam in semet ipso *sic* dedit et filio *habere uitam* in semet ipso
om. et	pater habet 1 *cod.* | ita *Qu.* 122 | uitam habere *Qu.* 122 | in semet ipso *om. Qu.* 97

*Io. v 46.

(Comm. in Rom. ix 28; cf. in Col. i 23—24)	(Qu. 72 (76), col. 2270, 51; qu. 127, col. 2380, 70)
de me enim scripsit Moyses	de me scripsit Moyses

*Io. vi 38.

(Comm. in Rom. xv 3)	(Qu. 91, col. 2282, 48)
non enim descendi de caelo ut faciam uoluntatem meam sed uoluntatem eius qui *misit me* patris	non enim descendi de caelo ut faciam uoluntatem meam sed uoluntatem eius qui me misit patris
me misit	

*Io. viii 44.

(Comm. in Rom. viii 14)	(Qu. 80, col. 2273, 55; qu. 90, col. 2282, 2; qu. 98, col. 2297, 48)
uos de patre diabolo estis	uos de patre diabolo estis
	nati estis (*qu.* 98) *ubi Colb. om.* nati

*Io. viii 56.

(Comm. in Gal. prol.)	(Qu. 117, col. 2360, 17)
Abraham cupiuit uidere diem meum et uidit et gauisus est	Abraham pater uester cupiuit ut uideret diem meum et uidit et gauisus est

Io. x 30.

(Comm. in Phil. ii 5—6)	(Qu. 97, col. 2291, 33; qu. 125, col. 2373, 37)
ego et pater *unum* sumus	ego et pater unum sumus
unus	

*Io. xiv 9.

(Comm. in 2 Cor. v 19 ff.)	(Qu. 97, col. 2291, 25)
qui me *uidet uidet* et patrem	qui me uidit uidit et patrem
uidit uidit	

*Io. xiv 11.

(Comm. in 2 Cor. v 19 ff.)	(Qu. 97, col. 2291, 37)
quia pater in me est et ego in patre	quod ego in patre et pater in me
totum locum om. duo codd.	

*Io. xiv 27.

(Comm. in Rom. xiv 17; in Rom. xv 33; in 1 Cor. xiv 33; in 2 Cor. xiii 11; in 1 Thess. v 23)	(Qu. 92, col. 2286, 2)
pacem meam do uobis, pacem relinquo uobis	pacem do uobis pacem meam relinquo uobis
Thess. et omnes codd. ubique add. meam *post alt.* pacem.	

*Io. xvi 15 (cf. xvii 10).

(Comm. in Eph. ii 3, cf. in Eph. iii 17)	(Qu. 125, col. 2373, 39)
omnia quae habet pater mea sunt; et mea patris	omnia quae patris sunt mea sunt, et quae mea sunt patris

*Io. xvii 3.

(Comm. in Rom. i 1 (excluded because wanting in some MSS): in 1 Cor. xv 24 ff.)	(Qu. 3, col. 2219, 39; qu. 113, col. 2340, 7)
haec est autem uita aeterna ut cognoscant te solum *uerum* deum et quem misisti Iesum Christum	haec est autem uita aeterna ut cognoscant te solum et uerum deum et quem misisti Iesum Christum
et uerum (*unus cod. om.*)	

*Io. xvii 24.

(Combined from comm. in Gal. iv 26 and in Eph. i 20—21)	(Qu. 79 (75), col. 2270, 25; qu. 122, col. 2368, 68)
pater quos dedisti mihi uolo ut, ubi ego fuero, et hi mecum sint et uideant gloriam meam	pater uolo ut ubi ego sum et *isti* sint mecum et uideant claritatem meam
sint mecum *Gal.*	ipsi *Mett.*

*Io. xix 11.

(Comm. in Eph. v 2)	(Qu. 78 (74), second version col. 2269, 24)
non haberes *aduersum* me potestatem nisi *data tibi* esset de super	non haberes potestatem in me nisi data esset tibi de super
aduersus | tibi data (datum tibi)	

Quotations from the Pauline Epistles.

Rom. iii 8.

	(Qu. 126, col. 2377, 56)
quorum damnatio iusta est	quorum damnatio iusta est

*Rom. iii 19.

	(Qu. 33, col. 2233, 75)
scimus *autem* quoniam, quaecumque lex loquitur, *iis* qui in lege sunt loquitur	scimus autem quoniam, quaecumque lex loquitur, his qui in lege sunt loquitur
autem *om.* | his | primum *post* lege	
	(Qu. 102, col. 2309, 39)
	scimus autem, quia quaecumque lex loquitur, his qui sub lege sunt loquitur

Rom. iii 23.

	(Qu. 47, col. 2248, 61)
omnes *enim* peccauerunt et egent gloria dei	omnes peccauerunt et egent gloria dei
enim *om.* | gloriam	gloriam

*Rom. iv 3, (Gen. xv 6).

	(Qu. 44, col. 2241, 46)
credidit Abraham deo et reputatum est *ei* ad iustitiam	credidit enim Abraham deo et reputatum est ei ad iustitiam
illi	deo Abraham *Aug.* | *om.* ei *Colb.*

Rom. vii 23.

	(Qu. 112, col. 2337, 9)
uideo autem aliam legem in membris meis repugnantem legi mentis meae	uideo autem aliam legem in membris meis repugnantem legi mentis meae

Rom. viii 9.

	(Qu. 125, col. 2374, 51)
siquis autem spiritum Christi non habet, hic non est eius	siquis spiritum Christi non habet, hic non est eius

Rom. viii 18.

	(Qu. 126, col. 2378, 15)
non *sint* condignae passiones huius temporis ad futuram gloriam quae reuelabitur in nobis	non sunt condignae passiones huius temporis ad futuram gloriam quae reuelabitur in nobis
sunt	

*Rom. viii 26—27.

	(Qu. 125, col. 2374, 66)
(27) qui autem scrutatur corda scit *quid* desideret spiritus, quia secundum deum postulat pro sanctis	(27) qui scrutatur corda scit quid *desideret* spiritus, quia secundum dei uoluntatem postulat pro sanctis
quod	desiderat *Colb.*
	(Qu. 125, col. 2374, 76)
(26) *nam quid* oremus *sicut* oportet nescimus	(26) nam quid oremus sicut oportet nescimus
quid enim | secundum quod	

*Rom. viii 29.

	(Qu. 106, col. 2320, 52)
conformes fieri imaginis filii sui	coimaginati filio dei
consortes	

*Rom. viii 32.

	(Qu. 91, col. 2283, 70; qu. 97, col. 2291, 10)
qui proprio filio suo non pepercit	qui proprio filio non pepercit
etiam *add. post* qui	

*Rom. ix 5.

	(Qu. 56, col. 2253, 21; qu. 91, col. 2284, 44 combined)
quorum patres et ex quibus Christus secundum carnem, qui est super omnia deus, benedictus in saecula	quorum patres et ex quibus Christus secundum carnem, qui est super omnia deus, benedictus in saecula

*Rom. ix 16.

	(Qu. 75 (79), col. 2272, 25)
non uolentis neque currentis sed miserentis est dei	neque uolentis neque currentis sed miserentis est dei

Rom. ix 18.

	(Qu. 75 (79), col. 2272, 26)
cui uult miseretur et quem uult indurat	cuius uult miseretur et quem uult indurat
deus *add. post* cui	

Rom. ix 25 (Osee ii 23).

	(Qu. 44, col. 2243, 9)
uocabo non plebem meam plebem meam et non dilectam dilectam	uocabo non plebem meam plebem meam et non dilectam dilectam

Rom. x 4.

	(Qu. 69, col. 2263, 56)
finis enim legis Christus	finis legis Christus

*Rom. x 10.

	(Qu. 102, col. 2311, 41; qu. 126, col. 2377, 33)
corde enim creditur ad iustitiam, ore autem confessio fit *ad* salutem	corde enim (*enim* not in 1st reference) creditur ad iustitiam, ore autem confessio fit in salutem
in	

Rom. xi 29.

	(Qu. 102, col. 2306, 30)
sine paenitentia enim *sunt* dona et *uocatio* dei	sine paenitentia enim sunt dona et uocatio dei
om. sunt | uocationes	

*Rom. xi 33.

	(Qu. 125, col. 2375, 51)
o altitudo diuitiarum sapientiae et scientiae dei! quam *inscrutabilia sunt* iudicia eius, et inuestigabiles uiae *ipsius!*	o altitudo diuitiarum *et* sapientiae et scientiae dei! quam inscrutabilia sunt iudicia eius, et inuestigabiles uiae *ipsius!*
sunt inscr. | eius	***om.* et | eius**

*Rom. xi 36.

	(Qu. 122, col. 2369, 29)
quoniam ex ipso et per ipsum et in ipso sunt omnia, ipsi gloria	quoniam ex ipso et per ipsum et in ipso sunt omnia, ipsi gloria
	add.* in saecula saeculorum *omn. exc. P* amen *P* (*post* saeculorum) *Aug.

*Rom. xiii 1.

	(Qu. 35, col. 2234, 47; qu. 110, col. 2330, 38)
omnibus potestatibus sublimioribus *subditi estote*: non *est enim* potestas nisi *a* deo; quae autem sunt a deo *ordinata* sunt	omnibus potestatibus sublimioribus subditi estote; non est enim potestas nisi a deo; quae enim sunt a deo ordinatae sunt
subiaceat | *om.* est | *om.* enim | ex ordinatae	**(second reference omits first *enim*; and in second ref. *Aug. Gand.* have *ordinata*)**

*Rom. xiii 3.

	(Qu. 69, col. 2264, 13)
qui principantur non sunt *timori bonis operibus*, sed *malis.* Vis autem non timere potestatem? *bonum facito* et habebis laudem ex illa	principes non sunt timori operi bono, sed malo. Vis autem non timere potestatem? bonum fac et habebis laudem ex illa
principes | timoris | opere bono | malo fac quod bonum est	**timeri *Brux.* timendi *Aug.* | autem *om. Nostrad.***

Rom. xiv 18.

	(Qu. 91, col. 2284, 20)
qui enim in hoc seruit Christo placet deo	qui seruit Christo placet deo
nam qui | *om.* in hoc, *post insertum*	

Rom. xiv 23.

	(Qu. 9, col. 2222, 69)
omne autem quod non est ex fide peccatum est	omne quod non est ex fide peccatum est

*Rom. xv 8.

	(Qu. 58, col. 2254, 43)
dico enim Christum *Iesum* ministrum fuisse circumcisionis *pro ueritate* dei *in hoc ut confirmaret* promissiones patrum	dico enim Christum ministrum fuisse circumcisionis pro ueritate dei ad confirmandas promissiones patrum
om. **Iesum | propter ueritatem (misericordiam) | ad stabiliendas**	

*1 Cor. i 19 (Esa. xxix 14).

	(Qu. 109, col. 2326, 5) (perhaps a recollection merely)
perdam sapientiam sapientium et intellectum prudentium reprobabo	perdam prudentiam prudentium

1 Cor. i 24.

	(Qu. 91, col. 2283, 6)
Christum dei uirtutem et dei sapientiam	Christum dei uirtutem et dei sapientiam

1 Cor. i 25.

	(Qu. 117, col. 2360, 56)
quod stultum est dei sapientius est hominibus	quod stultum est dei sapientius est hominibus

*1 Cor. ii 1.

	(Qu. 100, col. 2300, 67)
et ego *cum uenissem* ad uos, fratres, ueni non *cum* eminentia *sermonis* aut sapientiae	et ego ueniens ad uos, fratres, ueni non in sublimitate sermonis aut sapientiae
ueniens | in | uerbi	

*1 Cor. ii 8.

	(Qu. 66, col. 2261, 25; qu. 111, col. 2335, 32; qu. 115, col. 2358, 35)
quam nemo principum huius saeculi cognouit: si enim cognouissent, numquam *dominum* maiestatis cruci fixissent	quem nemo principum huius saeculi cognouit: si enim cognouissent, numquam dominum maiestatis cruci fixissent
dm̄ (deum)	**intellexissent (*codd. qu.* 111)**

*1 Cor. ii 9 (Esa. lxiv 4).

(Qu. 112, col. 2337, 21)

quod oculus non uidit nec auris audiuit nec in cor hominis ascendit quae praeparauit deus diligentibus *eum*	quod oculus non uidit nec auris audiuit nec in cor hominis ascendit quae praeparauit deus diligentibus se
se	

*1 Cor. ii 11.

(Qu. 125, col. 2375, 5; qu. 97, col. 2295, 52; qu. 125, col. 2374, 33)

quis *enim* scit hominum *ea* quae sunt hominis nisi spiritus hominis qui in ipso est? *sic* et quae *dei* sunt, nemo *nouit* nisi spiritus dei	nemo scit quid sit in homine nisi spiritus hominis qui in eo est: nemo scit quae sunt in deo nisi *spiritus* dei
autem | *om.* ea | ita | in deo | cognouit	in spiritu *Mett.*

1 Cor. iii 6—7.

(Qu. 102, col. 2312, 19)

ego plantaui, Apollo rigauit, sed deus incrementum dedit. itaque neque qui plantat est aliquid neque qui *rigat* sed qui incrementum dat deus	ego plantaui, Apollo rigauit, sed deus incrementum dedit. itaque neque qui plantat est aliquid neque qui rigat sed qui incrementum dat deus
inrigat	

1 Cor. iii 17.

(Qu. 97, col. 2296, 47)

templum enim dei sanctum est quod estis uos	templum enim dei sanctum est quod estis uos

1 Cor. iv 20.

(Qu. 100, col. 2300, 69)

nec enim in sermone est regnum dei sed in uirtute	quia non in sermone est regnum dei sed in uirtute
non	

1 Cor. v 6.

(Qu. 102, col. 2311, 16)

nescitis quia modicum fermentum totam massam corrumpit?	nescitis quia modicum fermentum totam massam corrumpit?

1 Cor. v 7.

(Qu. 96, col. 2290, 47)

pascha nostrum immolatus est Christus	pascha nostrum immolatus est Christus

*1 Cor. v 12.

(Qu. 102, col. 2309, 41; qu. 110 pr)

quo enim mihi de his qui foris *sunt* iudicare?

quid | est (*corr.*)

quo enim mihi de his qui foris sunt iudicare?

1 Cor. vii 23.

(Qu. 91, col. 2284, 23)

nolite fieri serui hominum

nolite fieri serui hominum

*1 Cor. vii 25.

(Qu. 127, col. 2384, 73)

de uirginibus autem praeceptum domini non habeo

de uirginibus imperium domini non habeo

*1 Cor. viii 6.

(Qu. 122, col. 2369, 23)

unus deus pater ex quo omnia et nos in *illo*, et unus dominus Iesus per quem omnia et nos per ipsum

ipso

unus deus pater ex quo omnia et nos in ipso, et unus dominus Iesus per quem omnia et nos per ipsum

*1 Cor. x 1—4 (cf. ap. xiv 32).

(Qu. 127, col. 2380, 60; *v.* 4 also in qu. 20, col. 2228, 27 and qu. 72 (76), col. 2270, 47)

nolo enim uos ignorare, fratres, *quia* patres nostri omnes sub nube fuerunt, et *omnes mare transierunt* et omnes in *Moyse* baptizati sunt in nube et in mari et omnes eandem escam spiritalem *ederunt* et omnes eundem potum spiritalem biberunt. bibebant *enim* de *sequente eos spiritali petra*: petra autem erat Christus

quod | per *inter* omnes *et* mare (*unus cod. habet* omn. m. pertransierunt) | Moysen | manducauerunt | autem (*corr.*) | spiritali sequenti petra (*om.* eos) (*unus cod.* consequenti spiritali petra)

nolo enim uos ignorare, fratres, quia patres nostri omnes sub nube fuerunt et omnes per mare transierunt et omnes in Moysen baptizati sunt in nube et in mari et omnes eandem escam spiritalem ederunt et omnes eundem potum spiritalem biberunt. bibebant enim de spiritali sequenti petra: petra autem *erat* Christus

fuit (*codd. exc. Mett. qu.* 20)

1 Cor. x 13.

	(Qu. 99, col. 2299, 41)
temptatio uos non adprehendat nisi humana	temptatio uos non adprehendat nisi humana

1 Cor. xi 3 (cf. Eph. v 23).

	(Qu. 24, col. 2230, 6)
caput autem mulieris uir	caput mulieris uir

*1 Cor. xi 6—7 (in the order 7—6).

	(Qu. 21, col. 2228, 64; qu. 106, col. 2319, 74 has v. 7 only)
(7) uir *enim* non debet uelare caput, cum *sit imago et gloria dei.* (6) uelet caput	(7) uir quidem non debet uelare caput, cum sit imago et gloria dei: (6, or paraphr. of 6, cf. qu. 106 l.c.) mulier autem uelet caput
autem | im. et glor. dei sit	quia imago et gloria dei est (*codd. qu.* 106)

*1 Cor. xi 27 and 29.

	(Qu. 102, col. 2311, 8) a paraphrase[1].
(29) qui enim manducat et bibit *indigne*, iudicium sibi *ipsi* manducat et bibit	qui indigne sumit gladium sibi sumit
om. indigne | *om.* ipsi	

*1 Cor. xii 11.

	(Qu. 97, col. 2295, 70)
omnia *autem* haec operatur unus atque idem spiritus diuidens uni cuique prout uult	omnia autem haec operatur unus atque idem spiritus diuidens uni cuique prout uult
om. autem | *om.* uni cuique	

*1 Cor. xv 19.

	(Qu. 91, col. 2285, 71)
si in hac uita tantum *in Christo sperantes sumus*, miserabiliores sumus omnibus hominibus	si in hac tantum uita sperantes sumus in Christo, miserabiliores sumus omnibus hominibus
sper. sum. in Christo	

[1] The editor of the 1531 Paris edition of Augustine (tom. IV) refers to this quotation as an instance of carelessness.

*1 Cor. xv 45, 47—48[1].

	(Qu. 123, col. 2370, 46)
(45) factus est primus homo Adam in animam uiuentem, nouissimus *autem* Adam in *spiritum uiuificantem* (47) Primus homo de terra terrenus, secundus homo *de* caelo caelestis. (48) qualis terrenus tales *et* terreni, et qualis caelestis tales et caelestes	(45) factus est primus homo Adam in animam uiuentem, secundus autem homo in spiritum uiuificantem (47) Primus homo de terra terrenus, secundus homo de caelo caelestis. (48) qualis terrenus tales et terreni, qualis caelestis tales et caelestes
om. autem | spiritu uiuificante | e | *om.* et	*et* ante *ult.* qualis *P*

2 Cor. iii 16.

	(Qu. 8, col. 2222, 49)
cum autem conuersus fuerit ad dominum, auferetur uelamen	cum conuersus fuerit ad dominum, auferetur uelamen

2 Cor. iii 17.

	(Qu. 20, col. 2228, 37)
ubi autem spiritus domini ibi libertas	ubi spiritus domini ibi libertas

*2 Cor. v 3.

	(Qu. 47, col. 2248, 38)
siquidem expoliati non nudi inueniamur	si expoliati non nudi inueniamur

*2 Cor. v 21.

	(Qu. 78 (74), col. 2268, 35)
eum *enim* qui non nouerat peccatum pro nobis peccatum fecit	eum qui peccatum nesciebat pro nobis peccatum fecit
om. enim	

2 Cor. vi 11.

	(Qu. 112, col. 2338, 71)
os nostrum patet ad uos, o Corinthii	os nostrum patet ad uos, o Corinthii

2 Cor. xi 14.

	(Qu. 27, col. 2231, 13)
ipse enim satanas transfiguratur uelut angelus luminis	ipse satanas transfigurat se in angelum lucis

[1] The Benedictine editor wrongly refers a quotation which occurs in qu. 27 (col. 2231, 25) to 2 Cor. ii 11: it really belongs to Apoc. ii 24, cf. qu. 102 (col. 2309, 27). The editor of the 1531 Paris edition had made the same assumption as his Benedictine successor.

*2 Cor. xii 9—10.

	(Qu. 119, col. 2363, 32)
sufficit tibi gratia mea; nam uirtus in infirmitate perficitur. libentissime itaque magis gloriabor in infirmitatibus meis, ut inhabitet in me uirtus *Christi*...cum enim infirmor tunc potens sum	sufficit tibi gratia mea; nam uirtus in infirmitate perficitur. gaudeo (in) tribulationibus meis, ut inhabitet in me uirtus Christi...cum infirmor tunc fortis sum
dei	

*2 Cor. xii 21.

	(Qu. 102, col. 2308, 41)
ne iterum cum uenero...lugeam multos ex *iis* qui ante peccauerunt et non egerunt paenitentiam super *inmunditia* et *fornicatione*...quam gesserunt	ne forte ueniens lugeam multos ex his qui ante peccauerunt et non egerunt paenitentiam super inmunditia et fornicatione quam gesserunt
hiis (his) | inmunditiam | fornicationem	inmundiciam (*Aug. corr.*) | fornicationem (*Aug. corr.*)

Gal. i 1.

	(Qu. 91, col. 2284, 25)
Paulus apostolus non ab hominibus neque per hominem sed per Iesum Christum et deum patrem qui suscitauit eum a mortuis	Paulus apostolus non ab hominibus neque per hominem sed per Iesum Christum et deum patrem qui suscitauit eum a mortuis

*Gal. i 12.

	(Qu. 91, col. 2284, 31; qu. 91, col. 2284, 40)
neque enim ego ab homine accepi illud aut didici sed per reuelationem Iesu Christi	neque enim ego ab homine accepi illud neque didici sed per reuelationem Iesu Christi
	edoctus sum (*pro* didici) v. 40[1]

Gal. ii 15

	(Qu. 81, col. 2274, 24)
nos natura Iudaei	nos natura Iudaei.

Gal. iii 12.

	(Qu. 9, col. 2222, 70)
lex autem non est ex fide	lex non est ex fide

[1] The second version is to be preferred, according to the sound rule of Bp Wordsworth and Mr White (*Nouum Test.* I p. 727 f. (epilogus)).

Gal. iii 13.

(Qu. 78 (74), col. 2268, 63)

factus pro nobis maledictum	factus pro nobis maledictum

Gal. iii 17.

(Qu. 10, col. 2223, 33)

post quadringentos et triginta annos facta est lex	post quadringentos et triginta annos facta est lex

*Gal. iii 27.

(Qu. 47, col. 2248, 36)

quotquot enim in Christo baptizati estis Christum induistis	qui in Christo baptizati estis Christum induistis
quicumque	

*Gal. iv 3.

(Qu. 82, col. 2275, 60)

et nos...sub elementis huius mundi eramus subiecti	eramus et nos sub elementis huius mundi seruientes

Gal. iv 14.

(Qu. 102, col. 2308, 63)

sicut angelum dei excepistis me	sicut angelum dei excepistis me

*Gal. v 1.

(Qu. 98, col. 2299, 25)

state *ergo* et nolite *iterum seruitutis* iugo *contineri*	state et nolite iterum seruitutis iugo cohiberi
om. ergo | seruitutis iterum | cohiberi	

Gal. vi 7.

(Qu. 126, col. 2377, 21)

deus non *deridetur*	deus non inridetur
inridetur	

*Eph. ii 3.

(Qu. 115, col. 2348, 68)

et eramus natura filii irae sicut et ceteri	eramus et nos natura filii irae sicut et ceteri
et *add. post* irae	

*Eph. iii 8—10.

(Qu. 47, col. 2248, 10)

mihi *omnium sanctorum minimo* data est *gratia haec ut in nationibus euangelizem* inaestimabiles diuitias *Christi* et *inluminem omnes* quae dispensatio mysterii absconditi a saeculis in deo qui uniuersa creauit ut *nota fiat* principibus et potestatibus in caelestibus per ecclesiam multiformis *sapientiae* dei

min. omn. sanct. | haec gratia | inter gentes euangelizare | Christi *om.* | inluminare (inlumine) | *om.* omnes | est *add. ante* disp. | innotescat | sapientia

mihi minimo omnium sanctorum data est haec gratia inter gentes euangelizare incomprehensibiles diuitias Christi et inluminare omnes quae sit dispositio mysterii absconditi a saeculis in deo qui uniuersa creauit ut innotesceret principibus et potestatibus *in caelestibus* per ecclesiam multiformis sapientia dei

in caelestibus *om. aliquot codd.*

Eph. v 18.

(Qu. 120, col. 2364, 45)

nolite inebriari uino in quo est luxuria

add. omnis *ante* lux.

nolite inebriari uino in quo est luxuria

*Eph. v 29.

(Qu. 127, col. 2384, 38)

nemo enim umquam carnem suam odit sed nutrit et fouet eam sicut *et* Christus ecclesiam

om. et

nemo carnem suam odio habet sed nutrit et fouet eam sicut et Christus ecclesiam

*Eph. vi 2—3.

(Qu. 7, col. 2222, 23)

honora patrem tuum et matrem, quod est mandatum primum promissionis, ut *et* bene sit tibi, et sis longaeuus super terram

om. et

honora patrem et matrem quod est mandatum primum in promissione, ut sis longaeuus super terram et bene tibi sit

*Eph. vi 12.

(Qu. 66, col. 2261, 39; qu. 110 pr; qu. 115, col. 2351, 72)

non est uobis *lucta* aduersus carnem et sanguinem sed aduersus principatus et potestates huius mundi *aduersus* tenebrarum harum rectores

conluctatio | *om.* aduersus

non est nobis conluctatio aduersus carnem et sanguinem sed aduersus principes et potestates aduersus huius mundi *tenebrarum harum rectores*

rect. ten. harum *Aug. Colb.* (*sed Colb. add.* rectoris *post* harum)

*Phil. ii 6.

	(Qu. 97, col. 2291, 11)
qui cum in forma dei esset non rapinam arbitratus est esse se parem deo	qui cum in forma dei esset non rapinam arbitratus est esse se parem deo

*Col. i 15—16.

	(Qu. 122, col. 2368, 37)
qui est imago inuisibilis dei primogenitus uniuersae creaturae quia in ipso *condita* sunt *omnia* in caelis et in terra uisibilia et inuisibilia siue throni siue dominationes siue principatus siue potestates omnia per ipsum et in *ipso condita* sunt	qui est imago inuisibilis dei primogenitus ante omnem creaturam quoniam in ipso condita sunt omnia in caelis et in terra uisibilia et inuisibilia siue sedes siue dominationes siue principatus siue potestates omnia per ipsum et in *ipsum* creata sunt
creata | uniuersa | ipsum creata	*codd. exc. Mett.* ipso

Col. ii 3.

	(Qu. 113, col. 2340, 26)
in quo sunt omnes *thesauri* sapientiae et scientiae absconditi	in quo sunt omnes thesauri sapientiae et scientiae absconditi
thensauri (*unus cod.*)	

*1 Thess. v 5.

	(Qu. 107, col. 2322, 20)
filii *luminis* estis et filii diei non estis noctis neque tenebrarum	filii diei estis et luminis non noctis et tenebrarum
lucis	

*2 Thess. ii 4.

	(Qu. 110 pr; qu. 113, col. 2341, 42)
ita ut in templo dei sedeat ostentans se ipsum *quasi* sit deus	ita ut in templo dei sedeat ostendens se quasi sit deus
tamquam	

2 Thess. iii 5.

	(Qu. 97, col. 2295, 40)
dominus autem dirigat corda uestra in dilectione dei et *patientia* Christi	dominus dirigat corda uestra in caritate dei et (in) *patientia* Christi
expectatione	pat. (*corr.* in pat.) *Nostrad.*

*1 Tim. i 9—10.

	(Qu. 4, col. 2220, 1; qu. 69, col. 2263, 71)
iusto lex non est posita *sed iniustis*... scelestis et profanis...*fornicatoribus*	iustis lex non est posita sed iniustis ...idola colentibus...fornicatoribus
iniustis uero | fornicationibus	non est lex *aliquot codd. qu.* 69

*1 Tim. ii 12.

	(Qu. 21, col. 2228, 67)
docere mulieri non permittitur neque dominari *in uirum*	mulieri docere non permittitur neque dominari in uirum
uiro	

*1 Tim. iii 7.

	(Qu. 101, col. 2302, 70)
oportet autem *et illum* testimonium habere bonum ab *iis* qui foris sunt	oportet enim hunc et testimonium habere bonum ab his qui foris sunt
eum et | his	

*1 Tim. iv 14.

	(Qu. 93, col. 2287, 15)
noli neglegere gratiam quae *est in te* quae data est tibi per prophetiam cum inpositione manuum presbiterii	noli neglegere gratiam quae est in te quae data est tibi per inpositionem manuum presbiterii
in te est	

*1 Tim. v 14.

	(Qu. 127, col. 2385, 6)
uolo itaque iuniores nubere filios procreare	uolo adulescentas[1] nubere filios procreare
	ad ulescentes (*spatio unius litterae inter* d *et* u *relicto*) *Aug.* adolescentas *Colb.* (*def. Nostrad.*) aduliscentas *Mett.*

*1 Tim. vi 8.

	(Qu. 115, col. 2354, 3)
habentes autem alimentum et *quibus tegamur* his contenti *simus*	habentes uictum et uestimentum his contenti *sumus*
alii om. alii tegimina | sumus	simus *P*

[1] This is a new reference for this form, marked as doubtful in the *Thesaurus*, and seems a better attested example than those given there.

*1 Tim. vi 15.

	(Qu. 97, col. 2292, 2)
rex *regum* et dominus dominantium	rex regum et dominus dominorum
regnantium	

2 Tim. i 6.

	(Qu. 120, col. 2364, 30)
ut recrees donum dei quod est in te	ut resuscites gratiam *dei* quae est in te
	dei *om. Nostrad.*

*2 Tim. i 12.

	(Qu. 113, col. 2340, 28)
scio enim cui credidi et certus sum quia potens est depositum meum custodire	nam scio cui credidi quia potens est depositum meum *custodire*
	seruare *Colb.*

2 Tim. ii 20.

	(Qu. 102, col. 2309, 76)
in magna autem domo non solum sunt uasa aurea et argentea *uerum* et lignea et fictilia	in magna autem domo non solum sunt uasa aurea et argentea sed et lignea et fictilia
sed	

*Tit. iii 4—7.

(grouped here also)	(Qu. 123, col. 2371, 13)
cum *uero* bonitas et humanitas inluxit salutaris *dei nostri* non ex operibus iustitiae quae *nos fecimus* sed secundum *misericordiam suam* saluos nos fecit per lauacrum regenerationis et renouationis spiritus sancti quem effudit in nos abunde per *Iesum Christum saluatorem* nostrum ut iustificati gratia illius heredes efficiamur secundum spem uitae aeternae	cum autem benignitas et humanitas adparuit *salutaris nostri* dei, non ex operibus iustitiae quas (*sic*) *nos fecimus* sed secundum *suam* misericordiam saluos nos fecit per lauacrum regenerationis *et renouationis* per spiritum sanctum quem *effudit* in nos abunde per Christum Iesum saluatorem nostrum ut iustificati gratia ipsius heredes efficiamur secundum spem uitae aeternae
enim (*corr.*) | nostri dei | fecimus nos | suam misericordiam | Christum Iesum | salutarem	salutaris (*corr.* saluatoris) *Aug.* | *om.* nostri *C* | fecimus nos *P* | suam *om. C* | et renou. *om. N* | effundit *B*

Of the twenty-six quotations from the third and fourth Gospels found in both works, three agree with the Vulgate. Of the remaining twenty-two, thirteen agree verbally, four almost verbally. There are real differences in the texts of Luc. ii 48; Io. xiv 11; xvi 5; xvii 24, and xix 11. Io. iii 13, as it appears in the MSS of the *Quaestiones*, is not a quotation, but a paraphrase.

There are ninety quotations from the Pauline epistles. Of these, thirty-seven, most of them very short, agree with the Vulgate, and may be dismissed. Long quotations are these:—1 Cor. x 1—4, Eph. iii 8—10 and Tit. iii 4—7. In the first, taking the variants into account, we find that there is not a single difference between the two texts. In the second the only differences are *inaestimabiles*)(*inconprehensibiles*, *est dispensatio*)(*sit dispositio*, and *innotescat*)(*innotesceret*. The first of the three is the only difference of importance; the second may be merely palaeographical; *innotescat* is the Vulgate reading. In the third quotation the following are the differences:—*enim* (*uero*))(*autem*, *bonitas*)(*benignitas*, *inluxit*)(*adparuit*, *spiritus sancti*)(*per spiritum sanctum*, and *illius*)(*ipsius*. *Autem*, *benignitas*, *adparuit*, *spiritus sancti*, and *ipsius* are Vulgate readings. Of the remaining fifty quotations, twelve agree exactly, twenty almost exactly; sixteen may be said to show real differences[1], and two may be set down as paraphrases[2].

Having regard to the considerations advanced at the beginning of this chapter, we can hardly doubt, I think, that the same bible lies behind both the commentaries and the *Quaestiones*. The parallels in the gospels are especially striking.

[1] Rom. viii 29; 1 Cor. ii 1; 11; vii 25; 2 Cor. xii 9—10; Gal. i 12; iv 3; Eph. v 29; vi 2; 12; Col. i 15—16; i Tim. i 9—10; iv 14; v 14; vi 8; 2 Tim. i 12.

[2] 1 Cor. i 19; xi 27—29.

CHAPTER III.

COMPARISON OF STYLE AND LANGUAGE.

In this chapter I propose to record some points of contact in style and language between the commentaries and the *Quaestiones*. The more I study both works, the more agreements in this respect do I find between them. To treat the subject adequately would require two volumes, one a complete concordance to both works, another an exhaustive study of the style modelled on that which Mr E. W. Watson has furnished for S. Cyprian[1]. A mere fraction of such a task is attempted here. Only two or three points of style are selected for comparison; but a more or less complete account of the uses of various particles is given. Professor von Wölfflin, whose great experience entitles him to speak with authority on such a point, lays it down that the way in which particles are employed forms the best means of deciding common authorship[2]. The entire agreement between both works in this respect is most striking, especially when we consider that the one work consists of short comments, the other of essays. The second part of the chapter consists of a list of words and expressions (other than particles) common to both works, which have struck me in the course of repeated reading. The subjective element enters largely into the investigation of these. Any other scholar going over the same ground would undoubtedly select expressions which have been passed over by me. Indeed Dr Langen in his brief comparison has quoted some phrases the occurrence of which did not strike me. As a general principle I have omitted all

[1] I cannot refrain from expressing the highest opinion of Mr Watson's work (in *Studia Biblica*, vol. IV, Oxford, 1896), which is an honour to British scholarship.

[2] *Archiv für lat. Lexikogr.* XI (1900) 577 f, where there are other important remarks on this subject.

those words the absence of which from our author would have caused us some surprise. The investigation, such as it is, has cost great trouble, but the result will, I hope, prove convincing.

(I) STYLE.

(1) *General.*

Scriptural quotations are in both works introduced in the same ways. A very frequent practice is to represent the statement as made inter cetera, 'amongst other things[1],' thus:—sicut hoc loco inter cetera *et unus* inquit *dominus Iesus* cet. (50 A): other examples are 63 A, 76 A, 85 C, 117 B, 122 B *bis*, 129 C, 148 B, D, 206 A, and very often; qu. 7, 11, 16, 20, 23, 27, 31, 41 *bis*, 44, 60, 66, 71, 72, 77 *bis*, 78, 86, 88, 89, 90, 91 *ter*, 94, 97 *septies*, 100, 102, 105 *bis*, 106 *bis*, 113, 120, 122 *ter*, 125, 127, 2 qu. V.T. 3, 2 qu. N.T. 26, 49 *bis*, 54, 57, 62. 'Inter alia' is comparatively rare, qu. 69, 71, 91, 97 *bis*, 106, 123: cf. *inter multa* (qu. 93). Another method of introducing a quotation is 'hinc est unde[2]—ait (inquit)' cet.: 222 C, 254 B, 338 B, etc., qu. 1, 44, 68, 69, 77, 97, 102 *quater*, 108, 110, 114, 115, 120, 125. The simpler form 'hinc—ait (inquit)' is also found: 117 B, 146 B, etc., qu. 115, 2 qu. mixt. 10 (*hinc apostolus...scribit*), etc. Another variety is 'unde—ait,' etc.: unde idem apostolus ait 117 B, unde dominus...ait 128 B, unde et Moysi dixit 142 A, unde saluator...inquit 182 B, unde dominus... inquit 186 C, unde et Salamon...inquit 232 C, cet.: unde et apostolus Paulus...inquit qu. 100, unde dicit Paulus apostolus qu. 102, unde Iohannes apostolus...inquit qu. 102, unde dicit in Esaia propheta qu. 106, unde dicit dominus qu. 110, cet. The present participle 'dicens' is very common, generally in the nominative or ablative case: sicut et Petrus apostolus testatur dicens 50 A, promotum se ostendit dicens 50 B, hic est populus quem increpat dominus sub nomine Hierusalem dicens 81 B, cet.,

[1] *Inter cetera*, not introducing a quotation, 163 B, 228 C, 235 C, qu. 117, 122, 2 qu. mixt. 9: *inter ceteros* occurs 53 A, qu. 106.

[2] *Hinc est unde* is sometimes used, where a quotation is not introduced, e.g. 142 B, 184 C, 185 B, 193 A, qu. 2, 127 (p. 2379).

qu. 125 pm, 127 pr, 2 qu. N.T. 2, 7, 10 *bis*, 23, 26, 27 and often. Examples of the ablative absolute (singular) are:—dicente Esaia propheta 50 C, dicente Cleopha et Emmau 52 B, cet., dicente et probante domino ad Iudaeos qu. 117 pr, dicente apostolo qu. 110 (new part), qu. 125 m, 2 qu. N.T. 19, dicente euangelista 2 qu N.T. 31, deo dicente qu. 127 am, dicente Samaritide ad dominum 2 qu. N.T. 51. There are also examples like 'apostoli uox est dicentis' (qu. 127 ex). Besides 'dico,' the verb 'testor' is often used in this connexion: Petro apostolo hoc testante; dicit enim quia 150 B, cet., ipso domino testante et dicente qu. 122 ex, ipso nobis testante qu. 125 ex, cet. We find also such expressions as 'teste apostolo,' introducing quotations, in both works. The writer displays much ingenuity in finding these introductory expressions, only a few of which are referred to here. No attempt at exhaustiveness has been made. One more, however, may be mentioned. To avoid the monotonous repetition of 'sanctus apostolus,' or 'apostolus Paulus,' the writer employs 'uas electionis'[1], as Langen has noted[2]: 419 C, qu. 2, 106, 115 (col. 2348).

There are certain formulae also, which follow quotations, introducing an explanation of their import, for example, HOC DICIT QUIA (quoniam), and HOC DICIT UT. Instances of the former are 88 D, 89 C, 95 C, 132 B, 133 C, 134 A, 149 D, 150 A, 212 B, 214 C, 104 C, and very often, qu. 112 ex, of the latter, 105 A, 440 B, 477 D, etc., qu. 102, 112. We find TESTATUR following on quotations, thus:—*per redemptionem quae est in Christo Iesu*: gratiam dei in Christo esse testatur 83 C; so 435 A, 443 B, etc. sicut praesens lectio testatur qu. 119.

I now select one or two stylistic features, which have struck me as specially characteristic of the works under consideration. The first is the employment of a pair of adjectives[3] or adverbs almost synonymous, where one might be regarded as sufficient[4].

[1] From Acts ix 15. Augustine introduces a quotation from S. Paul in this way, at least once (de bono uiduit. 2, 3). There are examples in other authors also.

[2] Diss. p. 21.

[3] Or participles, used adjectivally.

[4] The founders of the *Thesaurus Linguae Latinae* were, I believe, the first lexicographers to recognise the important principle that words, as well as men, are known by the company they keep.

This construction meets us of course in many authors, and is perhaps traceable to rhetorical training. *Inhonesta et turpia* 49 A, *turpe . et inhonestum* qu. 114, *inhonesta et turpia* qu. 114, *turpia et inhonesta* qu. 121 (*turpis* and *honestus* are used as opposites in qu. 114, cf. 107 B, C), *turpis et foeda* 110 A, *turpia et polluta* 305 A, *foeda et inlicita* 521 B, *concessa et licita* 64 A, *honestum et sanctum* qu. 114, *reprehensibile et turpe* qu. 114, *sanctum et inreprehensibile* qu. 114, *inhonestum et inlicitum* qu. 115, *sordidum et contaminatum* qu. 127, *turpiter et obscene* qu. 102, *turpiter et contaminate* qu. 126; *idoneum et efficacem* 450 A, *apti et digni* qu. 114, *friuola et inepta* qu. 114; *par et aequalis* 433 A, *par . et aequalis* qu. 97, *ratam et integram* 51 A, *humilis et stulta* 53 D, *humilem et mansuetum* 334 D, *stulti et hebetes* 94 A, *stultus et uanus* qu. 100, *stultum et inane* 2 qu. N.T. 47, *uana et inanis* qu. 114, *inprouidi . et stulti* qu. 114, *inprouidi et inconsulti* qu. 114, *inprouidum...et carens ratione* qu. 115, *non credendum et stultum* qu. 117, *stultum . et periculosum* qu. 117, *inprouida et infirma* 212 C, *tepidi et inprouidi* 223 B, *prouida et rationabilis* 261 A, *superfluam et inanem* 370 C, qu. 44, *neglegentem et inprouidum* qu. 5, *neglegentes et inprouidi* qu. 34, *neglegenter et inprouide* qu. 103, *neglegenter et indeuote* 435 C, *prouidenter et curiose* 67 B, *rationabiliter et prouidenter* qu. 113, *supplices et deuoti* 406 D, *sollicitis et deuotis* qu. 95, *sollicitus et fidelis* qu. 111, *sollicitos . et uigilantes* 2 qu. N.T. 62, *diligentes et sollicitos* qu. 102, *diligentibus ac sedulis* qu. 10, *deuoti et fidelis* 468 D, *deuote et fideliter* qu. 126, *prudentem et deuotum* qu. 5, *prudens . et astutus* qu. 31, *facinorosus et inprouidus* qu. 43, *inualida . et inanis* qu. 41, *inanem et infructuosam* qu. 102, *prouidus et praescius* qu. 46, *inualidis et inermibus* qu. 92, *horrendum et ualidum* qu. 102, *infirmum et inprobabile* qu. 108, *infirmum . et fragile* 2 qu. N.T. 50, *propitio et prouido* qu. 117, *alacri et deuoto* qu. 120; *releuati et reparati* 108 C, *munita atque firmata* qu. 106, *disrupta ac resoluta* qu. 121, *distinctis . et discretis* 2 qu. V.T. 20, *emortua et resoluta* 2 qu. N.T. 47 (see below, p. 105), *exstinctos et perditos* 2 qu. mixt. 11, cet.; *uerum et stabile* 69 A, *fundatos et stabiles* 411 B, *firmi et stabiles* 445 D, 501 A, *stabiles et firmi* 452 B, *uerum et manifestum* qu. 49, *uerum ac manifestum* 2 qu. N.T. 49; *lenis...et inturbata* 80 D; *inportabilis...et aspera* 109 C, *asperos et duros* 130 A, *graui et aspera* qu. 117, *aspera et difficilis* 2 qu. N.T. 19; *fragilis*

...et incerta 130 A, *corruptibilia et mortalia* qu. 28, *caduca et corruptibilia* 130 C, *caduca atque incerta* 511 A, cf. *infirmum et fragile* (quoted above); *subtilis et uersutus* 151 C, *subdolis et uersutis* 521 A, *callide et astute* qu. 114, cf. *prudens . et astutus* (quoted above); *inreuerens et blasphemus* 169 C; *pacifici...et quieti* 175 B; *diffidentes et perfidi* 196 A; *simplicem et incorporeum* 207 B, *aperta et simplex* qu. 127, *unum...et indifferens* 2 qu. N.T. 29, *unum...et singularem* 2 qu. N.T. 57, *simplici ac singulari* 2 qu. mixt. 9; *contemptibilis et despectus* 217 B, *despecti et humiliati* qu. 126 (col. 2376); *participes et consortes* 249 C; *intractabiles et inconsideratos* 223 B; *sublimis et ineffabilis* 280 A, *sublimis et magnifica* qu. 102, *ineffabiliter inconprehensibiliter* (sic codd.) qu. 21, *magnificum et mirabile* 348 C, *magnificum et gloriosum* 447 B, *magna et admirabilis* qu. 113, *magnus . et admirabilis* qu. 117, *praecipua et admirabilis* qu. 117; *plena et perfecta* 418 C; *plena . et abundans* qu. 69, *copiosi et abundantes* 479 C; *laboriosa et inefficax* 370 C; *inmensum et inaestimabilem* 406 B; *sobrii et modesti* 417 A; *infesta et inimica* 492 B; *humanus et pius* qu. 102; 117; *clemens et misericors* qu. 44, 114, *misericors et patiens* qu. 68, *bonus et misericors* qu. 119, *iniusti...et inmisericordes* qu. 103; *diuinum et supercaeleste* qu. 95, *diuinam et deificam* qu. 114; *superabundans . et inauditum* qu. 78, *noua et inaudita* qu. 104, *nouum et inauditum* qu. 123, *noua . et mirabilis* qu. 104 (cf. *nec mirum nec inauditum* qu. 44 and *nouum...et...inauditum* qu. 115), *inpossibilia et inaudita* qu. 117; *rebelles et contumeliosi* qu. 44, *perfidos et rebelles* qu. 126, *adrogantes...et rebelles* qu. 110; *iustam et salutarem* qu. 110, *sanctum et salutarem* qu. 121; *palam aperteque* qu. 89, *palam . et manifeste* qu. 114 (cf. *non palam neque manifeste* qu. 115); *uarius et mutabilis* qu. 46 (perhaps the only definite reminiscence of Virgil in this author); *indigni et inutiles* qu. 77 (73), *bona et utilis* qu. 127, *inutilia et abicienda* 237 A; *inperiti et rusticani* qu. 77, *inculti et agrestes* qu. 106; *uenenatam...et peramaram* qu. 102, *conexa...et indiuidua* qu. 106; *continentes et sancti* qu. 115; *inbecillem et aegrum* qu. 115; *intrepidus et securus* qu. 117; *cara et suauis* qu. 117; *gratum . et fructiferum* qu. 118; *modesta et tranquilla* qu. 119; *robustus et fortis* qu. 119; *felix et beatum* qu. 123; *pestiferi et superbi* 2 qu. V.T. 5, *superbis...et contumacibus* 2 qu. V.T. 10, *perfida . et contumax* 2 qu. mixt. 9; *pugnantia et inimica* 2 qu. N.T. 46 cet. Pairs of

comparatives are occasionally found :—*largior et uberior* qu. 102, *fortiores et uehementiores* qu. 114, *fortior . et plenior* qu. 117, *peritior et fortior* qu. 126. Pairs of superlatives are almost entirely absent: one example is *mitissima et clementissima* qu. 102. There are curious mixtures, *pessima eorum et pergrauis causa* 79 C (codd.); *pessima et impia genera* 459 A, *inpius et crudelissimus* (qu. 94); *inhonesta et uanissima* qu. 114 (col. 2344).

Similar pairs of nouns, though not so frequent, are also a feature of both works. Here are a few examples; *modum et rationem*[1] 47 A, *ambiguitas et diffidentia* 52 B, *turpitudinem et contaminationem* 64 A, *passionibus et pressuris* 87 D, *procellis et tempestatibus* 130 A, *error et delictum* 161 A, *uersutia et calliditate* 198 B, *dedecus . et deformationem* 305 B, *dolo et fallacia* 367 B, *animositati et audaciae* 370 A; *inbecillitas atque inperitia* qu. 18, *lamentationibus et gemitibus* qu. 102, *lamentatione et gemitu* qu. 126, *gemitu et dolore* 2 qu. V.T. 12, *caput et originem* qu. 111, *caput...et principium* qu. 113, *fons et origo* qu. 123, *subtilitate et astutia* qu. 114, *astutia et subtilitas* qu. 115, *formidine et metu* qu. 114 (col. 2345), *cura diligentiaque* 501 C, qu. 120, *ira...et indignatione* 2 qu. V.T. 5, *uitam et conuersationem* qu. 84, *conuersatio et uita* qu. 126, *pressuras et angustias* 2 qu. mixt. 6, cet.

Allied to this construction is another, intended to produce the same kind of emphasis. This is the employment of a special kind of 'constituent' genitive. Whereas in classical Latin the governing word is generally of wider scope than that of the word in the genitive, the two words may here be said to be identical in meaning[2]. Examples are :—*aemulatio zeli* 157 C, qu. 5, 2 qu. N.T. 7[3], *aemulatio inuidiae* 79 B, *aemulatio...inuidentiae* 153 D, *agonis legitimum certamen* 523 D, *patientiae longanimitas* 68 A, *tergiuersatio cauillationis* 88 B, *infirmitatis suae inbecillitate* 108 B, *subtilitate astutiae suae* 137 B, *caecitatis obtunsio* 158 B, 160 B[4], *subtilitate quadam diabolicae uersutiae* 450 C, *stultitiae inprudentia* 463 D, *conpendio breuitatis* qu. 73, *dolo simulationis* qu. 75, *astutiae*

[1] The words *modus* and *ratio* are usually identical in meaning, see infra pp. 107–8.

[2] This idiom is found in other late authors.

[3] *aemulatio* (2 Cor. vii 11) he explains by *zelus*, cf. 247 C.

[4] On *obtunsio* (πώρωσις) see Dean Robinson in *Journ. Theol. Studies*, vol. III (1901) 81–93, or *Commentary on Ephesians*, pp. 268 f.

calliditate qu. 97, *temeritatis praesumptio* qu. 101, *lamentatione paenitentiae* qu. 102, *liuoris sui inuidam uoluntatem* qu. 102, *simulatio commenticiae ueritatis* qu. 118, *ingenium naturae nostrae* qu. 120, *fornicatione idolatriae*[1] qu. 111, *crudelitatis saeuitia* qu. 118 cet.

The last peculiarity of style common to both works, to which I shall refer, is the use of the ablative absolute of personified abstract nouns[2] with the present participle of intransitive verbs. This construction is very frequent. With it may be coupled a kindred construction, the employment of another noun in apposition instead of the participle. Examples of the former usage are *dictante iustitia* 191 C, qu. 44 m, *hortante iustitia* 404 D, *paenitentia subsequente* 219 C, qu. 102 (cf. qu. 6: see also p. 141), *manente in ea peccato* 106 B, *manente sententia* 121 C, *manente iustitia* 143 B, *manente . fide* qu. 113, *modestia gubernante* 98 B, *gratia regnante* 104 B, *peccato regnante* 104 B, *superueniente . gratia* 104 C, *misericordia interueniente* 155 B, *interueniente misericordia sua* 183 B, *interueniente causa aliqua* 225 B, *interueniente mentis dolore* prol. 2 Cor.[3], *interueniente lamentatione paenitentiae* qu. 102, *misericordia . ueniente* 2 qu. V.T. 10, *misericordia adueniente* qu. 69, *accusante conscientia ipsa* 172 A, *suadente uirtute* 200 B, qu. 114, *inpellente lasciuia* 230 A, *refrigescente proposito* 234 A, *necessitate cogente* 346 D, *aequitate cogente* qu. 100, *perfidia obcaecante* 305 C, *recedente infirmitate* 314 A, *apparente ueritate* 456 A, *accedente . timore dei* qu. 115, *blandiente consuetudine* qu. 114, *imperante natura* qu. 115, *recrudescente...crudelitatis saeuitia* qu. 118, *operante inlecebrosa fallacia* qu. 114, *prohibente pudore* qu. 114. Of the kindred construction I may cite the following instances: *teste uirtute* 198 B, 201 C, 204 B, 212 C, 340 A, qu. 84 ex, 114 pr (cf. *testis uirtus posita est* 2 qu. N.T. 63; *testis doctrinae uirtus est* 52 D; *uirtus testis inuenitur* qu. 114[4]; *uirtutis testimonio* qu. 111 ex); *teste interiore conscientia sua* 71 C, *teste conscientia sua* 137 C, 501 D, *conscientia sua teste* qu. 102 *bis* (an expression suggested by ep. Rom. ix 1);

[1] *Fornicatio* is here used in the Old Testament sense.

[2] There are of course many examples of this construction with concrete nouns also; see above, p. 65, and cf. *suadente diabolo* qu. 116, *dicente scriptura* qu. 117, *deo adiuuante per fidem* 108 C, *corporis manente conpagine* 105 A, *manente in nobis spiritu sancto* 129 A cet.

[3] As published in *Journ. Theol. Studies*, vol. IV (1902), pp. 89–92.

[4] Cf. also *scientiam testem* 341 C; *testis est iustitia eius* 58 C.

teste promissione eius 518 C[1]; *magistra iustitia* 98 A, qu. 111; *magistra modestia* 464 C[2]; and the common expression *duce natura* or *natura duce* 71 A, 71 B, 75 B, 100 A, 111 A, etc., *natura ipsa duce* 162 C; qu. 118.

(2) *Particles.*

The study of the uses of particles in the later Latin authors may be said to be as yet in its infancy. I have used such works as were accessible to me and my own reading of these authors in estimating the importance of the usages I have brought forward. To me they are convincing, and I confidently leave them to the judgment of experts. I aim at exhaustiveness within the limits I lay down, and intend this part of my study to be a small contribution to the history of Latin syntax.

AC PER HOC introducing a sentence or a clause is very frequent in both works. It is unnecessary to give examples. Dom Morin has noted as many as 121 occurrences in the commentaries and more than 65 occurrences in the *Quaestiones*[3]. The expression occurs also in Cypr., Isaac ex-Iudaeo 1544 C, Hier., Aug., Daniel's Servius, the commentator on Virgil (R. B. Steele in *The American Journal of Philology* xx (1899) 376), and others.

NEC NON ET[4]: the presence of this expression in a good many late prose authors may be traced to the reading of Virgil at school. It occurs in Rom. ii 12; iii 29; in Gal. iii 2; in Col. i 20; in Col. ii 8–9 (some MSS *nec non*); in 1 Thess. v 22; qu. 51; 71; 97 ppr; 99 pm; 106 m; 109 ppr; 109 m; 114 pr; 114 m; 115 ex; 126 aex; 127 pm. *Nec non etiam* occurs in 2 Cor. vii 12, *nec non* in 1 Tim. vi 13–16. (*Nec non et* is found even in Scripture, e.g. Vulg. Exod. xxviii 27.)

[1] Compare too *testibus signorum prodigiis* 51 B with *testibus signis* qu. 3.

[2] With these expressions, cf. *ministro spiritu sancto* qu. 91, *ministris angelis* qu. 100, 115, 119, *ministris sideribus* qu. 115, *ministris elementis* 67 C, *membris... ministris* 107 A, cet.

[3] Dom Morin, *l.c.* p. 102.

[4] See *Archiv f. lat. Lexikogr.* VIII 181, n. 2; X 390 for examples, which could be greatly increased; add e.g. [Aug.] serm. 188, 1; 307, 3; 48, 1.

The pleonastic expression PORRO AUTEM introduces sentences:—in Rom. ii 8 porro autem *dei natura ab his passionibus inmunis est* (so one MS, where Migne has *nam*); in 1 Cor. vi 18; in 2 Cor. xi 4; in Col. ii 13 ff; qu. 2; 14; 27; 69; 102 *bis*; 106; 109; 114 *bis*; 115; 117. (This expression is common in Cyprian's latest writings and in some of his epistles: Mr E. W. Watson in *Studia Biblica* IV pp. 239, 316. It occurs also Boet. *cons. phil.* iii 11 (p. 79, 74).)

The remarkable combination, ADUBI autem[1], which is of rare occurrence in Latin, occurs several times in both works[2]. As the old editors were naturally rather suspicious of this strange expression, I have had to restore it sometimes from the manuscripts[3]: in Rom. v 13 (where the Cologne edition of 1616 corrupts to *at uero ubi*); in Gal. prol. (one good MS: Migne (358 B) *at ubi*)[4]; in Eph. iv 11 f. (410 B) *codd.*; in 1 Tim. iii 12 f (497 C) *codd.* (Migne *at ubi uero*); qu. 3 pr; 4; 37; 44 *bis*; 104; 106; 115 (col. 2350 l. 52); 127; 2 qu. N.T. 17; 2 qu. mixt. 3.

QUO MODO ERGO (interrogative "how then") is a frequent mannerism at the beginning of a sentence: a few examples are:—quo modo ergo *non inputabatur peccatum, cum lex non esset?* (in Rom. v 13); quo modo ergo *hoc ad corpus potest referri ut...?* (in Phil. ii 10 ff); quo modo ergo *possunt deum Abrahae scire, qui...?* (in Tit. i 16); quo modo ergo *personarum acceptio non est apud deum?* (qu. 32); quo modo ergo, *post quam baptizatus est, dictum ei a domino deo est* cet.? (qu. 54); 91; 102; 105; 107; 110 (new part); 114; 115 (col. 2354); 115 (col. 2357); 127 *quinquies*, 2 qu. N.T. 62 cet.

QUANTO MAGIS, interrogatively, is often used in argument: 60 C; 67 A: 90 A; 94 C; 96 A *bis*; 98 A; 99 C; 102 B; 130 A; 132 B; 133 C; 186 B; 196 C; 205 C; 224 A; 231 B; 237 C; 242 C; 245 C; 273 B; 298 C; 330 B; 335 B, C; 361 C, etc.[5]; qu. 27; 38; 45; 46; 91;

[1] In the MSS sometimes *atubi* (or *at ubi*) *autem*.

[2] See the article *adubi* in the *Thes. Ling. Lat.*, which has none of my examples.

[3] Here, and elsewhere often, I have refrained from mentioning Migne's wrong reading, where the MSS give a different but correct reading.

[4] Also in the text of scripture, Gal. iv 4, in three MSS, where *Migne* at ubi.

[5] Also in the text of Rom. xi 24.

97 *quater*; 101; 102 *bis*; 110; 111; 113; 114 *bis*; 115 *bis*; 117; 122 *ter*; 125; 127 *ter*; 2 qu. N.T. 50.

QUID EST UT, with the subjunctive, equal to *quid est cur*, *quid est quod*, *quid est quam ob rem*, *ut quid*, *quare*, *cur*, the latinity of which was denied by one of the old editors of the *Quaestiones*, occurs:—in 1 Cor. iii 23; iv 5; in 2 Cor. xi 26; in Gal. i 14; ii 3; etc.; the titles of qu. 14, 17, 22, 24, 37, 53, 57, 61, 62, 67, 85; and occasionally in the documents themselves as well, e.g. qu. 112, 115.

When a negative answer is expected, questions are introduced by NUMQUID, never by *num* or *numquidnam*[1]. The following are examples:—in Rom. i 22; in Rom. ii 3; in Rom. ii 6; also 88 A; 100 A; 104 B; 118 D; 120 A; 127 A; 209 C, D, and often: qu. 1; 41 *bis*; 43 *quater*; 44; 46 *ter*; 69; 83 *bis*; 91; 97 *ter*; 101 *bis*; 102 *bis*; 106; 107 *bis*; 112; 114 *bis*; 115 (twelve times); 122 *bis*; 123; 125 *bis*; 127 *quater*; 2 qu. N.T. 34, 61, 62 etc. (The word is found also in the following verses of scripture quoted by the author:—Gen. xx 4; Esa. xlii 14; xlv 9; Luc. xviii 7; Io. x 21; Rom. iii 5; ix 14; x 17; *sed dico: numquid Israhel non cognouit*; hoc est, cognouitne? x 19 (cf. qu. 107 (col. 2321, 73), qu. 123 (col. 2369, 64)); xi 11; 1 Cor. i 13; ix 4, 5, 8, etc.)

The reduplication of inferential particles, which is comparatively rare in Latin[2], is a feature of both works. IDEO ERGO is found:—in Rom. ix 22; in 1 Cor. vii 2; in 1 Cor. xiv 27; in 2 Cor. i 18; in 2 Cor. x 1; in 1 Tim. iv 10; qu. 37; 53; 75 (79); qu. 2 N.T. 19; 61; qu. 2 mixt. 3: ERGO IDEO occurs in 2 Cor. x 4 (where some MSS have *enim ideo*); in Gal. i 6; IDCIRCO ERGO: (*Migne* enim) in 1 Cor. xv 3; qu. 16; ERGO IDCIRCO: in 2 Cor v 16; qu. 107; IDCIRCO IGITUR: in Gal. ii 10[3].

Both works agree in placing ENIM third, and *est* second, if these

[1] *numquidnam* is common in Aug., and occurs even in Cic. In this author *aliquis* often = *quisquam*, and introduces interrogative sentences where a negative answer is expected, e.g. qu. 83 pr.

[2] The only outside examples I can find are *itaque ergo* Ter. eun. 317, Liv. 1, 25, 2; 3, 31, 5; 9, 31, 16; 28, 12, 12; 39, 25, 11; Peregr. Ether. (*Archiv f. lat. Lex.* IV 269); *ergo igitur* Plaut. trin. 756, most. 848, Apul. met. (Koziol, *der Stil des L. Apuleius*, p. 145).

[3] *Quare ergo* occurs qu. 104, perhaps oftener.

be two out of the first three words in the sentence; for example, *ipse est enim* (93 B codd.); *homo est enim*...(249 A); *officium est enim*...(261 C codd.); *ibi est enim* (314 C codd.); *hoc est enim* (319 C); *degenerare est enim* (399 B codd.); *non est enim* (449 B, 492 C); *praedestinatus est enim* 491 B; *quid est enim* (491 C); *superfluum est enim* (468 B); *asperum est enim* (502 C); *periculosum est enim*...qu. 97; *hoc est enim* qu. 97; *capax est enim* qu. 123; *signum est enim* qu. 123; *ipse est enim* qu. 125. The MSS should be altered probably in qu. 114 ex; 127 (p. 2382). For Cicero's rule see Dr Reid's *Acad.* Index.

ETENIM usually occupies the *second* place in a sentence[1]. Originally, as in the best prose, *etenim* comes first in the sentence, being really two words, *et enim*, where the *enim* occupies its natural place as second in the sentence. When it became one word, prose writers began to give it the place of *enim* in the sentence, influenced perhaps by the poets, like Lucretius, Horace and Propertius[2], who for metrical reasons gave it this position. The following prose writers[3] among others employ this construction, Tertullian, Apuleius, Novatian, Lucifer of Cagliari, Paulinus of Nola, and Jerome. I have noted no example in Augustine[4]. In the works concerned, we find: ostendere e. imminens periculum bonum est 114 A; duo e. genera hominum hic continentur 156 B; sunt e. pessimae uoluntatis 156 B; peccantibus e. ignoscere misericordia est 166 A; tribus e. discipulis gloriam suam in monte ostendit 209 A; indigni e. sunt resurgere cum sanctis 286 B; insultantis e. uerba sunt 286 D; ideo e. non dixit... 320 A; sic e. de domino dictum est 384 C; tunc e. exerta potest esse libertas 485 A; tunc e. addiscentes uera esse sciunt quae audiunt 485 B; fidei e. gratia hanc habet potestatem 492 D; praefectus e. potest... qu. 46 m; sic e. de carne... qu. 51 (*b*); ideo e. (*cf.* 320 A) a nocte... qu. 64 am; omnia e. suis uoluminibus... qu. 69 pr; omni e., inquit,... qu. 70; scripturae e. dominicae qu. 95 pr; Anania e. cum qu. 102 pr; utquid

[1] *Etenim* occupies the *first* place;—95 A (printed text), 258 D, 490 A; qu. 64, 72 (76), 90; 2 qu. N.T. 32. In this and in the following list the MSS are followed. They often offer *enim* for *etenim* of the printed text, and *vice versa*.

[2] See Georges *s.v.*

[3] Georges gives one passage from Plin. h. n., but *etenim* is not now read there.

[4] But it occurs in Cons. ap. Aug. ep. 119, 5.

e. C annis qu. 102 ppr; peccatores e. eos polluunt, qui consentiunt malis eorum qu. 102 aex; duo e. genera sacrificiorum qu. 103; sic e. inuenitur et Cain peccasse qu. 103; ideo e. (*cf.* 320 A *supra*) permissum est... qu. 104; triginta e. dies qu. 106 ppr; in principio e. qu. 106 ppr (in-principio counting, of course, as one word); sic e. dicit qu. 106 aex; quis e. hominum dicat... qu. 107 ppr; Moyses e. cui legitur qu. 109 am; nemo e. potest... qu. 109 pm; legimus e. in psalmo qu. 109 ex; sunt e. eius imago qu. 109 ex; ipse e. Abraham qu. 115 pr; mulieribus e. Romanorum qu. 115 ppr; cogitantibus e. nobis qu. 115 am; educens e. hunc dominus qu. 117 ppr; sub Hester e. regina (*cf.* qu. 106 ppr) qu. 120; nihil e. medium est qu. 122 ex; coquit e. ignis qu. 123 am; lucem e. habitat qu. 125 m; contuendum e. est qu. 125 m; hinc e. quis uidetur qu. 126 pr[1].

ALIQUANDO—ALIQUANDO: a. deum a. hominem significat 50 A; a. laudat a. commonet 126 A, B; a. corripit a. laudat 194 D; cet.: a. diligi a. timeri qu. 1 ppr; qu. 66; 80 pr; 97 ex; 99 m; 125 pm; 127 ex. *ter*; 2 qu. mixt. 6 *bis*; etc. For this double *aliquando* see *Archiv für latein. Lexikogr.* II 246 f.

DENIQUE always has the first place in the sentence, *cf.* 55 C; 63 C; 133 A; 247 D; 254 A, C; 280 D; 350 D; 357 B; qu. 2; 3; 47; 57; 61; 73 (77); 77 (73); 74 (78); 75 (79); 91; 95; 97; 98; 102 *bis*; 103; 107; 113; 115; 2 qu. N.T. 37: 46.

The usual equivalent for 'not only'—'but also' is NON SOLUM—SED ET; less common is NON SOLUM—UERUM ETIAM. *Non solum—sed et* occurs e.g. 88 A *codd.*; 219 A; 221 B; 224 A; 236 C; 239 A; 249 A; 251 D; 252 A; 261 B; 265 B; 269 B; 276 C; 281 B; 281 C; 294 A; 302 B; 305 A; 306 C; 313 C; 318 B; 330 B; 331 C (where there is an extra *et* clause); 332 B; 340 A, C; 346 C; 351 A; 352 A; 359 D (so Act. xxi 13 quoted); qu. 4; 13; 14; 28; 32; 41 *bis*; 44; 45; 46 *bis*; 47 *bis*; 56; 61; 78 (74); 81; 89; 97; 102 *bis*; 109; 111 *bis*; 112 *bis*; 114; 115; 118; 122; 123 *bis*; 124 *bis*; 127 *ter* (cf. *non solum—sed nec* qu. 115) (so Io. v 18

[1] The writer found this use in his Bible:—Act. xvii 28 ap. 2 qu. N.T. 51 sicut quidam ex uobis dixerunt: "huius *e.* genus sumus" [*Vulg.* ipsius enim et genus sumus]; Rom. viii 16 ap. 2 qu. N.T. 49 Spiritus e. testimonium perhibet cet. [*Vulg.* Ipse enim Spiritus testimonium reddit cet.]: in comm. with neither *etenim* nor *enim*.

quoted in qu. 97; 2 Tim. ii 20 in qu. 102). *Non solum—uerum etiam* occurs e.g. 233 D; 247 A; 404 B; 415 C; 431 D; 442 C; qu. 5; 23; 33; 34; 61; 76 (72) *bis*; 79 (75); 93; 95; 115; 127 *ter*. The following combinations occur only sporadically[1]: *non solum—sed etiam* (305 C; 395 A); *non solum—sed* (325 A *codd.*; 372 A; 468 A; qu. 43); *non solum—uerum* (446 A); *non tantum—sed et* (85 D; 505 D; qu. 2; 79 (75); 113; 127); *non tantum—uerum etiam* (529 C; qu. 118); *non . tantum sed* (qu. 102). These are all the combinations found, *non modo*, for instance, being entirely absent from both works.

SI QUO MINUS, 'but if not,' εἰ δὲ μή etc., is an expression which seems to have escaped the lexicographers and grammarians entirely. Dr Sanday and Mr C. H. Turner alone, as far as I am aware, have taken note of the expression, as occurring in one of the Old Latin texts of the New Testament[2]. It appears in the text of Ezech. iii 19[3], quoted both in the commentaries and in the *Quaestiones*.

I have collected all the examples:—nec dominus utique adorari se pateretur, nisi quia deus est: si quo minus, usurpasse dicendus est 138 D; hic enim induit Christum...si quo minus, non sunt induti Iesum Christum dominum 175 A; spiritus enim sanctus tunc permanet in eo, cui se infuderat, si permaneat in proposito regenerationis: si quo minus, abscedit 208 B; cuius filii sunt in utroque, si credant: si quo minus, peiores erunt gentilibus 232 A; ut...non quaerat uxorem; ita tamen ut a ceteris temperet. Si quo minus, quid prodest desiderium carnis premere? 234 A: missus enim seruus a domino facit, etiam inuitus, quod sibi praeceptum est: si quo minus, adstringatur plagis necesse est 243 C; forma ergo uult esse ceteris, ut ubi uident non expedire, etiam licitis non utantur: si quo minus, de licito fient rei 244 A; pro utilitate enim nostra gesta sunt, ut si terrore horum in dei timore manserimus, gloriam illis promissam accipiamus: si

[1] Perhaps the text ought to and will be altered in some cases.

[2] See *Old Latin Biblical Texts No. II*, p. cxxiii (two examples in the S. Matthew of *k*) and Dr M. R. James' *Apocrypha Anecdota* II (1897) p. 143. Add Ezech. iii 21. *Si quo minus* is found also in [Ambr.?] serm. 26, 5 (Migne, *P. L.* XVII 680 B). Dom Chapman points out to me that the expression occurs also (twice) in the Vulgate. Iren. (lat.) also has examples.

[3] In 300 B (in 2 Cor. ii 16) correct Migne's *sin* to *si* (MSS).

quo minus, geminabitur nobis poena illorum 248 B; ideo...dixit..., propterea quia illum sciunt dominum: si quo minus, non uidebitur eis dignus esse uocari dominus 250 B; despectis...exhortatio necessaria est, per quam addatur illis aliquis honor, ut fiant utiles: si quo minus, ipso contemptu neglegentiores circa se erunt 262 B; haec potestas est quam superius optat esse otiosam...si quo minus, exercere se in hac 356 B; quid iam sonat, nisi quia cessit...? Si quo minus, quo modo uerba aut sensus sequerentur? 368 A; omnia enim eius manifesta sunt, ut seruans legem uiuat: si quo minus, necesse est plectatur 374 B; ecclesiae caput est Christus, si tamen omnes unum sentiant caelestes et terreni, ut sint Ecclesia...: si quo minus, truncati capite totius corporis..., amentia quadam et uanitate bacchantur 448 A; si...accipiantur, bona sunt: si quo minus, mala erunt 488 D; expectat ut impii credant, et peccatores emendent: si quo minus, plectentur qu. 68; suspendit sententiam, ut hic...habeat spatium paenitendi: si quo minus, redit in illum sententia cumulata qu. 69 ex; deus...non ex se habet quod deus est: si quo minus, nec apud deum deus esse diceretur neque...appellaretur qu. 122 pr; propterea mandata data sunt...ut ex his dei cultura appareat: si quo minus, audient qu. 126 ex.

PROPTER QUOD is the prevailing form in both works. Other forms are almost entirely absent[1]. *Propter quod* is found in Apuleius, Cyprian[2], Irenaeus (lat.), the Vulgate, and the Bible used in the works before us[3], for example. Examples are:—50 B; 84 C; 100 A; 101 B; 128 A; 132 A; 153 C; 162 A; 177 A; 189 A; 262 A codd.; 307 A; 315 B; 319 B codd.; 338 A; 395 B; qu. 37; 46; 47; 76 (72) *bis*; 81; 100; 101; 102 *ter*; 104; 106 *ter*; 110; 112 *bis*; 114; 116; 122 *bis*; 127; 2 qu. N.T. 55. *Enim* is never put between the two in the MSS, but always after, thus:—*propter quod enim*. *Propterea quod* occurs 127 B; 260 D; 276 C; 330 C; 359 A; qu. 59 (only ex.); and *propterea quia* (126 B)[4] 176 A; 250 B; 470 A codd.; qu. 41; 97.

[1] E.g. *quapropter*, qu. 62; the MSS at 319 B have *propter quod*.
[2] See Mr Watson, *op. cit.* p. 316.
[3] E.g. Rom. xv 7; 22.
[4] Some MSS omit *propterea*.

QUIPPE CUM = 'since,' with the subjunctive, is a favourite usage in both works. Examples are:—56 A; 67 C; 73 B; 76 D (sed v. n. crit.); 79 B; 83 A; 98 A; 109 C; 117 A; 130 D; 142 B; 159 C; 171 A; 179 C; 186 B; 204 D; 208 A; 213 B, D; 221 D; 229 B; 260 C; 281 D; 283 A; 308 A; 366 A; 370 D; 377 D; 383 D; 406 A; 413 D; 419 B; 457 B; 469 A; 478 C; 493 D; 496 C; 500 A; 502 C; 504 B: 508 C; 510 C; 511 A; 521 B; 524 C; qu. 1; 2; 20; 31; 38; 46; 61; 66; 79 (75); 81; 83 *bis*: 91 *ter*; 94; 97 *bis*; 101; 102 *ter*; 108; 111; 112; 113; 114 *bis*; 115 *bis*; 122; 2 qu. N.T. 57; 62.

PER ID QUOD is a favourite mannerism. Examples are:—per id quod neglegit, non bona se fecisse quae fecit ostendit (in Rom. ii 3); per id quod praescientiam non habet (in Rom. iii 4 (codd.)) ut, per id quod inhabitat in eo, iustificatus appareat esse filius dei (in Rom. viii 10); se uerum praedicatorem per id quod a Christo dei uoluntate missus est adseuerat (in 1 Cor. i 1); 216 C; 226 D; 227 C; 232 A; 382 C; 446 D; 448 C; 472 A; 499 C; ut...gaudeat in sese per id quod opere suo uidet se meliorem qu. 1; qu. 20; spem...esse...uult intellegi per id quod subiecit dicens qu. 39; qui per id quod inpraescius est uarius et mutabilis est qu. 46; potest enim homini suaderi quod nescit per id quod scit qu. 59; qu. 89; qu. 97; qu. 106; qu. 112; qu. 115 *bis*; qu. 123; qu. 125 *ter*. Where another particle also occurs at the beginning of the clause, the writer places the complete expression first and then the other particle. The printed text must be altered to agree with the manuscripts; e.g. *per id quod ergo* 226 D; qu. 20; *per id quod autem* qu. 59; *per id quod enim* qu. 97; qu. 114 (col. 2344) are the correct readings where the editors have transposed the *quod* and *ergo*, etc. In conformity with this rule I do not hesitate to emend *per id enim quod* of 2 qu. N.T. 61 to *per id quod enim*[1].

To Mr E. W. Watson belongs the credit of first pointing out the expression CUM QUANDO[2]. I am glad to be able to add the following examples: ostendit quam uim creatura patiatur nostri causa, cum quando nos...ingemescimus (in Rom. viii 23); quid

[1] I have since found it in the chief MS.

[2] In Hilary of Poitiers (Mr Watson in *Journal of Philology* XXVIII (1901) p. 84).

enim opus erat summam hanc ponere totius deuotionis, cum quando singula membra...memoret (*memorat?*) (in Rom. xii 11); solet per iram peccari cum quando quis furore commotus plus exigit quam postulet causa delicti (in Rom. xii 19); hoc est, nequid contra legem admittatur, cum quando quod lex non prohibet uitatur (in 1 Cor. vii 2); presbyterum autem intellegi episcopum probat Paulus apostolus cum quando Timotheum quem ordinauit presbyterum instruit cet. (qu. 101: so all MSS); quo modo ergo anteriores se putant pagani, cum quando quod colunt post deum est? (qu. 114 col. 2346: so all MSS).

(II) LANGUAGE.

(*An asterisk indicates that a word, sense, or construction is wanting in Georges' Handwörterbuch and Benoist-Goelzer's Dictionnaire.*)

abdico: abdicatis Iudaeis qu. 44 pr; abdicatis Iudaeis 146 A; nihil ultra potuit donare credentibus, quam ut filii dei dicantur, perfidis abdicatis 92 B; ne laborum suorum fructibus abdicentur 349 D; ne similes gentibus inuenti adoptionis nomine abdicentur (abdicantur is misprint in Migne[1]) 473 D.

absolutus (cf. *Thes. Ling. Lat.* I col. 178 53 ff.): absolutum *est* ei qui legi factorum...subiectus est...non inputari meritum ad mercedem 86 C; absolutum est quia accedens ad Christum relinquit legem 371 B; absoluta sunt haec, nec interpretatione egent 436 A; absolutum *est* non nos lunam colere qu. 84; ecce absolutum *est* donum dei multo plus gratiae concessisse homini tempore saluatoris qu. 123; cf. the adverb *absolute*: *ut* absolutius doceat quia...conspiciuntur 59 C; *ut* hoc absolutius ostenderet 233 C; quod *ut* adhuc absolutius traderet qu. 122. I must mention here a usage which occurs several times in the *Quaestiones*, though it does not as yet appear in the printed form of the commentaries. It is **in absoluto est**: cum in absoluto sit inmundum bonum dici non posse qu. 9 pr (this is the correct

[1] I use throughout the exceedingly careless reprint of 1879. Volume IV is as bad as the other three, stigmatised in *Theolog. Litteraturzeitung*, 1903, no. 3, by Jülicher. The *Quaestiones*, on the contrary, is well printed: I have counted about ten misprints only.

reading, to which the MSS point); non otiose illud mandasse Ioseph filiis Israhel in absoluto est qu. 25; in absoluto est Samuhelem minime fuisse sacerdotem qu. 46 (col. 2246 l. 1); in absoluto est per septem mulieres septem ecclesias esse significatas qu. 47 pr; quia autem et hic possent fieri in absoluto est qu. 115 (col. 2349).

acceptabilis: 52 D; 198 B; 203 C; 208 D; 210 D; 215 C; 299 D; 327 B; 340 A; 387 A; 473 A; 504 D; 515 B: qu. 120; qu. 2 N.T. 1.

accipio: in the phrase **accepto ferre**[1] = the classical acceptum referre: accepto ferri ambobus iustitiam fidei 70 A; quod a deo Abrahae accepto feratur fides Iudaeorum 183 C; ut... sacrificium eorum possit accepto ferri sanctificationis causa 184 B codd.; in re quae accepto ferri non posset fidelis 280 D codd.; accepto tulisse Christum, cuius legatione fungebatur 298 C; putantes iam non accepto ferre deum 347 B; non dubitent illa accepto ferri apud deum 443 C; accepto ferre deum 444 A; hoc enim libenter accepto fertur 445 C; ut per haec quae bona sunt accepto ferantur et mala 478 A; ut sub nomine eius epistula accepto ferri non possit quae non fuerit manu eius subscripta 486 D; dignum est plane et accepto ferendum pro spe, quae est in deo, pati persecutiones 501 A; accepto ferri putant quod non probant mandatum qu. 114 pr; ut etiam id...accepto ferri debeat qu. 127 am; hoc dicit quia oblationes et holocausta tunc accepto ferri haberent qu. 112 ex.

accuratus: laetum est caput siue cetera membra si pedes fuerint accurati uel sani 262 D; mundum spernendum adserunt et semper accurati procedunt 521 B; nemo enim imperatori ministrat non accuratus qu. 127 ex; bonae uoluntatis hominibus qui accurati magis uita sunt quam *sermone* qu. 100; causa accurati *sermonis* 339 C.

adaeque: sanctum praecipit creari episcopum adaeque et diaconum 496 C and probably oftener[2]; Ionas adaeque propheta praeceptum...inrupit qu. 109 (col. 2326); et malum recusatur cum adaeque (*Migne* illud aeque) natura hoc praestet qu. 115 (col.

[1] The phrase occurred in his Bible: Rom. iv 6, beatitudinem hominis, cui deus accepto fert iustitiam sine operibus. (Cf. 671 A of Migne, 17.)

[2] The word caused difficulty to scribes, and may be lurking in some passages.

2348 4); alius adaeque (*Migne* qui aeque) naturae suae rem exsequens (*Migne* exsequitur) praemiis adficeretur qu. 115 (col. 2348 13); condiscipulus autem eius adaeque sanctus Petrus cet. qu. 127 (col. 2384).

adbreuio, and cognates: multa quae misericordia dei adbreuiarit 49 B; quae (fides) adbreuiata ex lege est 146 D; adbreuiata ergo lege 146 D; adbreuiatio facta legis est 49 B; tempus pressurae adbreuiabatur 350 A; sola fides...adbreuiata ex lege 357 C; breuiatum legis uerbum qu. 44 am; semper breuiata propositione sensum occultas qu. 74 (78); nisi breuiati fuerint dies illi qu. 102 am; breuiatos uult esse dies dominus 249 A; adbreuiatio facta legis qu. 44 pm; per adbreuiationem legis qu. 44 pm.

addisco: not in the sense of "to learn on and on," or "to learn in addition," but = *the simple *disco*[1]: (a) *c. acc. obi.* addiscere spiritalia 56 D; addiscentes bonam vitam 110 A; aliquid ex lege Moysi addiscentes 111 A; fides (non) operibus addiscitur sed corde creditur 113 C; res dei non potest sine Spiritu dei addisci 205 D; naturali...lege...addiscitur 207 A; ut perfectionis verba mererentur addiscere 208 C; ut addisceret (*Migne errore* addiceret) dei maiestatem 265 A; quaestionum solutionem addiscit 267 D; integram praedicationem se addidicisse 312 B; addiscentes caritatem apostoli erga se 322 C; cum nihil amplius ab illis addiscatur 339 A; temperantiam...debent addiscere 422 C; ut donum dei addisceret 439 D; per quod...fidei suae addiscerent sensum 452 B; addiscunt mysterium dei 454 B; ut...addiscerent ueritatem qu. 83 pr; hinc enim addiscitur nobilitatis eius aeternitas qu. 97 ppr; ut...regem gloriae Christum addisceret qu. 111 aex; addiscere sacramentum qu. 113 pr; nulla in hac causa alicuius documenta addiscens qu. 118 pr codd.; dum sacramentum Creatoris addiscit qu. 127 am.—(b) *c. acc. et inf.* ut in hoc ceterae gentes addiscerent non esse alium deum... 144 B; magnalibus Christi addiscere hunc non posse fallere 157 A; carnem non edere bonum esse addiscunt 180 A; ut nullam illi gloriam...dandam addiscerent 197 C (codd.); (*pass.*)

[1] *Disco* itself is, however, found often: 266 C (?); 267 C; 312 B; 363 D; 364 A *bis* cet; qu. 91 pm *bis*; 118; 2 qu. N.T. 53 cet: also the compound *edisco* 472 D, 474 C, qu. 113 pr, 2 qu. N.T. 53; but no other compound.

(Marcus) Barnabae adfinis addiscitur 465 B; ut addiscerent non impune sibi futurum qu. 14 pm.—(c) *c. indir. interrog.* addiscerent principes huius saeculi quid admisissent mali 206 D; addiscentes quae promissa sunt bene uiuentibus 322 B (*fort. sub* (*a*) *inserendum*); ut per hanc quid agendum sibi esset addiscerent 466 B; ex imagine, quam praecellat ueritas, addiscitur 511 A; ut, adhaerentes ei, addiscerent, unde illi calumniam facerent 515 A.—(d) *c.* quia (= "that," in statements): a Tito autem addiscens quia dolorem paterentur 324 B; addiscentes quia in aduentu domini priores resurgent 475 A; addiscens quia "uerbum caro factum est" qu. 76 (72).—(e) *c. inf. simpl.* legem per quam addiscerent rectum a peruerso distinguere 76 B; ut bene uiuere addiscerent 489 A.—(f) *absol.* tunc etenim, addiscentes, uera esse sciunt quae audiunt 485 B.

adimpleo: non utique lex exinanitur per fidem, sed adimpletur 85 B; ut adimpleret exhortatione sua uoluntatem illorum in opere bono 328 B; omnia in passione saluatoris consummata et adimpleta sunt qu. 105.

adinuentio: rectum et manifestum est non nos adinuentioni Adae...obsecundare debere 127 C; mendacium adinuentio diaboli est qu. 113.

adiudico: (a) **c. inf.* quippe cum Sodoma et Gomorra per ignem adiudicatae sint deperire 98 A; Achar quoque filius Charmi, cum peccasset, consumi cum omnibus suis adiudicatus est qu. 127 pm.—(b) *simpl.* cognouerunt adiudicatum esse principem huius mundi qu. 89; nam solemus de aliquo dicere "adiudicatus est" 2 qu. mixt. 6.—(c) *c. dat. poenae*: non utique sine corpore adiudicabitur bono aut malo 311 C.—(d) *c. obi. interrog.* unum quemque adiudicat quid mereatur qu. 34.

adstruo: (a) *c. acc. obi.* hoc nulla ratione adstrui potest 227 A; ut heretici animum suum uerbis, non sensu, legis adstruere uideantur 496 D; proprium enim sensum (legis) uerbis adstruunt legis 532 A; ad causam istam adstruendam qu. 41 pr; ut causam furoris sui adstruat 2 qu. N.T. 50; stabile esse quod uerbis adstructum erat qu. 93; sed tu hoc sic adstruis, ut... uidearis qu. 102 ex.—(b) *c. acc. et inf.* adstruentes nihil posse fieri praeter quam mundi continet ratio 125 B (so Hier.).

aduerto is used = "to observe," almost to the entire exclusion of *animaduerto*, which occurs, e.g. qu. 12; 73 (77). Examples are:—cognomen Iudaeis tripartito genere significatum debemus aduertere 73 A; Iudaeos pro noxiis (so most MSS) suis traditos sibi non aduertebant 74 C (animaduertebant *cod.*) cet.; si uelis aduertere, non incongruum uidebis qu. 12; ut nimis impium facinus Sodomitarum possit aduerti qu. 13; the word occurs also in qu. 64; 98; 102 (p. 2310); 103; 105; 113; 115 (p. 2348).

adultero in the metaphorical sense: libenter acceperant doctrinam sub nomine Christi adulteratis uerbis 55 A; uerba legis adulterat 100 D (*cf.* non sunt adulteri legis 111 C; mala enim et adultera doctrina 211 A); sophistae Graecorum... adulterarant scripturam 366 B; si enim in carnem, quae ex se est, peccat, bis utique se ipsum adulterat 2 qu. N.T. 50 cet.

ago: in the phrase **sub lege agere**[1]: sibi uiueret aliquis, si non ageret sub lege 176 C; scirent se sub lege agere non debere 53 A; sub lege enim agentes male intellegunt Christum 53 B; sub lege agebant simpliciter 55 D; ad eos loquitur qui agunt sub lege 84 C; nam sub lege agentes obnoxii sunt (peccato) 122 C cet.; sub lege agens qu. 47 m; agentes sub lege qu. 59 ex; agentes enim sub dei lege qu. 99 pr; sub dei lege agentes qu. 110 ex; sub dei lege agere qu. 33; sub lege agere qu. 15 cet. (*Esse* (e.g. 108 A; qu. 47; 102 (p. 2307)) and *uiuere* (e.g. 112 B; qu. 22) are much rarer.)

ambigo, ambiguus with negative words, or in quasi-negative sentences: *nemo* ambigit animae esse peccatum 62 B; facta quae hominibus *non* ambigerent displicere 64 B; qui *non* ambigitur cuncta ex nihilo fecisse 208 A etc.; *non* ambigit sed nefariis pernegat uocibus 2 qu. mixt. 9; quam...dare *non* ambigit qu. 117 pr; *non* ambigens impleri debere quod iubet deus qu. 117 ex; *non* ambigitur etiam ipse esse de deo, ut in sancto spiritu patris esse substantia et diuinitas *non* ambigatur qu. 125 am; *nemo* fidelium ambigit 2 qu. N.T. 64; *non* ambigeremus qu. 95 pr; *non* ambigebant qu. 91 (p. 2283); *non* ambigeretur qu. 97 (p. 2293); 104; *non* ambigitur qu. 97 (p. 2295); *non* ambigantur qu. 106 (p. 2319); *non* ambigatur qu. 109 (p. 2326); *non* ambigit qu. 109 (p. 2326); ut *nemo* ambigeret qu. 114 aex. Examples in quasi-negative sentences are:—quid ambigitur

[1] Cf. *sub* potestate *agere* 172 A; *sub* principe *agere* qu. 110 (new part); *sub* fato *agere* qu. 115.

qu. 125; 2 qu. N.T. 11; quis ambigat qu. 91 (p. 2284); quis ambigeret qu. 109 (p. 2325); quis ambigit qu. 110.

non est ambiguum with acc. and inf. Instances are:—201 A; 248 A;' 263 D; 371 C; qu. 56; 91 (p. 2283); 95; 97 (p. 2295); 123: also, non fuit ambiguum qu. 43; non esset ambiguum qu. 91 am; ambiguum non est qu. 102 aex; nulli est ambiguum qu. 108 pm.

amputo: in a *metaphorical* sense; nearly always *perfect participle passive* in the *ablative absolute* construction: amputato errore 75 D; amputatis erroribus 393 B; qui errorem hunc amputaret qu. 12; ut errorem amputet qu. 122 pm; omni enim amputata discordia 152 C; amputata omni discordia erroris humani 187 B; amputata enim sollicitudine rei uxoriae 235 C; ut amputata caligine...digni fierent uidere gloriam dei 358 B; amputata erroris nebula 437 D; amputata totius traditionis humanae cultura 453 C; superbiam ergo amputat 248 B; fide et uigilantia sua omnem offensionem neglegentibus amputat 316 A; ut hac tergiuersatione fructum amputet paenitentiae qu. 102 pr; non uoce sed effectu paenitentiam amputas qu. 102 pm.—ut illis amputet quod prius per errorem uolebant audire 278 A.—amputandum est tamen ne sibi uel de eo ipso blandiatur iniquitas qu. 97 am. (Literally amputauit auriculam qu. 104.)

apertus: in the phrase **apertum est**[1]**:** apertum est quod dicit 307 C; 387 B; 476 C cet.; qu. 110 pm: quid tam apertum (sometimes followed by *quia*[2])? 222 C; qu. 46; 59; 91; 97; 98; 123; 127 ex: apertum est quia followed by the indic.: 140 A; 157 C; 214 A; 266 A; 296 C; 350 B; 352 D; 356 B; 361 A; qu. 44 (col. 2242); etc.: apertum est with acc. and inf.:—152 B; 267 A; qu. 97 (col. 2296); 2 qu. V.T. 3 etc.

apophoretum: ut quasi dedicatio regni Christi hanc gratiam credentibus pro apophoretis largiretur 405 B; in magna uota maxima dantur apophoreta 404 B; cum id elaborare soleant diuites, ut in die festo natalis sui exquisita inuitatis dent apophoreta qu. 123 aex.

[1] Frequent varieties are *uerum est*, *manifestum est* (see below), *nulli dubium est*, *non est obscurum*, *non est ambiguum* (see above), followed by *acc. et inf.* or *quia*.

[2] Cf. *quid tam euidens quia* qu. 47 (col. 2249) (codd).

apostasia: 'quo modo cecidit de caelo Lucifer' casum et apostasiam significans 157 B; si uirum suum causa fornicationis dimiserit, aut apostasiae 230 A; participes apostasiae suae uolens efficere homines 454 A; adsentientes apostasiae eius (diaboli) 506 C; diaboli apostasiam qu. 2; nemo fidelium dubitet diabolum apostasiae suae auctorem non habere qu. 98; ut post apostasiam regressis remittat peccata qu. 102 (col. 2305).

apostato: diabolus cum alta sapuit apostatauit 168 B; si tamen apostatauerit uir, aut usum quaerat uxoris inuertere 230 A; filii Hierusalem terrenae apostatarunt a deo qu. 40.

apparentia (never *apparitio*): ut multifaria apparentia fidem resurrectionis (Iesus) firmaret 276 A; apparentia enim sua dum (saluator) lacessit desiderantes liberari, 'cepisse' illos dicitur 408 D; de antichristi apparentia et damnatione 479 B; apparentia maiestatis suae inbecillitatem mentis eius roborauit 489 B; apparentia comminantis angeli qu. 16; sub dei apparentia et nomine qu. 46 (col. 2245); per stellae apparentiam Christum regem Iudaeorum natum intellexerunt qu. 63; et in aduentu et in apparentia spiritus sancti qu. 93 (col. 2286); ex apparentia ineffabilis gloriae qu. 114 (col. 2346).

audacia in the exclamatory expression **qua audacia**, etc.: qua praesumptione et audacia legatis dei non solum exitia, sed et mors inrogatur 425 A; qua igitur audacia dicunt Iudaei non nostra nos lege uti qu. 44 (col. 2242); qua audacia diceret infra *templum* cet. qu. 97 (col. 2296); quod uisibile est et sentitur et tangitur qua audacia uocatur aeternum! qu. 28'; quae audacia est presbyteris ministros ipsorum pares facere! qu. 101 (col. 2301).

baiolo: grandis animi erat in baiulandis infirmitatibus fratrum 317 A; si aequo animo fuerint baiulatae (tribulationes) qu. 119.

baiolus, in the ablative absol. construction with another noun: baiulis nubibus 475 C; baiulis leuitis qu. 46 (col. 2246).

brutus: sensu bruta est omnis caro 321 A; creaturam hylicam...quae utique sensu bruta est qu. 41 (*a*) aex; (gens) quae... sensu bruta erat 153 D; (caro) brută natura 121 B.

cado: in the phrase **non cadere in**[1]: quia non cadit in deum, ut iniquus sit 78 D; in rerum naturam non cadit 91 B;

[1] Morin, 8.

uidens hoc in rerum naturam non cadere 281 B; (res) in humanum sensum non caderet 205 C; ea quae .. in uituperationem non cadunt 442 C; natura eius in reprehensionem non cadit qu. 73 (77).

calco: *met.* (Hier. etc.): calcata iactantia 432 D; inpudentia calcata qu. 121; calcata morte 409 A; partem legis naturalis... calcauerunt 98 B; si desideria eius (carnis) calcentur 106 B; ad calcandam horum maliuolentiam 429 A; legis auctoritas rationem calcat fatorum qu. 115 pm.

caligo: especially in the phrase **caliginem abstergere**[1]: ut... abstergeretur caligo ab oculis mentis eorum 160 C; ut purificati homines dono dei, abstersa caligine, possint uidere gloriam Christi 302 D; carnalis error obstabat, caliginem praestans humanis cordibus, ne cognoscerent creatorem...Christus, qui hanc caliginem abstergeret qu. 12; *cf.* nondum adhuc discussa erroris caligine 2 qu. mixt. 9, cet.

causa: the ablative case, governing[2] the names of both persons and things (or qualities) in the genitive, prefixed or postfixed to the governed word indifferently, is one of the most frequent constructions in both works[3].—I. Genitive of *Persons*: (*a*) *Nouns.* causā patrum 58 B; 70 A; qu. 14 ex; c. Corneli 183 B; causa Achar qu. 36; hominis c. 406 C; qu. 127 pr; hominum c. qu. 114 pm; inimicorum...discipulorum c. qu. 104.—(*b*) *Adjectives.* multorum c. 293 B; infidelium c. 436 C; malorum c. qu. 115 pm.—(*c*) *Pronouns.* nostri c. 135 A; 415 B; tui c. qu. 102 ex; sui c. 326 D; 439 B; 440 A; 443 B; horum c. 324 A; 368 A; qu. 106 pr; illorum c. 357 B; cuius c. 487 A; qu. 102 ex; quorum c. 79 B; 242 B; 294 C; 409 A; 472 B; 518 B.—(*d*) *Present Participles.* c. credentium[4] 292 B; 321 A; credentium c. 394 A; perstrepentium c. 299 A.—II. Genitive of *Things or Qualities*: (*a*) causa *prefixed*—(1) the noun being unqualified in any way—c. peccati 82 C; 93 A (see below);

[1] Which, by the way, I have found in Paulin. Nol. ap. Aug. ep. 94, 1, *caligine dubitationis abstersa*: see *Thes. Ling. Lat.* s. u. and C. Weyman in Bursian's *Jahresbericht* Bd. cv (1900 II) p. 79.

[2] Not to the exclusion of such expressions as *hac causa*, *nostra causa*, cet.

[3] *Propter* is occasionally found, however; *e.g.* 409 C, 468 D, 469 A. In each section, examples, where *causa* comes first, are first given.

[4] This writer uses *credentes* and *diffidentes* practically as nouns, *e.g.* 72 A, see below *s. u.*

303 C; 308 B; 315 B; 358 B; 365 A; 371 D; 379 B; 379 C; 491 C; qu. 27 m; qu. 112 aex; c. credulitatis 151 B; c. incredulitatis 161 A; c. indignitatis 218 B; c. fornicationis 230 A; 234 A; c. apostasiae 230 A; c. delictorum 292 A; c. delicti 323 C; c. fidei 309 B; c. deuotionis 532 D; c. uirtutum 318 B; c. quietis 348 A; c. legis 349 C; 365 B; c. terroris 397 A; c. dilectionis 421 A; c. inuidiae 435 A; c. blasphemiae 491 C; c. administrationis qu. 25; c. facinoris qu. 68 (*a*); c. magisterii qu. 79 (75); c. sanctitatis qu. 123 aex; c. gaudii 2 qu. N.T. 37; c. deitatis qu. 88; c. uentris 225 C—(2) With a pair of nouns; or, sometimes, a qualifying adjective or genitive with one noun—c. suae religionis 56 B; c. timoris illorum 370 B; c. timoris dei qu. 111 m; c. tam admirabilis et inuisibilis praemii 440 B; c. conuersationis mundanae 464 C; c. communis fidei 508 B; c. fidei sincerae 513 A; c. impietatis et stupri et ceterorum qu. 76 (72); c. peccati Adae qu. 123 aex.—(*b*) causa *postfixed* (95)—(1) the noun (pronoun) being unqualified in any way—peccati c. (93 A (*codd.*)); 111 D; 126 C; 127 A; 128 C; 164 B; 287 A *bis*; 463 C; 532 D; qu. 64 (*a*); qu. 111 am; peccatorum c. 292 A; qu. 42; qu. 102 ppr; castitatis c. 461 A; orationis c. 497 D; amoris c. 502 C; affectus c. 532 B; incredulitatis c. 77 A; 153 C; 159 C; 385 B; eius c. 131 A; 131 C; horum c. qu. 115 ex; perfidiae c. 159 B; peregrinationis c. 187 C; fidei c. 188 C; 191 B; qu. 76 (72); qu. 108 ppr; gloriae c. 197 C; generis c. 191 B; contaminationis c. 220 A; ventris c. 317 A; caritatis c. 239 A; 240 C; peritiae c. 240 B; dedicationis c. 247 B; delicti c. 249 B; 323 B; qu. 112 pr; uenerationis c. 251 C; schismatis c. 255 B; ordinis utique c. non proprii meriti 263 B; inoboedientiae c. 265 C; correptionis c. 291 C; salutis...c. 293 A; quaestus c. 293 D; 469 A; infidelitatis c. 303 C; reatus c. 304 C; iactantiae c. 313 A; auaritiae c. 341 D; signaculi c. 357 D; firmitatis c. 369 A; legis c. 383 A; infirmitatis c. 432 C; terroris c. qu. 4 m; purificationis c. qu. 49; paupertatis c. qu. 32; dignitatum c. qu. 46 m; exempli c. qu. 59 pm; misericordiae c. qu. 60; necessitatis c. qu. 61 (*a*); sanctitatis c. qu. 91 m; idolatriae c. qu. 102 pm; signorum c. qu. 104; antiquitatis c. qu. 114 aex; inimicitiarum c. qu. 127 ppr.—(2) With a pair of nouns; or, sometimes, a qualifying adjective or genitive with one noun—commendationis suae c. 213 C; non religionis c. sed quaestus 225 C; peccati et imprudentiae c. 232 C; subiectionis suae c. 254 B;

unitatis et mysterii c. 255 C; peccati proprii c. 297 C; proprii honoris et quaestus c. 300 D; libertatis c. et purae conscientiae 318 B; gaudii et laetitiae c. 404 B; condicionis c., non naturae 421 C; quaestus c. aut gulae 441 A; peccatorum suorum c. 454 B; malorum (*subst.*) memoratorum c. 459 C; plebis solius c. 466 C; humanae salutis c. 468 B; qu. 104; uentris c. aut pecuniae 485 A; non quaestus c. magis quam defensionis 503 A; caritatis c. et magisterii 515 B; non deuotionis c. sed quaestus 527 A; praeteriti peccati c. qu. 42 (*a*); diffidentiae et malae uitae c. qu. 68 (*b*); incredulitatis suae c. qu. 74 (*b*); iustitiae et sanctitatis c. qu. 105 pm.

certus of persons, followed by a noun clause, either acc. and inf., or **quia**: certi quia quod sub dei creatoris nomine editur non potest polluere 251 B; certus deinceps quia et uitia eorum paulatim corrigerentur prol. 2 Cor. (published in the *Journal of Theological Studies* IV (Oct. 1902), no. 13, pp. 89—92); certi quia pro salute fidelium animas suas traderent usque ad mortem 321 A; certus quia obaudirent bona opera facere 329 B; certus apostolus quia exitia...auctore diabolo ministrantur 423 C; certi quia omnes...odio habentur 522 A; certi quia pro salute sua corripiuntur 530 B; certus ex hoc quia obsequeretur et mandatis eius 533 B; certus quia...possit occidi (qu. 5); certus uanitatem uulgi mortuos magis ut deos uenerari quam uiuos (qu. 25); certus dei uoluntatem non debere ab homine retractari (qu. 109 col. 2326); qu. 115 (2352), etc. Cf. certum est ergo quia non ascendit (qu. 74 (78)); and certi ergo sancti uiri quod deus iudicium...exceperit (qu. 119).

cesso, regularly of the Law or the Old Dispensation, is a very frequent expression in both works, for example, in the phrase *cessante lege.* I give some references merely: 49 B; 55 D; 67 B; 85 B; C *quater*; 87 A; 89 C; 108 A; 111 C; 113 C; 128 B *bis*; 142 A; 160 C; 180 A; 229 A codd. etc.: qu. 44 *passim*; 50 *bis*; 69 *bis*; 107; 112; 115 *bis*; 125; 127 *passim*; 2 qu. N.T. 15 *ter*; 26; 29; 31 *bis*; 60; 2 qu. mixt. 11, etc.

ceterus: in the phrase **de cetero**: ut *d. c.* scirent quid euitare deberent 103 A; *d. c.* non peccantes 104 C; ut *d. c.* hanc uitam sequamur 105 B; si...*d. c.* non peccemus 105 C; ne *d. c.* peccet 108 A; ut *d. c.* non peccaretur 108 B; qui *d. c.* abstinent se a peccatis 110 B; ut *d. c.* Christi simus serui solius 112 B; sciens hominem ad Dei iudicium *d. c.* pertinere 114 C; ut ea...*d. c.* uitarentur 116 A; ut *d. c.* inimico dei resistat 117 B; ut...genus humanum... *d. c.* possit resipiscere 120 B; ut *d. c.*...detinere non audeat 124 B; ut *d. c.* nihil tale agamus 128 C; ne *d. c.* possint ueritatis uiam aspicere 156 B; ne *d. c.* possit fidem recipere 156 B; ne *d. c.* possint credere 157 A; ut...*d. c.* non intellegerent 157 A; ut *d. c.*... dei amorem in nos prouocemus 164 A; ut *d. c.* corrigant 255 C; *d. c.* accepturos se boni operis mercedem a domino 287 B; ut *d. c.* obaudientes facti laetificarent eos 296 D; si *d. c.* desinat 298 A; ut iustificati *d. c.* non peccent 302 A; ut *d. c.* mors eos...tenere non possit 315 C; ut *d. c.* timeatur 354 C; ut *d. c.*...a morte non tenerentur 354 D; si quis *d. c.* legem seruandam putat 362 A; sed uult illos *d. c.* perseuerare in bono 383 B; *d. c.* nulli eorum credentes 386 D; ut...*de cetero* thesaurizet sibi *in futurum* 414 C; *d. c.* orandum hortatur ut...484 B; *d. c.*...iudicii diem expectent 488 D; ut...homo *d. c.* in dei fide maneret 493 B; ut *d. c.*...ab ea teneri non posset 493 C; iam *d. c.* se ab usu feminae cohibentes 497 B; ut *d. c.* appellarentur ciues Romani 524 A; ut *d. c.* sciret quid faceret qu. 5 am; ut *d. c.* cessaret circumcisio qu. 50; *d. c.* aperta est ad caelum uia qu. 83 pm; ut *d. c.* traditio ista...crederetur...ut...*d. c.* inuisibiliter dari non ambigeretur qu. 93 pm; ut *d. c.* permaneant in mandatis eius qu. 98 aex; ut *d. c.* corrigentes emendarentur qu. 102 pr; ut *d. c.* acceptae legis redderent rationem qu. 102 pr; ut *d. c.*...nullo modo ueniam consequantur qu. 102 m; *d. c.* temperare ab his quae admiserat qu. 102 m; ut *d. c.*... actus sui redderent rationem qu. 112 pr; ut *d. c.*...relinquerent errorem qu. 113 pm.

christianitas appears 204 A; qu. 39; 114 *bis*; **christianismus** 49 B; 111 B *bis*; qu. 3 *bis* (codd.).

circumspectus: non, sollicitus de cura Timothei, *tam* circumspectus est, sed propter successores eius 510 B; nec enim *tam* circumspectus potest aliquis esse, ut nusquam erret qu. 111 (col. 2333).

coimagino: mori mundo, et commori Christo, aeternae quoque uitae ac salutari coimaginari 106 B; ut autem imago dei esset homo, quia dono dei coimaginari haberet filio dei qu. 106 ex. (The word is cited once from Hilary: see also chap. ii p. 48.)

commendo often in the passive with **testimonio** as an instrumental ablative: his dictis commendat credentes Iudaeos 77 A; iniustitia nostra dei iustitiam non commendat (= Rom. iii 5). Si autem commendaret... 78 C; ut et caritatem dei commendaret in nobis 94 A; uirtutis, quae maior res est, testimonio commendatur 94 B; adfectum saluatoris erga nos commendare 94 D; commendans apostolus fidem 103 C; nec enim Iudaeos poterit commendare praerogatiua patrum 151 B; originem commendat Iudaeorum 182 B; aliorum ideo refutare personas, ut suam commendaret 197 B; ut doctrinae ueritas ipsa se commendaret 198 B; deus praedicationem suam non testimonio uerborum uoluit commendari sed uirtutis 203 C; per hypocrisin commendati 208 D; commenta erroris commendare non possunt 210 C; ipsis nos magis, quia meliora sunt, commendemus 213 A; eloquentia commendati 215 C; quod tantis testimoniis commendat 243 B; etc. etc.; uir laudabilis et dei testimonio commendatus qu. 46; nullo diuino testimonio commendatur qu. 46; signorum uirtutibus commendata qu. 95; per hoc commendatur Christus non inclinatur qu. 97; nullo testimonio commendati qu. 100; ita tamen ut duarum rerum testimonio commendentur qu. 120; commendet orationem cum ieiunio qu. 120; orationem et ieiunium Corneli misericordia commendauit qu. 120; si dei iudicio commendetur qu. 127 etc.

The comparative of the past participle passive occurs :—233 C, 390 C; qu. 93.

commixtio: nihil dicit posse fieri sine commixtione 199 A; nihil enim existimat posse fieri sine commixtione 207 B; cf. ne (credendum sit) aliquid corporeum sine rerum admixtione generari 452 D cet.[1]; quia nihil sine commixtione generatur in hoc mundo qu. 97 am; ut nihil aestiment posse fieri sine commixtione spiritali et simplici 2 qu. N.T. 47; ex commixtione filii hominum homines sunt qu. 122 (p. 2366).

compago and cognates, **compagino**, **compaginatio**, are frequent: corporis manente compagine 105 A; compaginatio humani generis 410 D; compaginati fidei eius subministrante

[1] *e.g. sine commixtione* uiri uirginem peperisse 112 C; *sine elementorum commixtione* 246 C; *commixtione elementorum* qu. 20.

euangelio 456 C, cet.; discretis enim ab inuicem substantiis facta compaginatione mundus uocatur qu. 2 ppr; primum oportebat domum compaginari qu. 23 pm; cum ergo corporis liniamenta compacta non fuerint, ubi erit anima? qu. 23 aex; ante compaginationem mundi qu. 106 ppr; nunc enim compaginatur in specie mundus qu. 106 m; substantias ex quibus mundum compaginaret quo compacto qu. 106 pm; ...ex quibus compaginatus est mundus qu. 107 pr; compaginata in speciem linguae unius qu. 108 aex.

comparatio: in the phrase **ad comparationem** *c. genit.* (Hier.) = "in comparison with": ad comparationem legis 113 B; ad comparationem eius 127 B; ostendit parua esse, quae hic possunt a perfidis inrogari, ad comparationem decreti muneris in futuro saeculo 129 D; ad comparationem aeternorum uana sunt 130 D; ad comparationem earum 237 A; in hac ergo uita paruuli sumus ad comparationem futurae uitae 267 A; ad comparationem spiritalium haec nulla sunt 309 C; homo enim ad comparationem sancti spiritus caro est 391 B; haec omnia detrimenta deputans ad comparationem promissionum saluatoris 439 A; ad comparationem autem ceterorum, qui res diuinas neglegentius curant, perfecti dicendi sunt 440 B; aliquando ad comparationem meliorum immundum dicitur qu. 9; ad comparationem pulcherrimarum rerum qu. 9; plumbum ad comparationem auri immundum est qu. 9; ad comparationem temporum et gratiarum qu. 20; ad comparationem ceterorum qu. 42 (*a*); ad comparationem domini qu. 91 pr; ad cuius comparationem minimus dicitur Abraham qu. 109 pr; sed ad comparationem eius imperfecta sunt qu. 123 ppr; ad comparationem enim infidelium nos perfecti sumus qu. 123 am; ad comparationem lucernae tenebrae non tantum obscurae sed et sordidae sunt, ad comparationem autem stellarum lucerna caligo est, ad solis uero comparationem stellae nebulosae sunt qu. 127 ex.

compendium: the *abl.* ***compendio** (Hier.) is characteristic, also ***per compendium,** etc.—(*a*) *abl.* compendio: abbreuiatio facta legis est, quae compendio daret salutem 49 B; ut possit compendio medellam uulneris inuenire 90 A; docens quo compendio citius itur ad deum 237 A; et non potius compendio per fidem salutem quaerere 488 A; compendio loquitur scriptura qu. 16; aliquando compendio loquitur scriptura qu. 16 (*b*) per compendium: per compendium dixit hoc saluator qu. 16; hoc quod per compendium propositum est qu. 77; ut securi per compendium possint deo seruire spiritaliter 2 qu. N.T. 46. (*c*) Ordinary use: ut utar compendio 143 C; compendium est male agentibus si citius moriantur quam si diutius in peccatis uersentur 221 C; *solent qui* compendium *quaerunt errare* 228 B, almost exactly repeated in—frequenter, *qui* compendium *quaerit, solet errare* qu. 72 (*a*); compendio breuitatis studens euangelista qu. 73 (77); do compendium qu. 95 ex.

competo[1]: never in any part but *present tense, indic., subj., infin.* or *pcpl.*; when any case follows, it is the *dative*: *(*a*) *c. dat.* quod utique homini competit 50 B; quia hoc homini competit 78 C; fructus est competens naturae 95 B; sicut competit eius diuinitati 133 C; nec enim competit ei ut iniustus sit, cuius beniuolentia tanta apparet 145 A; hoc competit deo 155 B; quod nec loco ipsi competit 167 A; scit non sibi competere in quo illi potest inuideri 250 B; non competit fidelibus audire linguas quas cet. 271 A; cum sciant sibi magis competere ut in domo dei precibus uacent 273 C; quod soli conditori competit 417 C; ei hoc competit 434 D; ut ipsi soli magis competat in ueritate 490 C; quid cuique personae competat demonstravit qu. 3 ex; quod nec animae ipsi competit qu. 23 pr; planctum Rachel filiis dicit competere qu. 62; persona cui competat detur. quare Christo non competat cet. qu. 91 pm; quod deo non competit qu. 97 pr; nec iusto uiro competit aliquem accusare qu. 102 aex; dei nomen non competit creaturae qu. 122 pr; haec nulli alii possent competere nisi filio dei qu. 122 ppr; quamquam enim bona sunt, dei tamen personae non competunt qu. 127 ex; his competit 2 qu. N.T. 55. (*b*) *absol.* uindictam competentem 170 A; damnatio enim in eo competit quia uoluerunt 416 D; competens locus 493 D; tempore competenti qu. 46 aex; qu. 110 pm. The substantive *competentes* appears in neither work.

complector met. = 'include': totum enim hic complexus

[1] A favourite word of Augustine also, in the same sense, "to fit, suit."

uidetur 99 D etc.; omnia enim peccata complexus est qu. 102 (col. 2307) etc.

condignus followed by the dative, of which construction there are only two examples in Georges: tria ergo alia posuit incredulitati condigna 69 B; ne...solus habeat nomen deitatis sibi soli condignum 459 B; illa sectari quae iusta sunt et legi (codd.) dei condigna 527 C; maiestati suae minime hoc condignum opus qu. 48; illam puram et ipsi professioni condignam cognouissemus (codd.: *Migne* ipsa professione dignam) qu. 114 (col. 2342). There are examples of the absolute use in qu. 111; 112 *bis*.

confoueo metaphorically used (Hier.): confouens animos illorum 244 B; animum suum confouet mentis alacritate 513 B; also 179 D; 244 C; inpudentia calcata, uerecundia confota, animabus ad caelum data facultas qu. 121.

confugere ad deum etc. is a characteristic phrase: magis gratia dei et donum in plures abundauit confugientes ad se 101 C; fides enim data est quae iustificat confugientes ad se 122 C; praedicata misericordia est quae ad se confugientes saluaret 162 C; ideo est ad dei misericordiam confugiendum 117 B etc.; ad dei auxilium confugere qu. 2; (dominus) uult nos ad auxilium suum confugere qu. 102 (col. 2306); dominus ad auxilium suum uult confugere seruos suos qu. 112 (col. 2336); confugere ad dei clementiam qu. 112 (col. 2338); ad auxilium eius confugiens qu. 115 (p. 2352); confugientibus ad deum qu. 115 (p. 2353).

confusio: in the phrase ***ad** or **in confusionem** cet.: haec ad Iudaeorum confusionem pertinent 81 C; ad confusionem Iudaeorum 265 B; (dum coeperint) omnia falsa commenta uel dogmata in confusionem deduci 151 A; hoc decreuit ad confusionem illorum, qui cet. 204 B; auctoritatem...conseruare, ad confusionem diaboli 253 C; ad confusionem (*v. l.* destructionem) prudentium mundi 94 B; 468 B; qu. 121; hoc saluator ad confusionem illorum fecit 2 qu. N.T. 33; ut superior creatura ad confusionem suam...disceret qu. 2 am cet.; ad confusionem gentilium 264 C; ad confusionem Photini qu. 56; ad confusionem obstrepentium qu. 109.

congruus and **congrue:** si congruam paenitentiam agant qu. 102; nec gratias congruas possunt ei agere qu. 123 ex; congruas poenas qu. 44; 126; in auctorem congrua (codd.) datur uindicta qu. 14; congruum fuit *c. acc. et inf.* 2 qu. N.T. 1; congruum est enim creaturae credere et uenerari suum conditorem 71 C (some MSS differently) etc. etc. Qui congrue intellegunt Christum 372 B; cui congrue respondit 282 A etc.; iam uide si non congrue illa in parte uel tale signum accepit qu. 12; ut dies pentecostes unde et qua ratione tractus sit congrue dinoscamus qu. 95 (col. 2289) etc. *Incongruus* and *incongrue* are also used (see below).

conloco: in the phrase ***conlocare meritum,** with **(sibi) apud deum** usually added.—(a) *c. sibi ad deum*: ut discant quemadmodum *apud creatorem* meritum collocatur 98 B; ideo non magna iustitia legis est, nec meritum collocat *apud deum* 150 B; *apud deum sibi* collocat meritum 168 A; meritum *sibi* collocat *apud deum* 232 C; *apud deum* meritum illi collocat 237 C; quae (uia) meritum collocat *apud deum* 264 B; spiritalia enim sunt, quae seruata meritum collocant *apud deum* 362 B; ad haec eos facienda hortatur, quae meritum collocant *apud deum* 461 B; ex diuersis causis meritum collocatur *apud deum* 526 A; ut...uoluntas...meritum *ei* collocet *apud deum* qu. 115 ex.—(b) *simpl.*: sic meritum quis collocat, dum in tribulationibus patiens inuenitur 133 A; meritum sibi collocat et coronam 234 A; non quia mala sunt, sed quia parua sunt ad meritum collocandum 440 A; meritum *sibi* collocans per laborem 2 qu. N.T. 63; uti maius meritum collocares 2 qu. mixt. 6.

constituo: in the phrase **reum constituere:** reus constituitur qu. 61 (*a*); lex per Moysen data reos constituit peccatores qu. 76 (*a*); ut nec gloriari possit de bonis, nec reus constitui de malis qu. 80 (*a*); reum constituens a quo occiditur 200 D; omnes rei sunt constituti 128 C; qu. 2 *bis*; 102; 112; etc. (*Reum facere* and *reum tenere* are also common: *reum facere* occurs e.g. 108 A; 219 A; qu. 61; 116; 124; *reum tenere* e.g. 103 C; 108 A; 111 B *bis*; 113 B; 122 C; D; 162 C; qu. 31; qu. 69.) *Constitutus*, for the missing present participle of *sum*, is conspicuous by its rarity (218 D; 362 D; qu. 111; 113; 2 qu. V.T. 17): *positus* is the regular equivalent in these works (see below, p. 125 f.).

consto: the phrase **cum constet:** cum constet omnes subditos esse legi naturali 70 A (cod.); cum enim constet omnes inimicos fidei falsa tenere pro ueris 207 D; cum constet dominum et auctorem nostrum Christum aliter...interfatum 208 D; cum constet multis officiis opus esse 261 A; cum constet...homines resurgere 285 B codd.; cum constet hunc legem defendere et custodire 392 B; cum constet primum mandatum ita contineri 422 A; cum constet Christum hominem esse et deum 434 A; cum constet uiuere illum cum his omnibus 458 B; cum constet apostolum exemplo usum domus diuitis et opulentis (*u. l.* locupletis) 519 B; cum constet omnem instructionem uiri ecclesiastici in epistula contineri 524 A; cum constet nos semper omnia aspicere qu. 1 ex; cum enim mundum constet hominis causa fabricatum qu. 3 (col. 2218); cum constet apud omnes personae sublimi maxima debere offerri munera qu. 5 (col. 2220); cum constet omne factum sententiam secum habere qu. 6; cum constet fidem stultam...minime prodesse qu. 43; cum constet exempli causa locutum hoc saluatorem qu. 59; cum constet a Dauid...XVII esse generationes qu. 85; cum constet utique omnes...non fuisse in templo qu. 94; quem cum constet scire ac facere posse bonum qu. 98 (col. 2299); cum constet omnes ante quam credant in deum peccare qu. 102 (col. 2307); cum constet omnia dei esse qu. 106 (p. 2318) codd.; cum constet dei auxilio ipsum etiam ab hominibus uinci qu. 113; quos cum constet homines fuisse qu. 114 (col. 2342); cum constet in scripturis omnes bonos oboedire prophetis 2 qu. N.T. 34.

constringo (as also **adstringo**[1]) in a metaphorical sense, especially the participle **constrictus:** 'angustiae' uero sunt quibus constrictus sententia tribulabitur in poena 69 B; Iudaeis in peccatis constrictis 81 D; ideo non debet quis constringi 229 B; non ita lege constringitur uir sicut mulier 230 B; lege maritali constricta (uxor) 236 B; constrictus *carnali ratione* 489 B etc.; sibi prius subueniret in eadem necessitate constricto qu. 112; in multis constrictus qu. 118; *carnali* constrictus[2] *ratione* qu. 59 (col. 2254) etc.

consubstantiuus (never *consubstantialis*): mulier consubstantiua uiro est 420 C (here the Benedictines, following "alii

[1] See the *Thes. Ling. Lat.* s. u. and qu. 102 (col. 2304) adstrictus *lege*; qu. 6 acrius adstringendum *eum*.

[2] *Migne* corruptly *instructus*.

MSS," have *consubstantialis*, for which I have no MS authority: the MSS have either *consubstantiua*, or *consubstantia*, which points to it): sp. s....consubstantiuus ei (*i.e.* deo) qu. 41; quod uerbum idcirco filium nuncupauit ut ostenderet de se illum exstitisse et esse sibi consubstantiuum qu. 48; per id quod enim consubstantiui sunt, qui unum uidet ambos uidet qu. 97 (col. 2291); consubstantiuus esse deo Christus non ambigeretur qu. 97 (col. 2293); aequale esse et consubstantiuum cum eo quod aeternum est qu. 97 (col. 2293); quo modo ergo dici potest de spiritu sancto quia nescit natiuitatem filii dei, si consubstantiuus est ei qu. 125 (col. 2373); si consubstantiuus non est deo et Christo qu. 125 (col. 2375).

contrarius, used absolutely, is very common: ne ueniens introeat atque animo contraria suadeat 121 B; quae aut ante petuntur quam peti debeant, aut sunt contraria, non sinit fieri 133 A; non euitans hanc uelut contrariam 176 A; ab eis quae infructuosa sunt et magis contraria declinantes 179 B; ut res contrarias et absurdas nominis dignitas faciat acceptabiles 210 D; hoc *quantum ad uerba pertinet uidetur* contrarium 416 C etc.; quod si cui adhuc forte *uidetur* esse contrarium qu. 64 (p. 2259); qui suggesserunt faciendum quod contrarium est qu. 115 (p. 2351); non se ingerunt ad contraria suggerenda *ibid.*; suggerunt cum blanditiis contraria *ibid.*; *quantum ad uerba pertinet uidetur* contrarium 2 qu. mixt. 7; hoc quantum uidetur contrarium est qu. 71; fecit enim et non fecit contrarium est qu. 78 (74); quid *uidetur* contrarium... qu. 74 (78); non est contrarium qu. 97 (p. 2295); contrarium non est quod unius corporis est qu. 114 (p. 2345); also 118; 127 *bis* (p. 2381; 2384); 2 qu. N.T. 1; 36; 46; 54; 62.

contueor: contuendum est unum esse sensum et in nullo differre 102 A cet.; contuendum itaque est quia non a Pilato sed a Iudaeis saluator crucifixus est qu. 65; contuendum etenim est quo modo dictum sit qu. 125 (p. 2375); contuens apostolus Petrus uenenatam malitiam hominis qu. 102 (p. 2310); contuens factum apostoli Petri qu. 104; hoc contuens iudex qu. 112 (p. 2337); magnam prouidentiam in hoc opere et ordine contuemur qu. 106 (col. 2320); quem sensum contuemur in lege qu. 127 (col. 2379).

conuello, metaphorically used: ideo ut haec temptatio conuellatur admonet cum terrore 248 C; nunc excusationem iracundiae conuellit 534 B; multa poterunt diuinis solidata oraculis unius conuelli degeneris testimonio qu. 97 (col. 2293); quod facile puto conuelli qu. 102 (col. 2310); ut prauam adseuerationem conuellat qu. 106 (col. 2318); conuellatur si alienum est a meritis Abrahae qu. 108 (col. 2323).

conuenio: in the phrase **conuenit**[1]: sed non conuenit, quia... qu. 23 pr; non conuenit quia... qu. 23 aex; istud et rationi conuenit qu. 91 aex; abnuatur si non conuenit rationi qu. 108 (p. 2323); sed hoc non sic conuenit rationi qu. 108 ex; quomodo conuenit ut...sit in aeternum? qu. 109 ex; illud facit quod conuenit rationi qu. 83 ex; ex aliqua parte conuenient rationi qu. 113; ut omnia deificae rationi conueniant qu. 114 (col. 2346).

corrigo *intransitively, like the English 'reform': ut corrigatis 217 B; solent enim aliqui pudorem pati et corrigere, cum de se audiunt bona 224 C; ut de cetero corrigant et sciant hoc uerum 255 C; 270 C codd.; non uos abicio sed ut corrigatis moneo 320 C; accepit autem cum didicit corrigere uelle 324 A codd.; 324 B codd.; ut corrigant in quibus reprehenduntur 334 A; si corrigant 347 B; non enim destruuntur qui arguuntur ut corrigant (so best MSS: others and edd. *corrigantur*) 356 B; ut de cetero corrigentes emendarentur qu. 102 pr. The evidence for this use is too strong to be upset by palaeographical considerations. Compare the intrans. use of *emendo* (below) and *reformo* (qu. 126 codd. p. 2377, 67).

coruscus, as a masc. substantive, is rare in Latin; it occurs once in each work: datur illi prudentia non ex litteris sed corusco *spiritus* sancti, ut *cor* habeat *inluminatum* 259 C codd. (*igne* after *sancti* is an editorial insertion); *corda* eorum *inluminata* sunt *spiritali* corusco qu. 112 (col. 2337).

credo: the *present partic.* ***credens**, used in the *sing.* and *plur.* as a *subst.* = "believer(s),"[2] opp. to ***diffidens** "unbeliever(s)": credens honorificentior est propter Abraham, diffidens autem

[1] Morin, p. 8.

[2] Also in Ambrose and in Vulg. act. 4, 32 etc. (See Achelis in *Theologische Literaturzeitung* xxix (1904) 242.)

peius tractandus est 69 C; sicut per conscientiam suam laudantur credentes, ita et per conscientiam suam accusantur diffidentes 72 A; 76 D (codd.); honorabilior erit credens 92 A; quae (lex fidei) credentes liberaret a dominio legis 113 B; credentes accepto spiritu prophetabant 165 B cet.; propensior credentis est merces et minor poena diffidentis...credentibus...diffidentibus qu. 122 am.

crementum is used almost to the entire exclusion of *incrementum*. Its opposite is *detrimentum*. The printed texts sometimes offer *decrementum*[1], which is probably a 'ghost-word,' a mere scribes' error for *detrimentum*. Examples are:—luna crementum (some MSS) et detrimentum *facit* 94 C; non poterit qui tribuit iuxta dei uoluntatem dei nutu non augeri crementis (*codd.*) huiusmodi ad amplificandum fructum iustitiae 332 B; crementum enim *faciunt* scientiae et plenius fundantur in fide 429 D; crementum *faciunt* deo quia ex perditis adquiruntur 456 C; crementum (*codd.*) operum eorum cum scientia uult *fieri* 445 D; ut praedicatione eius crementum (*codd.*) *faciat* in saluandis disciplina dominica 511 C etc.; ipsi filii nequissimi crementum *faciunt* malitiae qu. 14; huiusmodi crementum *faciunt* bonorum qu. 34; ex magna deminutione lux quae dies est crementum incipit accipere qu. 53; ex eo dies coepit crementum accipere qu. 55; usque dum fidei semina iacerentur ad crementum qu. 93 (col. 2287); post crementum solis ac lunae qu. 105 (col. 2316); cursus facit lunae in *detrimentis* et crementis qu. 106 (col. 2318); ut semen fidei per hanc crementum *faceret* qu. 114 (col. 2345); cuius ut superabundans crementum (*codd.*) fidei nosceretur qu. 117 (col. 2361); non haec a deo permitti nisi ad crementum (*codd.*) meritorum nostrorum qu. 119; nisi crementum (*codd.*) *faceret* in dei perceptione qu. 127 (col. 2382); nec enim deus aliquid dehabet, ut crementum *faciat* per nos 2 qu. N.T. 49; crementum *facit* in nobis diuinitas, ideo in eis qui ab eo recedunt *detrimentum* est 2 qu. N.T. 49. It is interesting to observe how the editors have treated the commentaries differently from the *Quaestiones*. The former they regarded as an important work, which must not bear the taint of

[1] E.g. *Adam ad hoc reuocatur ad quod fuerat factus sed cum* detrimento (*codd.*; *M.* decremento) qu. 127 (p. 2384). I am aware that the form is cited from other authors.

the unclassical form *crementum*, and altered nearly all the examples of it to *incrementum*. The *Quaestiones* was not valuable enough to make it worth while to alter the form which appeared in the manuscripts.

cumulus: hoc ad cumulum uerae protestationis adiecit 51 B codd.; ut ad cumulum nobis iustificationis proficeret, resurgens praeceptis suis auctoritatem tribuit 92 D; haec tamen ad cumulum adhuc addens grauat causam 243 A; ut augeantur his ad cumulum possessionis aeternae 349 D; ut...factum diaboli ...ad cumulum reatus eius proficeret qu. 2 m (*cf.* 92 D *supra*); ut addant ad cumulum confessionis suae qu. 114 (p. 2344, 32) codd.; accedit ad cumulum gloriae eius qu. 119 ex (cf. Cic. Clu. 74).

custodire in the sense 'keep' (the law, etc. as in Plin. ep.), is common in both works. I have not collected examples. **Custodire se ab** also occurs: membra nostra custodientes ab omni turpitudine 107 D; custodiens se a peccato qu. 19 cet.

defendo with acc. of the thing and dat. of the person, in the sense of *uindicare*[1], 'to claim': inde enim *sibi* defendunt generis praerogatiuam 343 A etc.; dum uult *sibi* regnum impia praesumptione defendere qu. 2 (col. 2216); ut tibi hoc defendere uidearis qu. 102 (col. 2311); *sibi* locum uolentes defendere qu. 110 (col. 2331); quae res...arbitratur rationis *sibi* ueritatem posse defendi qu. 114 (col. 2346)[2].

defero *with dat. of person, 'to defer to one': personis deferentes et alterum alteri praeponentes 353 C; sic ei deferentes quasi ipsi auctori domino 382 C; qua ratione Dauid Saul...christum domini uocat et defert ei? qu. 35 (MSS); putantes enim se deo patri deferre qu. 97 (col. 2292); quippe cum uideant non sic deferri sacerdotibus qu. 101 (col. 2302).

dehabeo: ut inuicem sibi praestent quod dehabent (*Migne* debent) 260 C; ab alio sumat quod dehabet (*Migne* non habet) 263 C; quare pater dicitur dedisse, cum ipse qui homo factus erat nihil dehaberet? 433 C; hominis natura dehabet scientiam qu. 125 (col. 2373); nec enim deus aliquid dehabet 2 qu. N.T. 49.

deputo is very common, I. esp. *c. acc. et dat.* (a) the *dat.* being

[1] Which is also common: e.g. 84 D; 197 A; qu. 14; 46; 97; 106 *ter*.

[2] Without the dative, *si enim ex solo nomine putant hoc debere* defendi qu. 108 (p. 2323).

a *person*: promissio regni caelorum iustis deputata est 90 B; nec eius claritas et maiestas alicui de creaturis deputetur 98 B; qui baptismatis eius gratiam hominibus deputabant 197 C; antiquitatem promissi Christi aliis deputat 216 C; interitus carnis homini deputatur 219 C; ut quod illi soli debitum est deputetur creaturae qu. 1 aex (cf. 98 B *sup.*); hoc apostolus sancto spiritui deputat qu. 97 aex; si gloriam et nomen eius aliis deputauerint qu. 114 ppr; ideoque deputatum est ei ad iustitiam (cf. Gen. xv 6) qu. 117 am; gloriam eius aliis deputant qu. 127 am—(b) the *dat.* being a *thing* or *quality*: omne uisibile carni deputatur 126 A; Adam...carni deputatus 128 A; uitia et delicta...carni deputantur 128 A; omne enim quod uidetur carni deputatur (cf. 126 A *supra*) 457 A; omnis error carni deputatur 478 B; ut qui...eligeret carni deputaretur qu. 115 m; partem Israel... perditioni deputatam 154 C; ipsa officia deputata membris 165 A; ius diuinum humanis auctoritatibus deputatum 171 B; mali actus tenebris deputantur 174 A; gentes istud risui deputant 199 A; hoc personae suae deputat 216 A; ceteri ergo Iudaei filii sunt carnis...nec deputari possunt merito Abrahae 140 A; "diuisiones autem gratiarum" sunt officiis ecclesiae non humanis meritis deputatae 259 B; quod non humanis meritis deputat 305 A; hoc enim deputatur naturae quod sequitur 399 A; qui singulis elementis diuinitatis diuersitatem deputant ad culturam 453 A; cum uiderit membrum quod sibi deputatum officium est 165 A; auctoritatem harum (legum) idolis deputantes 222 B; deputatus est gregi satanae 496 A; nox enim diei deputata est qu. 106 ppr; dominus...diei deputatur qu. 107 pm; ut quidquid... dicitur stultitiae deputetur qu. 115 pm.—II. *c. acc. et inf.*, the *infin.* (as with habeo) *not* being *expressed*, or with *inter c. acc.* cet.: (a) *c. predicative acc.* haec omnia detrimentum deputans (Phil. iii 8) ad comparationem promissionum saluatoris 439 A; non paricidium hoc deputans sed holocaustum qu. 109 ppr.—(b) *c.* inter *et acc.* cum inter Leuitas deputatus esset qu. 46 ex; inter quas et nos deputamur qu. 47 pr; inter perfidos deputatus qu. 115 m.—(c) *c.* extra *et acc.* si *extra* unius dei honorem deputetur et gloriam qu. 97 ex.—(d) *c.* cum *et abl.* neque scium cum inscio deputari qu. 125 ex.—III. = *credo, committo, trado*: (in) officio deputato 516 B.

desum: *non deesse* often appears in the MSS of both works in the curious form ***de non esse**[1]: et de non sunt qui dicant 'mala est' qu. 3 (col. 2219); hodie de non sunt qui latratus canum intellegant qu. 31 (col. 2233); Samuhel non egit sacerdotium quia de non erant sacerdotes qu. 46 (col. 2245, 70: corrupted to *qui dei non erat sacerdos* (Migne)); cetera autem de non est qua subrepant qu. 110 (*Journ. Theol. Stud.*, Oct. 1904); quamuis de non sint qui diffidant qu. 122 (col. 2367); de non erunt qui imitentur 442 A; quibus de non erat, qui...praestaret 518 B; de non sunt qui prope cottidie baptizentur aegri 497 C.

So ***de non fieri**: non ut abundet sed ut de non fiat 506 A (*cod. Casin.*: *alii* non desit; *Migne* non deficiat) (never in *Quaest.*).

deterioro: with its opposite, **melioro**[2]: a fidelibus enim et bene agentibus *melioratur* natiuitas: ab infidelibus autem et male agentibus deterioratur qu. 127 m.—II. **intrans.* ut calliditate sua non solum nihil profecisse se doleat, sed et deteriorasse qu. 127 pm; aliqui enim profecerunt in melius, alii deteriorauerunt, alii permanserunt 2 qu. V.T. 6; Iudaei...qui proficere magis debuerant, deteriorauerunt 147 D; putantes aliquid se proficere doctrina pseudoapostolorum deteriorauerant 248 B[3].

detineo: a secunda morte detineri 58 A; detinebat homines in inferno propter delictum Adae, ut de cetero...detinere non audeat 124 B; ab ira detinemur 170 A cet.; ut animas eorum duabus ex causis in errore detineret qu. 84 (col. 2279); hac uersutia paganos detinet in errore qu. 84 (col. 2279); hi detenti sunt apud inferos qu. 83; ut iam detentus aurem quae abscisa fuerat restitueret qu. 104; detinent homines quasi compedes desideria saecularia 2 qu. N.T. 19.

deuinco, in the phrase **deuicta morte**: cognosci se uoluit...

[1] Cf. the correct text of Phil. ii 30, preserved by the Padua MS, id quod de ex uobis erat. This and the parallel form *prode esse* (=*prodesse*), which is preserved once or twice in the best MS of the *Quaestiones*, and in other authors, seem to indicate that some compounds of *esse* were not as thoroughly formed as others. Prof. Conway tells me that inscriptions frequently have DE ESSE.

[2] For which, see below: the writer uses also *minoro* (e.g. qu. 116). Compare the words *certioro*, *deminoro*, *peioro*, which he does not use.

[3] I have since found this use in ps. 37, 6 (ap. [Ambr.] *Epistula Nicetae episcopi de lapsu Susannae deuotae*, ed. Burn § 49) computruerunt et deteriorauerunt (*vulg.* corruptae sunt) cicatrices meae.

morte deuicta 51 D; deuicta morte *resurgens* 150 B; Christus ...descendens ad inferos deuicta morte 315 C; Christum suscitauit a mortuis deuicta morte 403 B; Christum...*resurrexisse* deuicta morte 468 B; quam diu deuicta morte *resurgeret* a mortuis 498 C etc.; deuicta morte *resurgens* clarificatus est dominus qu. 93 (col. 2286); ut deuicta morte liberarentur de inferno qu. 105; morte per mortem deuicta qu. 116; quando mysterium dei declarari haberet deuicta morte qu. 123 (col. 2371) etc. (Varieties are *mortis euictae* 58 A; 92 C, which ought perhaps to be altered; *uicta mors* 93 A, *uicta morte* qu. 123. Compare the indicatives *mortem uicit* 111 D, and *mors deuicta est* qu. 121.)

dicatio appears, in addition to *dedicatio* (which occurs e.g. 405 B; qu. 95; 123; 127): dicatio idolorum 258 D; per quod et dicationem suam et meritum eius probaret qu. 5 (col. 2220); ne quod dicationi eius impedimentum adferret qu. 117 (col. 2361).

dignitosus: ut ostendat et dignitosos credere 188 B (my certain emendation, agreeing with old editions); quando enim uident dignitosum uirum erroris causa corripi, necesse est ut sibi caueant 506 B; dignitoso enim homini negotiari deforme est qu. 102 ppr codd; dedecus est enim dignitosi filium esse sine honore qu. 44 am codd.

dignus is frequently used with the PLAIN INFINITIVE: ne digni iam essent addiscere spiritalia 56 D; ut digni fiant dici filii dei 90 A: other exx. of the constr. are 92 C *bis*; 107 C; 139 C; 218 C *bis*; 250 B; 271 A; 302 B; 303 C; 358 B; 369 B; 386 A; 514 A; ut dignus esset accipere qu. 79 (*b*); digni fuerunt in Tartaro remanere qu. 83; qui filii dei digni sunt appellari qu. 91 m; dignos eos fieri sacerdotes qu. 101 ex; dignus erit stare qu. 111 am; digni sunt et uidere qu. 111 pm (so 358 B); dignum esse Christum dici regem gloriae qu. 111 ex; ut...dignus sit accedere qu. 112 pm; saluatorem uidere dignus exstitit qu. 117 pr; dignus existit ab omnibus liberari peccatis qu. 126 pr; ut dignus fieret etiam in praesenti uidere cet. qu. 127 m; filium generare dignus qu. 127 aex, etc.

Another frequent construction is **dignum est** with **ut** and the subjunctive:—dignum fuit ut...illum promitteret 51 B, C; dignum est ut pereant 70 B; dignum est ut...haec non adipiscatur

247 A; dignum est ut filii caput pater dicatur 252 D; dignum fuit ut cuperet uidere Petrum 364 A; nec dignum est ut deus inmutetur in carnem 434 A etc.; dignum ergo fuit ut in alto appareret qu. 42; dignum fuit ut...praeuideret qu. 117; dignum enim erat ut ipse...esset qu. 49; sic enim fuit dignum ut... largiretur qu. 102 (col. 2306); non est enim dignum ut his detur remissio peccatorum qu. 126 (col. 2377). *Dignum est* sometimes takes the accus. and infin. construction, e.g. 62 A; 208 C; qu. 33; 102. The expression is also used absolutely, e.g. qu. 114; 2 qu. mixt. 3.

There are various phrases with *dignus*, common to both works: *deo dignus* (usually of persons) 75 B; 208 C; 502 D; qu. 5; 46; 77 (73); 112; 114; 117; (*domino dignus* qu. 117); *poena dignus* 65 B; qu. 114; 115 *ter*; *laude dignus* 91 C; qu. 97; 115; 118; 123; 126.

The word is found with the genitive and dative, as well as the ablative, cases: *mortis* 159 C; *gloriae* 305 A; *honoris* qu. 101: *creatori* qu. 5; *operi* qu. 6; *ei* qu. 97 (col. 2294) (so *indignus*: *rem sibi* indignam qu. 113 (col. 2340); see also *condignus*); with *ad* and the accusative gerundive, ut digni fierent ad excipiendum annum domini qu. 111 (col. 2334) etc.

dilucido: saepe repetit, ut dilucidet 118 C; diuersa sunt ingenia, ut disputatione planiore dilucidentur 272 B; idem sensus est, quem ut dilucidet, repetit 334 A; haec...obscura sunt, ac per hoc adhibita cura dilucidanda sunt 454 C; omnis quaestio, ut dilucidari possit, ad originem reuocanda est qu. 99 (*b*).

discordare a: discordabat *a* doctrina apostolica 58 A; *a* natura animarum et loquendi ratione non discordat 150 C; non discordat *a* bene agentibus 169 B; per id quod discordarent *a* traditione apostolica 213 C; 353 B cet.; nisi enim discordauerit *a* diabolo qu. 92; hic ergo *a* mundo discordat qu. 92; si *a* mundi lege discordant qu. 115 (col. 2352).

dissimulo: in the construction ***dissimulare ab**[1]: a lege dissimulans[2] 50 C; dissimulant a ueritate 59 B; dissimu-

[1] As this interesting construction seems to be nowhere noted (except 1 ex. fr. Aug. in Georges), I append all the examples I have seen: Tert. Scap. 4 ppr; Aug. Serm. 351, 1; 355, 2; ep. 44, 9; 88, 6; 113 *bis*. Georges' example, de ciu. Dei 1, 9, 1 is simply thrown into his article, with a translation.

[2] Occasionally we find *dissimulo* used otherwise e.g. with *de*, 199 B; C; *absol.* 419 B.

lantes ab eo (*neut.*) 60 B *var. lect.*; intellegat autem ideo a se dissimulari, quia non in hac uita iudicium Dei promissum est futurum 68 A; ab ira dissimulandum monet [explanation of "date locum irae"] 169 D; ab hac (lege) praesenti dissimulare 171 A; dissimulare ab ea (creatura) 176 B; ab intentione edendi aut non edendi dissimulare nos docet 179 A; a quo crimine mali doctores aut dissimulabant aut neglegentius arguebant 220 B; si enim ipsi discesserint, dissimulandum ab his (*masc.*) 231 D; ab scientia dissimulandum docet caritatis causa 240 C; ceteris apostolis propter scandalum ab hac re dissimulantibus 241 B; doctus dissimulare a Iudaismo 365 A; si, praesentibus Iudaeis, dissimulasset a gentilibus, timens scandalum 370 B; auaritia, a qua dissimulamus 417 A; ut...dissimulet ab eo (*masc.*) 419 B; ab his autem omnibus, quae in firmamento et sub firmamento sunt, dissimulandum 458 B; si enim rector populi ab his (*neut.*) dissimulat, neglegit gratiam datam sibi 501 C; ideo dissimulandum ab his (*masc.*) est 520 B; a quibusdam neotericis dissimulat qu. 2 pm; deus a tali sacrificio dissimulauit qu. 43 pm; si uero dissimulet ab iniuria qu. 69 ex; a potestate sua dissimulans 2 qu. N.T. 7;—a notable use derived from the above is:—auctorem legis ***hinc dissimulare** non posse qu. 115 pm.

dubius: **sine dubio** is very frequent in both works: 51 C; 78 A; 84 D; 155 B; 196 C; 200 C; 240 C; 282 A; 342 B etc.; qu. 2; 3; 6; 16; 30; 40; 46; 51; 62; 76; 81; 83; 90; 97; 100; 102; 105; 108; 109; 111; 114; 115 *bis*; 125; 127 *ter*; 2 qu. N.T. 15; 53. *Procul dubio* is rare (195 C; 491 B; qu. 3; 102): *absque dubio* is, I think, entirely absent.

Various other expressions with **dubius**: (1) *dubium non est*: dubium non est omnes Graecos reos esse mortis 82 A; quod de Iacob multi sint perfidi dubium non est 140 C etc.; non est dubium non datum esse credentibus spiritum qu. 93; dubium non est qu. 102; 112; 125 etc. (2) *nulli dubium est* (Hier. Aug.): nulli enim dubium uerba uirtuti cedere 58 A; nulli enim dubium est quia pagani obruti sunt 81 D; quod nulli dubium est 86 A; and often; nulli dubium est bona omnia a deo esse qu. 34; nulli dubium est diabolum esse hominis inimicum qu. 70; paganos elementis esse subiectos nulli dubium est qu. 82; itaque nulli dubium est prodesse ieiunia qu. 120;

nulli dubium arbitror mundum istum hominis causa esse fabricatum qu. 127 pr etc. (3) *in dubium uenit*: ipsum decreuisse *nulli* in dubium uenit 60 A, and often; ea quae latebant aut in dubium ueniebant qu. 72 (76); quod temptatur in dubium uenit qu. 99; also in 91; 101: cf. *in dubium uocari* 2 qu. N.T. 10.

dumtaxat is employed in both works in a restrictive or explanatory sense, 'at least,' 'of course,' as in Hier. This word is probably wanting in many Latin authors[1]. Examples are:—gratias ergo agere se dicit, deo suo dumtaxat, quia cet. 54 A; ut eminentia uirtutis eius appareat, per homines praedicatores dumtaxat 307 A; ut efficaciam eorum tam ueram probet quam est et praedicatio eius ad eos, in correptione dumtaxat 324 C; deum testem dat ut quae dicit facile credantur, et propter eos dumtaxat qui eum non ut uerum apostolum honorificabant 347 C; manifestato creatore et ratione ostensa quam sequi debeat creatura, in fide dei sui dumtaxat, contestatur illos cet. 412 B; apparere enim debere significat exercitii profectum, in doctrina dumtaxat et in gestis 502 A; temptatio ut nos adprehendat exoptat, sed humana dumtaxat qu. 99; non enim qualiscumque honor est antistiti dei seruire, in ecclesia dumtaxat, ut sacerdos totius honoris ecclesiastici dignus habeatur qu. 101 (col. 2302); constat autem ex quattuor elementis terra aere aqua igne, deo auctore dumtaxat qu. 108 (col. 2323); *lucem* etenim *habitat inaccessibilem*, creaturae dumtaxat qu. 125 (col. 2374).

ecclesiasticus is employed with the same or similar substantives: examples are:—officium 259 A; qu. 109; salutatio 357 A; disciplina 491 B; regula 492 A; ordinatio 531 D; potestas qu. 93; ius 524 A codd.; qu. 93 *bis*; 102 *bis*; traditio qu. 93; honor qu. 101. In qu. 127 (col. 2385) ***ecclesiasticus** must be a subst. 'an ecclesiastic': ante quam ecclesiasticus quis sit, licet ei negotiari. So also 516 A 'ecclesiasticus idcirco deo se probat,' and 509 B 'ecclesiasticus maxime qui sublimis loci est.' So Hier.

emendo used intransitively *'to amend,' 'to reform': qui emendare nequiuerant prol. 2 Cor.; componentes se qui adhuc non emendauerant 333 D; non omnes adhuc quos in prima epistula corripuit emendauerant 353 B (editors add *se*); sine

[1] There is one example only in Tacitus. See also Prof. J. S. Reid's note on Cic. Mil. § 5 (Pitt Press Series).

dubio enim prodest ei qui corripitur, ut emendet 353 B; si emendare promittunt 507 C (one MS and edd. add *se*); Iudaei autem dum emendare erubescunt non cogitant futurum iudicium qu. 44 ex; exspectat enim ut impii credant et peccatores emendent qu. 68 (editors add *se*) (see *corrigo* above). It will perhaps be argued that the above examples are errors, and that the passive should be read, or *se* added. I submit that the excellence of the manuscripts and the number of instances are strong enough evidence that the usage existed.

emorior: compare 'ut non credat resurgere resoluta *et* emortua *corpora (edd.* soluta et mortua) 282 B with 'et emortua *et* resoluta *corpora* non posse rursus reddi ad uitam' 2 qu. N.T. 47. (The phrase was doubtless in part suggested by Rom. iv. 19.)

euangelicus is used similarly in both works: examples are:—doctrina 56 A; sermo 115 D; ueritas 153 A; 185 C; disciplina 172 C; 2 qu. N.T. 55; opus 188 D; ius 223 C; qu. 95; praedicatio qu. 95; auctoritas qu. 107.

examen: in the sense of 'judicial examination': tibi examen datum est potestatis iudicandi de malis 67 B; dum enim examen coeperit fieri omnium rerum in die iudicii 151 A; gaudium uero fretum futurae spei testatur examen 166 B; infidelium potius examina requirebant 193 B; examen futurum est accipientium corpus domini 257 B etc.; ut examen circa se iudicis mitiget qu. 112. (*Examino* and *examinatio* also occur.)

excludo in a metaphorical sense especially, 'to put out of court,' is a favourite word: ut omnem tergiuersationem cauillationis excludat 88 B; ut et diaboli regnum excluderetur et dei imperium ignorantibus praedicaretur 104 C; ut...ueritas omnem fraudem excludat 221 B; ut fornicationem excludat 229 A; excluditur promissio 376 B; ne pauci temporis diuitiae excludant aeternas qu. 32; uerum excludere nituntur qu. 100; exclusa est ergo Nouatiani impie composita adsertio qu. 102 (col. 2304); exclusa est adseueratio tua qu. 102 (col. 2307); exclusum est fatum qu. 115 (col. 2349); ratio fatorum...exclusa est qu. 115 (col. 2357); exclusit omnem controuersiam et argumenta terrena qu. 122 (col. 2367); ut...excludat ueritatem qu. 127 (col. 2380); excluditur desperatio 2 qu. mixt. 11.

exemplum is used in many phrases common to both works,

but only one use, that of the ablative of manner with a genitive dependent on it, will be mentioned here. Instances are:—exemplo eius 92 B; exemplo corporis 165 A; exemplo legis 170 B; exemplo domini 181 C; exemplo (this is the correct reading: *edd.* ex ore) asinae qu. 46 (col. 2245); huius exemplo qu. 117.

exhibeo: compare 'spiritus animalium magno gemitu artatur ad exhibenda seruitia' 131 B, and 'propter timorem dei iusta et fidelia uult hominibus exhiberi seruitia' 423 A with 'ut... inciperent exhibere seruitia dominicis caerimoniis' qu. 46 (col. 2247): compare also 'neque aliquam legi reuerentiam exhiberent' qu. 115 (col. 2348).

exsuscito *met.*: exsuscitatur dolor 141 C; dilectio in his dei exsuscitatur memoria patrum 161 C; (2 Cor. iv. 14 ap. Ambrst.): tunc exsuscitatur libido...qu. 120; exsuscitatur enim desiderium animae erga opera salutaria qu. 120 codd.; exsuscitantur ad sollicitandos nos qu. 115 (col. 2351) codd.; (declaratio mysterii) maiores exsuscitauit diffidentibus poenas qu. 122 (col. 2367).

fabrica: in the expression **fabrica mundi:** fabrica mundi testificante 59 B; notitia dei manifesta est ex mundi fabrica 59 C; ipsa enim fabrica mundi praedicat creatorem 153 B; cet.; descripta mundi fabrica qu. 3 aex; ex ipsa mundi fabrica intellegi...diuinitatem suam qu. 83; ad mundi fabricam profecerunt qu. 107 pr; ad mundi fabricam proficerent qu. 122 pr; mundum fecerunt uocari, cuius in fabricam profecerunt qu. 106 (col. 2318). *Cf.* caeli f. 59 A.

fiducia: *freti fiducia fidei* 68 C and qu. 115 (col. 2347), same order.

firmo is constantly used in the meaning and with the constructions of *confirmo*[1], and is very much commoner than the latter. References are:—56 A; 58 A; 72 A (cod.); 77 A; 79 D; 82 C; 85 B; 91 C; 98 B; 110 C; 116 D; 138 C; 153 A; 165 B; 180 D; 183 C; 185 B; 189 B; 205 C; 226 A; 232 B etc. etc.; qu. 29; 54 *ter*; 59; 75; 77; 97 *ter*; 104; 105; 106; 108; 114; 123 (codd.); 2 qu. N.T. 10; 14; 37; 46; etc. etc.

fomes[2]: *metaph.* qui fomitem *praebeant delictis* illorum 66 B;

[1] Which occurs e.g. 94 A; 182 A; 186 C; 192 A etc.

[2] As this metaphor is fairly common, its occurrence in both works has

quod.. *peccandi* fomitem *praebeant* 79 C; nec illi (uirgini) ingerat fomitem nuptiarum, quam uidet nubendi uoluntatem non habere 237 B; satellitibus in hac re fomitem conspirationis *praebentibus* qu. 2 ppr; *delinquendi* illi fomitem praestat 2 qu. N.T. 49.

The extreme rarity of **forinsecus**, which is a favourite word of S. Augustine, is significant. The word occurs once only in the *Quaestiones* (qu. 108), not at all in the commentaries. *Foris* is common in both works, by itself, and in *de foris*.

The words **fragilis** and **fragilitas** are often used of the human race (so Hier.). Examples are:—homo autem fragilis est 117 B; fragile est *genus* humanum 302 A; humana fragilitas in 1 Cor. xv 45 (some MSS); fragilitatem humani *generis* qu. 102; fragile *genus* humanum qu. 102; 126; fragilitatis humanae qu. 108, cf. qu. 109.

fulcio in the passive, metaphorically: qui *dignitate* doctoris fultus erat apud Iudaeos 363 A; dei legem quam utique uidet non uerborum strepitu fulciri sed rerum uirtutibus qu. 100; legem uirtutum testimoniis fultam qu. 114 (col. 2342); quis enim *dignitate* fultum uirum et diuitem arguere audeat? qu. 124 (col. 2372).

genus (=modus): in the phrases **hoc genere**[1] =hoc modo: hoc igitur genere reos facit eos 144 C; hoc etiam genere antiqui medici cet. 59 C; hoc utique genere, id est, per sacerdotem qu. 46 am: **eodem genere**[2]: eodem genere iudicandos angelos a nobis, *quo* et mundus iudicabitur 223 A; eodem genere uisus est et a Iacob 447 A; eodem genere, *quo* Ioseph uocabatur filius esse Iesus, ita erat... qu. 56; eodem genere sacerdos est Christus in aeternum *quo* et Melchisedech qu. 109 ex; see also below. Most characteristic

probably only a cumulative force: see lexx.; Index to Peiper's *Cypriani Heptateuchos* s.v. (Vindob. 1891); Mayor's *Latin Heptateuch* 106 35; add Aug. serm. 153, 2; Acad. 2, 5 pr.; [Aug.] serm. 7, 1; 66, 2; 175, 2; Anthol. (Riese and Bücheler) II 546, 6; [Ambr.] epist. 1, 3; prec. 1, 3; paen. 14; 26; hymn. 75, 23.

[1] Morin 8. *Hoc modo* (103 B; 135 C; qu. 34; 59; 81; 89; 107; 115; 2 qu. V.T. 8) and *hac ratione* (qu. 2; 64; 91; 107; 112; 122; 2 qu. N.T. 57) are, however, also found. The latter expression occurs in Martial at least twice, though the word *ratio* finds no place in Friedländer's index.

[2] But also *eodem modo* (99 A; qu. 44; 59; 95; 97; 110; 115); *eadem ratione* (qu. 34; 56; 91).

of all is **duplici genere**[1] = duobus modis. It occurs 70 B; 72 A; 114 C; 170 B; 198 B; 220 C; 222 B; 263 A; 293 D; 315 C; 336 B; 352 C; 375 B; 381 C; 383 C; 425 A; 515 A; 527 A; qu. 14; 20; 103; 110; 112 *bis*; 115 (p. 2355); 119; 124; 2 qu. N.T. 36. I can find no example of this expression in any other author. *Triplici genere* occurs 124 B[2]; *tripartito genere* 72 D[3]. *Simili genere* is much less common than *simili modo*[4] or *similiter*[5]. It appears 91 A. *Nullo genere* occurs 309 A (haec subiecit quibus nullo genere deficere se probat quo minus...); 433 C (quod nullo genere *nulla ratione* conuenit); qu. 78 (74) (qui non solum nullo genere peccauerat sed et multis uitam donauerat); qu. 75 (79) nullo genere ex his liberi arbitrii poterit causa turbari[6]. *Omni genere* occurs 437 D; 457 B; qu. 59 ex[7]. *Uno atque eodem genere* occurs 208 D; qu. 127 pm. *Eo, quouis* and *quo* (except with *eodem*) *genere* are wanting in both works[8].

gesta (plur. neut.) is very commonly used for **deeds*, especially Divine achievements. *Actus* is also used for *deeds*, rarely, if ever, *acta*. Examples of *gesta* are :—uerbis et gestis dominicis 71 D; ne...cum dei serui dicimur, gestis serui diaboli inueniamur 108 C; ut dei gestis repugnent 125 C; nolebant enim uerba gestis comparare 149 A etc. etc.; gesta ueterum qu. 95 (col. 2289); gesta dominica qu. 102; humana autem natiuitas beatitudinem adquirit per gesta qu. 109 (col. 2326); quamuis enim quis posset gesta eius imitari qu. 118 (col. 2361); formam praebens mirabilium gestorum qu. 118 (col. 2362); gesta saluatoris qu. 127; gesta et dicta domini 2 qu. N.T. 1; 2 etc.

[1] But *duplici modo* 59 D; 278 D; 403 D; qu. 44; 45; 69; 78; 102. *Duplici ratione* does not, I think, appear, but *gemina ratione* qu. 52.

[2] *triplici ratione* qu. 110.

[3] *tripartita ratio* (nom.) 87 B.

[4] *simili modo* (often first in the sentence): 99 A; 102 C; 104 A; 127 B; 141 B; 163 A; 176 C; 199 A; 202 C; 211 C cet.; qu. 7; 20; 37; 44; 52; 91; 97; 102; 109; 115; 127; 2 qu. V.T. 8; 2 qu. N.T. 9; 49; 60; 2 qu. mixt. 6.

[5] *similiter* e.g. 102 C. It is characteristic of these works to have *similiter* as the first word in the *sentence* (e.g. 165 B; qu. 93; 102; 109; 115; 2 qu. N.T. 9).

[6] *nullo modo* 129 B; qu. 97; 102 *bis*; 109: *nulla ratione* 433 C (*supra*); *nullo pacto nulla ratione* qu. 113.

[7] *omni modo* is apparently wanting in both works; *omni ratione* 459 A.

[8] *una ratione* 85 B; qu. 115; *ea ratione* qu. 97; 122; *quauis ratione* 180 C; *qua ratione* 108 B; 163 B etc.; qu. 58; 91; 95 *bis*; 97; 107; 109; 114; 115 *ter*; 123; 125 *bis*; 127; 2 qu. N.T. 47 etc.

The combination **gloriosus apparere** (perhaps from 2 Reg. vi 22 or Prov. xxv 6) is strangely frequent; quid est ut elati iudicemur quasi pro nostra propria utilitate praedicare, ut gloriosi appareamus 306 A; ut gloriosus in his appareat magister gentium 427 D; dignum est enim ut, qui pro illo obprobria patitur et exilia, in regno eius gloriosus appareat 517 B etc.; Moyses ergo quia non peccauerat gloriosus apparuit qu. 8; nonne partem ipsam humanis uultibus ingerit ut appareat gloriosus qu. 12; nullus sanctorum in mundo gloriosus apparuit qu. 115 (col. 2354); in regno Christi gloriosi appareant qu. 126 (col. 2376) etc.

habeo (= 'must') followed by pres. inf. pass.[1] (cf. Hoppe, *Syntax u. Stil des Tertullian*, p. 44). The editors sometimes alter to *debeo* against the MSS. Examples are:—quia nebula carnis circumcidi haberet qu. 12; quia per fidem saluari haberent homines qu. 29; quia dono dei coimaginari haberet filio dei qu. 106 (col. 2320); quia oblationes et holocausta tunc accepto ferri haberent qu. 112 (col. 2339); quando mysterium dei declarari haberet qu. 123 (col. 2371). No examples appear in the printed text of the commentaries.

The writer is very fond of **hebes, hebeto,** and **hebetudo.** Examples of the second and third will suffice; occurrences of the first are numerous. We have:—(homines) *stupore* quodam *hebetasse ad honorandum deum 60 A (the intransitive use is unknown to the dictionaries): ut magis ac magis hebetati ad omnia mala admittenda fierent promptiores 64 B; nemo sic poterit hebetari qu. 53; in tantum hebetati ut ipsum dominum sub fato egisse contendant qu. 115 (p. 2358); mirabatur enim *stupore* hebetatus 2 qu. N.T. 9: quanta hebetudo quanta stultitia hos sapientes appellare 61 B; recte fides hebetudini comparatur qu. 117 (col. 2360); qua tamen hebetudine...praedicant qu. 97 (col. 2293).

honorifico, honorificentior, and **honorificentia** are characteristic expressions. *Honorifico* occurs e.g. 60 B; 100 B; 158 A; 280 A *bis*; 347 C; qu. 32; 35 *bis* (cf. Io. v 23 as quoted); *honorificentior* 69 C; 158 A; *honorificentia* 60 C; 61 B; 76 B; 96 B; 99 B;

[1] The active, which appears in Cicero, is found also: *deus...despicere* habet deuotum sibi cet. qu. 102 (p. 2312).

253 B; 259 A; qu. 8. (*Honoro* (61 C; 182 C; 188 C; qu. 35) and even *inhonoro* (62 C, codd.; 74 B; 182 D; 422 C) also appear.)

ignis, with a personal noun in apposition: ignem tortorem *patietur* 391 C; igne ultore poenas *pateretur* qu. 115 (col. 2348).

ignoro: non ignoro is very common, e.g. 60 A; B; 66 A; 67 A; 82 C; 97 C; 137 B (*nec ign.* 98 A; *neque ign.* qu. 91) etc.; qu. 14; 16; 58 *bis*; 102 *bis*; 113; 114; 115; 120; 125 *quater*; 127. (Cf. *non ignotum* 97 C; *non nescius* qu. 94, *nec nescius* qu. 115 ex; *non ignarus* qu. 109.)

***impraescius**[1]: permisit se diabolo saeuienti sed impraescio 83 D; inimicus (i.e. diabolus) impraescius futurorum contra se 416 D; (homo) qui per id quod impraescius est uarius et mutabilis est qu. 46 ppr; ne ergo uelut impraescius (dominus) haec pati uideretur qu. 104 am.

impulsus: in the *abl. sing.* **impulsu**: *non uoluntate*, sed impulsu eius uidebuntur peccare 79 A; omnem dixit concupiscentiam operatam in homine impulsu diaboli 114 B; cuius (peccati) impulsu 118 A; loquitur non impulsu aeris...sed sicut competit eius diuinitati 133 C; contra hanc regulam fidei impulsu malorum doctorum sentientes 224 C; si impulsu *carnis* perseuerare se uiderint non posse 229 C; *non uoluntate* haec facit, *sed* impulsu naturae qu. 2 aex; ea quae impulsu *carnis* suggeruntur qu. 115 am cet.

in, with accusative, of purpose, this accusative representing *a person[2]. This usage is scriptural e.g. 1 Reg. iii 20 ap. qu. 46 *fidelis est Samuhel* in *prophetam* (so MSS: Migne *propheta* without *in*) *domino* (εἰς προφήτην τῷ Κυρίῳ LXX (B); *propheta esset domini* Vulg. cf. LXX (A)), and Ps. xcviii 6 ap. qu. 46 *fiant Moyses et Aaron* in *sacerdotes eius* (ἐν τοῖς ἱερεῦσιν αὐτοῦ LXX; *in sacerdotibus eius* Vulg.). The following examples occur:—a deo adoptamur in filios 92 B; deo in filios adoptari 159 C; ex perditis iterum reformauit sibi illos in seruos 177 A; ut *suscipiat* nos in *filios* 319 C; Agar ancillam suam obtulit uiro suo Abrahae in concubinam 383 C; ut...adoptarentur in filios deo 395 B; in filios hos adoptare 467 A; credentes sibi adoptare in filios 473 B; adoptatos...a deo in filios 474 B; in filios sibi adoptauit 491 A; istos in *filios suscepit* qu. 44

[1] *impraescientia* occurs 416 D.

[2] Cf. of things *haec luminaria* in *signa temporum* qu. 84; *in turres* qu. 105.

(col. 2242); eis qui in reges unguebantur qu. 49; Dauid iam unctus in regem qu. 61; hunc esse Christum qui patribus apparuisset in deum qu. 71; semper in deum uisus a patribus est qu. 71; principum Iudaeorum quos propheta significauit in turres qu. 105 (p. 2315) codd.; natus de deo patre in regem non inmerito Christus appellatur qu. 114 (col. 2346); apud maiores enim nostros qui in reges unguebantur qu. 114 (col. 2346).

inaestimabilis[1]: used of God and his attributes: *inmensum* et inaestimabilem cognoscere deum, omnia excedentem maiestate uirtutis suae 406 B; igitur deus est...lux inaccessibilis, inuisibilis, inaestimabilis, *infinitus*... qu. 1 pr; qui potentiam dei inaestimabilem praedicas qu. 97 m.

inanio, in a metaphorical sense: ut gloriam diaboli...inaniret 103 D (codd.); non utique legem inaniri dicit per fidem sed impleri 85 B (codd.); ne gratiae beneficium inanire uideamur 113 B; hic inanit (*Migne* exinanit) fatum qu. 115 (col. 2356); ut omnia quae fati putantur esse inanirent (*Migne* exinanirent) qu. 115 (col. 2357); inanitus *infernus* qu. 121; mors per peccatum inaniuit *infernum* 315 C, etc. Much commoner in these works are *exinanio, euacuo*, in the same sense.

incarno: gerundive **incarnandus:** deus deduxit illum (Iesum) in caelum cum corpore unde *uenerat* incarnandus 151 A; cur dominus noster de sacris et caelestibus sedibus ad terram incarnandus *uenisset* qu. 113 (p. 2340).

inclino transitively and metaphorically, *'to humble,' often with the reflexive **se**, and sometimes with the dat., of that before which one humbles oneself: ne uentris causa inclinaretur 317 A; uim auctoritatis inclinant 326 A; etiam a licitis temperaret ne inclinaretur 333 C; hic...inclinat se et comparat se inferioribus 335 C; inclinat se ut manifestet etc. 350 C; auctoritatem potestatis...non inclinat 353 B; humilitas enim etiam superbos solet inclinare 390 B; si nos erigeremus inclinaremur 390 C; ut...inclinemus nos 432 A; ante quam se inclinari permitteret 432 B; caro factus hominibus se inclinauit 433 A; his inclinari quorum gubernaculis humanum regitur genus 457 D; qui enim uult audiri inclinare se debet 494 A etc.; quo soluto non solum scandalo non

[1] The epithet is doubtless derived from the famous verse, Baruch iii 36 *hic deus noster: non aestimabitur alter ad eum* (quoted in qu. 97, p. 2292, 50).

esset exactoribus neque inclinaretur requisito auxilio ad soluendum qu. 79 (75) (col. 2270); cuius auctoritati inclinandum hunc putant qu. 97 (col. 2292); nihil de se praesumentes diuinae se uoluntati inclinant qu. 100; uanitas cui qui se inclinat cet. qu. 111 (col. 2333); magnificum si hic qui dignitate et copiis commendatur inclinet se qu. 124 (col. 2372) etc. The opposite is *erigo*.

inconcessus, especially in the phrase **inconcessa praesumere:** ne ab licitis se abstinentes inconcessa praesumerent, sicut faciunt Manichei 228 B; corrumpit autem corpus qui inconcessa praesumit 391 B; dum aut inconcessa praesumuntur aut concessa inordinate fiunt qu. 1 (col. 2215); qui enim inconcessa praesumit reus est qu. 110 (col. 2331); in qu. 46 and 127 without *praesumo*. (Cf. *inlicita* praesumerent qu. 46 (col. 2247).)

incongruus in the phrase **incongruum est*: imago enim dei incongruum est ut celetur 253 B; incongruum est ut pater subiciatur filio 280 A; non esse incongruum inquiunt his inclinari 457 D; incongruum erat ut facta uiro subiecta diceretur esse imago dei 460 C etc.; non incongruum uidebis quod putas diuersum esse a ratione qu. 12; incongruum enim erat ut dei filius in corpore peccatis subdito nasceretur qu. 49; incongruum deprehendimus tenebras ante lucem creatas adserere qu. 107 (p. 2322); incongruum enim uidetur personae eius hoc opus subisse qu. 113 (cf. Veget.); incongruum est enim ut...apud inferos teneatur qu. 123 (col. 2371) etc. (The adverb *incongrue* qu. 97.)

incresco occurs e.g. increscere cupientes mala 66 B; ne peccata increscerent 102 D; dies super noctem increscere qu. 55; ut ex eo nox increscat super diem qu. 106 (col. 2317); coepit dies increscere super noctem qu. 106 (col. 2317); increscit illi calor qu. 115 (col. 2351).

incurro: (1) *c. acc. obi.* ne diu hic positi damnum incurrant (faciant *cod.*) promissae uitae 68 C; ne...poenam, quam euasimus, incurramus 104 D; ultionem legis incurreret 115 C; omnis enim cogitatio foras respiciens incurrit delictum 128 A; ne...ea omnia quae euasimus...incurramus 128 D; ne incurrat sententiam euangelicam dicentem... 151 A; homo qui possit culpam incurrere nescius 214 A; ne et damnum ad praesens et offensionem forte incurrat 223 D; ne...illi incurrant *quod* nos *timemus* 235 A; egredientibus fluminibus incurrebat periculum 345 C; ne... incurrant uindictam 473 D; per quam rem elatus incurrit laqueum diaboli 495 C; diuisio incurrit peccatum qu. 5 am; ne incurrerent peccata patrum qu. 14 m; maledictum nos incursuros qu. 127 ppr; non natiuitas crimen incurrit qu. 127 m; incurris *quod times* qu. 91 pr; nimia iustitia incurrit *peccatum* qu. 15; non incurrit peccatum qu. 110 (*Journ. Theol. Stud.* Oct. 1904) cet.—*(2) *absol.* solent uiduarum iuniores incurrere ("to be guilty") 238 A.—*(3) *c.* ut *et subi.* ex quacumque causa incurrebant ut inmundi essent 148 A; incurrit ut patiatur quod sibi fieri non uult qu. 69 (*a*) humana conuersatio...incurrit ut peccet qu. 110 (*J. T. S.* l. c.); omnis inquietus...frequenter incurrit ut membra corporis laedat qu. 112 aex.

indisciplinatus: cuius exemplo indisciplinata coercenda iuuentus est 501 B; non solum male sentientibus amarum est, uerum etiam indisciplinatis qu. 76 (72); omnis inquietus uel indisciplinatus frequenter incurrit cet. qu. 112 (col. 2339); qui de turpibus honestos facit, de indisciplinatis modestos qu. 114 (col. 2342). (Cf. *indisciplinatio* qu. 97 (col. 2294).)

inexcusabilis occurs e.g., ut inexcusabiles deperirent 145 C; qui enim audientes legem peccant inexcusabiles sunt 171 C; ut his infidelitas accusata inexcusabilis pereat 498 A; qui ad hoc surgit ut peccet, inexcusabilis effectus pergrauem habet causam qu. 126.

ingenitus, 'unborn,' of God the Father, as contrasted with Jesus, the Son: pater ingenitus est, filius uero genitus 472 D; pater ingenitus est, filius uero genitus (the identical words) qu. 97 (col. 2292); in carne uisus neque patrem neque matrem habuit, hoc est ingenitus apparuit qu. 109 (p. 2329).

ingero: *met.* (Hier.) nec illi (uirgini) ingerat fomitem nuptiarum, quam uidet nubendi uoluntatem non habere 237 B; ut passim et importune uerba religionis ingererent tempore inimico 167 B; diaboli qui per subiectam sibi carnem suggestiones malas ingerit animae 121 A; nonne partem ipsam humanis uultibus ingerit, ut appareat gloriosus? qu. 12; di paganorum... non se ingerunt ad contraria suggerenda qu. 115 (col. 2351): aliquando occupatae menti non se ingerunt qu. 115 (col. 2358).

inmerito: non (nec) inmerito is a favourite litotes, e.g.: 47 A; 93 D; 149 A; 266 B; 315 B; 407 D; 418 B; 451 D; 459 B; 474 B; 509 C; 513 A; 524 B; qu. 56; 85; 98; 102; 105; 106; 110 (new part); 111; 112; 114; 116; 123; 125.

inmunis a, with the ablative of something objectionable, such as punishment (Hier.): *poena* occurs 67 B; 82 C (codd.); 416 C; qu. 67; 111 (col. 2333); qu. 115 pr; 2 qu. V.T. 17: *passionibus* 69 B; *morte* 97 B; *crimine* 119 A; 219 A; 247 B; *criminibus* 224 B; *malitia* 95 B (codd.); *seueritate sententiae* qu. 14; *eis quae dei legi aduersa sunt* qu. 110 (col. 2331); *fornicatione idolatriae* qu. 111 (col. 2333); *uulnere* qu. 118 (cf. Prov. xx 9 ap. qu. 112, *peccatis*) etc. The word is absolutely used e.g. 219 A; 251 A; qu. 115 (col. 2351).

inpossibilis, especially in the expression **inpossibile est:** credidit enim quod mundo i. *uidetur* 91 B; quod mundo inpossibile est 92 A; inpossibile est non peccare 99 B; quod enim i. iudicabat possibile declaratum est 199 B; quod humanae rationi i. *uidebatur* 205 C; quod omnino creaturae inpossibile est 206 A etc.; quod i. *uidetur* qu. 6; quamuis...fallere eum inpossibile sit qu. 10; inprobabile et inpossibile est qu. 28; serpentem subtilitatem istam composuisse inpossibile est qu. 31; inpossibile est enim discordare unius spiritus uiros qu. 66; quem falli utique inpossibile est qu. 71; inpossibile prorsus est ut... qu. 73 (77); quidquid hominibus i. *uidetur* qu. 97 (col. 2294); also qu. 102 (col. 2306) inpossibile est enim homini ut non peccet (cf. 99 B above); inpossibile est non peccare qu. 110 (*Journ. Theol. Stud.*, Oct. 1904); 112; 115 (col. 2353); 117 (col. 2361); 2 qu. N.T. 10; 46; 60 etc.

inprobabilis: peregrini hominis i. origo in terra aliena est 94 B; hic enim qui laudatur inprobabile est an dignus sit 214 D etc.; i. et inpossibile est qu. 28; quod i. est qu. 56; ut adseueratio nostra non inprobabilis uideatur qu. 112 (col. 2339) etc.

instruo is used once or twice passively, implying *a construction in the active with two accusatives, such as *doceo* has in classical Latin: 'ab his tamen uiam domini diligentius instructus est' 188 A; compare that with:—'Aegyptiorum, a quibus etiam Moyses fuerat instructus omnem peritiam Aegyptiacam' qu. 3 pr.

interuenio in the abl. absol. constr.: for example:—quid est enim paenitere nisi iam ab errore cessare, interueniente mentis dolore? *prol.* 2 Cor. (*Journ. Theol. Stud.*, Oct. 1902, p. 90); nunc, interueniente causa neglegentiae uel erroris, dissidere inter se uidentur apostoli 369 C; nulla interueniente lamentatione paenitentiae qu. 102 (col. 2306); interueniente gemitu et fletu qu. 102 (col. 2306); cf. *interuentu* paenitentiae qu. 102 (col. 2308); *interuentu* misericordiae qu. 105 (col. 2315).

intimo (verb): legem...spiritus, non litteris utique scriptam, sed per fidem animis intimatam 304 B; non illis hoc intimarunt 352 C; ordinem ipsum...exponit...sancto spiritu intimante 475 A; etc.; caelestibus huius modi intimatur doctrina qu. 47 (col. 2248); qui sensum istum prior intimauerat dicens qu. 57; Marcus autem rem quae ab illis praetermissa fuerat uoluit intimare qu. 65; noua per Christum praecepta populis intimata qu. 127 (col. 2379) etc.

inuenio is frequently found (with a personal subject) in the passive, almost with the force of *sum*, and generally with an adjective or participle in the predicate: a few examples out of the great number are:—cum diffidunt, peiores inueniuntur 70 C; ne ...cum dei serui dicimur, gestis serui diaboli inueniamur 108 C; inuentus est in eo reus in quo accusabat 111 D; semper diffidentes inuenti sunt Iudaei 153 C; hominibus adsentientes inuenti sunt 157 A; si in altera (re) inaequalis fuerit inuentus qu. 108 (col. 2324); Tobias in temptatione robustus et fortis inuentus est qu. 119.

irritus: in irritum with various *verbs:* dei gratiam in irritum *deducentes*[1] 79 D; accusatio illorum in irritum iam *deducta* est 207 D; affectum et gratiam *dei* patris in irritum habuerunt 138 A; qui *beneficium* eius in irritum *ducunt* 256 D; iudicium enim saluatoris in irritum *ducunt* 377 B; promissio... in irritum uenit 89 B; *beneficium* et misericordiam *dei* in irritum *deducentes* qu. 44 pm.

ianua in *ianuae tartari:* obligatus peccatis exire ianuas tartari non potest 446 B; tartari ianuae confractae qu. 121.

iuxta: *prep. c. acc.* = "in accordance with," or "in respect of" is frequent (Hier.): e.g. verbis quae infirma iuxta uirtutem sunt 203 C; libere enim et i. ueram fidem sine aliqua adulatione

[1] *Cf. in* dubium *deducitur* 311 D.

Christum praedicantes 216 D; *i. historiam* (so in Jerome), intrauerunt in Macedoniam 321 B; tertius psalmus *i. historiam* post quinquagensimum est qu. 102 (p. 2304); propositum suum, quo prius i. carnem uigebat 362 C; i. physicam rationem mundum factum a deo 245 A cet.; qui sine dubio i. ea quae supra dicta sunt septem uindictas exsoluit qu. 6 cet.: also *iuxta quod* introducing a clause (Hier.): ad dei filium pertinet iuxta quod deus est 50 B; iuxta quod deus est, a patre hunc non separari sed unum esse cum patre 377 D; qui iuxta quod scriptum est sciebat... qu. 18; iuxta quod Hieremias prophetauit qu. 44 (col. 2243); (cf. iuxta illud quod Petrus apostolus dicit (Hier.) qu. 66); a Christo iuxta quod deus est et a patre deo esse qu. 91 (col. 2284) and often. Cf. *secundum quod* supra ostendimus qu. 106 (col. 2316); *secundum quod* statuerat Moyses qu. 46 (col. 2247). Hier. has *secundum illud quod.*

latet, impersonal or semi-impersonal, with the accusative of a person is very frequent in some late authors, for example, Augustine, and is common in both works:—quem nihil utique latet 61 A; quem utique nihil latet 214 D; latebat quis esset 74 A; ut quid unus quisque dignus esset non lateret 99 C; quos nihil latet 137 D; quod latuit genus hominum 192 B; (res) quae ...caelestes potentias lateret 205 C etc. etc.; nec non et ipsum puerum latet usque ad horam necis qu. 109 (col. 2326). Cf. quid proficiant, quamuis non lateat, taceri tamen non debet qu. 120; quod non latet qu. 114.

liquidus: the adverbial phrase **ad liquidum:** si ad liquidum quaeras, nullus hominum dignus potest uideri uicarius esse Christi 514 A; ad liquidum non colligimus qu. 44 ex. (*Liquido* (Hier.) occurs e.g. qu. 14; 102.)

magia (*subst. fem.*): magi uel uenefici Aegyptiorum qui arte magiae suae uirtuti dei...resistere se putabant 521 C; non nulli gesta dominica magias appellant qu. 102 (p. 2307, 14).

magis is occasionally found with adjectives and adverbs already in the comparative (cited from Plaut., Iust., and Apul. only in lexica, but see more authorities in *Journ. Philol.* XXII (1894) 194; *Arch. f. lat. Lex.* XIII (1902) 148): magis melius 429 D (codd.); magis dignior 495 B; magis subtiliora qu. 1; magis potentioribus qu. 102; magis propensior (but see *propensior*) qu. 122; magis amplius qu. 14; magis honorificentiores qu. 32; magis honorabilior 92 A.

magister gentium is often applied to S. Paul (never *doctor gentium*): instances are on 57 C; 184 B; 335 A, B; 385 C; 407 C; 427 D, and in qu. 112; 113, and often.

magnalia is used occasionally for 'miracles,' e.g. 52 B; 157 A; 467 C; qu. 102 (p. 2307); 2 qu. N.T. 57. *Mirabilia* is found (e.g. qu. 114 (p. 2346); 127 (p. 2380)). But far the commonest terms are *uirtutes*, *signa*, *prodigia*, which correspond respectively to *δυνάμεις*, *σημεῖα*, *τέρατα*, and are commonly found in groups of two. *Miracula* is, I think, entirely absent.

maior and other comparatives are sometimes employed with *a genitive after them, where in classical Latin the superlative would be employed: (in the text of 1 Cor. xiii 13 *maior* autem horum est caritas: cf. the text of Apoc. ii 19 (qu. 102 col. 2309, 16) opera tua nouissima meliora priorum); omnium sublimior 422 C; omnium maior 461 C; qu. 26 (where Migne *omnibus*); fortior omnium qu. 92 (codd.; *Migne* fortissimus); Melchisedech non ideo melior Abrahae dicitur qu. 109 (col. 2325); meliores Moysi non sunt qu. 111 (col. 2334).

***malignum** as a noun: facientem maligna et consentientem facientibus morte dignos ostendit 66 C; ut malignum eorum nullum interuallum haberet qu. 85; ut cum maligna praedicat bona putentur qu. 110 (col. 2331). (Cf. *maligni* 156 A, *malignantes* 185 B; 190 A (from Ps. xxv 5), and especially qu. 85, which throughout rings the changes on *malignus* and its derivatives.)

mancipo: *c. acc. et dat.*: malis mancipati bonos, si posset fieri, deuorare uolebant 80 B; dei dominio mancipati 92 A; priusquam se manciparet morti 117 C; quia enim mancipauit se per assensum peccato 119 A; ne...turpiter abiectus tenebris mancipetur 175 A; ut sub nomine Christi aliis dogmatibus populum manciparent 185 A; manciparunt se legi factorum 360 B; per eum mancipabitur gehennae 412 D; uoluptates mundanae, quae omnibus illecebris mancipatae sunt 519 D; cui (corpori peccatorum) mancipati, facti sunt potestatis eiusdem 65 C; ut non sit quod nos...mancipet mundo 2 qu. N.T. 19.

manifestatio, manifeste, manifesto (verb[1]), **manifestus** are

[1] *manifesto* (adv.) does not appear, being entirely displaced by *manifeste*.

favourite words, especially the expression **manifestum est**: *manifestum est*[1] with the *accusative* and *infinitive* or **quia* and the *indicative:* manifestum est quia occurs 355 A; 372 A; 374 A; 396 D; 403 D; 405 A; 437 D; 471 C; 495 B; 522 C; 533 A cet.: manifestum est quia...erat qu. 106 am; manifestum est quia ...facit qu. 110 m; manifestum est quia...distat qu. 112 m; 2 qu. N.T. 7 cet. The acc. and inf. construction is less common: e.g. 2 qu. V.T. 12, 2 qu. N.T. 57.

medella[2] is a characteristic word for 'cure': 79 B (cod.); 90 A; 108 B; 143 B; 259 D; 396 B; 493 A; qu. 49; 112 (col. 2336); 120. *Remedium, medicina* and *medicamentum* are also found: the first e.g. twice in qu. 102, the second in qu. 112, the last in qu. 83.

melioro[3]: *exercitio* enim *bonum naturae suae* iustus meliorabit 95 B; ad fidem hanc melioratae resurrectionis 282 C; meliorata tantum *substantia* 282 C; quidam ex Cretensibus melioratus per disciplinam dominicam 527 B; si quid amplius ad culturam melioratae conuersationis excogitauerint 440 B; si *bonum naturae suae exercitio* melioret, honore sit dignus...non dedit operam ut melioraret se bonis qu. 1 m; Abraham fidei suae signum accipiens, non deformatus est, sed melioratus qu. 12; meliorati temporis qu. 60; non solum est instauratus sed et melioratus qu. 123 *et iterum*; a fidelibus enim et bene agentibus melioratur natiuitas: ab infidelibus autem et male agentibus *deterioratur* qu. 127 m; meliorata *substantia* qu. 116; quo (corpore) reparato et meliorato per fidem qu. 127 m; per culturam melioranda erant semina qu. 127 pr; omnia...multiplicata et meliorata super terram qu. 127 pr; meliorari se credit dum sacramentum creatoris addiscit qu. 127 am; melioratur natiuitas ut plus mereatur...qu. 127 am; **intr.* uidentes domini meliorasse seruos et in reddendis obsequiis fideliter profecisse 422 D.

mereor with an infin. (Hier.) is a characteristic phrase: 304 A, B; 310 D; 346 C: 416 B; 460 B; 470 D; 480 B and often: qu. 8; 26; 115; 121 etc. etc. (in qu. 115 (col. 2349) *consumi mererentur* appears in our texts as *consumerentur*, a double case of haplography).

[1] *Cf.* apertus, *s.v.*

[2] Such is the correct spelling given by the first hand of MSS nearly always, but often altered later. It conforms to Lachmann's rule (see Munro on Lucr. I 39).

[3] *Cf.* its opposite *deterioro* supra, with note.

meritum as a subst., especially in the instrumental ablative singular, occurs an enormous number of times: e.g. 67 B; 69 A; 70 A; 73 A, B *bis*; 75 A *bis*; 76 A, B, C; 79 D; 85 B; 86 B, C; 89 A; 91 C; 92 D; 93 C; 95 A; 104 C; 129 B; 132 B, D; 138 B; 140 A; 141 D; 143 D; 144 A; 151 B; 161 C; 162 A, C; 232 A; 306 B etc. etc.: qu. 11 *ter*; 22; 26 (five times); 27; 35; 37; 43 *bis*; 44 *ter*; 81; 83; 85 *quater*; 102 *bis*; 105; 108 *ter*; 109 *ter*; 111 *bis*; 113; 117 (five times); 118; 119 *quater*; 122 *bis*; 123; 126; 127 *ter*; 2 qu. V.T. 18 *ter*; 2 qu. N.T. 4; 46; 2 qu. mixt. 6 *bis*, etc.

mirus, in the expression **quid mirum?** ('what wonder?'): et quid mirum cum hodieque tales mulieres reperiantur? 63 C; et quid mirum si serui moriantur pro bono domino 136 B; sed quid mirum si in hoc loco Christum deum...loqueretur 138 C; quid ergo mirum si post resurrectionem corpus...inmortale futurum credatur 349 A cet.; quid mirum ergo si imminentem prope mortem potuit praeuidere qu. 27; nam quid mirum si diabolus sapientior erat bestiis qu. 31; sed quid mirum cum inter cetera dicat qu. 91 (col. 2284); et quid mirum cum, quem...viderit,... dicat qu. 97 (col. 2295); et quid mirum? qu. 97 (col. 2296); et quid mirum si auctor mundi fecit quod non potest mundus qu. 115 (col. 2352) etc. (cf. nec mirum si qu. 44; 64).

multifarie intellegere: in carne esse multifarie intellegitur 112 B; hoc multifarie intellegendum est 166 A; inquinamentum carnis (2 Cor. vii 1) multifarie intellegendum est 320 A; consilium impiorum (ps i 1) est conspiratio malignorum multifarie intellegenda qu. 110 (the new part, first printed in *Journ. Theol. Stud.* Oct. 1904).

mundi or **mundana ratio** is frequent; the former occurs e.g. 91 C; 92 A; 125 A; 199 A; 212 B; qu. 43; 97; 115 *ter*; the latter, e.g. 94 A; 200 A, C; in the plural, 125 A etc.

mustela: it is remarkable that the author should single out this particular animal in referring to the prohibitions of the Mosaic law (cf. Leu. xi 29): cessat enim factorum lex, id est obseruatio sabbatorum neumeniarum circumcisionis, escarum discretio, animalis mortui aut sanguinis mustelae obseruatio 89 C, D; haec Iudaeis data sunt propter duritiam cordis illorum: ut si mustelam forte quis mortuam calcasset, aut tetigisset aliqua morticina, aut si sorex in uas ruisset, inmundum diceretur 148 A; si autem sanguis mustelae pauimentum maculasset 148 B; de escis aut coniugiis aut neomeniis aut sanguine mustelae uel domo inmunda 527 C; sanguinem mustelae magna cura expiandum 531 B; onera legis quae ad duritiam cordis Iudaici fuerant data in escis neumeniis mustelis (*Migne* sabbatis et caeteris) qu. 69.

mysterium: in the combination **mysterium Trinitatis**[1]: dei cognitionem in mysterio Trinitatis 76 A; ostendit mysterium Trinitatis 52 A; ueritas est mysterium Trinitatis 202 A; Trinitatis mysterium a nullo sic potuit explanari 206 A; ut Trinitatis mysterium in unius dei natura et potestate claudatur 259 C; cf. the evidence of C. Marold, *Der Ambrosiaster nach Inhalt und Ursprung* (*Zeitschr. f. wissenschaftl. Theol.* t. XXVII, 1884, pp. 415—470), p. 465, "sehr häufig gebraucht der Ambrosiaster den Ausdruck *mysterium Trinitatis*"; intra unius dei fidem sensum nostrum concludentes mysterio Trinitatis qu. 97 ex; colere unum deum in mysterio Trinitatis qu. 114 ex (a definition of Christianity); unus deus sciatur in mysterio Trinitatis 2 qu. N.T. 26.

nebula like caligo[2], is common in a metaphorical sense: erroris nebula[3] is five times in Comm. 60 B; 76 A; 182 C; 357 C; 437 D; quia nebula carnis circumcidi haberet a cordibus hominum per fidem Christi qu. 12.

nociuus (1 Tim. vi 9): omnia enim sola insuauia sunt et nociua; quia nec panis solus bene editur, nec reliqui cibi sine admixtione grati sunt, sed nociui 238 C; utilia solet iudicare quae nociua sunt qu. 127 am (*inutilis*, like ἀνωφελής, carries with it sometimes the idea of *hurtful, injurious*).

nomen, in the phrase **sub nomine**[4] with genitive (Plin. ep. Tac. Iust.), is very frequent: the genitive is usually *Christi*; *s. n.*

[1] Cf. Morin p. 103, whose list is not quite complete. I should perhaps not have cited the expression, which is in Tert. and Cypr., had others not done so: *mysterium* is frequent in combination with almost everything divine, *dei, natiuitatis, fidei, diuinitatis, saluatoris, ecclesiae*, cet.; the word is almost banished from Cyprian, see Watson's model study (*Stud. Bibl.* IV p. 195).

[2] See above, p. 85.

[3] Perhaps from Iuu. *Sat.* 10, 4; see *Classical Review* for October, 1900: *erroris tenebrae* occurs in this author, and in Aug. ep. 93, 3; see also *Archiv für latein. Lexikogr.* XI (1898) 245.

[4] But *eius nomine* simply (qu. 114, p. 2343).

Christi 55 A, C; 185 A, B; 193 A; 210 C; 338 C cet.; 2 qu. mixt. 10 cet.; *s. n. saluatoris* 56 D; 2 qu. N.T. 57; *s. n. Hierusalem* 81 B; *s. filii sui n.* qu. 44; *s. n. eius* qu. 99; *s. eorum n.* qu. 107; *s. eius n.* qu. 107; *s. dei n.* qu. 110 *bis*; 127; *s. uno misericordiae n.* 166 A; *s. uno fallacis n. idolatriae* qu. 114; *s. n. fatorum* qu. 115; *s. unius dei n.* 2 qu. N.T. 29 (cf. with adjectives:—*s. uno n.* qu. 102 *bis*; *s. tuo n.* qu. 102; *s. eodem n.* qu. 108, and the analogous expressions **sub uocabulo animae* 127 A; *sub uno uocabulo* 166 A; *sub uocabulo noctis* qu. 107 (col. 2321): *sub eorum specie* 196 C; *sub specie idolorum* 99 B: *sub hac significatione* 73 B: *sub bona professione* 505 B.

notabilis 'notorious,' 'disgraceful'; with it the adverb **notabiliter**: dignitoso enim homini negotiari deforme est et popinam ingredi notabile est qu. 102 (col. 2305); multum expedit nubere quam sub bona et pia professione notabiliter incedere 505 B (this sense of the adjective is quoted only from Rufinus, and this sense of the adverb is unrecorded).*

notitia, nearly always **notitia dei,** of the knowledge of God (objectively); *cognitio dei* is also used: 47 A; 59 B; 98 B *bis*; 149 A; 173 C; 299 C etc.; qu. 3; 4; 5; 83 *bis*; 114 *bis*; 119; 125; 127; 2 qu. mixt. 3 etc. All these are examples of *notitia.*

nouellus is used of persons in a way which is unrecorded: ipsi etiam nobiles, per quos superstitionis suae originem antiquitati adsignant nos nouellos dicentes 201 A; quamuis futura credant fideles, tamen inter ipsa primordia pressurae nouellis faciunt scandalum 292 C; 'uitulos' ergo dicens, populum nouellum significauit qu. 112 ex.

noxia, which scribes were apt to confuse with *noxa*: Iudaeos pro noxiis (*codd.*) suis traditos sibi non aduertebant 74 C; in Aegypto pro noxiis (*codd.*) patrum plexi sunt filii qu. 13. The author's knowledge of law would prevent him from using *noxa,* which is technically *the crime of a slave.*

nudus, in the words **nudis uerbis**: e.g. destruitur ergo dum sine *testimonio* nudis uerbis *adseritur* 201 C; hi non uerbis nudis sed *uirtute* operum spiritalium dignos se ostenderent ab apostolo uisitari 218 C; qui contra disciplinam hanc sentiunt errare noscuntur, quia nudis uerbis *adsertionem* suam adlegare nituntur qu. 3 (col. 2218); ut hoc subiecto non nudis uerbis sed cum *testimonio* regem gloriae Christum addisceret qu. 111

(col. 2335); quod si nudis uerbis diceret, non erat ei credendum qu. 114 (col. 2342); nullis *uirtutum* signis adtracti sed nudis uerbis quae sacra uocant percepimus qu. 114 (col. 2344); cum nudis uerbis credidimus aut cum rebus qu. 114 (col. 2344).

nullius egere is used of God (perhaps suggested by Act. xvii 25): quod quidem obsequium non illi utique proficit qui nullius eget 127 D; solum deum esse qui nouerit omnia consilia et hunc unum esse qui nullius egeat 163 A; ille cum sit dominus et nullius egeat obtulit se pro nobis 400 D etc.; deus est... inaestimabilis infinitus perfectus nullius egens aeternus qu. 1 (col. 2215); deus certe perfectio est et nullius egens qu. 48; haec enim uera laus est si sic illi proficiat quaesita dignitas ut nullius egeat qu. 81; Christus enim nullius egens pacem offert inualidis et inermibus qu. 92; si sic perfectus factus esset ut nullius egeret, non fuerat homo sed deus qu. 123.

nunc usque = the classical *usque adhuc*, quoted by the lexica from Ammian only, but found in other authors[1] also: traduntur nunc usque ut contumeliis adficiant corpora sua 62 B; originis enim illius nunc usque sunt homines qui dicuntur corpora sua dehonestare inuicem 62 B; ex quibus rami aridi exstant nunc usque 194 A; cuius filius nunc usque iniurias patitur pro nobis 449 C (N.B. *usque modo* of 1 Cor. iv 13 is explained by *usque nunc*) etc.; post deum enim patrem diabolus deus dici uoluit, quod et nunc usque contendit qu. 113 (col. 2340); cum gestarum nunc usque appareat umbra...uirtutum qu. 114 (col. 2345).

nutus, in the ablative, **nutu dei,** 'by the will of God[2]': eius (dei) nutu ac prouidentia 67 C; nutu eius (dei) 79 A; qu. 115; cuius (Christi) nutu 190 A; ipsius nutu dei 229 B; dei nutu 282 B; 331 B; 332 B, C; 336 C *bis*; 447 D; 467 B; 513 C; qu. 122

[1] I have noted it in [Aug.] serm. 164, 2; Ioh. v 17 ap. Aug. gen. Man. I 33; Aug. spec. praef.; retr. I 13, 7 *bis*; gen. ad litt. 5, 23 *bis*; qu. hept. 7, 49: *usque nunc* is in Hier. (Lewis-Short): *usque modo*, in the same sense, I have found in Gen. xxxii 4 ap. Aug. loc. hept. I 119; Ioh. v 17 Vulg.; 1 Cor. iv 13 ap. Ambrst.; [Aug.] serm. 1, 9.

[2] The editors in one passage (qu. 55) have taken the trouble to alter *nutu* to *uoluntate*. The word has been left unharmed in other places. These old editors evidently skimmed over the pages of the works they were 'editing,' and capriciously made alterations here and there, which were based upon very slender knowledge of the language.

(col. 2367); qu. 127 *bis*; nutu patris qu. 55; diuino nutu qu. 56; 63; etc. (cf. alterius nutu qu. 75 (79)).

obligo, metaphorically: cum obligati essent terrenis et carneis (*Migne* carnis) nexibus 236 C; totos se dei rebus obligantes 332 C; quid est ut libertatem suam obligauerint uinculis legis 363 A; obligatus peccatis exire ianuas tartari non potest 446 B etc. (cf. 2 Tim. ii 4 nemo enim militans deo obligat se negotiis saecularibus); ita ut huic malo etiam filios suos obligarent qu. 98 (col. 2299); non nulla autem sunt quae sola corpora obligant infirmitatibus qu. 115 (col. 2351); non illis mundus praestat per quae obligati teneantur humanis rebus obnoxii qu. 115 (col. 2354); nos obligatos impedimentis carnalibus 2 qu. N.T. 19 etc.

oblittero: non potest enim in aliquo omne bonum penitus oblitterari 142 B; hos tamen omnes in baptismate oblitterari 87 C; cum consuetudo peccandi hoc oblitterasset 115 B; ut oblitteratis peccatis utilis reuerteretur 534 A; quia...mala, quae oblitteranda erant, exemplauerunt qu. 14 pm; non ergo iustitia in uindicta oblitterata est qu. 69 (*a*) ex; lamentatione et gemitu impetrat oblitterari peccatum qu. 126 pm; de cetero peccatis oblitteratis qu. 112 pr; non quod penitus (lex) oblitterata esset qu. 4; ut eorum opera oblitterarentur qu. 13; cum peccatum suum...sacrificii oblatione oblitterari putaret qu. 112 (col. 2339); cum unius dei notitia oblitterata esset in mundo qu. 114 (col. 2346); Solon et Lycurgus multa statuerunt...quae paulatim...oblitterata sunt qu. 115 (col. 2350).

obnoxius, with the dative of something evil, 'liable to (suffer)': *damnationi* 59 D; 504 C; *legi* 70 A; 86 B (codd.); *peccatis* 82 A, B; 86 D; 387 D; 478 D; *peccato* qu. 112 *bis*; *uiro* 253 B (the irksome authority of the husband is referred to); *maledicto* 374 C; *corruptelae* 391 B; *perditioni* 104 A (codd.); 447 D; qu. 102; 110 *bis*; 112; 114; *morti* 108 B (codd.); 493 C; qu. 106; 115; 119; *abolitioni* qu. 28; *passioni* qu. 28; *poenae* qu. 110; *delictis* qu. 111; *desperationi* qu. 114; *contradictioni* qu. 114; *seruituti* qu. 115; *humanis rebus* qu. 115; *punitioni* qu. 115 etc. (The *absolute* use is also common to both works: e.g. 108 C; 121 B; 122 C; qu. 36.)

otiose, in the phrase ***non otiose**[1], = 'without force, meaning':

[1] Also employed by Ambrose frequently, e.g. neque *enim* otiose *dictum est homini* (expos. Luc. prol. 6 (p. 7, 14 Schenkl)).

non otiose ergo prohibitum se dicit 56 D; quos non otiose Romam uenisse manifestum est 188 A; quod puto non otiose iteratum 191 C, codd. etc.; non otiose aliquid[1] aut inprouide diuina loquitur scriptura qu. 10; non otiose illud mandasse Ioseph filiis Israhel qu. 25; non enim otiose hoc factum ratio probat qu. 108; etc. (Cf. nihil otiose dicit apostolus 222 C; non est itaque otiosum quia uoluerat ire 294 C; unam dixit esse generationem requirentium deum, et quaerentium faciem dei Iacob, quod non est otiosum qu. 111 (col. 2334); non est otiosa carnalis natiuitas qu. 115 (col. 2351).)

pario, in a metaphorical sense, is a favourite word; examples are:—nequitia, cuius adfectus inuidiam parit et homicidia 64 C; omnis contentio et zelus inimicitiam parit 174 C; disceptatio discordiam parit 179 A; ne horum forte segnitia offensionis occasionem pareret discipulis 316 B cet.; ne neglegentia pareret uitae praecipitium qu. 1 (col. 2315); offensio legis parit egestatem qu. 34; diuina temptatio perniciem parit qu. 99; uides quid pariat uana praesumptio qu. 101 (col. 2302); officium eius offensionem non parit qu. 102 (col. 2307); est corruptio quae parit mortem qu. 110 (col. 2330); inuidia quam parit defensio ambarum partium qu. 114 (col. 2343); illud adserere quod perniciem pariat qu. 114 (col. 2343); per luxuriam et uoluptatem fit intemperantia et inquietudo quae parit incontinentiam et iracundiam qu. 115 (col. 2350). It will be observed that the verb commonly occurs in the pres. indic., third sing., and in general sentiments.

Paulianus, a follower of Paul*; Pauliani (codd.) et Petriani et Apolloniaci dici uolebant, non Christiani 193 A (prol. 1 Cor.); cum apostolus condemnet si quis dicat se Paulianum aut alterius alicuius qu. 102 ex.

perduro: *in* opere sibi decreto perdurant elementa rerum 60 A; si homo *in* eo quod factus est perdurasset 121 B; *in* malis suis perdurauit 144 A; *in* coepto malo perdurant 145 D; si *in* inimicitiis perdurauerint impietate mentis suae 170 C; qui *in* fide eius perdurat 371 C; cet.; quia *in* eo (peccato) perdurant qu. 112 ppr; sententiam...*in* qua assiduis uocibus perdurantes qu. 65.

[1] *aliquid = quicquam* here, and usually, but not always, in this author.

perhibeo (cf. Rom. ix 1; x 2): in the phrase **testimonium perhibere**, usually with dative: 71 A; 93 C; 134 C; 152 B; 218 A; 295 C; 313 B; 324 C; 350 C; 367 C (cf. Act. xvi 2); 373 C codd.; 386 A; 465 B; 524 A; qu. 44 m; 84; (95); 115 *bis*; 118; 2 qu. N.T. 10; 2 qu. mixt. 8.

permitto with the accusative and infinitive construction[1], especially of our Lord in the phrase **cruci figi (pati) se permisit**: pro peccatoribus filium suum deus occidi permisit 95 C; saluator noster corpus suum diabolo cruci figere permisit 111 C; ut non illam permittat ire quo uult 119 B; quem Christus ut redimeret, cruci figi se permisit 240 C; permisit eos loqui linguis 271 C (so 272 B); deus...qui pro nobis filium suum mori permisit 400 C; (deus) illum occidi permisit 416 C; ante quam se inclinari permitteret 432 B etc.; non utique uir iustus permisisset se adorari qu. 27; quid causae fuit ut illo tempore cruci figi se permitteret dominus qu. 55; quare autem cruci figi se permiserit qu. 114 (col. 2345); cum ille uoluntatis suae horam significauerit qua se pati permiserit qu. 115 (col. 2358); descendit, hoc est, pati se permisit 2 qu. V.T. 17; tempus quo se pati permisit qu. 104; etc.

plecto, "punish," is a characteristic expression. I have found even the perf. partic. pass., previously unknown, **plexus* (see below). Examples of this word are:—necesse est enim seueriori poena ut plectatur 68 B; cum *iustum* esset plecti illos 102 A; similiter et in Aegypto pro noxiis patrum plexi sunt filii qu. 13; quam ob rem *iuste* plectendus est quem cum constet scire ac facere posse bonum agit malum qu. 98 (col. 2299).

positus, as in Ambr. Hier. supplies the place of the missing participle* of *sum*, very rarely *constitutus*[2], which is Cyprian's favourite[3]. The most characteristic phrase in which it occurs is **in cruce positus**, of our Lord: in poena enim positus sine fructu paenitentiae paenitebit 68 A; ne diu hic positi damnum incurrant promissae uitae 68 C; *in carne* positi (reference to S. Paul's 'non

[1] This construction is found with all verbs of command, request, or permission: e.g. *mando* 167 A; *peto* 110 C; qu. 68; 112; *praecipio* 97 A; 173 B; *postulo* 143 A; qu. 30; 68 *bis*; 112; *precor* qu. 112; *hortor* qu. 102.

[2] *constitutus* e.g. 218 D; 362 D; qu. 111; 113; 118; 2 qu. V.T. 17.

[3] Cf. Mr E. W. Watson, *Studia Biblica* IV 311, and in Wordsworth and White's Vulg. Ioh. v 13, Marx's index to Filastrius, *s.v.*

estis in carne' (Rom. viii 8)) dicuntur non esse in carne 126 A; prius *in carne* positi exemplo Adae uiuebamus subiecti peccatis 127 D; *in* domini et creatoris *potestate* posita creatura non utique sponte subiecta est uanitati 130 C; habet in labore posita (creatura) hoc solacium 131 A; *in dolore* positi 132 D; Iudaei in lege positi...deteriorauerunt 147 D; *in necessitate* aliqua posito uel oppresso opem ferre misericordia est 166 B; iam in manifestatione positi 173 C; quis enim in poena positus iacturam non facit 211 B; Moyse in monte posito apud deum 247 B; deus praesidia sua non negat *in necessitate* positis 293 B; in inopia positis adfuit pastor deus 307 B; in corpore positi spiritaliter uiuimus 334 B etc.; in postremis positi qu. 13; eis *in carne* adhuc positis qu. 20; inter errores positi 2 qu. N.T. 15; amisit meritum spiritale quod positus *in carne* quaesiuerat qu. 27; *in* ipsa enim *necessitate* positus qu. 118 (col. 2362); gentilem in potestate positum qu. 35; in itinere positus qu. 61; in Galilea positus qu. 74 (78); Aegyptius positus in obscuro qu. 97 (col. 2293); in ignorantia positus qu. 126 (col. 2376); si autem *in* ipsa *necessitate* posito auxilium feras qu. 83 (col. 2276); alicui *in dolore* posito 2 qu. N.T. 62; in misericordia positis lege...uti non licet aspere qu. 104; aliis se subiciat *in potestate* positis qu. 110 (col. 2330) etc.; adhuc in cruce positum 52 B; et dominus in cruce positus postulat pro inimicis 173 B; quid est quod in cruce positus saluator ait...? qu. 67; quippe cum etiam in cruce posito insultarent ei qu. 94 etc.

possibilitas: unus quisque iuxta uotum suum donum dei habet ut si uelit ipsius nutu dei possibilitatem consequatur 229 B; ambigenti Mariae de conceptu possibilitatem angelus praedicat qu. 51; sic enim deus instituit genus nostrum ut sine sensu nascamur, possibilitatem tamen habeamus discendi siue bona siue mala qu. 80.

praeiudicare, with the dative, is common: nihil (*adverbial acc.*) ergo praeiudicatur deo patri cum adoratur Christus ut deus 138 D and often[1]; illis qu. 61; filio dei qu. 125; spiritui sancto qu. 97; 125; uni deo qu. 97; ueritati qu. 84; 114 (p. 2345); unitati qu. 122.

[1] I have accidentally omitted to record further examples from the comm.

praerogatiua: semper Iudaeum anteponit praerogatiua patrum 69 C; nec enim praerogatiuam *generis* sequitur 70 A; ex praerogatiua parentum est ut dicantur Israelitae 72 D; non recipiendo saluatorem praerogatiuam patrum et promissionis meritum perdiderunt 138 B; *sibi* praerogatiuam *defendunt,* quod filii sint Abrahae 141 B; nec enim Iudaeos *commendare* poterit praerogatiua patrum 151 B; qui praerogatiua patrum digni erant 159 B; filii sunt bonorum, quorum praerogatiua et *merito* plurima a deo beneficia perceperunt 161 C; Iudaei, qui sibi praerogatiuam *uindicant* patrum 185 A; inde enim sibi *defendunt generis* praerogatiuam 343 A; praerogatiuā praeteritorum operum uidua *commendatur* 504 A; dum quidam eorum (Iudaeorum) sibi *uindicarent* praerogatiuam originum patriarcharum 531 B; eo quod *commendentur* praerogatiua illorum qu. 13; legis ueteris praerogatiua qu. 95 pr; (res) nullā munitur praerogatiuā signorum qu. 100 ppr; pauper enim, cum nullā praerogatiuā *commendaretur* qu. 124; quasi istud ad praerogatiuam pertineat magnitudinis qu. 101 aex; praerogatiuă enim honoris eius ac *meriti* fides est qu. 117 pr; cognitio dei hanc habet praerogatiuam, ut...qu. 126 pr; ut per hoc non *sibi* praerogatiuam *generis uindicarent* 2 qu. V.T. 6.

praescius, of God, with *a noun clause dependent on it: examples are:—praescius itaque *deus* malae illos uoluntatis futuros 141 C; praescius utique quod futurus esset bonus 142 C; cui praescius eram quod misericordiam daturus essem 142 D; praescius *deus* errores futuros in mundo 204 B; praescius quia Iudas proditor erat futurus 255 A; praescius enim Iudaeos se inimicum legis dicturos 2 qu. N.T. 8; and often.

(Also absolutely used: e.g. qu. 104; 2 qu. V.T. 11, and with genitive, e.g.: deum qui omnium praescius est 275 A; praescium se huius rei qu. 104.)

praesens: in the adverbial phrase **ad praesens**[1] "for the present," "at present": 67 D; 98 A codd.; 150 B; 323 B; 332 C *bis*; 378 A; 441 C; 452 D; 469 C; 477 B; 507 D; 508 D; 509 C; 531 A cet.; qu. 68 (*b*); qu. 99; qu. 105 pm; qu. 110 (new part); qu. 124; qu. 126 aex; 2 qu. mixt. 5 *bis* cet.

[1] *in praesenti* occurs, however, 98 A (but see above), 238 A, qu. 124 *ter* perhaps oftener; *hoc in tempore*)(*in aeternum* 332 B.

praeuaricatio: praeuaricatio Adae of Rom. v 14 (so Vulg. also) is referred to also 106 C mortale corpus est ex causa praeuaricationis Adae, qu. 112 peccatum quod ex praeuaricatione Adae humano generi imperabat, and qu. 127 pm per praeuaricationem autem Adae.

praeuarico, active (as sometimes in Old Latin versions, cf. Rönsch *Itala und Vulgata*[2], p. 298): hic (Adam) beneficium dei perdidit dum praeuaricauit 97 B; praeuaricauit enim (Adam) putans se hominem futurum deum 99 A; neque circumuentus praeuaricasset (Adam) qu. 123 (col. 2369); Eua uirgo adhuc praeuaricauit 2 qu. V.T. 8; necesse est ut praeuaricetis 2 qu. N.T. 46 (col. 2403).

primordium is a favourite word[1] for 'beginning'; ut ipsa primordia peccati ostenderet 96 C; ostendit hoc *inter* primordia fidei non requiri 161 C; sicut in primordio epistulae memoraui 175 B; sicut in primordio epistulae memoraui 180 C; hoc est quod in primordio epistulae dicit 190 C; *inter* illa primordia, cum ambo utique essent gentiles 230 C; quod dudum in primordiis ipsi didicerant 255 D cet.; lex...in primordiis suis seueritatem exercuit qu. 102 (p. 2303); in primordio renascibilitatis qu. 115 pr; in primordio legis 2 qu. V.T. 10; *inter ipsa* primordia pressurae 292 C cet.; *inter ipsa* primordia (without genitive) 348 A; 409 C; 410 C; qu. 83 (col. 2277); qu. 87; qu. 102 (col. 2303).

pristinus: ut...*ad* pristinum *statum reuocaret* meliorata substantia qu. 116; *ad* pristinum *redditus statum* qu. 123 pr; ut *reddamur ad* pristinum *statum* Adae qu. 127 m; *ad statum* pristinum *reuocata* sunt 2 qu. V.T. 8; *ad* institutum pristinum *reuocatur* qu. 127 ex; non redeamus ad mala pristina 104 D; reparatus...*ad statum* pristinum 121 C; *ad* pristinum *statum redditus est* qu. 102; *ad statum* suum pristinum reformari qu. 102; *reddita* pristinā uita 448 A; pristinae calliditatis suae qu. 118; pristina conuersatio qu. 126; errores pristinos 381 C; etc.

professio, as a Christian term, is ignored by the *dictionaries: it is very frequent; ut in professione et fide sua essent perfecti 55 D; ratam habentes fidei suae professionem 57 A; qui non

[1] *exordium* and *initium* also appear: *inter initia sua* qu. 102.

solum bonae professionis sunt sed et uitae 69 A; non solum facta significat sed et perfidiae professionem 69 B; ut professio *nostra* animi iudicio promatur 109 A; propter *unius dei* professionem 138 B; gratia dei...non quaerit gemitum aut planctum aut opus aliquod nisi solum ex corde professionem 161 C; cum sint unius professionis 191 A; quidquid sub dei creatoris professione fit sanctum est 231 A; nescire religionis et professionis suae fidem 355 B etc.; propter quod integrae professionis sunt qu. 76 (72); ut professione *nostra* ab eo cuius mundus est condemnemur qu. 79 (75); sub *unius dei* professione qu. 97 (col. 2296); trinitas quam in salutari professione retinemus qu. 97 (col. 2294); mundus hic diuersae professionis continet homines qu. 102 (col. 2310); ut...alterius essent et professionis et conuersationis qu. 108 (col. 2323); ut professionem sine bona uita non ualde proficere ostenderet qu. 111 (col. 2333); illam (legem) puram et ipsi professioni condignam cognouissemus qu. 114 (col. 2342); etc.

proficio: (1) a very favourite construction is **proficio ad** or **in** with the *Acc.*, expressing growth in a **bad*[1] direction[2]: iam enim deprauati proficiunt in peius 80 B; in peius proficiant 180 D; quod deterius est, in peius profecisse 217 B; uidebat eos in peius proficere 381 C; dant enim quibusdam occasionem, ut in peius proficiant 518 A; ut in peius proficiant qu. 76; ne in peius proficeret qu. 101 pr;—sciens hoc ad iniuriam proficere creatoris 132 B; contaminatio erit, quia ad iniuriam proficit creatoris 393 D; ut ad eius iniuriam proficiant 499 C; quod ne ad iniuriam eius proficeret qu. 44 ex; ut deo proficiat ad iniuriam patris qu. 97 ppr; ne ad iniuriam dei proficeret qu. 122 pr; ne ad dei iniuriam proficeret qu. 25; quod quidem ad iniuriam proficit saluatoris qu. 123 aex; ad iniuriam promissionis patrum proficiebat 2 qu. N.T. 17; in iniuriam creatoris, quae proficiet ad perditionem dubitantis 178 B; non illis ad iustificationem proficiebant sed ad exitium qu. 44 m; istud ad

[1] The use is not unknown to Scripture: plurimum enim *proficiunt ad inanitatem* 2 Tim. ii 16; nequam autem homines et deceptores *proficient in peius* (frequent above) 2 Tim. iii 13.

[2] The good sense is often seen in our author, too, e.g. 106 C; 181 C; qu. 99; 122 pr; cet.; the word is used *absol.* too, e.g. 364 D, 430 A, 502 A.

necem proficere Iudaeorum qu. 44 pr; eis qui pro Christo tribulantur, (fides) ad salutem *proficit:* illis uero qui tribulant, ad perditionem 430 B; ut celeri motu proficiant ad perditionem 500 D; quod sic sumunt, ut ad detrimentum proficiat 244 A; illa ei dare quae ad uitam proficiant, non ad luxum 246 A; ad dedecus enim et deformationem eius proficit 305 B; ne illis in scandalum proficeret 341 B; ad contumeliam eius proficere, si... 371 D; superstitione humana, quae ad nihilum proficit, nisi ad damnum 456 B; mali in deterius proficiunt 522 A; ad accusationem eorum hoc proficere qu. 60; ut ergo ad condemnationem proficeret Iudaeorum qu. 71; ad diminutionem nostram hoc proficere qu. 99 ex; obsequia proficient illis ad poenam 170 C; ad poenam proficiet, non ad praemium qu. 114 pr; ut ista omnia ad sanctorum proficiant gloriam, ad diaboli uero poenam qu. 118 ex; horum enim natiuitas proficit ad poenam qu. 127 am; proficiens in interitum carnis 2 qu. N.T. 49.

(2) The second frequent construction is **proficio** with a **Dative*, of persons or things[1]. (*a*) *Dat. of Persons:* quod quidem obsequium non illi utique proficit...quod proficit nobis 127 D; proficit enim hominibus natis in mundo, ut...discant 130 D; nos quibus obsequium eius proficit 132 B; nostra obsequia proficient illis ad poenam 170 C; non sibi proficere vult, ne libertatem arguendi humiliet 243 B; sciens hoc sibi magis proficere ad futuram salutem 243 B; scientia...proficiens omnibus ad utilitatem 267 C; ut proficiat ceteris studium eius 269 A; ad occultandos sensus incredulis proficiunt linguae 271 A; refectus est spiritus eius in his, quibus profecerant; sibi enim dicit datum, quod proficit his quibus uoluit 290 B; ac per hoc commendatio haec istis magis proficit 301 A; ut (euangelizare) nobis proficiat forte ad tempus 306 A; ut abundans donum...multis proficiens afflueret... 308 D; si...intelligitur...Corinthiis proficere dicit 312 C; ut mors iusti peccatoribus proficeret 315 C; certus hoc sibi proficere apud deum 316 D; ut nobis proficiat 326 D; ueritas haec his magis quam ei proficeret 338 C; in tantum eis proficere uoluit, ut... 341 A; ne illis in scandalum proficeret 341 B; auxilium dei mitibus proficit, non elatis 348 B; commendatio enim haec istis proficit 364 D;

[1] like *prosum.*

ut gentibus proficeret 365 D; ut illi ad meritum proficiat in die iudicii 374 C; ut non illi sed nobis proficeret. Nos enim etiamsi nobis non proficeret 400 D; omnibus enim proficit mors saluatoris 401 C; ut praedicatio ecclesiastica etiam his proficiat 404 C; hoc enim dicit sibi ad uitam proficere 429 A; hoc secutus est quod proficeret fratribus 430 A; eis qui pro Christo tribulantur ad salutem proficit: illis uero qui tribulant, ad perditionem 430 B; labores eorum qui adquisiti sunt proficient eis, quorum... 442 B; nec enim sibi natiuitas sua proficit, sed nobis 447 B; (discipuli) bona conuersatio proficit magistro 471 C; ut etiam illi proficiat, qui facit 477 B; quamuis ad praesens proficiat sumenti, nihil tamen *proderit* in futuro *danti* 477 B; eis dicit fallaciam iniquitatis prodigiorum eius proficere 483 A; difficile proficient audientibus 485 B; medicina...quae neque dubiis proficit, neque inuitis 492 D; nec enim possunt bene illi proficere, qui sic illa sumit 499 D; quod rectori plebis duobus proficit modis 502 A; quod non solum ordinatis proficit, sed et plebi 506 B; pauci conderent quod pluribus posset proficere cum eorum ipsorum emolumento 509 B; ad hoc enim data est (scriptura), ut proficiat imperitis, et instauret deformes 522 C; non illis ad iustificationem proficiebant, sed ad exitium qu. 44 m; ut passio eius proficeret nobis qu. 78; oblatio enim Iudaeorum profecit gentibus... qu. 74 (*b*); sic illi proficiat quaesita dignitas qu. 81; ut proficiat sibi qu. 92; ut deo proficiat ad iniuriam patris qu. 97 ppr; donum dei proficere posse deuoto sibi qu. 102 ex; bona eius mihi possent proficere qu. 102 ex; non enim erant adhuc quibus proficerent officia eorum qu. 106 pm; ut et nobis proficiat qu. 118 pr; donum dei his proficere qui... qu. 126 m; quod illis proficiat ad salutem 2 qu. N.T. 62.—(*b*) *Dat. of Things:* actus nostri iustitiae dei proficientes, non mundanae iustitiae 107 C; ut alimentis seruorum dei proficiant 132 B; in fructibus, qui humanae proficiunt utilitati 261 B; ut...nihil proficeret aduentus eius saluti illorum 288 D; ut potestas data saluti proficiat non elationi 336 B; ut proficiat saluti plebis suae 501 C; ut saluti eorum proficeret 2 qu. N.T. 51; ut...bonum opus proficiat mercedi promissae 391 D; uidens monita sua proficere utilitatibus nostris 415 A; cui rei proficit humana cupiditas...? 509 A; semen fluxu quodam non proficit natiuitati qu. 23 pm; quod quidem errori profecit Iudaeorum qu. 60; hoc proficere religioni qu. 102 ex.

promereri, especially in the formula **ad deum promerendum:** ad deum...promerendum suffragatore non opus est 61 A; seruitus quae ad deum proficeret promerendum 131 B; ad deum promerendum animus eruditur 235 C; quaerens causas ad promerendum eum (Christum) 439 B; pietas cuius opera multorum precibus adiuuatur ad dominum promerendum 500 B; ut ad dominum promerendum orationibus uacet 503 C; qui *propter* deum promerendum uirgo manere uult 237 A; interpositis temporibus ad deum promerendum 228 C codd.; nec ille deum promeretur 232 B; promerebitur dominum 463 A; etc.; ut non utique iam multis utatur praeceptis ad deum promerendum qu. 44 (col. 2241); haec satis non faciunt ad deum promerendum qu. 47 (col. 2248); formam praebens mirabilium gestorum ad deum promerendum qu. 118 (col. 2362); ut uitam suam frenaret ad promerendum eum (creatorem) qu. 127 (col. 2379); quaestus pecuniae *propter* deum promerendum repudiatur qu. 115 (col. 2350); deum promereri 2 qu. N.T. 34.

propensior (*compar. adj.*) and **propensius** (*compar. adv.*) are both characteristic: the positive and superlative of both are absent[1]: (*a*) *Adj.* tanto magis in dei rebus propensiores essemus 129 C; propensius enim malum est dignitatem perdidisse, quam non habuisse 138 B; propensiores enim erant *in dei deuotione* 188 A; ostendit in qua re melius est esse propensiorem 229 B; sub creatoris ueneratione nati sunt propensiore ex parte 231 A; propensiores et *uigilantes* in diuinis operibus 234 D; ut monitis eius...propensiorem poenam mereamur inoboedientes 248 A; propensior in hac parte fit 268 D; ut propensiores simus in eius amore 303 B; ut enim *deuotionem* suam adhuc propensiorem in dei rebus ostendat 309 A; in dei rebus propensior erat 322 A; eadem fecit, quae faciebant apostoli, qui propensiores (*v. l.* potiores) uidebantur 339 B; uerum est quia faciliores et propensiores in bono circa fratres esse debemus 391 D; propensiores

[1] An interesting study would be that of adverbs used almost entirely in the compar. and superl., or one only of these two, e.g. *expressius* in Aug. cet.

fient circa excolendam religionem...propensiores fient necessario, cum cognouerint 396 D; nunc alacritatem suam propensiorem factam ostendit 443 A; hos significat propensiorem affectum habere circa eos, qui... 444 C; quanto *magis* propensior erit *in dei deuotione*, quem... 463 A; propensiori delicto rei facti 483 B; propensior ad peccandum est qu. 1 pm; *in dei creatoris deuotione* propensior qu. 25; propensiores in idolis erant qu. 33; in eo enim quis iudicatur in quo propensior est qu. 73; erat enim propensior in seueritate qu. 102 pr; propensiores in exercitio implendae legis qu. 110 ex; tanto *magis* propensior credentis est merces qu. 122 am[1]; propensiori dei testimonio qu. 127 ex.—(*b*) *Adv.*[2] cum utique propensius deberet seruiri deo quam diabolo 109 C; solemus enim in alienis causis propensius uigilare 131 C; propensius domino nostro seruire debemus 227 D; diminuta enim sollicitudine saeculi, in dei rebus propensius uigilatur 235 C; ut...propensius illi seruiant 313 C; sua pro eis impendere et propensius impendere (with reference to "superimpendam" of 2 Cor. xii 15) paratum se dicit 352 A; ut propensius gratias agant deo per Christum 400 B; propensius agnita uoluntate dei 445 C; commonet tamen ut propensius id agant 474 A; propter dei timorem propensius obsequuntur suis uiris 529 A.

propositum: *ut impleret* propositum *uoluntatis* suae 55 C; propositum et uotum suum ostendit 56 B; ut in proposito erroris et malignitatis permaneant 96 A; propositum gratiae dei erga genus humanum ostendit 96 C; ut et nos de proposito nostro abstrahat 170 D; propositum suum non custodit 175 C; ut unus quisque in proposito cordis sui maneat 180 B; remitti illos in proposito cordis sui 180 C; confirmans propositum eorum in Christo 184 B; dei enim propositum est ut ueritatem eius...disceremus 202 A; si permaneat in proposito regenerationis 208 B; propositum liberum est 214 B; propositum religionis custodit 231 A; quo modo propositum deo deuotum custodiat 236 A; significat confabulatione malorum hominum euerti posse bonum propositum 281 C, and often: *ut* propositum mysterii

[1] *magis* is elsewhere found joined to a compar.: see above; but, in the absence of *propensus*, it is here more natural than in other cases.

[2] Not, apparently, in *Quaest.* but the examples are added for completeness.

impleretur qu. 54; ut mali propositi impleant uoluntatem qu. 115 (col. 2348); propositum deo dicatum qu. 118 (col. 2362); qui degenerem dicunt spiritum sanctum dei pulsant propositum qu. 125 (col. 2375) etc. etc. The word is not found in the plural in either work.

protectio, in the phrase **dei protectio** (Ps. xc 1): tutus enim est protectione et misericordia dei 393 A etc.; quippe a quibus dei protectio amota uidetur qu. 27; securi de eius (i.e. dei) protectione qu. 115 (col. 2359): (cf. protectione diuina qu. 36: precibus deum inuocabant ad protegendum populum suum qu. 46 (col. 2246)).

prudens in the expression **prudentes mundi**[1]: *ad confusionem* prudentium mundi 94 B; o prudentes mundi, qui putant... 125 B; ne stulti uiderentur prudentibus mundi 198 B; prudentibus mundi qu. 109 ppr; prudentes mundi qu. 100; *ad confusionem* prudentium mundi qu. 121 (*cf. sapientes* mundi in carne sunt 125 C; *sapientibus* mundi qu. 100; quidam mundi *sapientes* qu. 117 am; sophistae et nobiles mundi qu. 114 ex); per prudentiam mundi 194 B; mundi *sapientia* et ratio 198 B. Cf. prudentes saeculi 53 D; qu. 109.

***pseudo-apostolus** occurs in both works with its parts separated: pseudo enim apostoli erant qui et nocebant illis 320 C; pseudo enim apostoli formam auaritiae dari sibi optabant 469 B; pseudo enim apostoli, cum circumuenirent gentiles credentes,... 2 qu. mixt. 10. (Some MSS in the passages of the commentaries give *pseudo apostoli enim.*)

quaestionem facere: *de* edenda carne et non edenda quaestiones fiebant 48 A; non habet *unde* incipiat facere quaestionem 88 B; quaestio *hinc* fieri non debet 175 D; eadem dicit non debere fratri...fieri quaestionem 180 A etc.; non est *de* hac re facere quaestionem qu. 103; quaestiones non *de* deo fiunt sed de uerbo dei qu. 122 (col. 2366); sic solent dubii facere quaestiones 2 qu. N.T. 46 etc.

quantum ad...pertinet, as a parenthetical expression, the origin of French *quant à,* occurs frequently. Though the verb is

[1] The expression is derived from 1 Cor. i 20; 21; iii 19, where, however, *sapientia,* not *prudentia,* is the word; *prudentia carnis,* however, is in Rom. viii 6 and is glossed =*sapientia* by our writer. Rom. viii 7, too, has *sapientia carnis.*

omitted in some authors, it is always present here. Examples are:—q. ad locum istum p. 95 A; q. ad sensum et prouidentiam p. 120 B; q. ad te p. 169 C; q. ad Iudaeorum uotum p. 205 B; q. ad honorificentiam dei p. 209 D; q. ad ministerium p. 209 D; q. ad ...magistrum p. 229 A; q. ad mentem loci p. 247 D; q. ad idoneos praedicatores p. 295 B; q. ad praesentem uitam p. 318 B; 501 A; q. ad Iudaeos p. 375 A; q. ad legis culturam p. 438 A; q. *ad personas* p. 472 D; q. ad scientiam eius pertinebat 497 D; q. ad praesentem uitam p. ... q. uero ad promissam salutem 501 A (this and the following examples are not really exceptions to the rule above given); q. ad aetatem p., iuuenis erat; q. ad mores et conuersationem, senior et grauis 501 B; q. ergo ad comparationem ceterorum p. ... q. uero ad rem ipsam 514 A; q. ad tempus p. illud Iudaeorum 531 B; q. ad ordinem lectionis p. non q. ad dignitatem qu. 107; q. ad mundi rationem p. qu. 107; q. enim p. ad Petrum qu. 104; q. ad numerum p. qu. 87; q. ad bonam mentem p. qu. 97; q. ad sensum p. qu. 78; 97; q. ad causam nostram p. qu. 102; q. ad conscientiam eius p. ... q. autem ad praescientiam qu. 11; q. ad historiam p. qu. 31; 62; 112; q. *ad personam* p. qu. 97; q. ad leges Romanas pertinuit qu. 65; q. ad euangelistam p. 2 qu. mixt. 2; q. ad fidem ueri p. qu. 71; q. ad nomen p. qu. 108; q. p. ad ritum Iudaeorum qu. 115; q. ad reliquas p. partes qu. 115; q. ad effectum p. qu. 122; q. ad uerba p. qu. 10; qu. 2 mixt. 7.

qui enim **fieri potest ut?** is found several times in the MSS of both works, but is generally corrupted by scribes and editors; e.g.: qui fieri poterat ut tempore Christi prohiberentur? 98 A; qui enim poterat fieri ut sine apostolis regnarent? 215 D; qui enim (quomodo autem *Migne*) fieri potest ut auarus fidelis sit? 509 D; qui (*Migne* quomodo) enim fieri poterat ut arte magica adtraheretur uir...? qu. 27; qui fieri potest ut ista, quae clemens est, non recipiat paenitentes? qu. 102 (p. 2304); si enim apud ueteres nostros paenitentia habuit locum, qui (quomodo *Migne*) fieri potest ut hoc tempore locum non habeat? qu. 102 (col. 2306); qui (quomodo *Migne*) enim fieri potest ut aliquis super haec sit quae colit? qu. 84; also qu. 109 (p. 2327, 4) cod. *Quo modo* in the same phrase is common in both works (e.g. 94 D; 434 D; qu. 46 (*posset*); 66 (*poterat*).

refuto 'to reject' (**oblata** offers, gifts): donum promissum patribus refutauit 69 C; non pecuniam refutaret 352 C; gloria pseudo-apostolorum in pecuniis erat accipiendis, ideo apostolus hoc refutauit 341 D; oblatos sumptus refutauit 340 B; non refutabat at sumptus oblatos 241 C; si praepositus ideo oblata refutet, ut libere arguat 353 B etc.; utquid Abel sacrificium acceptatum est et Cain refutatum? qu. 5 (col. 2220); ut etiam oblata munera refutarent qu. 115 (col. 2350); illorum testimonium refutauit 2 qu. mixt. 8; Dauid (*genit.*) precem suscepit et Saul (*genit.*) refutauit qu. 18 etc.

***remissa**[1] (plur. neut. = *remissio*[2]): et necesse est ut sit sub lege, quam diu remissa non accipit 108 A; quando coeperunt homines remissa (*Migne* remissam) peccatorum accipere 514 B; sciens dominus conuersis dari debere peccatorum remissa (*Migne* remissionem) qu. 102 (col. 2304); duae causae sunt quae habent peccatorum remissa (*Migne* remissam[3]) qu. 126 (col. 2377); cognitio dei hanc habet praerogatiuam ut peccatorum consequatur remissa (*Migne* remissam) qu. 126 (col. 2376).

***renascibilitas**[4]: in caritate renascibilitatis 189 A; forma renascibilitatis est a Christo coepta qu. 50 (*a*); renascibilitatis donum qu. 54; in primordio renascibilitatis qu. 115 pr; non ergo accusat renascibilitas natiuitatem qu. 127 m.

reparo, used reflexively or in the passive, of 'moral reformation': examples are:—ut possent reparare se ad uitam 113 B; digesto enim impedimento reparat se uoluntas robustiore uirtute 229 C; qui enim semel peccauerit reparare se debet ne denuo peccet qu. 1 (col. 2215); ne in re aspera uictus abscedat et fiat reus, uix aut tarde se reparans qu. 1 (col. 2216); ut post peccata

[1] For the form see C. Weyman in *Archiv f. lat. Lexikogr.* IX 138; Rev. E. W. Watson in *Studia Biblica* IV 249, n. 2: add Aug. *Migne P. L.* XLIII 217 last line, and 218, l. 3 (in cod. Bodl. Laud. 130).

[2] *Remissio* is of course very much commoner (e.g. 79 C; 87 D; 92 C; 102 A; 104 A, B; 108 B; 110 A; 111 C; qu. 102; 126; 2 qu. N.T. 29).

[3] This example of the feminine form, derived doubtless from Paucker, must be struck out of Benoist-Goelzer's *Dictionnaire*. The fem. form occurs, however, 385 B (codd.).

[4] Cf. Morin p. 102, who quotes examples of *nascibilitas*, *innascibilis* and *innascibilitas* from Isaac ex-Iudaeo: *nascibilis* is in Tert.; *innascibilis* is in Tert., Victorin. Petab., Hil.

haberent quo modo se repararent qu. 102 (col. 2308); qui se dolet uictum reparat se qu. 126 (col. 2376); de hoc spes est quia potest se reparare qu. 126 (col. 2376); ut autem totus homo minime reparatus fuisset Christi gratia *ad* statum pristinum 121 C; per ipsum reparatum est genus humanum 147 B; eruti a lege quae illos habebat obnoxios et releuati et reparati... uitiis...*repugnarent* 108 C; ut uirtute eius reparati fortiter *repugnemus* qu. 102 (col. 2306); Niniuitis, peccata deflentibus, imminente morte reparata est uita qu. 102 (col. 2305); nulli est ambiguum idcirco in ipso reparatum esse quod fuerat amissum qu. 108 (col. 2324); omnibus maculis ablutus et reparatus qu. 112 (col. 2338); neque emortua et dissoluta corpora rursus reparari *ad* uitam qu. 114 (col. 2344); animae autem peccato maculatum est corpus quod reparato et meliorato per fidem consilio abluitur qu. 127 (col. 2382).

retracto, a legal term, 'to revise' (a judgment): iustus est deus: scit enim quid faciat, nec retractandum est eius iudicium 142 C; in deo cuius consilium retractari non potest 212 C; hoc placuit deo cuius consilium retractari non potest 395 C etc.: dei iudicium retractari non conuenit qu. 18; ut iudicium dei retractari prohiberet qu. 75 (79); dei uoluntatem non debere ab homine retractari qu. 109 (col. 2326); factum eius retractari nefarium ducit qu. 115 (col. 2347); uerba saluatoris retractare infidelis est 2 qu. N.T. 20; horum testimonium retractandum putat 2 qu. N.T. 26.

rubor: ut ipso rubore non se iactarent 161 D; plures credunt, quam non credunt, ad illorum ruborem 201 B; non ut ruborem uobis faciam 217 B; ad ruborem eorum ait 223 B; ruborem ergo incussit eis 341 A; ruborem illis incutit 382 B; ut duplici genere (= modo) confundantur, et de errore suo et rubore apostoli, quem patiebatur apud eos 383 C; nec in apostolo est, quod ad ruborem pertineat 513 C cet.; cui ignoscitur, non est sine rubore, nisi loco suo fuerit redditus, ut dignitas loci ruborem excuset qu. 112 m; etc.

securus de (Cic. Liv. etc.) is frequent; e.g.: 79 C; 94 A; 114 D; 135 C; 178 B; 190 C; 195 C; 215 D; qu. 14; 111; 112; 115; 117; 119; 124 *ter*; 126. The word is also often used absolutely, and is even followed by *quia* (qu. 100).

spurcus, as *substantive: sententia paganorum turpis et foeda est, maxime quae in Phrygia inuenta est, in qua nisi spurcus intersit, sacramentum mutum est et torpescit religio 110 A; et maligni et spurci habent pacem 356 D; meretrices et spurci 2 qu. N.T. 53.

stupor (especially modified by *quidam*): stupore quodam *hebetasse* ad honorandum deum 60 A; stupore quodam non considerant 71 D etc.: omnes enim stupore quodam in morte domini dubitarunt qu. 77 (73); res enim inaudita...stuporem hominibus faciebat qu. 91 (col. 2283); admirationem autem et stuporem facit cum dicitur quod auditum est numquam qu. 111 (col. 2335); mirabatur enim stupore *hebetatus* 2 qu. N.T. 9.

subaudio: in the 3 sing. pres. indic. pass. **subauditur**[1], "is understood," only: quid "dominus corpori"? subauditur: immortalitatem resuscitato praestabit 225 D; "et uirum uxorem non dimittere": subauditur autem, excepta fornicationis causa 230 B; si enim ii...facultatem habent accipiendi, quanto magis nos? et subauditur, uestri apostoli 242 C; "quid et nos periclitamur?" et subauditur: nisi quia speramus futuram resurrectionem 281 A; "gratia domini nostri Iesu Christi uobiscum": et subauditur, qui diligitis dominum Iesum 290 D cet.; hoc est "neminem uoluit scire": et subauditur, a suis noluit nuntiari alicui... qu. 77 (*a*).

subiaceo, metaphorically, with the dative: examples are:—(uita) quae occasui subiacet 107 B; uitiis et peccatis subiacebamus 112 C; ut *uoluntati* subiaceant 175 D; (cum ipse pro aliena salute periculis cottidie et morti subiaceat Prol. 2 Cor. in printed editions)[2]; sic enim ea condidit ut *uoluntati* eius subiaceant qu. 115 (col. 2352); in saeculo sunt obprobrio et iniuriis subiacent qu. 126 (col. 2376).

subicio = "to add"[3] (in statement), is a very favourite expression: a common phrase is **subiecit,** with or without **dicens**

[1] See *subintellego* below.

[2] I have rejected the prologue in *Journ. Theol. Studies* (Oct. 1902), but give this quotation from it, as it may belong to another edition.

[3] Not to the exclusion however of *addo*, *e.g.* 346 B; 366 B; *subdo*, *e.g.* qu. 112 pm; *adicio*, *e.g.* 80 A; 288 C; qu. 77; qu. 106 pm.—In the sense, "I subject," *subicio* occurs 360 C *bis*, 363 A, 399 A cet., qu. 80 (*a*) qu. 82 pr. cet.

added: post autem subiecit etiam de eis gentibus, quae non credunt 72 A; ac per hoc subiecit: "si autem..." 78 A; C; ideoque subiecit "quorum damnatio iusta est" 79 B; peiora subicere 80 A; other examples are:—101 B; 131 A; 167 B; 174 C; 191 C; et quae esset subiecit, dicens "hoc autem dico..." 196 C; et ideo non subiecit, dicens 230 B; et quae sit subicit, dicens[1]: "numquid non...?" 241 C; other examples are 242 A; 252 C; 276 D; 280 C; 290 C; 305 B; 309 A; 316 B; 328 C; 341 A; 349 C; 361 C; 367 D; 372 B; 384 C cet. cum dixisset,...subiecit qu. 26; per id quod subiecit, dicens qu. 39; subiecit euangelista dicens qu. 57; denique subiecit...inquit qu. 59; et subiecit "in testimonium illis" qu. 60 (*a*); item subiecit quia qu. 93 pr; statim subiecit, dicens qu. 93 ppr; et subiecit... qu. 97 pr; et subiecit... qu. 107 in cet.

Specially characteristic is the use of the *neut. plu.*[2] *participle perfect passive,* as a *noun, in the sense of "the following," "what follows": **subiecta**[3] (**-orum**), nearly always in **in subiectis**: his subiectis cumulauit ad poenam hebetudinis 61 B; quod in subiectis monstrabimus 98 D; possunt tamen credere, quod ex subiectis aperit 141 C; exemplum Isaiae prophetae in subiectis ponit 160 D; quorum doctrinam prauam in subiectis significat 196 C; qualis autem ipse erat, mox in subiectis ostendit 229 A; quae sit scientia, non statim dicit, sed in subiectis ostendit dicens 238 B; per haec subiecta declarauit in idolio edere... inimicum esse deo 251 D; hoc mox in subiectis absoluit 264 B; uerum hoc ad meritum non ascribi sed ad dei gloriam subiectis ostendit 265 A; quod supra significauit et adhuc in subiectis plenius manifestat 334 A; in quo erratum est, in subiectis ostendit 370 A; *et* in subiectis: "tollite portas..." 404 C; quod in subiectis aperit, dicens 432 C; statim ipsum in subiectis esse deum agnoscimus 475 B; quo ordine populum disciplina ecclesiastica imbueret, in subiectis ostendit 491 B; si tamen non ab iis declinet, quae in subiectis habentur 495 A; *et* in subiectis...

[1] Cf. Aug. ep. 98, 3 non eorum defensionem continuo *subiceret, dicens.*

[2] 155 C hoc *subiectum* in Isaia legitur "dedit illis..." is perhaps an example of the *sing.*

[3] A solitary example of the phrase in the literal sense is:—ut lux, quae in supernis erat, fieret in subiectis, ut lampas in domo qu. 107 aex.

inquit qu. 41 ppr; *et* in subiectis: "Ego dedi..." qu. 44 m; in subiectis propheta testatur dicens qu. 47 aex; hunc sonum in subiectis uocem appellat qu. 59 (*a*); denique in subiectis ait qu. 91 pm; *et* in subiectis: "Ego locutus sum..." qu. 97 pm; quod in subiectis pandemus qu. 101 pr; ait enim in subiectis qu. 102 am; sicut in subiectis apparet qu. 106 pr; *et* in subiectis "et die tertio cet." qu. 107 m (codd.); *et* in subiectis... inquit qu. 122 am; *et* in subiectis qu. 122 aex; *et* in subiectis 2 qu. V.T. 12; cf. fit quaestio...de subiectis qu. 110 (the newly discovered part in *Journ. Theol. Stud.* Oct. 1904).

subintellego: esp. in the form **subintelligitur:** et subintelligitur: quid est ut uos... 366 C; quia supereminentis est scientiae, et subintelligitur humanae 406 C; haec in prima tabula contineri subintelliguntur 422 A cet.; nam aliquando compendio loquitur scriptura, quae subintelligi uult ex proposita ratione qu. 16; sine dubio per compendium dixit hoc saluator, ut subintelligantur sacerdotes Iudaeorum qu. 16; multa enim subintelligi uult scriptura qu. 26.

subintro (see Benoist-Goelzer[1] s. u.); subintrantibus gentibus quae sine deo prius erant 141 C[2] etc.; non aliter principi tenebrarum nisi per noctem potuit subintrari qu. 64; si dominum non uidisset subintrantem qu. 64; quo modo quos male tenebat amitteret et subintraretur ei qu. 83 (col. 2277); illud autem quo modo subintrauit quod tradidit Moyses? qu. 115 (col. 2349); si per sensus non subintrarent peccata ad animam qu. 115 (col. 2351); per mortem ergo morti interitus subintrauit qu. 116; ut alii significarentur subintrare 2 qu. V.T. 6 etc.

sublimo[3]**:** honore *patrum* sublimantur 75 A; omnes aut confundi propter diffidentiam dicit aut sublimari causa credulitatis 151 B; qui nulla commendatione sublimati sunt 159 C etc.; et *patrum* et sua iustitia sublimantur qu. 14; quanto magis qui potiores sublimandi sunt qu. 101 (col. 2302); quorum incredulitate plus sublimatur fidelissimus Abraham qu. 117 (col. 2361) etc.

subsequor: in the phrase **paenitentia subsequente:** si...

[1] Georges gives 'eccl.' merely.

[2] Cf. Gal. ii 4.

[3] The best collection of examples of this word is in Mayor's *Latin Heptateuch*, p. 79, 15 ff.

erubesceret,...non interiret, paenitentia subsequente 219 C; ut...Nineuitis ignosceretur paenitentia subsequente qu. 102 (p. 2306); quia paenitentia subsequente erratum suum amarissime fleuit qu. 102 (p. 2304); qui paenitentia subsequente circumuentum se dolet qu. 110 (*Journ. Theol. Stud.* Oct. 1904).

suffragium simply = "help"[1]; saluatorem ergo relictum nobis dicit ad suffragium uitae 147 A; ubi enim deficiebat humanum eis suffragium, aderat Christus 246 D; sequebatur enim ut humanis suffragiis deficientibus adesset ad auxilium tribuendum 272 D; sanctorum suffragio 328 A; ut dei suffragio liberaretur 348 A; uidens enim ex nulla parte se *habere* suffragium 503 B; ab aduersa parte suffragium quaerit 526 A etc.; nullum suffragium *habet* iustitia qu. 27; ab idolis suffragia requirentes qu. 44 (col. 2240); ut...humilitate suffragii quaereret a quo solueretur qu. 79 (75); nullo requisito suffragio qu. 81 (col. 2275); ut nullius lateris esset suffragium qu. 85: (compare *suffragor* (always abl. absol. pres. pcpl. plur.) qu. 14; 120; 124; *suffragator* 61 A).

suggero and **suggestio** are characteristically employed of the actions of the Evil One and those under his influence; dum *mala* suggerit 119 D; ut suggestiones aduersarii reprimere non posset 116 B; ut decipiat hominem suggestionibus *malis* 118 B; diaboli qui per subiectam sibi carnem suggestiones *malas* ingerit animae 121 A; animus...spiritu sancto adiuuante *malas* suggestiones potest spernere 121 B; ut de suggestionibus diaboli non sit sollicitus 122 A; qui suggestioni quae efficitur per carnem obtemperat 124 C etc.: inimicis qui suggesserunt faciendum quod contrarium est qu. 115 (col. 2351); numquid aliquis ad aliquam rem alicui dedito aliud suggerit qu. 115 (col. 2351); suggerit *mala* contra eundem spiritum 2 qu. N.T. 61 (in the same document occurs the opposite:—spiritus enim bona suggerit); officialitas quae per suggestiones *malas* seu bonas nunc plurimum potest qu. 101 (col. 2302). In comparing the

[1] *Auxilium* is frequent; *adiutorium*, which occurs hundreds, perhaps thousands, of times in Augustine, is found only five times in the *Quaestiones*, and a corresponding number of times in the commentaries. It may be recalled that the *comitia* had ceased to meet in the early part of Tiberius' principate (A.D. 14—37). The word *suffragium*, if kept, had to change its meaning.

large number of examples from the commentaries with the few in the *Quaestiones*, it must be observed that most of the examples in the former work occur in one context (in Rom. vii and viii).

superaddo: nunc enumerat omnia mala quae illis superaddita sunt 64 B; superadde adhuc ad caput primi mensis dies septem et decem qu. 95 (col. 2290).

supercaelestis[1]**:** qui supercaelestia cogitant 458 A; quae inuisibilia et supercaelestia sunt qu. 84 pr; diuinum et supercaeleste qu. 95 am.

supergredior: supergredi enim uidetur ipsam iustitiam, cum, quod licet, ut melior sit, non facit caelestis iustitiae imitator 168 D; incipit iterum nox de magnitudine, qua supergreditur diem, minorari usque ad finem quarti temporis qu. 106 (col. 2317).

supra memoro[2]**:** ex supra memorata praescientia dicens 144 D; sicut supra memoraui 145 B; 148 B; 161 B; 198 C; 212 B; 243 B; 266 A; 267 B; 349 C; 389 C; 478 B; qu. 93 (*a*) ex; 2 qu. mixt. 6; hoc dicit quod supra memoraui 157 B; 298 C; 399 D; illos autem quos supra memorauit 159 D; sensus et ratio est, quam supra memoraui 247 B; ita ut...sanctis proficeret supra memoratis 287 D; secundum quod supra memoraui 324 A; in tribulatione Pauli et Sileae, quam supra memoraui 325 B; hos fratres memorat, quos supra 330 B; illa...quae supra memorat 346 D; qui legem per supra memoratos angelos acceperunt 377 A; hoc dixit quod supra memoraui 378 B; lex...haec, quae supra memorauit, fructificat 389 B; hoc est quod supra summatim memoraui 401 B; sicut et supra memoraui 433 B; istos et potiores supra memoratis fratribus ostendit 444 C; hoc est quod supra memorauit 448 C; desiderii supra memorati causas expressit 471 D; quam regni Romani abolitionem superius intellegendam memoraui 482 B; illi...quos supra memorat 515 B; sicut superius memoraui 519 B; cet.; ex parte...qua supra memoraui qu. 82 (*a*); ut supra memorauimus qu. 95 pm; ad decem et nouem supra memoratos qu. 95 pm; sicut supra

[1] Georges 'Eccl.'; Benoist-Goelzer, 'Hier.'

[2] With variations, such as:—sicut in primordio epistulae *memoraui* 175 B; **praememoro* 362 B; *supra* dico, e.g. qu. 82; 2 qu. N.T. 11. Two exx. of *compar.* superius also are noted in Comm., and 1 in Qu.

memoratum est qu. 98 pm; supra memorati Iudaei qu. 102 m; haec omnia supra memorata qu. 107 pm; quae supra memorata sunt qu. 110 pr; hoc est quod superius memorauit qu. 111 pm; principes supra memorati qu. 111 aex; hic sensus est quem supra memoraui qu. 112 pm; Herodes filius supra memorati Herodis 2 qu. N.T. 11; talis est etiam supra memoratorum uersutia qu. 127 ppr; cet.

suscipio[1] (with a personal object), and **susceptus** (subst.), cum suscipit confugientes ad se, iustitia dicitur, quia non suscipere iniquitas est 83 A; aliquanti exierunt cum illis in heremum Aegyptii, quos suscipere iubentur 85 A; generi quod te ut ex malo bonus esses suscepit 158 D; regressi ad fidem suscipientur cum laetitia 161 C; credentes suscipi, ut saluarentur 163 B; dominum nostrum Iesum...suscepturum nos in adfectu caritatis suae 320 A; Titus ab apostolis...susceptus est incircumcisus 366 C; cet.; istos in filios suscepit, quos uidet imitatores esse suae gloriae qu. 44 m; ultro...uenientes ad fidem non suscipere inuidiae erat qu. 73 (77); qui confitentes sibi suscipit peccatores qu. 112; quis enim medicorum non arguat susceptum suum neglegentius se tractantem 293 A; numquid si malae uitae sit aduocatus, contra susceptum eius pronuntiabitur?...hoc est officium aduocati...ut suscepti sui causam peroret...obesse causae suscepti...suscipiuntur a iudice (and *thrice* more in this qu.) qu. 102 ex cet.

tango 'touch on,' 'allude to,' 'strike': tangens et Romanos ut his oboediant quos ad profectum gentium audiunt laborare 188 A; per quod etiam tangit illos quos neque Christus miserat, neque uerum erat quod dicebant 193 C; nunc hos tangit qui in idolio recumbentes putabant non esse peccatum 247 B; quos occulte tangit 344 A; tangit horum contumaciam qui emendari nequiuerant Prol. 2 Cor. (*J. T. S.* IV (Oct. 1902) 90) etc.; nunc ipsa genera peccatorum tangit qu. 111 (col. 2333); ipsum ratio tangebat qu. 113 (col. 2340); auctorem tangit uituperatio qu. 115 (col. 2348); etiam nunc lex tangitur qu. 115 (col. 2355) etc.

[1] Cf. *susceptus* subst. = "patient (of a physician)," 293 A; for which add also Migne XVII 659 A to lexx. In above sense, we have in *susceptione* hominis M. XVII 1197 C.

tegmen: in the phrase, **sub tegmine**[1], used *metaphorically sub tegmine continentiae alias decipiunt 234 A; sub tegmine melioris spei uitam et conuersationem suam mundiali cura et sollicitudine occupantes 236 C; sub tegmine simulacrorum diabolus colitur 249 D; sub tegmine amicitiae lateat hostis qu. 109 pm.

tempus: the phrase **ad tempus:** ad tempus caecatos illos ostendit 159 D; illos quos excaecauit ad tempus 160 A; ad tempus caecitatis obtunsio data est Iudaeis 160 B; qui ad tempus aliquo pacto euadunt 171 B; etsi seruus sit ad tempus...libertus fit domini 232 C; dei uirtute sine elementorum commixtione ad tempus creata 246 C; ut semper imitentur, non ad tempus, sicut pridem 383 B; quamuis enim deus haec dederit, sed ad tempus 401 B cet.; ad tempus non intelligi qu. 51 (*b*); ad tempus uindicet qu. 68; data ad tempus est 2 qu. N.T. 15 cet.

tergiuersatio[2] is a favourite word: examples are:—neque tergiuersatione aliqua poterat tegi crimen 219 B; tergiuersatione hoc agere apostolum adserebant 353 A; atrocissimos hostes et omni tergiuersatione callidos 424 A; alius qui calliditate tergiuersationis rem ueneno plenam *proponit*, ut est Arrius et Fotinus 531 B; ut omnem tergiuersationem cauillationis excludat 88 B; qui per potentiam leges contempserunt aut tergiuersatione inluserunt qu. 4; aliud iterum adsolent sua tergiuersatione *proponere* qu. 97 (col. 2294); ut hac tergiuersatione fructum amputet paenitentiae qu. 102 (col. 2304); quia enim aperte repugnare non audet auctori, tergiuersatione id agit ut et deo iniuriam faciat qu. 115 (col. 2347).

titulo (verb): tam enim deuota uidetur fuisse, ut omnis domus eius signo titulata esset crucis 466 B; hic liber euangelium est quod CATA IOHANNEM titulatur (*Migne* intitulatur) qu. 76 (72): psalmus quinquagensimus titulatus est (*Migne* intitulatus est) qu. 112 (p. 2335).

titulus in the ablative (as in Livy): prior peccans mortem

[1] Cf. apud nos nihil astute nihil *sub *uelamine* 271 B; *quasi sub uelamine* 482 B; diabolus *sub uelamine* latens qu. 27, quae *sub uelamine* erant qu. 72 (76); *quasi sub uelamine* erat intellegentia eius 2 qu. V.T. 3.

[2] The scribes sometimes write as two words, not knowing the existence of *tergiuersor*. *Tergiuersator* appears also, e.g. 481 C; qu. 14.

nobis hereditatis titulo dereliquit 127 C; his duobus titulis subtilitatem fallaciae suae prodidit inprouidus satanas qu. 27; strange examples of the word are: signa temporum certis titulis necessaria qu. 106 (p. 2319, 2); uariis titulis obsequentes 500 C.

torpesco in connexion with the opposite idea, **uigeo** (**uigor**)[1]: ne causā uentris *uigor* euangelicae ueritatis torpesceret 225 C: ne *uigor* euangelicae auctoritatis torpesceret 242 D; ne *uigor* euangelicae potestatis torpesceret 340 C; numquid utile corpus est, cuius quaedam membra uigent, quaedam torpescunt? qu. 127 pr.

***tractare apud se**: quamuis enim sibi uideatur minime reus qui non credidit, quia apud se tractare istud non potuit, ratione tamen conuincitur 72 A; nec enim (deus) tractat apud se quid faciat aut quid non faciat, deliberans an expediat qu. 125 (col. 2375); qui enim audiuit et tractauit apud se et uotum habet peccandi...durum est ignosci ei qu. 126 (col. 2377); gentilis si coeperit infirmari et in ipsa uitae desperatione tractet apud se de fide et spe promissa qu. 126 (col. 2377). Hier. says *tractare secum*.

tradux, employed exactly as in Tertullian, is very common: I merely give some references:—99 B; 119 B *bis*; 140 B; C *bis*; qu. 23; 46; 56 *bis*; 81 *bis*; 83; 106; 108; 110; 112 *bis*; 114 *bis*; 123.

transpungo, peculiarly *used: quia aduersarius eius deuictus potentia Christi non auderet, transpuncta sententia primae mortis, hominem sibi defendere 121 C; qui enim accipit eum (*i.e.* spiritum sanctum) et manet in eius dilectione, transpuncta (*Mig.* transacta[2]) hac uita, pergit in caelos ad eum cuius spiritum habet qu. 123 (col. 2371). The abstract noun **transpunctio,** hitherto known only from an Old Latin version of Esai. xxix 10 ap. Cypr. laps. 33[3], occurs once:—propter spem uitae futurae quam hi idcirco ridendam censent, ut iure dehonestare se et aliena adpetere auida cupiditate uideantur, quasi post hanc transpunctionem nulla sit uita 412 D.

[1] So Sil. in lexx.

[2] This very phrase occurs 304 C (*transacta hac uita*).

[3] The reference is given by Benoist-Goelzer. Georges and others want the word entirely.

triumpho as a transitive verb: ut gloriam diaboli quam de triumphato homine quaesierat inaniret (deus) 103 D; triumphata morte qu. 112: perhaps elsewhere also.

tuitio (some MSS *tutio*): examples are:—calicem mysticum sanguinis *ad* tuitionem corporis et animae nostrae percipimus 256 B; habebit et dilectionem simul et deum eorum *ad* tuitionem perpetuam 356 D; quia post ascensum domini non minorem aut degenerem *ad* tuitionem habituri essent pastorem aut regem qu. 93 (col. 2286); tuitionem etiam deferens deuotis fidei qu. 93 ex; dei nostri tuitio (*Migne* assistentia[1]) imploranda est ad tutelam qu. 115 (col. 2351).

uices: in the phrase **uicem reddere**[2] 'to pay one back,' 'to give tit for tat': iustificati sunt gratis, quia nihil operantes, neque uicem reddentes, sola fide iustificati sunt dono dei 83 C; quando enim uicem malis reddere non uult, pacificus est 169 B; inimicis non solum uicem reddere prohibet dominus per Salomonem, uerum etiam humilitate ad amicitiam prouocare hortatur 170 C; ne uicem reddamus inimicis 170 C; si prouocati ab illo uicem illi non reddamus 170 D; non resistendo ulli neque uicem in malis reddendo, sed semper se subiciendo 217 B; qui ergo pretio emitur, magis seruire debet, ut aliquatenus uicem reddat emptori 233 A; ministris euangelii reddere uicem 290 A; uicem reddere, in quantum possumus, debemus beniuolentiae dei 303 B; ut uicem ei reddant 312 D; non quasi homini uicem reddentes sed deo 313 C; haec est aequalitas ut...reddantur (some MSS *reddatur*) illis uices in futuro 327 D; prouocat eos ad sanctitatem, ut et ipsi audeant reddere uicem sanctis in salutatione 357 A; sibi pro iustis actibus in die iudicii uicem reddere 423 A; ut uel in aliquo illi uicem possit reddere 439 B; senioribus uicem reddentes parentibus 500 B; necesse est reddi illi uicem a suis, sicut et illa reddidit propinquis 503 B; iuxta hoc ergo conuenit uicem nos ex aliqua parte reddere redemptori 513 D; dum uicem non reddit malo...reddere enim uicem iustitia est

[1] I have shown in *Arch. f. lat. Lexikogr.* XIII 2 (1903) p. 286 f. that this is a 'ghost-word.' The part of Gradenwitz *Laterculi Vocum Latinarum* (Leipzig, 1904), containing it, was printed off before my note appeared.

[2] (Once *plur.* uices reddere.) The phrase is in 1 Tim. v 4 mutuam uicem gratiarum reddere parentibus. Cf. quasi *uicem rependentes* ministerio illorum 327 C (so Prop. in lexx.).

qu. 69 ex: si pro hac misericordia *uices (*nom. sing.*) illi aliqua redderetur[1] qu. 83 pr; se illi uicem reddere profiteantur qu. 83 (*a*).

I had at first thought of adding to this chapter an epitome of its results, but have now decided to omit this, as it partakes too much of the nature of a series of arithmetical calculations. Besides, the use of clarendon type and asterisks at once 'insulates' the expressions. The eye of the cursory reader easily fixes itself on the *lemmata*, while the minute investigator of style and language must read the chapter in detail; and for him a summary is unnecessary.

Many will think the chapter too long. It could be made much longer, and profitably longer, if I had made much use of the earlier edition of the *Quaestiones*, contained in manuscripts of the "second" class, and if it were at present possible to undertake several fresh lines of investigation into the language. A valuable criterion of diction in Christian authors is the use of theological and ecclesiastical terms, which in Cyprian's case has been so well carried out by Mr Watson[2]. It is a very great mistake to bundle all the Christian authors together and label them 'eccl.', as lexicographers down to our own time have been too much in the habit of doing. Every writer employs definite expressions according to his taste or school, and avoids other expressions, which are employed by authors of a different taste or school. Many students have forgotten that men, on coming over to Christianity, did not cease to be human beings, but retained the most definite traces of their early environment and education. Nothing could more vividly illustrate this than the likeness between the style of two such men as Apuleius and S. Cyprian. How different their spirit was, it is hardly necessary to say. The Christian author is no mere ecclesiastical machine, turning out so many theological terms with more or less regularity, but a being,

[1] The existence of a nom. sing. is denied by Georges, and Benoist-Goelzer. We have now two examples, if *reddatur* be read in 327 D, as I believe it ought to be. See 'A Nominative for *Vicem*' in the *Classical Review* XVII (1903) Feb. There is a third example in Schol. Iuu. 9, 82 *tantorum beneficiorum quae in te contuli nulla gratia uel* uices *rependitur* (where Jahn wrongly altered to *merces*).

[2] *Studia Biblica* IV (Oxf. 1896), p. 243 ff.

pulsing with thought and feeling, eager to instruct or inspire his fellow men. As often as not, he is a highly educated person, a lawyer like Tertullian, a government official like Ambrose, or a professor like Augustine. To the investigator these authors present different characteristics in the use of theological terms, as they do in temperament, and in language and style generally. Cyprian's hostility to Greek terms has been noted by Mr Watson. This hostility is not shared by our author.

Another test is the spelling and declension of Hebrew or Hebraeo-Greek names. A striking instance in our works is *Moyses*, which in the manuscripts, which we ought to follow, invariably makes the genitive *Moysi* and the accusative *Moysen*.

A third line of investigation would be to take all the particles and discuss their uses thoroughly.

Finally, I am confident that the most remarkable results would be elicited from the compilation of a list of words, found in contemporary authors, which are absent in our author, and yet might well have been used by him. Such, for example, are *absconsus*, *adpropio*[1], *subsano* (Tert. Hil. Hier. Aug. cet.[2]), and *typhus* (Aug.). Ambrose and Jerome seem to be nearest to this author in vocabulary. Some words noted above occur in Jerome.

I may find it possible at some future time to perform some or all of these tasks. Such delicate investigations, however, cannot be carried out until Professor Brewer's edition of the commentaries is published.

[1] For which see Mayor's article *Visio Pauli* in *Journal of Philology* XXII (1894) 196.

[2] Exact references in Mayor, l.c. p. 197.

CHAPTER IV.

IDENTITY OF THOUGHT.

A comparison of the theological positions in the commentaries and *Quaestiones* has satisfied Langen and Harnack among others that the two works proceed from the same pen. I do not propose to enlarge on this subject here. If any further treatment of the question be desired, it must come from one who has made a close study of the theology of the Western Church in the early centuries, and can distinguish the elements which are special to particular Latin writers. In studying the genesis of Ambrosiaster's theology the Latin writers of most importance are perhaps Irenaeus, Tertullian, Pseudo-Clement, Victorinus of Pettau, and Hilary of Poitiers[1].

Two tasks of a much humbler character are attempted here: the first is to show that the favourite texts of Scripture in the one work are as a rule favourites in the other also[2]; the second to prove, by a comparison of the interpretations of various Scripture passages commented on in both works, that these interpretations proceed from one mind. I include some instances of favourite topics of this author, such as 'the second death.'

[1] Father Brewer first pointed out to me the connexion with Hilary and Irenaeus. I regard the expressions *creatura hylica* (qu. 41 (*a*), qu. 106, p. 2318), *hylicae substantiae* (qu. 106, p. 2318), and *hylicae res* (qu. 127, p. 2381) as borrowed from Irenaeus (e.g. i, 1, 9). Our author knew only the translation of Irenaeus, which I believe to be a fourth-century product. For Pseudo-Clement, cf. p. 40. For Tertullian and Victorinus, see pages 38—39. The interpretation of Esai. iv 1 in quaest. 47 is derived from Victorinus (Migne *P. L.* v p. 320 BCD, p. 321 A).

[2] Ezech. iii 19 (21) is a notable exception. It occurs three times in comm., nowhere in quaest.

§ 1. Favourite Texts of Scripture.

Every person who reads Scripture frequently has favourite texts, and the Christian writers of antiquity are no exception to this rule. A very interesting and curious book could be written on this subject. While it is true that there are certain great texts, which occur in all theological authors, there are others which may almost be said to be peculiar to an individual, and which would never have struck any other person in the same way. Augustine, for example, is extremely fond of a verse, which is seldom quoted by others, Wisdom viii 1 *adtingit ergo a fine usque ad finem fortiter, et disponit omnia suauiter*[1]. I venture to think that some verses quoted below are unfamiliar even to attentive students of the Bible. The quotations are given in the order in which they occur in the Septuagint of the Old Testament and the Vulgate of the New. I omit the Gospels of Luke and John, and the Pauline Epistles, quotations from which have been already collected in the second chapter for a different purpose.

Ps. lxxv 2 *notus in Iudaea deus:* quoted 101 A, 146 B; qu. 109 (p. 2329), qu. 111 (p. 2334).

Ps. lxxxiv 12 *ueritas de terra orta est:* quoted 52 B, 397 C; qu. 47 (p. 2248), qu. 109 (p. 2327), qu. 113 (p. 2341).

Eccle. vii 17 *noli iustus esse multum:* quoted 170 A, 414 A; qu. 15 (subject).

Esai. xiv 12 *quo modo cecidit de caelo Lucifer:* quoted 157 B; with the next clause, *qui mane oriebatur* 285 D; qu. 2 (p. 2216).

Esai. xlii 14 *tacui: numquid semper tacebo?* quoted 67 D (note 64); qu. 1 (p. 2215), qu. 68[2].

Esai. lix 20, 21 (Rom. xi 26, 27) *ueniet ex Sion qui eripiat et auertat impietatem ab (a, ex) Iacob; et hoc illis (erit) a me testamentum, cum abstulero peccata eorum:* quoted 50 C, 148 C, 378 B; qu. 44 (p. 2240, without *cum—eorum*), qu. 47 (p. 2248, only down to *Iacob*), qu. 76 (*a*) (p. 2271, as far as *Iacob*).

Hier. xxxviii (xxxi) 31, 32 (Hebr. viii 8, 9) *ecce uenient dies (dies uenient), dicit dominus, et consummabo domui Israhel et domui Iuda testamentum nouum, non secundum (testamentum) quod disposui (dedi) patribus illorum (eorum) in die qua adprehendi manum illorum, ut educerem illos de terra Aegypti, quia ipsi non permanserunt in testamento meo, et ego neglexi eos, dicit dominus:* quoted 85 C (as far as *eorum*), 148 B (a paraphrase, *dabo illis testamentum nouum, non quale dedi patribus illorum*), 270 B (as far as the

[1] Peiper has not recognised this quotation in Boet. *cons. phil.* p. 84, vv. 59, 60.

[2] For Esai. liii 9, see p. 153.

first *illorum*) ; qu. 44 (p. 2240), qu. 60 (exactly the same paraphrase as in 148 B).

Bar. iii 36—38 *hic deus noster: non aestimabitur alter ad eum. Hic adinuenit omnem uiam scientiae, et dedit eam Iacob puero suo, et Israhel dilecto sibi. Post haec in terra uisus est, et inter homines conuersatus est:* quoted 134 B (*hic deus noster* only), 319 C (with the omission of *non aestimabitur—dilecto sibi*, the other two parts being given apart from another) ; qu. 97 § 4 (p. 2292) (portions twice).

Ezech. xviii 4 (or 20) *anima quae peccauerit (peccat) ipsa morietur:* quoted 107 A, 127 A, 343 A ; qu. 14 (p. 2225).

Ezech. xviii 32 (cf. xxxiii 11) *nolo mortem morientis, quantum ut reuertatur et uiuat:* quoted 298 D ; qu. 102 § 2 (p. 2304), § 4 (p. 2306), qu. 111 (p. 2333).

Ezech. xx 25 *propterea ego dedi illis praecepta non bona et iustificationes, in quibus non uiuent in eis:* quoted 148 B (without *ego* and *et—in eis*) ; qu. 44 (p. 2242, without *propterea*), 2 qu. N.T. 46 (without *propterea ego* and *et—in eis*), *cf.* 2 qu. V.T. 10.

Ezech. xxxiii 12 *iusto nihil proderit iustitia eius, in qua die exerrauerit, et iniusto nihil oberit iniustitia sua, cum se conuerterit:* quoted 178 C (a paraphrase, *iustitia iusti non proficiet, si errauerit:* this quotation and the surrounding words are wanting in the older Bodleian MS) ; qu. 102 § 9 (p. 2309) (in the form *iustitia iusti non liberabit eum, in die qua errauerit, et iniquitas iniusti non nocebit ei, cum conuerterit se*), qu. 126 (p. 2376).

Matth. xii 31, 32 *omnia peccata et blasphemia remittentur hominibus ; spiritus autem sancti blasphemia non remittetur hominibus, et qui dixerit uerbum contra filium hominis, remittetur ei ; qui (cumque) autem peccauerit in spiritum sanctum, non remittetur ei, neque hic neque in futuro (futurum)* : quoted 227 B (omitting *spiritus autem—remittetur ei*) ; qu. 102 § 3 (omitting *omnia —remittetur ei* : *cf.* v. 55 of same section), qu. 102 § 6 (omitting *omnia—hominibus* (first) and *quicumque—futuro*).

Act. iv 12 *nec enim aliud datum est nomen sub caelo, in quo oporteat saluos fieri:* quoted 51 A, (with *non est aliud nomen datum*) 88 C ; 2 qu. N.T. 26 (exactly as 88 C, with the addition of *nos* before *saluos*).

Act. xv 10 *quid inponitis iugum super ceruicem fratrum, quod neque nos neque patres nostri potuerunt portare?* quoted 148 C, *quid inponitis iugum fratribus, quod neque patres nostri neque nos potuimus portare?* 374 A, *quid inponitis iugum supra ceruicem (ceruices 527 D) fratrum, quod neque patres nostri neque nos potuimus portare?* 401 B, 527 D ; 2 qu. V.T. 10 (same as 148 C, except that it has *potuimus*), 2 qu. N.T. 46 (p. 2402—3) (same as 401 B, except that it has *super*). The author's Bible doubtless had the verse as it appears in 2 qu. N.T. 46.

1 Petr. v 8 *sobrii estote et uigilate, quia aduersarius noster diabolus circu(m)it fremens sicut leo quaerens quem deuoret:* quoted 228 D (*ecce diabolus ut leo rugiens circuit quaerens quem deuoret*), 525 A (without *sobrii estote et uigilate*) ; qu. 2 (p. 2217) (with *uester* for *noster*, and *tamquam leo rugiens*

circuit), qu. 102 § 5 (p. 2306) (with *uigilate sobrii estote, uester, fremens sicut leo circuit*).

1 Ioh. iii 2 *scimus quia cum apparuerit similes ei erimus* quoted 105 c, 129 c, 304 c; qu. 105 (p. 2316) (*cum enim apparuerit, similes ei erimus*), qu. 106 (p. 2320).

Apoc. ii 24 *ignoratis altitudinem satanae* is quoted correctly in its context in qu. 102 § 8 (p. 2309), but elsewhere it appears as a question, *an ignoratis altitudinem satanae?* The references are 137 A; qu. 27 (p. 2231), qu. 31 (p. 2232). Some of the old editors, thinking the quotation was from 2 Cor. ii 11, poured scorn on the author's inaccuracy.

Apoc. xiii 8 *agnus qui occisus est a constitutione mundi:* quoted 101 B, 275 B; qu. 3 (p. 2219).

I have little doubt that, given complete indexes, the number of such quotations could be increased.

§ 2. Interpretations of Scripture.

'Man is the image of God, but not woman' is the opinion advanced in quaest. 21, 24, 45, 106, and also on 1 Cor. xi 5–7 (253 B), xiv 34 (273 B) and on Col. iii 8–11 (460)[1]. The argument is the same in both works. The Pauline statements that the husband is head of the wife, and must not veil his head because he is the image of God, while the wife must veil hers, are taken as proofs of the inferiority of the latter and the impossibility of her likeness to God. That man and wife are, nevertheless, of one substance is not denied.

The dignity of the priests' order has nothing to do with the moral character of the holder of the office, but is transmitted by and depends on ordination only. Of this Caiaphas is a standing example, who, though an evil man, prophesied. Compare quaest. 11, 101 (p. 2302), 102 (§§ 12, 13), 109, etc., with in 1 Cor. xii 28 and in 1 Cor. xiii 2. In quaest. 46 and in 1 Cor. xiii 2 the parallel case of Balaam is brought forward, and he is in both places called *ariolus*.

The treatment of the text, 2 Cor. v 21 *eum qui non nouerat peccatum* (*peccatum nesciebat*), *pro nobis peccatum fecit*, is the same in the commentary on that place and in Question 78 (74). Christ

[1] For the passages, see Morin, *Revue d'Hist. et de Litt. Relig.* iv (1899) 104 f.

was made sin in two ways, first, by the incarnation, by which He received a body of sinful flesh, and second, by being offered for sin. In both passages the analogy with the *hostia* of the Old Dispensation, which was called 'sin,' is mentioned. The same verse, Esai. liii 9 *qui peccatum non fecit, nec inuentus est dolus in ore eius,* is brought into connexion in both places:—

In 2 Cor. v 21

homo ergo factus est Christus causa peccati, quem non tangebat sors *neque dignitas* nasci hominem...*et quoniam oblatus est pro peccatis, non inmerito* peccatum factus dicitur, quia et hostia in lege, quae pro peccatis offerebatur, peccatum nuncupabatur.

Qu. 78 (74)

primum enim fecit illum peccatum, dum incarnari illum uoluit, ut quem sors non tangebat *de peccatrice carne corpus acciperet, per quod* dicitur factus peccatum. *Deinde dum* offert *illum* pro peccatis, *fecit illum peccatum.* Hostia enim in lege pro peccatis oblata peccatum nuncupabatur.

Qu. 74 (*b*).

hic utique quem sors *et condicio* non tangebat hominem procreare...peccatum *ergo* factus dicitur, *quia* secundum legem hostia, quae pro peccatis offerebatur, peccatum nuncupabatur.

At the close of the first version of quaest. 78 (74) and in the middle of the second, Gal. iii 13 *factus pro nobis maledictum* appears with comments, and on turning to the treatment of this verse in the commentaries we find it identical.

The attack on Novatian, quaest. 102, on which Harnack has written a long and valuable paper[1], is paralleled in the commentary on 2 Tim. ii 20, *in magnu autem domo non solum sunt uasa aurea et argentea, uerum (sed) et lignea et fictilia, et quaedam quidem in honorem, quaedam uero in contumeliam.* Novatian, says our author, interprets the 'great house' not as the Church, but as the whole universe, which contains men of different types (519 A; qu. 102 § 9 p. 2309f). Hymenaeus and Philetus, as well as the church of Corinth, are mentioned in illustration in both passages. The reason for this interpretation by Novatian is that he regards his own church as the pure church, composed of perfect Christians

[1] *Abhandlungen Alexander von Oettingen gewidmet* (München, 1898) pp. 54—93 'Der pseudoaugustinische Traktat Contra Nouatianum.'

only. One sentence appears in almost exactly the same words in both works: thus

Tract. in 2 Tim. ii 20 (519 c)	Quaest. 102 § 9 (p. 2310)
nam in una domo omnes sub uno sunt nomine: uno *enim* domini sui nomine censentur *omnes*. mundus autem diuersae professionis continet homines, ita ut dispares profiteantur se habere deos et dominos.	in una enim domo omnes sub uno sunt nomine; *quamuis enim moribus diuersi sint*, uno *tamen* domini sui nomine censentur *in professione*[1]. mundus autem *hic* diuersae professionis continet homines, ita ut dispares profiteantur se habere *et* deos et dominos.

1 Cor. v 12, *quo mihi de his, qui foris sunt, iudicare?* is quoted in both contexts.

There is another parallel in the note on 2 Cor. xii 21, a verse which is quoted in quaest. 102. In the commentary and in the Question the writer shows that the certain inference from this text that some Corinthians repented of fornication disposes of Novatian's doctrine that it is an unpardonable sin.

In both books it is stated that the name *Hebrei* is to be derived from *Abraham*, and not from *Heber*, as some say. Naturally, the name would be *Habruei*, but the letter was changed for euphony, just as *medidie* became *meridie* (in Phil. iii 5; qu. 108, *cf.* qu. 44, p. 2242). The treatment in qu. 108 is the longest, but is in perfect agreement with the first.

A remarkable, perhaps unique, interpretation of Psalm xxiii (xxiv), verses 7 and 9, is found in both works. Not only is the interpretation wonderful, but the text on which it is based is equally so, and is perhaps worthy of a place in Dr Swete's list[2]. It reads in this author, and not uncommonly in authors, such as Hilary of Poitiers, who employ an old Latin version, thus: *tollite portas principis uestri; et eleuamini, portae aeternales*[3]. Here are the comments:—*dicitur ergo his principibus, qui in errore sunt in caelestibus, siue ministris eius in terris, ut auferant portas* principis sui, id est diaboli, *de mentibus suis, per quas* multorum deorum *adserendorum* error *intrauit.* Sunt *enim* temporales, *quia omnis*

[1] *professio* is the ἀπογραφή, the returns made at the census.

[2] *An Introduction to the Old Testament in Greek* (Cambr. 1900) p. 330 ff.

[3] The MSS of course confuse this with the ordinary reading.

fallacia tempore clauditur : 'iter enim impiorum peribit' (Ps. i 6). *Ut autem aeternas portas eleuent, hortante iustitia ammonentur, quia ueritas in sempiterna saecula perseuerat* (in Eph. iii 10 p. 404 C, D) : *hi ergo dicunt ad principes et potestates aduersus quas nobis conluctationem esse dicit apostolus* (Eph. vi 12), *ut tollant portas* principis sui, id est diaboli, *qui est princeps principum in errore constitutorum, per quas itur in gehennam. Hae portae perfidia est et fallacia idolatriae...illae autem* portae *quas dixi perfidiam esse et fallaciam idolorum*, temporales sunt, *quia omne mendacium non permanet....Docentur ergo ut tollant portas* principis sui, *id est, ut amoto* multorum deorum errore *unius dei fides introducatur in Christo...tollendas dicit fallaces portas diaboli subtilitate conpositas* (qu. 111 p. 2334). The same passage is quoted, with the same interpretation, also in qu. 113 (p. 2341).

The 'second death' holds an important place in the author's system of thought. The expression appears in Scripture only in the Apocalypse, a favourite book with the writer, who is chiliastic in tendency[1], and greatly interested in 'the last things.' The longest Scripture quotation he makes is from the second chapter of the Apocalypse[2]. The definitions of the expression 'second death' are alike in both works. Compare in Rom. v 12 (97 B) *mors autem separatio animae a corpore est. Est et alia mors, quae 'secunda' dicitur, in gehenna, quam non in peccato Adae patimur, sed eius occasione propriis peccatis adquiritur ; a qua boni inmunes sunt tantum, quod in inferno erant, sed superiore, quasi in libera*[3], *qui in caelos ascendere non poterant*, etc., with qu. 47 (p. 2248) *per fidem enim peccatis ablutus et a morte secunda, quae ex sententia data in Adam homines apud inferos detinebat, alienus, nullo detinente, pergit in paradisum dei patris*[4].

The author twice compares the treatment meted out to Saul and David after committing sin, in a note on Rom. ix 16, and in

[1] See *Journal of Theological Studies* v (1904) pp. 611—615.

[2] Chap. ii 17—26 in qu. 102 § 8.

[3] This is short for *libera custodia*, and is as yet unparalleled.

[4] See also 51 A, 92 C, 99 C, 102 A, 106 D, 110 A, B, 112 A, C, 116 B, 120 C, 122 A, 127 C, 164 B, 298 A, 313 B, 371 D, 448 D, 459 C ; qu. 34, 78 (74), 115 pr (Langen, diss. p. 22).

Question 18. The subject is referred to in almost identical terms in both works: *Saul peccans, cum petisset ueniam, nec accepit; contra Dauid peccans et ignosci sibi postulans ueniam consecutus est* (in Rom. ix 16, p. 143 A); *quare Saul peccans petit orari pro se ut ignosceretur ei, et inpetrare non potuit, Dauid autem peccans postulauit et ueniam consecutus est?* (qu. 18 title).

In the note on Rom. xii 13 *hospitalitatem sectantes*, Abraham is mentioned as one who obeyed this command. In quaest. 109 (p. 2325) Abraham is said to have obeyed the Saviour's commands before they were proclaimed. This clause is then quoted[1], and it is suggested that the Apostle learned the value of hospitality from Abraham, who exercised it conspicuously.

Pascha is defined as *immolatio*, not *transitus*, as some[2] think, both in 1 Cor. v 7, and in quaest. 96, where the question is asked whether the Greeks are to be followed in interpreting the word as *transitus*, or not.

Practically the same words are used about manna in 1 Cor. x 3, 4 and in quaest. 20: *hic ergo panis aut cibus* non mundi lege *creatus est* commixtione elementorum, sed *de super uenit* spiritali *ratione prouisus*...ideo *autem* 'angelorum panis' dictus est, quia *ea* uirtute creatus est qua angelica natura subsistit *et uiuit* (qu. 20); *manna et aquam...dicit* spiritalia, *quia* non mundi lege *parata sunt*, sed *dei uirtute sine* elementorum commixtione *ad tempus creata*... ideo *et* 'panis angelorum' dictus est, quia uirtute qua angeli subsistunt creatus est (in 1 Cor. x 3, 4).

The same account of the original relation between *episcopi* and *presbyteri* is given in both works: (in 1 Tim. iii 8–10) *post episcopatum tamen diaconatus ordinationem subicit. quare, nisi quia episcopi et presbyteri una ordinatio est? uterque enim* sacerdos *est, sed* episcopus primus *est, ut omnis episcopus sit presbyter, non tamen omnis presbyter episcopus: hic enim* episcopus *est, qui* inter presbyteros primus *est. Denique* Timotheum presbyterum ordinatum *significat, sed quia ante se alterum non habebat, episcopus erat* etc.: (qu. 101) presbyterum autem intellegi episcopum probat Paulus apostolus, *cum quando* Timotheum quem ordinauit pres-

[1] Not Hebr. xiii 2, as the editors wrongly suppose.

[2] Jerome (*epist.* 78 § 2) holds with 'the Greeks.'

byterum *instruit qualem debeat creare episcopum. Quid est enim* episcopus *nisi* primus presbyter, *hoc est summus* sacerdos?[1]

The frequent mention of the impurity of contact with the *mustela* is common to both writings, as may be seen from the occurrences of the word given in Chapter III, page 119.

Such are some of the striking parallelisms between the two works, and the only relation between them to which they point is that of common authorship[2].

[1] Cf. chap. i, pages 37, 38. I append a translation of this passage: 'after dealing with the office of bishop, he treats also the appointment of deacons. Why does he do this, except that the bishop and presbyter have one position? For both are *sacerdotes*, but the bishop is the chief: so that every bishop is a presbyter, but not every presbyter a bishop: for *he* is a bishop, who is first among the presbyters. So he indicates that Timothy had been ordained a presbyter, but, because he had no one higher in rank, he was a bishop?' See also in Eph. iv 11 quoted and translated in chap. v, section 4. The Editor would compare with this account the system obtaining in the monastery church of Nitria: *ὀκτὼ δὲ ἀφηγούμενοι πρεσβύτεροι ταύτης τῆς ἐκκλησίας εἰσίν, ἐν ᾗ μέχρις οὗ ζῇ ὁ πρῶτος πρεσβύτερος ἄλλος οὐδεὶς προσφέρει, οὐχ ὁμιλεῖ, οὐ δικάζει, ἀλλ' ἡσύχως αὐτῷ προσκαθέζονται μόνον* Palladius, *Hist. Laus.* VII (p. 26, 9 of Dom Butler's edition, in *Texts and Studies*, Vol. VI, No. 2 (1904)). Surely this passage offers an important analogy to what must have been the usual polity in the Early Church.

[2] The identity of opinion in both works is dealt with excellently and at great length by Langen, Diss. pp. 19—31.

PART II

THE AUTHOR AND HIS BIBLICAL TEXT.

CHAPTER V.

THE AUTHOR AND HIS WORKS.

§ 1. *His Name.* If all ancient authors had imbedded their names in their works as Thucydides did, the problems of the authorship of ancient books would be sensibly reduced in number. As it is, the fact that the title of a work written on papyrus was usually inscribed on a slip pasted on to the edge of the roll, and therefore easily detached, has contributed to our ignorance of the actual or complete names of many early writers. Whether our author's works were first issued in the roll form is a matter of doubt, as he belongs to the transition period, in which the *codex* was first becoming really popular. However that may be, as it appears that nearly all the author's books were issued anonymously, it will be seen that we have here a problem of no ordinary difficulty. How are we to recover the name of an author, who lived in a particularly prolific literary age, when he, or destiny, seems to have done everything possible to conceal it?

Clearly our first step is to see what the manuscripts can tell us, if anything. But here we are met by a diversity of testimony. The oldest manuscript of the commentaries, *Casinensis* of the sixth century, gives in the subscriptions merely the titles of the epistles, and presumably the author's name was wanting also in the general heading to the book, which is now lost. All the other manuscripts of the commentaries, in number about seventy, attribute them to S. Ambrosius, with or without the designation *episcopus Mediolanensis*[1]. Even where this designation is wanting, it is certain that the great Ambrose of Milan is meant, as no

[1] One attributes that on Romans to Origen (Arnold in Herzog-Hauck's *Real-Encyclopädie*, s. v. Ambrosiaster).

other Ambrosius of that period is known[1]. If, as is highly probable, our commentaries are the commentaries attributed to Ambrose which Cassiodorus had heard of but had never seen, then we have authority coeval with *Casinensis* for the attribution to Ambrose. There is another ascription, that to Hilarius. This occurs in no existing MS of any book of the commentaries, but the celebrated reference by S. Augustine to *sanctus Hilarius*[2], showing that the commentary on Romans existed under that name in Africa in the early part of the fifth century, has recently been reinforced by evidence proving that the same part of the commentaries was known in Ireland, probably about the same period, and certainly as early as the eighth century, under the same name[3]. That this title was solely due to the reference in S. Augustine seems hardly possible, even in a country where Pelagianism was a great force and the Anti-Pelagian treatises of S. Augustine were doubtless well known. The Irish authorities as yet noted are three, the Book of Armagh[4], the codex Paulinus Wirziburgensis[5] and the old catalogue of the library of the Irish foundation of Bobbio[6]. The first contains the preface to the Romans, giving it as 'Hilarii'; the second cites amongst its numerous Latin glosses on Romans some from '*hl*', '*hel*'[7], which are found on examination to be Ambrosiaster[8]; the third gives 'Hilarii super Romanos' as one of its books.

[1] M. Schanz, *Geschichte der römischen Litteratur* IV 1 (München 1904), has no other.

[2] See page 3.

[3] See H. Zimmer, *Pelagius in Irland* (Berl. 1901) pp. 117—120 and Mr C. H. Turner's review in *Journal of Theol. Studies* IV (1901—2) p. 132 ff. This is not the only trace of connexion between Africa and Ireland. The gospel codex *k*, which gives a pure African text, was brought by S. Columban to Bobbio. (Cf. *Old-Latin Biblical Texts, No. II* p. xii ff.)

[4] S. Berger, *Les Préfaces Jointes aux Livres de la Bible dans les Manuscrits de la Vulgate* (Paris, 1902), p. 26. I owe this reference to Dean Robinson.

[5] See Stokes and Strachan, *Thesaurus Palaeohibernicus* I (Cambr. Press), p. xxiii ff, 503.

[6] G. Becker, *Catalogi Bibliothecarum Antiqui*, No. 32, p. 65.

[7] The contraction *hel* is due to the spelling *helairius*, which is found, e.g., in the Old Irish MS, Rawlinson B. 512 of the Bodleian Library (l. 138), edited by Kuno Meyer in *Anecdota Oxoniensia*, Mediæval and Modern Series, part VIII (Oxford: 1894).

[8] I take the passages from Zimmer's book, p. 117. They are Rom. i 22, 24; ii 5, 7, 8 (four times), 9, 13, 14; iii 2; iv 6, 17, 20; ix 6, 24; x 8, 12; xi 12, 24; xii 6; xiv 5, 16, 17, 18; xv 4; xvi 14. At each of these verses occurs a citation

This triple testimony belongs to the eighth and ninth centuries, but in view of the fact that the Irish church occupied a position of isolation for a long period before that time, we may treat it as though it belonged to the fifth century. We thus reach the conclusion that in two widely removed countries of the Western world, Africa and Ireland, the commentary on Romans was known as the work of Hilary in the fifth century. It appears then that neither Augustine nor the Irish had anything but the commentary on Romans, which is often found by itself still, and sometimes occurs in conjunction with commentaries of Remigius on other epistles[1]. It seems likely that copies of Romans with the name Hilarius attached represent the first edition of that commentary. If the later edition (or editions) was issued anonymously, the discrepancy of title in the manuscript tradition would be sufficiently explained.

The titles of the manuscripts of the *Quaestiones* need not detain us. There is no MS which gives the work as anonymous, but the tone of the one hundred and first Question DE IACTANTIA ROMANORVM LEVITARVM makes it practically certain that, whether it was issued by itself or in the whole collection only, there can have been no name attached to it. The case of Question 109 DE MELCHISEDECH, if, as is generally believed, it is identical with the *uolumen* ἀνώνυμον ἀδέσποτον which Euangelus sent to Jerome in 398[2], points the same way. It is highly probable that all three editions of the *Quaestiones* were issued anonymously, and that their attribution to S. Augustine is a guess of the fifth or sixth century. The ascription of a section of the third edition to Ambrose in the Görres MS may be due to knowledge of the commentaries on the part of the scribe, but is in any case an absurdity, as both sections are clearly from the same pen[3]. Alcuin used the *Quaes-*

from Ambrosiaster after the symbol *hel* or *hl*. There are altogether 29 quotations from Ambrosiaster among the glosses of this codex. Rom. ii 10 has *hl* attached by mistake for *pl* (i.e. *pilagius* or *pelagius*); contrariwise *pl* is attached instead of *hl* at Rom. i 19, 23, 24, 25, 28; ii 21; iii 8; iii 19 (cf. Zimmer pp. 127 f). Ambrosiaster is also the origin of many other explanations, where the glossator has forgotten to add the name.

[1] As in Paris and Florentine MSS which I have examined.

[2] Hier. Ep. 73.

[3] See page 19.

tiones for his own *Quaestiones in Genesim*, but, in the ancient manner, without any acknowledgement whatsoever[1]. The work was also known in Ireland, as an extract from Question 79 (75) is found on one page of the 11th century manuscript of the Irish *Liber Hymnorum*. There also no author's name is mentioned[2].

I have attempted to claim a recently published fragment on the twenty-fourth chapter of Matthew for this author. This piece is found in the celebrated eighth century MS at Milan, which contains the Muratorian Canon, and, like the other pieces comprised in that strange farrago, is anonymous[3].

Dr Sedlmayer has unearthed from a notable Vienna papyrus a fragment *contra Arrianos*, which is in proximity to Hilary of Poitiers on the Trinity, and which Dom Morin has with great probability claimed for our author. The mistaken combination would be explained, if our author's name were also Hilary[4].

The name Hilary was not so rare as the names Augustine and Ambrose, and it seems probable that one of 'Ambrosiaster's' names was Hilarius. I shall return to this point later in the chapter, where I seek to follow Dom Morin in identifying the author. The alternative is to consider Hilary to be Hilary of Poitiers, and to regard this ascription as on the same plane with those to Ambrose and Augustine. If this view be adopted, then the first edition of Romans was very possibly issued before the death of Hilary of Poitiers, which took place in 367.

§ 2. *His Locality.* When the study of late Latin authors has reached such an advanced stage of development that the peculiarities of each are well known, then and then only will it be possible to tell from a writer's style the district to which he belonged or the school in which he was trained. Some features pointed out in the third chapter will doubtless have some value in the attempt to reach a definite conclusion as to the part of the Roman world in which our author spent his youth. But they can have little

1 See the foot-notes in the Benedictine edition to quu. 4, 5, 11, 12, 13.

2 See the Irish *Liber Hymnorum* I (London: 1898) p. 42.

3 The fragment was published by G. Mercati in *Studi e Testi*, No. 11 (Roma 1903) and C. H. Turner in the *Journal of Theological Studies*, Vol. V (1904) 218—241; see my paper in the latter, pp. 608—621.

4 *Sitzungsberichte der Kais. Akademie der Wissenschaften in Wien* (phil.-hist. Kl.), Band CXLVI (1903) II, 21 pp.

value until the texts and styles of all surviving writings of his period are known. By far the majority of distinguished Roman writers were not natives of Rome, or even of Italy, if we except the great plain in the North. The great Christian authors of the second half of the fourth century came from other countries than Italy: Prudentius was of Spain, Hilary and Ambrose of Gaul, Jerome of Dalmatia. Ambrosiaster very likely came from one of these regions.

This, however, is little more than conjecture. What we do know is that the writer lived in Rome at the time of writing the *Quaestiones*, and probably the commentaries also. In question 115, which, like question 114, breathes a thoroughly Roman atmosphere, he expressly says 'hic *enim* in urbe Roma, quae sacratissima appellatur, *licet mulieribus uiros suos dimittere*' (page 2349). A natural misinterpretation of the force of the adjective *Romanus* led the Benedictine editor to the conclusion that Questions 55 and 84 must have been written somewhere else. The passage in quaest. 55 is as follows: *in regno itaque agens Romano, non nisi* VIII *Kal. Apr. pati debuit, quando aequinoctium habent* Romani; that in 84 reads thus: *in primo mense, in quo aequinoctium habent* Romani, sicuti et nos, *ea ipsa obseruatio ab his custoditur.* It is quite clear from the context that *Romans* here are contrasted, not with inhabitants of other cities, but with Christians, who had adopted an equinox at the Council of Nicaea: 'Romans' is in fact practically the equivalent of pagans[1]. The acquaintance with church affairs in Rome, shown in Questions 101 and 102, 'on the boastfulness of the Roman deacons' and 'against Novatian' respectively, proves conclusively that the author was resident there. The former sheds a gleam of light on the conduct of these influential and self-important officials; the latter shows us that even in the second half of the fourth century Catholic Christianity had to defend itself against the followers of Novatian in Rome. The author several times lays stress on the primacy of S. Peter, as for example in quaest. 127 (p. 2384), where it is mentioned that marrying and begetting of children did not hinder Peter from holding the chief position among the apostles. The manner in which he speaks of Damasus, and the liturgical usages to which

[1] Dom Morin, *Revue d'Hist. et de Litt. Relig.* XV (1899) p. 99 f.

he refers lead to the same conclusion[1]. Other references in quaest. 115 point to Rome: *quaedam mulier fuit in* urbe Roma *quam constat undecim maritos habuisse* (p. 2357), and *ne quis de* urbe Roma *transuolet in Hispaniam* (p. 2349). On page 2357 there is a tale of a girl in Campania, who became a man and was afterwards conveyed to Rome. On the same page we hear of a man, named Samsucius, whose devotion to the emperor Constantius led him to pretend insanity for thirty years, that he might by his oddities afford that prince a relaxation from cares of state. It has been shown by M. Franz Cumont in a learned paper that the references to definite pagan worships in Question 114, CONTRA PAGANOS, are specially applicable to Rome[2].

§ 3. *His Date.* The period at which our author wrote is happily easy to determine. In the commentary on First Timothy, chapter iii, verse 15, we find the words: *ut cum totus mundus dei sit*, ecclesia *tamen domus eius dicatur*, cuius hodie rector est Damasus: which show that he wrote that book between the years 366 and 384. As some, however, have regarded the sentence as an interpolation, it will not be out of place to gather together all the other indications of date, which show conclusively that the author wrote at that period. The sentence just quoted does seem strange at first, and its character rather supports the idea of interpolation. But this view is not supported by any manuscript which has been examined, and most scholars who have recently written on Ambrosiaster regard the sentence as genuine. It must be explained as either an assertion of the supremacy of the Roman Church over the Catholic Church, an idea which probably arose in Damasus' time and is quite in accordance with Ambrosiaster's thought; or we must regard it as an emphatic statement of the side the writer took in the quarrel between the party of Damasus and the party of Ursinus. If the latter be the correct view, it entirely disposes of the claim of Isaac the ex-Jew to be considered the author, as he was one of the most strenuous opponents of Damasus: nor is the former view much more favourable to the idea.

The author mentions the emperors Nero, Vespasian, Domitian,

[1] Dom Morin, *l.c.*, p. 99.

[2] *Revue d'Hist. et de Litt. Relig.* VIII (1903) p. 417 ff.

Diocletian, Constantine, Constantius[1] and Julian, but no later emperor. Julian's reign lasted from 355 to 363, and the manner in which the author speaks of him shows that he had been dead some little time. The following are the references to him: *mysterium iniquitatis a Nerone coeptum est, qui zelo idolorum apostolos interfecit, instigante patre suo diabolo, usque ad Diocletianum* et nouissime Iulianum, qui arte quadam et subtilitate coeptam persecutionem implere non potuit, quia desuper concessum non fuerat (482 B.C.); *quantum autem possit timor legis, hinc aduertamus. Ante* Iuliani edictum *mulieres uiros suos dimittere nequibant. Accepta autem potestate, coeperunt facere quod prius facere non poterant: coeperunt enim cottidie licenter uiros suos dimittere* (quaest. 115, foot of p. 2348)[2].

That Julian's reign was not long past is shown by the vivid way in which the author speaks of persecution in both works. Compare (in 2 Thess. i 6—9, 480 B.C.): *quid tam 'iustum' quam ut hi, qui* in saeculo deprimunt bonos et extorres eos faciunt persecutionibus, *in futuro eadem patiantur quae faciunt; illi autem ut sint in requie cum ceteris sanctis, qui de magna tribulatione uenientes regnum accipient aeternum in aduentu domini de caelo, cum coeperit uenire cum caelesti exercitu suo et ministro igne* ad dandam uindictam in paganos...et Iudaeos: with (quaest. 102 § 12 p. 2311) *nonne* persecutor odio Christiani nominis professionem persequitur, *non conuersationem? primo in loco sciens hoc proficere religioni, cum confitemur esse nos Christianos,* sacrilegus[3] confitentibus nobis credit *quod non uult audire quia odit...ut quid* a sacrilego persecutionem patior, si non hoc sum quod tu (Nouatiane) es? *nam si hoc de me profiterer quod tu de me dicis,* persecutionem non paterer. There is another passage similar in view in § 6 of the same Question, where we read: tortus huius modi et exungulatus *hoc uerum esse dicit quod sequitur* (p. 2307), of the courageous Christian. In another place he speaks of the rest from persecution which

[1] Nero 482 B; Vespasian *quaest.* 44; Domitian *quaest.* 76 (72); Diocletian 482 B; 521 B; Constantine *quaest.* 115 (p. 2357); Constantius *quaest.* 115 (p. 2357, MSS). For (Constantine's) edict abolishing crucifixion, see page 29.

[2] Cumont is certainly wrong in supposing that the jurisconsult Salvius Iulianus is meant here (*Revue d'Hist. et de Litt. Relig.* VIII (1903) 419 f.).

[3] Sacrilegus = *hereticus* (*cf.* Mommsen, *Römisches Strafrecht*, p. 600, n. 4), and includes of course pagans and Jews.

Christians enjoyed at the time: *in hoc tempore quo pax est* (in Rom. xii 11). The contrast between the quotations admirably suits the period of Valentinian (364—375), who held paganism and Christianity in equal esteem[1]. We see from Question 35, *hinc est unde gentilem, in potestate tamen positum, honorificamus, licet ipse indignus sit, qui dei ordinem tenens gratias agit diabolo,* that the Christians of the day were alive to the possibility that another pagan emperor might come to the throne. The fear of persecution was continually before their minds.

In Question 44 (p. 2243) it is stated that about three hundred years have passed since the destruction of Jerusalem. This brings us to about 370. In Question 115 (p. 2353) there is another means of dating: *quid dicemus de Pannonia, quae sic erasa est ut remedium habere non possit?* These words refer to the devastation of that province by the Quadi and Sarmatae in 374, and must have been written shortly after the disaster, as Pannonia recovered and flourished[2]. A rather interesting point of contact seems to me to connect this Question in time with the commentary on 1 Timothy. The first words of quaest. 115 are: *Nihil tam contrarium Christiano quam si arti matheseos adhibeat curam.* This turn of expression is exactly reproduced only in two passages, as far as I have observed, of the commentaries, and these are in close proximity to one another. They are in 1 Tim. v 14, 15 (505 B) *nihil enim tam periculosum est quam si professioni gesta repugnent*; in 1 Tim. vi 9, 10 (509 B) *nihil tam asperum tamque perniciosum est quam si ecclesiasticus...diuitiis huius saeculi studeat.* In view of the extreme rarity of this form in the author, and the way that such phrases have of repeating themselves when an author is in a particular condition of mind, it seems not altogether fanciful to suggest that quaest. 115 and the latter part of the commentary on 1 Timothy were written about the same time. Doubtless quaest. 115 was written first, as the author would take special care with the beginning of such an important pamphlet. An argument like this will appeal very differently to different minds.

[1] Cf. Harnack *Abhandlungen Oettingen*, p. 76.

[2] Cf. Morin, *l.c.*, p. 99; Cumont, *l.c.*, p. 419 f, who shows that Jerome, *Chron.* 2388, uses the same word *eradere* of the same disaster, and holds that it is derived from some official document.

Question 114 has also a voice in settling the date. In it paganism appears in full force. The worship of Bacchus, the Great Mother, Isis, Mithras, and many other divinities is openly carried on. Cumont points out that such a state of affairs is an impossibility after the year 382, in which Gratian confiscated the property of the temples and deprived the pagan priests of their privileges[1]. He rightly remarks that if this blow had fallen on them before the time of writing, the author could not have failed to refer to it. For the best commentary on Questions 114 and 115, dealing with the paganism and astrology of the period, I must refer the reader to Cumont's article.

In quaest. 125 we find another indication of date. There Eusebius of Vercelli, who died in 371, is referred to in such a way that he must have been dead at the time. The words are ADVERSVS EVSEBIVM. *Memini me in quodam libello* Eusebii quondam, egregii in reliquis uiri[2], *legisse quia nec spiritus sanctus sciat mysterium natiuitatis domini nostri Iesu Christi, et admiror* tantae doctrinae uirum *hanc maculam spiritui sancto inflixisse.* The bald reference to Eusebius points to an Eusebius, who would be well-known to his Latin readers. This can be none other than Eusebius of Vercelli. It looks, too, as if the author were resident in North Italy when this Question was composed. The works of Eusebius may, however, have been known in Rome also.

Question 101 contains the name of a Roman deacon, veiled by the phrase *quidam igitur qui nomen habet falsi dei.* In all the editions the sentence reads *quidam igitur qui nomen habet Falcidii.* It is strange how such a sentence could have passed muster for over four centuries. In the eyes of some people anything is good enough to be Christian Latin. Yet the writer shows clearly by the use of the word *quidam* that he could give the name of the Roman deacon if he chose, and from friendship does not so choose. For the correct reading, now recovered from the manuscripts, is *falsi dei,* and Falcidius must disappear from the biographical

[1] Cumont, *l.c.*, p. 421, where he refers to Wissowa, *Religion und Kultus der Römer*, p. 88.

[2] This is the correct punctuation, as *quondam* belongs to *legisse.* Morin, *Revue Bénédictine*, xx (1903), p. 115, n. 2, seems to punctuate at *Eusebii.*

dictionaries. Who is then to take his place? I think it probable that the deacon meant is Concordius, who is known to have lived at that time[1]; then the divinity alluded to will be Concordia. This Concordius, according to the *Liber Pontificalis*, was a deacon of Rome and one of the prosecutors of Damasus on a capital charge. He was expelled from the Church by a synod of bishops about the end of 378, or the beginning of 379. If he be the person meant by Ambrosiaster, then Question 101 was written before 378.

This very Question 101 is largely drawn upon by Jerome in his 146th letter (to Evangelus). No one can read the two compositions without seeing that there is a close connexion between them. Vallarsi considered the Question to have been composed from the letter; I hold the contrary view. Both tracts are an answer to a statement of *quidam*, that deacons are superior to priests. In Jerome he is simply *quidam*: in Ambrosiaster he is *quidam qui nomen habet falsi dei*. It is unfortunate that the date of the letter is uncertain. If it be really, as is believed, addressed to the same Evangelus as epist. 73, the only other addressed to a person of that name, and if we may state it as a probability that both were written about the same time, this brings us down to 398, and is sufficient proof of the side on which the borrowing lay. But the contents themselves, I think, support my view. The Question is nearly twice as long as the letter. There is an air of reality about the circumstances of the Question which is not shared by the letter. The writer of the Question is obviously in close touch with the circumstances, is anxious to obey the dictates of affection, and is afraid of censure. Jerome is interested only in the false teaching, and plunges at once into his argument. The proof-texts of Scripture are not the same in both cases. Ambrosiaster has more from the Old Testament than Jerome; Jerome more from the New than Ambrosiaster. But the order of topics corresponds. Both works mention that originally presbyters and bishops were the same. About the middle of each piece the peculiar position of the church of Alexandria is mentioned. Ambrosiaster refers to the fact that in Alexandria and throughout

[1] Duchesne, *Liber Pontificalis*, I, p. 212. *Cf.* M. Rade, *Damasus, Bischof von Rom* (Freib. i. B. 1882), p. 33, n. 2.

Egypt, when a bishop is not present, a presbyter confirms[1]. Jerome, who was well acquainted with the church of Alexandria, mentions that from the time of Mark the Evangelist till the episcopate of Heraclas and Dionysius the presbyters always chose one from among themselves and appointed him bishop. Compare also the following passages, given in the order of their occurrence:—

AMBROSIASTER	JEROME
istos (diaconos), quibus consessus in ecclesia datus est minime...nunc enim uidemus diaconos temere quod sacerdotum est agere per conuiuia, et in oratione id uelle ut respondeatur illis, cum istud solis liceat sacerdotibus... tollunt hoc de memoria adsiduae stationes domesticae et officialitas...'sed testimonio,' inquit, 'diaconi fit presbyter'...imperator,· ut imperator appareat, ordinatur obsequio militari.	*presbyteri ... episcopum nominabant, quo modo si exercitus imperatorem faciat...sed dices 'quo modo Romae ad testimonium diaconi presbyter ordinatur?'...in ecclesia Romae presbyteri sedent et stant diaconi, licet...inter presbyteros, absente episcopo, sedere diaconum uiderim et in domesticis conuiuiis benedictiones presbyteris dare.*

There is enough originality in Jerome's letter to save his credit, but he has clearly borrowed argument and illustration from his predecessor.

The title of the set of gospels in our author's Bible was EVANGELIVM, and the special headings were CATA MATHEVM, CATA MARCVM, CATA LVCAN (in 1 Cor. XV 5) and CATA IOHANNEM (quaest. 76 (72)). It was the same in Cyprian's Bible, and probably universally in the West till the publication of the Vulgate Gospels, which bore SECVNDVM in their superscriptions. The CATA is still found in Filastrius (383), Etheria's *Peregrinatio*, and the commentary on Mark attributed to Jerome.

The author's attitude to the *Epistle to the Hebrews* is also characteristic of the same period, but not of a later period. Just at the time he wrote, the West was coming into line with the East in regarding the epistle as Pauline. Ambrosiaster showed sufficiently that he agreed with earlier Western opinion by writing commentaries on the thirteen letters which were accepted everywhere as Paul's, and leaving out the Epistle to the Hebrews. But he also shows it in the few instances where he has occasion to

[1] Jerome confines this to bishops (*dial. contra Lucifer*. 9).

quote the epistle. As the editors have garbled the evidence of the *Quaestiones* on this point, and modern books on the Canon have suffered in consequence[1], it will be necessary to present the evidence in full. In the commentary on 2 Tim. i 3—5, we find the words: *nam simili modo et in epistula ad Hebreos scriptum est quia Leui, qui decimas accepit, decimas dedit Melchisedech*[2], *etc.* (p. 512 D). In Question 109 there are several passages which must be mentioned, one of them because it has been falsely referred to the Epistle to the Hebrews, when it undoubtedly belongs to the Epistle to the Romans. The first is on page 2325, first line: *Legimus in libro geneseos de Melchisedech, simili modo et in epistula data ad Hebreos, quia* obuiauit, *inquit*, Melchisedech sacerdos dei summi Abrahae reuertenti a caede regum, et protulit panes et uinum, et obtulit ei, et benedixit eum, dicens; Benedictus es, Abraham, a deo excelso, qui fecit caelum et terram, qui tradidit inimicos tuos sub manus tuas[3]. *Et ut significaret quid intellegendus esset idem Melchisedech, adiecit*: sine dubio enim, *ait*, quod minimum est a meliore benedicitur[4]. The next reference is not to Hebrews, but to Romans. The Benedictines were very careful and full in their references, but here they have taken over a reference from earlier editors without verification. On page 2325, line 64, occur the words *apostolus* hospitalitatem sectandam *magnopere docet*, and this is referred by them to Hebr. xiii 2, which reads in the Vulgate *hospitalitatem nolite obliuisci*. The reference, however, is certainly to Rom. xii 13, which in Ambrosiaster and the Vulgate reads *hospitalitatem sectantes*; and *apostolus* is quite in place. The third passage is on page 2327, lines 11 and 19, where the first part of Hebr. vii 1–4 is introduced by the words *si legem respiciamus, plurima adhuc et potiora dicentur*, and the second by the

[1] Cf. Jülicher's *Einleitung in das Neue Testament* (3—4te Aufl., 1901), page 427; Zahn's *Grundriss der Geschichte des Neutestamentlichen Kanons* (2te Aufl., 1904), page 68, note 10.

[2] Cf. Hebr. vii 9.

[3] As far as *regum* this is Hebr. vii 1: *et protulit panes et uinum* is Gen. xiv 18; *et obtulit ei*, is not Scripture at all; the rest is Gen. xiv. 19, 20, with the omission of one clause, καὶ εὐλογητὸς ὁ θεὸς ὁ ὕψιστος, before *qui tradidit*.

[4] Hebr. vii 7. The editors have altered the reading of the MSS in five places in this short passage, the most serious alteration being the insertion of *apostolus* before *significaret*.

words *adiecit* and *ait*, without any subject expressed. So is it throughout the rest of the Question. Where quotations are made, they are introduced by *dicit, adiecit, addit, ait,* but without *apostolus* or any other subject. Ambrosiaster is consistent throughout. To him the author of the epistle was unknown; and this is another indication that he wrote at the period for which I have argued.

It cannot be a mere accident that the five questions sent by Damasus to Jerome for solution in the year 384 are all included in the first twelve of Ambrosiaster's collection. Further, the order in which they are given is, with one exception, the same in both collections. Here are the titles:—

AMBROSIASTER	DAMASUS-HIERONYMUS
quaest. VI. Si Lamech occidit Cain, sicut putatur? (The verse quoted opposite is referred to in the body of the Question.)	quaest. I. Quid sibi uult quod in Genesi scriptum est *omnis, qui occiderit Cain, septem uindictas exsoluet?*
VIIII. Si omnia deus bona fecit, et bona ualde, quid est ut dicat ad Noe *de mundis et inmundis induc tecum in arcam*, cum in absoluto sit inmundum bonum dici non posse? (Acts x 14 is quoted in the body of the Question.)	II. Si omnia deus fecit bona ualde, quare Noe de mundis et inmundis animalibus praecepit, cum inmundum nihil bonum esse possit? et in nouo testamento post uisionem, quae Petro fuerat ostensa, dicenti *absit, domine, a me, quoniam commune et inmundum numquam introiuit in os meum*, uox de caelo responderit *quod deus mundauit, tu commune ne dixeris?*
X. Cum deus dicat ad Abraham de filiis Israhel, quod quarta progenie exituri essent de potestate Aegyptiorum, quid est ut e contra lex dicat *quinta progenie exierunt filii Israhel de terra Aegypti?* Valde uidetur contrarium.	III. Cur deus loquitur ad Abraham, quod quarta progenie filii Israhel essent de Aegypto reuersuri (*v.l.* exituri), et postea Moyses scribit *quinta autem progenie exierunt filii Israhel de terra Aegypti?* quod utique nisi exponatur, uidetur esse contrarium.
XII. Quare Abraham fidei suae signum circumcisionem accepit?	IV. Cur Abraham fidei suae signum in circumcisione suscepit[1]?
XI. Si uiri iusti uoluntas bona est, quid est ut Isaac, non Esau quem uoluit, sed Iacob quem noluit benedixit?	V. Cur Isaac, uir iustus et deo carus, non illi cui uoluit, sed cui noluit deceptus errore benedixit?

[1] Read *accepit:* the confusion is exampled elsewhere.

That the connexion between the two sets is close no one will deny. Observe the substance, language and order of the questions. The two which are omitted; namely the seventh and the eighth, dealing respectively with the contents of the tablets of the law and the brightness of Moses' face when he was descending the Mount, are of an obviously simpler nature. Most of the first five are of a very general character, and would have tempted Jerome to be more discursive than Damasus desired. It seems to me clear that what happened was this. Damasus had taken up the *Quaestiones* after publication, perhaps some years after publication, as men who are full of official business can never keep pace with current literature, and had been dissatisfied with the answers to some of the Questions. He therefore writes to Jerome, whom he obviously regarded as his most learned friend, to get better answers. This happened in the year 384, according to Vallarsi's dating; and it can be inferred that the *Quaestiones* was published before that date.

Further considerations which indicate the same period are the theology, which Langen has shown to be pre-Augustinian[1], the pre-Vulgate biblical text quoted, and the language, which has many analogies with that of Jerome. The heretics named are especially the Arians, the Photinians, the Marcionists, who are dying out (499 B), and the Manichaeans. These were the chief enemies of the Catholic Church in the period 370 to 380[2].

It is clear from the considerations advanced that the professed date of Ambrosiaster is correct, and that he wrote between 366 and 382 A.D.

§ 4. *His Status and Circumstances.* It will be well to begin by trying to decide whether the author was a clergyman or a layman, as his works supply some material for arriving at a conclusion. A failure to consider this question is conspicuous, perhaps pardonably so, among all investigators prior to Dom Morin.

If the author was, like nearly all the ancient Christian writers,

[1] See my fourth chapter, p. 157, n. 2.

[2] Harnack, *Abhandlungen Oettingen*, pp. 55, 73, gives other arguments as to date, which I have omitted, as I cannot estimate their value.

a clergyman, it is likely that he was bishop, presbyter, or deacon[1]. He cannot have been a Roman deacon, because no deacon could have written against his fellows in the contemptuous and scathing manner of the 101st Question. His references to bishops, '*our* bishops,' lead one to suppose that he did not himself hold the office: see in 1 Tim. ii 1–4 *haec regula ecclesiastica est, tradita a magistro gentium, qua utuntur* sacerdotes[2] nostri, *ut pro omnibus supplicent*, etc., a most important passage historically: quaest. 109 (p. 2325) nostri sacerdotes *super multos cottidie nomen domini et uerba benedictionis inponunt, sed in paucis effectus est. Est iterum quando meliores se benedicunt*: and a little before in the same tractate, *hic Melchisedech non utique sic benedixisse intellegitur Abraham, sicut faciunt* homines sacerdotes, where *homines sacerdotes* is not to be interpreted contemptuously, but with reference to the context in the Epistle to the Hebrews[3]. There is nothing to *prove* that he was not a presbyter. An important passage in this connexion is in Eph. iv 11, 12, of which I append a translation to the text. *Ideo non per omnia conueniunt scripta apostoli ordinationi quae nunc in ecclesia est, quia haec inter ipsa primordia sunt scripta. Nam et Timotheum, presbyterum a se creatum, episcopum uocat, quia primi presbyteri episcopi appellabantur, ut, recedente eo, sequens ei succederet. Denique apud Aegyptum presbyteri consignant, si praesens non sit episcopus. Sed quia coeperunt sequentes presbyteri indigni inueniri ad primatus tenendos, inmutata est ratio, prospiciente consilio*[4] *ut non ordo sed meritum*

[1] The minor officials *lector, exorcista*, etc., need not be taken into account.

[2] The best account known to me of the meaning of *sacerdos* in Christian Latin is contained in Professor E. W. Watson's article in *Studia Biblica et Ecclesiastica* IV (Oxford, 1896), p. 258, n. 1, where he states that 'Jerome is the earliest writer to waver in the matter' of the use of *sacerdos*. The name of our author should be substituted for Jerome here. *Sacerdos* is clearly 'bishop' in 1 Tim. ii 1—4 above, but it is equally clearly 'presbyter,' 'priest,' in 1 Tim. iii 8—10 *uterque* (i.e. bishop and presbyter) sacerdos *est, sed episcopus* primus est (see chap. iv, p. 157, and also in this chapter, p. 175 f.). The author uses for 'bishop' also *episcopus, rector* and *praepositus*.

[3] Hebr. vii 8 *et hic quidem decimas* morientes homines *accipiunt*, or vii 28 *lex enim* homines *constituit* sacerdotes *infirmitatem habentes*.

[4] The printed texts read *concilio*, which was referred by Lightfoot to the *Apostolical Constitutions*. The MSS are, I think, unanimous for *consilio*, and it is less likely that *concilio* would be altered by scribes, than the reverse.

crearet episcopum, multorum sacerdotum iudicio constitutum, ne indignus temere usurparet et esset multis scandalum. 'The Apostle's writings are not in entire agreement with the system now existing in the Church: for they were written at the very beginning of all things. For example, Timothy also, whom he had himself made a presbyter, he calls a bishop (for the presbyters first in rank were named bishops), so that on his retirement the next in order might succeed him in that office. Indeed in Egypt presbyters confirm, if no bishop is present[1]. But because the presbyters next in rank came to be found unworthy to take the first places [i.e. to succeed as bishops], a change of method was made, the design of which was to secure that merit and not rank should make a bishop, who should be appointed by the judgment of a number of priests [i.e. bishops, at least three in number] that no unworthy person might lightly take office and be a stumbling-block to many.'

His attitude to clerical matters is that of an external observer and critic. He thrice uses *ecclesiasticus* as a substantive, for 'an ecclesiastic,' a use of which the dictionaries have no example (see page 104). He is the earliest authority for the expression *ius ecclesiasticum*, which means 'the power of the Church to forgive sins[2].' He certainly did not coin the expression, and the reason why he and the Donatist bishop Macrobius are the only two men of their time who employ it, is probably the fact that both occupied a position apart from the Catholic clergy. Those in the inner circle would naturally use the pronominal adjective of the first person in referring to this power. It seems, then, that the author was not a clergyman. There is, however, a difficulty to be removed. Questions 100 and 116—121 are notes for sermons, and qu. 120 commences in a way which seems to make it certain that the author was a bishop: *congruum est, fratres carissimi*...dei sacer-

[1] This is introduced as bearing out the idea that, if 'primus presbyter' is not to the fore, 'sequens' naturally takes his place.

[2] I have used here Harnack's paper in the *Sitzungsberichte der kgl. preuss. Akad. der Wissenschaften* for 1903, pp. 212—226, entitled '*Ius ecclesiasticum.* Eine Untersuchung über den Ursprung des Begriffes.' See also his *Die pseudocyprianische Traktat* De Singularitate Clericorum, ein Werk des Donatistischen Bischofs Macrobius in Rom (Texte u. Untersuchungen, Neue Folge IX 3, Leipsic 1903). The references are [Aug.] quaest. 93; 102 *bis*: [Cypr.] de singularitate clericorum 36 (p. 212, 1 Hartel).

dotem et praepositum plebis Christi *exhortari populum, sub cura sua positum, in doctrina sana*. This sentence, however, cannot outweigh the strong evidence against it. We shall probably be right in regarding these Questions, either, with Dom Morin, as mere notes for sermons, jotted down for the sake of some bishop who was lacking in eloquence[1], or as exercises not actually intended for delivery. It may be noted that none of these Questions are in the earliest edition, and some will in consequence say that the author became a bishop before he died.

Having, then, concluded that the author was a layman, we must seek for some indications of his position in society, his circumstances generally, and his experience of life. These must be gathered from his works, and, being inferences with an unavoidable subjectivity behind them, may be regarded as fanciful. Such as they are, it seems best to put them before the reader, as they have not been lightly arrived at.

First, then, it seems clear that the writer was of high birth. We have seen that he draws many illustrations from the emperor, the highest state officials, and the senatorial order. He has a keen sense of what it is fitting for them to do. He has a respect for dignities and class distinctions, such as aristocrats and their servants alone have. He knows exactly the duties of all officials, the significance of the *programma* of a prefect of the praetorian guard, the dress of various classes[2], etc. Such illustrations come readily to him, and the only way to explain their occurrence in this author, marking him out among the Latin Christian authors, is to suppose that he himself was a senator and a high official in the state. References to his works need not be repeated here[3]. His Question 124, that any particular sin differs (in sinfulness) according to the wealth or poverty of the person who commits it, is in complete harmony with this view. In it he compares

[1] *Revue Bénédictine* xx (1903) 118.

[2] In quaest. 46 (p. 2246) he mentions that in his day deacons, as well as bishops, wore the dalmatic. I have not found this reference in any book on church antiquities.

[3] See chap. i, pp. 23—31; *cf.* Morin *Rev. Béned.* xx (1903) 119—121, who gives one or two passages omitted by me. See also Cumont *Rev. d'Hist. et de Litt. Relig.* VIII (1903) 437—440.

throughout the sinfulness of the chief sins, when committed by a rich and a poor man respectively, and shows much fairness and knowledge of the world. Compare quaest. 16 *uiri sublimis culpa graue peccatum est. Quanto enim persona eius suspicabilis est, tanto magis leue delictum eius acerbissimum est peccatum*[1], and quaest. 102, § 3 (p. 2304) '*sed forte regi ignosci oportuit, humilibus autem ignosci non debet?*' *cum magis potentioribus difficilius ignoscendum uideatur. Deus enim personam hominis non accipit. Quanto enim quis sublimior est, tanto magis, licet leue peccatum eius, graue est crimen*, etc. In quaest. 5 we are told that every one knows that the greatest gifts ought to be offered to a person in high position. The same thought is repeated in quaest. 103, *qui offert potentiori, munera electa offert.* I may add that only a man of high position could have been on terms of friendship with the Roman deacons[2], of whom there were only seven, and these persons of great consequence.

References in both works seem to point to the fact that he had also held high administrative posts. I have noted in the first chapter references to definite statutes, the *iudices*, etc. I have not there, or elsewhere, given any collection of examples of his legal terminology. It is not highly technical in character, but exactly such as an experienced administrator would employ. It runs the whole gamut of legal procedure, from the decision of the magistrate that there is a case up to the declaration of the verdict, and even to the revision of a judgment and the recall of a sentence. A few examples are *accusationem recipere, reum tenere, reum constituere, iudiciis offerre, accusare, causam dicere, professio, suscipere* (cf. p. 143), *iudicare, rennuere causam, pronuntiare, sententiam dare, absoluere, damnare, iudicium retractare, sententiam reuocare, ignoscere.* Tertullian's language forms a good contrast. He was a trained lawyer, and employs terms such as are never found in our author, *circumscribere, elogium, libripens*, etc. Cumont's conclusion is 'Les passages ici rassemblés, et dont le nombre pourrait être aisément accru, me paraissent démontrer suffisamment que l'auteur des *Quaestiones* et des *Commentaria* avait fait des études

[1] The editions have corrupted the text badly here.

[2] Quaest. 101 pr.

juridiques. Peut-être même avait-il occupé quelque fonction publique avant de devenir un docteur de l'Église.'

The author's interest in law and custom is remarkable; though, as far as I know, one modern author alone has given him his rightful place in the history of thought[1]. Ambrosiaster was not a mere mechanical administrator of the law as he found it, but one who had thought much on what was behind law in general. He was profoundly interested, for example, in natural law and its relation to the Mosaic Law, in the origins of Roman law, in the problem of slavery, in the position of the emperor and his special relation to God, in the question of woman's relation to man. Church law has no less interest for him. The proper method of blessing and its significance[2], the procedure followed in becoming a member of the Church[3], the *ius ecclesiasticum*, for the mention of which he is the earliest authority[4], and the rules governing the conduct of ecclesiastics: for example, they must be celibate, and must not engage in trade or business of any kind[5]. He has a consciousness of the fitting place, not only of the secular magistrate, but of each order in the Church. His whole attitude marks him out as an experienced administrator, with no slavish worship of the letter of the law, but an independent mind, which can discern the eternal principles implicit in it. His position is that of a highly placed and detached observer and critic.

As we might expect in the case of an experienced governor, there are indications that he had travelled much. These indications consist of both general and particular statements. Of the former, there occurs in Rom. v 5 the following: *Peregrini hominis improbabilis origo in terra aliena est*, an illustration which would hardly drop from any one who had not travelled, or had much to do with foreigners in court. A number of countries are referred to in the *Quaestiones*, especially the 115th. Such are

[1] Rev. A. J. Carlyle in *A History of Mediaeval Political Theory in the West*, vol. I (London: 1903). See the excellent index, *s.v.* Ambrosiaster.

[2] Quaest. 109.

[3] Quaest. 102, near the end.

[4] Cf. Harnack, *Abhandlungen Oettingen*, p. 73 f. See also page 176.

[5] Quaest. 127, near the end; in 1 Tim. iii 8—10, where the correct reading is *negotia tamen publica turpia uilia non habentes*, etc.

Africa, the country of the Garamantes, Egypt, Sicily, Sardinia, Spain, Gaul, Pannonia, Asia, Phrygia, Persia, besides Italy, and in it Etruria and Campania. It is true that most of them are mentioned only once, but they are mentioned with a naturalness and ease quite alien to erudition and perfectly suited to personal experience of them. The recital of the riding customs of ancient countries (quaest. 115, p. 2350) is, I think, unique. A man who had lived all his life in one country would not draw so many or so ready illustrations from other countries. Africa and Egypt are oftener mentioned than the others, and it seems very likely that the author had lived in these countries. The passages referring to Egypt have already been given in the first chapter. Their character can best be explained by the supposition that the writer had held office there, had been perhaps either *dux* or *comes Aegypti*.

It was perhaps in Egypt that he acquired his remarkable interest in the Jews. He is interested primarily in the Mosaic Law, but also in the customs of the synagogue and the position of Jews in the world. Though, like some other great Christian authors of the West, he wrote his polemic against the Jews[1], there is throughout his works a breadth of attitude towards them that has nothing either patronising or hostile in it. He has in his commentaries the insight to see where Jews are meant, though not explicitly mentioned, and shows from time to time that customs of the synagogue have been taken over by the Church. Several pages could be filled with quotations from his works, in which the Jews are spoken of, but here I must confine myself to the most striking and important. 'The name *Iudaei* dates from the time of Judas Maccabeus (58 B, quaest. 81),' but is derived from Judah, son of Jacob (73 A). Romans, chapter vii, verse 5, *uitia peccatorum quae per legem ostenduntur* is meant as an attack on the Jews, he tells us; and chap. ix, verses 11 to 13, also refer to them: cf. verse 28, 'Not a few of the Jews have believed' (155 A). He wrongly confines the reference in the 'altar' of First Corinthians ix 13 to Jews, while the 'temples' refer to Gentiles. Chapter ix of First Corinthians, verse 20, 'to them that are under the law,' is

[1] Quaest. 44.

referred to the Samaritans: *legem enim solam accipiunt, id est, quinque libros Moysi.* The 'doctores' of 1 Cor. xii 28 are defined as those *qui in ecclesia litteris et lectionibus retinendis pueros imbuebant more synagogae.* Verses 30 and 31 of the fourteenth chapter, 'but if a revelation be made to another sitting by, let the first keep silence, for ye all can prophesy one by one, that all may learn, and all may be comforted,' are explained thus: *haec traditio synagogae est quam nos uult sectari, quia Christianis quidem scribit, sed ex gentibus factis, non ex Iudaeis, ut sedentes disputent, seniores de dignitate in cathedris, sequentes in subselliis, nouissimi in pauimento super mattas.* Some of the false apostles of 2 Cor. ii 17 had a zeal for the *traditio Iudaica.* The Jews are specially meant in 2 Cor. iv 3, 'them that are perishing.' The analysis of Galatians, chap. iii 17, is an excellent example of the author's skill, but is much too long for quotation. The 'magistri' of Eph. iv 11 are defined in the same way as the 'doctores' of 1 Cor. xiii 28, with an alternative meaning: *magistri uero exorcistae sunt, quia in ecclesia ipsi conpescunt et uerberant inquietos, siue hi qui lectionibus imbuendos infantes solebant imbuere, sicut mos Iudaeorum est, quorum traditio ad nos transitum fecit, quae per neglegentiam obsoleuit.* In Philippians i 13 he strangely interprets *praetorium* as *Iudaismus,* and the *ceteri omnes* as the *uniuersae ecclesiae gentium.* His interest in the derivation of *Hebrei* has been already referred to in the fourth chapter (page 154). On Col. ii 16—17 he says that the Jews attack the Christians for disdaining to have anything to do with their festivals, or their new moons, or their sabbaths, which they pass in ease, banqueting and luxury. The opponents of Paul's gospel in 1 Tim. i 3—4 are Jews, who will perhaps give the people a delight in the *fabulis, quas narrare consueti sunt Iudaei de generatione suarum originum, de Abraham Isaac et ceteris patriarchis, et de circumcisione et his quae postea tradita sunt a Moyse.* On Titus iii 9 occurs this passage: *fabulosa autem non lex, sed heresis est, quantum ad tempus illud pertinet Iudaeorum, dum quidam eorum sibi uindicarent praerogatiuam originem patriarcharum, qui de matrimoniis orti sunt, cum ex hoc nullum meritum sit apud deum. quidam uero urceorum et ceterorum uasorum baptisma et sanguinem mustelae magna cura expiandum, et quia ideo Moysi sepultura abscondita est, ne a magis excitaretur; quod si uerum esset, et ceterorum sanctorum abscondenda fuerat sepultura: et quia Solomon adiutorio daemoniorum templum aedificauit, in quo opere ingens multitudo laborauit, quid tam fabulosum?* Perhaps our author had read some of the Jewish apocryphal books[1]. On First Timothy, chapter v, verse 1, he remarks *apud omnes utique gentiles honorabilis est senectus, unde et synagoga et postea ecclesia seniores habuit, quorum sine consilio nihil agebatur in ecclesia. Quod qua neglegentia obsoleuerit nescio, nisi forte doctorum* (the bishops, of course) *desidia aut magis superbia, dum soli uolunt aliquid uideri.* His interpretation of the 'cloke' passage (2 Tim. iv 13) is so important and interesting, that it must be quoted in full. "Paenulam quam reliqui Troade apud Carpum ueniens adfer, et libros, maxime autem membranas." *Apostolus natura Iudaeus fuit, nec quicquam habuit alienum. unde ergo illi paenulam? sed quia erat a Tarso, quos constat in societatem Romanorum receptos, ut de cetero ciues appellarentur Romani*[2], *idcirco necesse est eos et curiam habere, in quam more Romanorum paenulati conueniant. quicumque enim illo tempore cum muneribus obuiam exissent Romanis, inmunitate perpetua donati, ciues Romani et fratres eorum nuncupabantur, teste eodem apostolo. Potest ergo fieri, ut, si non suam, quia totum se legi dederat, patris sui haberet paenulam.* From this passage it seems clear either that the *toga* had been given up as the official dress of Roman senators, or that paenula had changed its name, and come to mean toga. It was at one time deemed unbecoming for a senator to wear the *paenula*[3]. We hear of pleaders in court wearing it in late times, but this is the only passage, seemingly, where it appears as the official dress of a senator. The author knows perfectly well what he is speaking about, and we may safely conclude that about 375 A.D. senators wore the *paenula* in the senate. In Question 127 (p. 2379), in speaking of the blessing of created things by their Creator, he says: *quo modo ergo dici potest male fieri aut non licere, quod ex*

[1] See also chapter i, p. 40.

[2] Some MSS put *ciues* before *Romani*. It is better, probably, to leave it out altogether, *cf.* qu. 107 m. *nam quia Romani regnum habent, Hispani et Galli et Afri et ceteri subiecti eis sub eorum nomine Romani uocantur.*

[3] Gellius *Noct. Att.* 13, 22 (21), § 1.

dei benedictione et ipso fauente augmentum facit? cuius rei traditio et in synagoga mansit et nunc in ecclesia celebratur, ut dei creatura sub dei benedictione iungatur; non utique per praesumptionem, quia ab ipso auctore data est forma. In quaest. 115 ppr the reason is asked why, in spite of the great multitude of the Jews throughout the whole world, there is never a case among them of conversion to paganism, while there are—though rarely—cases of conversion to Judaism among the pagans. In quaest. 82 (*a*) the rudiments of the world, under which the Jews are in bondage (Gal. iv 3), are thus described: *obseruant enim neomenias, sabbata, pecorum sacrificia, initio mensis septimi tuba canere, quinto decimo autem die mensis septimi medullas palmarum et ramos ligni spissos et ramos salicis circumferre et in casis septem diebus habitare*[1]. These passages will suffice to show the author's great interest in Judaism[2], and may close this section of our chapter.

§ 5. *Suggestion as to his Identity.* Dom Morin, after long study of this author and his period, has suggested the name of Decimius Hilarianus Hilarius as that of the author. This suggestion is, I think, the best that has been made, and those who differ from it will have to read the works of the author carefully in the forthcoming Vienna editions before coming to a conclusion on the subject. Much light will be thrown on the surroundings of the problem, if specialists in all branches will be kind enough to give the author their attention, and report what they find in him of interest in their departments. At present, one like myself, who seeks to treat the subject as a whole, is continually checked by inability to find an answer to many questions. But when the students of liturgies, creeds, Church organisation, Biblical criticism, the Christian literature of the first four centuries, and the Latin language, have studied him, then the problem will be easier. I hope I have shown that authorities on the general history of the period cannot safely neglect our author, though Tillemont alone seems to have read him.

Decimius Hilarianus Hilarius, who is commemorated in an inscription[3] of Bedja (anciently Vaga) in the Roman province of

[1] This passage is omitted in quaest. 82, which I regard as the later form.

[2] See Dom Morin *Revue d'Hist. et de Litt. Relig.* IV (1899) 111—114.

[3] *Corp. Inscr. Lat.* VIII 1219.

Africa, which corresponded in extent to the region which is now Tunis, was a Christian layman, who flourished in the second half of the fourth century and the early years of the fifth. He was proconsul of Africa in 377; a law was addressed to him as *praefectus urbi* (*Romae*) by the emperors Gratian, Valentinian and Theodosius on February 19th, 383[1]; in 396 he was *praefectus praetorio Italiae*, and had four laws addressed to him by the emperors Arcadius and Honorius during his tenure of that office, on March 19th[2], May 30th[3], June 16th[4], and December 28th[5], respectively. He held the office of *praefectus urbi* (*Romae*) a second time in 408, as we know from the fact that a law was addressed to him by the emperors Arcadius and Honorius on January 15th of that year[6]. Letters 38—42 of the third book of his pagan contemporary Symmachus are addressed to him. These letters belong probably to the year 397.

In connexion with this family Professor Otto Seeck, of Greifswald, has made what may be regarded as a certain conjecture. Jerome in his 54th letter, section 6, addressing a Roman lady of the name of Furia, uses the following words: *pater tuus, quem ego honoris causa* (*i.e.* with all respect) *nomino, non quia consularis et patricius, sed quia Christianus est,* impleat nomen suum, laetetur *filiam genuisse Christo, non saeculo.* Furia's father, then, must have had a name connected etymologically with the idea of rejoicing. The name cannot have been Gaudentius, as Jerome would then have used *gaudeat,* such plays upon words being in good taste in ancient literature. Again, no important person of the name of Laetus is known in that period. The word *hilaresco,* apart from its comparative rarity, is rather too long to

[1] *Codex Theodosianus* v 1, 3 IMPPP. GRAT. VALENTIN. ET THEOD. AAA. AD HILARIVM P.V. The corresponding passage of Justinian gives HILARIANVM.

[2] *Cod. Theod.* XIII 11, 7 IMPP. ARCAD. ET HONOR. AA. HILARIANO. It is doubtful whether this be the same person.

[3] *Cod. Theod.* VII 4, 22 IMPP. ARCAD. ET HONOR. AA. HILARIO P.P.

[4] *Cod. Theod.* VII 4, 23 ,, ,, ,, ,, ,, ,, ,,

[5] *Cod. Theod.* XI 21, 2 ,, ,, ,, ,, ,, HILARIO.

[6] *Cod. Theod.* XIIII 4, 8 ,, ,, ,, ,, ,, HILARIO P.V. I mention this law because Morin has done so, but no doubt we ought with *Theodosiani Libri* XVI ed. Mommsen and Meyer, I (Berol. dated 1905, really 1904) to regard this Hilarius as a different person.

express just the kind of point that is wanted. Yet there can be little doubt that the name *Hilarius* is meant. His rank, his age, and his religion suit the situation perfectly. We know that the wife of Hilarius had been Titiana, deceased at the time (about 394). She was the daughter or sister of Furius Maecius Gracchus, who, when prefect of Rome in 376—377, showed his zeal for Christianity in a very striking manner by destroying a *speleum* or cave, devoted to the worship of Mithras. The three mentions of the *speleum* in our author[1] acquire new meaning in this light. Other particulars of the family are also known.

It will be seen that there is much to recommend this hypothesis, but its weakness must be pointed out. There is not a scrap of evidence to prove that this Hilarius wrote books. Of course there is also no evidence to show that he did not. Further, the suggestion is difficult to reconcile with the silence of Jerome. Neither in the *De Viris Inlustribus* nor in the preface to his commentary on Galatians does he mention the commentaries of Ambrosiaster. The former was composed at Bethlehem in 392, the latter at the same place in 386. It seems incredible that Jerome, with so many friends and an eager thirst for biblical literature, should have been ignorant of this important work. Marold thinks[2] that he knew it well enough, and used it. If he did, then he had some strong reason for ignoring it on these two occasions. It is difficult to see what reason he could have had, if Decimius Hilarianus Hilarius were the author. Perhaps its anonymity was the cause of its omission; or Jerome hated the author, who may have been a rival for Damasus' favour and was certainly as good a catholic as himself, though with no interest at all in monachism. Perhaps some day it will be possible to elicit from Jerome's works a hint as to the identity of this author.

§ 6. *The Author's Editions of the Commentaries and the Quaestiones.* By a new edition of an ancient book I mean the same as authors in the present day mean, namely, that there are a considerable number of changes in the way of amplification, curtailment and the correction of minor errors: I do not mean what publishers in modern times sometimes mean by the term,

[1] In 1 Cor. xiv 24—25; quaest. 114 *bis*.

[2] See page 8, note.

the mere correction of a few misprints. There was something in ancient times corresponding to that, namely, the correction of clerical errors, which had been made by the original copyist. But it is to be understood that I use the term here in the former sense.

The subject of authors' editions of ancient books is one about which we hear very little from the authors themselves, and we must sometimes judge from the manuscript tradition what really happened. We know that Cicero made two editions of his *Academics*. Of the original edition the second book survives; of the second edition, which was in four books, we possess only the first book (incomplete) and fragments of the others[1]. The poet Martial tells us that he prepared a selection from Books X and XI of his Epigrams for the use of the Emperor Nerva; this is no longer extant[2]. The researches of Blass have led him to suggest that the author of the third gospel and the book of *Acts* issued two editions of each work. Such are some of the instances of which record has been preserved. There are also instances of works which were revised in ancient times, but not by their authors. The discovery by Mercati of the 5th century Quirinian fragment of Cyprian's *Testimonia* has shown that at an early date this collection of biblical quotations was carefully worked over to bring them into harmony with the *Vulgate*. It is this recension which von Hartel gives in the Vienna edition. The case of Niceta's *Ad lapsam uirginem libellus*, just edited by Dr A. E. Burn, is not so certain. There exists a longer recension, quoted in his critical notes, which is in some MSS attributed to Jerome, and in others to Ambrose. While there is no doubt that the shorter form is by Niceta, it is not as yet possible to say definitely who was the author of the longer form.

Of all instances of authors' editions known to me the most interesting and important is that of Ambrosiaster. We possess in complete form three editions of the *Quaestiones*, of which two at least emanate from the author. We also have represented in our MSS two editions at least of the commentary on the Epistle to the Romans, and two of the commentaries on the First and

[1] Middleton and Mills, *The Student's Companion to Latin Authors*, p. 80 f.

[2] Epigr. xxii 5; Middleton and Mills, p. 300.

Second Epistles to the Corinthians. The proper treatment of these editions of the commentaries must be reserved for Father Brewer. I content myself here with a proof resulting from my own researches in the Bodleian MSS, premising that this question has been discussed between us since my notes were made.

In spite of the well-known instance of Blass's *Attische Beredsamkeit*, it is the almost invariable rule that later editions are longer than their predecessors. This amplification results from the inevitable increase of knowledge, as the author continues working, and also from the fact that clearness is generally best achieved by expansion. We shall be justified then, I think, in considering that the shorter form represented by cod. Bodl. 756 amongst others, represents an earlier form than that given by many MSS. By way of anticipating the likely objection that the additions in the longer form were really made by another person, and are therefore interpolations, I must state that the additional parts are unquestionably of the same style as the main body of the work. There is at least one interpolation in all the editions[1]; there may be others. But the instances I am about to give—few, out of a large number—cannot be regarded as such. The thick type represents what is common to both editions, the italic type the additions of the later recension.

The prologue to Romans, which is often found apart from the commentaries in MSS, differs very greatly in some authorities from the form which is found in the Benedictine edition. Zimmer has shown the form it has in Irish authorities[2]. The text of the Bodleian MS, just mentioned, is also considerably different. Apart from minor omissions and differences, the whole block, p. 49, lines 19—28 (*non tota, quia* —— *omnino non essent*) is wanting; as also the section, p. 50, lines 34—38 (*sed non* —— *peccata eorum*). In Rom. i 16 **Igitur uirtus dei est quae inuitat ad fidem et dat salutem omni credenti, dum peccata remittit et iustificat, ut a secunda morte detineri non possit signatus mysterio crucis. Praedicatio enim crucis Christi indicium est mortis euictae,** *dicente apostolo Iohanne* AD HOC ENIM VENIT FILIVS DEI VT SOLVERET OPERA DIABOLI,

[1] The words *quia cetera* —— *carnalis. unde subditur* (1 Cor. vi 18).

[2] *Pelagius in Irland*, p. 118 f.

ut omnis credens non teneatur a morte, quia signum habet quod uicta mors est. **IVDAEO PRIMVM ET GRAECO, etc.** Here we get a glimpse into the author's study. After the publication of the first edition he had thought of a Scripture proof of his statement, and now adds it.

There is another example on the same page, lines 33—39 (in Rom. i 17) **IVSTITIA ENIM DEI IN EO REVELATVR EX FIDE IN FIDEM: quia in illo qui credunt, siue Iudaeo siue Graeco, iustitia dei manifestatur.** *Iustitiam dei dicit, quia gratis iustificat impium per fidem,* SINE OPERIBVS LEGIS, *sicut alibi dicit*: VT INVENIAR IN ILLO NON HABENS MEAM IVSTITIAM QVAE EX LEGE EST SED ILLAM QVAE EX FIDE EST. *Quae ex deo est iustitia in fide, ipsam iustitiam dicit reuelari in euangelio, dum donat homini fidem per quam iustificetur.* **Ostenditur enim in ipso ueritas et iustitia dei dum credit et profitetur etc.**

The note on the clause SED EVANVERVNT IN COGITATIONIBVS SVIS (Rom. i 21) appears in different language in both recensions, but both are by the same author.

B.	*Migne.*
Vere uanitas est hoc, ut cognoscentes ueritatem cogitarent aliud colendum quod nesciebant uerum esse, ut dissimulantes a deo colerent idola.	*'Euanuerunt': uidentes enim mundum miro ornatu aptatum ab eo, quem eius opificem cognouerant, dissimulauerunt.*

The note on Rom. i 25 is very different in different MSS, as the Benedictines have observed. There is also a great discrepancy at verses 29 and 30 of the same chapter, and again in verses 31 and 32. Many others are recorded with fair accuracy in the Benedictine notes. From *et tamen* (in Rom. ii 17) down to *Iudae defendunt,* in other words, nearly the whole of the comment, belongs to the later recension: there is no word of this omission in the Benedictine notes on MSS. The Bodleian MS is an excellent one, as may be seen for example from the fact that it provides *callosis* rightly, where the MSS cited by the Benedictines in their note on Rom. v 6—7, give *callidis*; and also from the character of its text in the later epistles. It omits *unde idem apostolus* —— *esse satanae* (in Rom. vii 14); *hoc est quod singuli* —— *mundi nos teneri* (in Rom. viii 23); *exempla igitur prophetarum* —— *unde audiunt a saluatore* (in Rom. xi 8—10), for which it has *quam sciens prudensque abnuit; aut sibi ipsi —— quod contra nos est* (in Rom. xii 19); *in tantum denique —— miserebitur deus* (in Rom. xv 27).

The verse 1 Cor. x 24 with the comment is wanting. There are great disturbances in 1 Cor. xii 21 and the following verses. The whole block, verses 34 and 35 of 1 Cor. xiv, with commentary, is transferred to the end of the chapter, after verse 40. The notes on chapter xv, after verse 51, as represented by the Benedictines, do not exist in the Bodleian MSS, and there is confusion from that point to the end. There are two prologues to Second Corinthians, both of which are probably by the author. There are also considerable differences in the authorities for the first few verses of the first chapter.

These notes may suffice to show that the author really issued two editions of the longer epistles.

We have already seen that the *Quaestiones* exists in three editions. Of these, that preserved in the manuscripts of the Benedictine Coustant's second class must be regarded as the earlier. It gives the tractate against Arius in a very much shorter form than it has in the edition of the 127 *Quaestiones.* The title *Quaestiones* is also more descriptive of this collection than it is of the 127. The latter contains many documents at the end which are not *Quaestiones* at all, but the old title was kept because the later edition contained much that was common to the first. In the collection of 127 there are wanting many short Questions which are found in the other, while no long ones are absent in the 127. Those which are discarded are brief, and of little value. It seems then certain that the collection of 127 is the later of the two. As to the third class, it was very likely put together out of the other two by someone of a later period than the author.

I propose first to give a specimen of the alterations made in a Question between the publication of the earlier and the later editions; and for this purpose I select quaest. 79 (of the 127) = quaest. N.T. 59 of the other collection.

N.T. 59.

CVR SALVATOR PRO SE TANTVM ET PETRO DIDRAGMAM SOLVIT, NON ET PRO CETERIS APOSTOLIS, QVIPPE CVM OMNES EVM SECVTI SVNT, DERELICTIS OMNIBVS SVIS?

Didragma capitum uel tributi exactio intellegitur non praediorum, quod nunc pannosum aurum appellatur, quia et pauperes exiguntur. nec enim saluator aliquid possidebat in mundo, cum sit dominus mundi; et mortuus alienis inpendiis sepelitur: et nos, quibus mundus extraneus est, facultates augere cupimus, ut, morientes, mundum a nobis inuasum non tantum uoce sed et litteris contestemur, ut professione nostra ab eo, cuius mundus est, condemnemur. Hinc dominus qui non, inquit, reliquerit omnia et secutus fuerit me, non potest meus discipulus esse.

Didragma igitur ab his exigenda est, qui aliquid negotii gerunt, uel danda pro artibus: saluator igitur, qui nihil horum curabat, neque discipuli eius, exigendus non erat. Sed quia diabolus inimicus semper in insidiis erat, occasionem quaerens inclinandi saluatorem, exactorum didragmae animos occupauit, ut eius facerent uoluntatem; et accedentes ad Petrum, qui primus inter discipulos erat, solui debere ab eorum magistro dicunt didragma, qui ab his oneribus liberi erant. nihil enim agebant in mundo quod esset mundi; quia non erat unde soluerent, aut his scandalo esset, aut certe humilitate suffragii quaererent a quo solueretur. et dominus, ut inprouidum diabolum et aduersus se ipsum semper machinas instruentem inluderet, ad mare ire Petrum apostolum iubet, quasi cui

LXXVIIII (LXXV).

CVR SALVATOR PRO SE TANTVM ET PETRO DIDRAGMAM SOLVIT, NON ET PRO CETERIS APOSTOLIS, QVIPPE CVM OMNES EVM SECVTI SVNT, DERELICTIS OMNIBVS SVIS?

Didragma capitum exactio intellegitur, non praediorum; nec enim saluator aliquid possidebat in mundo, cum sit dominus mundi.—mortuus autem alienis inpendiis sepelitur—: et nos, a quibus mundus extraneus est, facultates augere cupimus, ut, morientes, mundum a nobis inuasum, non tantum uoce, sed et litteris contestemur, ut professione nostra ab eo, cuius mundus est, condemnemur. hinc dominus qui non, inquit, reliquerit omnia et secutus me fuerit, non potest meus discipulus esse. quicumque ergo sic habet facultates suas, ut spem in illis non habeat, paratus autem sit pro fide illas abicere, uiam ambulat qua itur ad Christum dominum nostrum.

Didragma igitur ab his exigenda erat, qui aliquid negotii gerebant aut artibus operam dabant. saluator autem, qui nihil horum curabat, neque discipuli eius, exigendus utique non erat; sed quia inimicus diabolus semper in insidiis erat, occasionem quaerens si posset inclinare saluatorem, exactorum didragmae animos occupauit, ut eius facerent uoluntatem, ut accedentes ad Petrum, qui primus inter apostolos erat, solui debere ab eorum magistro dicerent didragmam, qui ab his oneribus liberi erant. nihil enim agebant in mundo quod esset mundi; ut, quia non erat unde solueret, aut his scandalo esset, aut certe humilitate suffragii quaereret a quo solueretur. tunc dominus, ut inprouidum diabolum et aduersus

N.T. 59.

curam domus delegauerat, et capti piscis os aperire et illic inuenire modum exactioni debitum, ut non esset scandalo exactoribus, neque humiliaretur requisito auxilio ad soluendum, et ut signum uirtutis maximae demonstraret, per quod captos a diabolo ad se traheret, ut argumento et astutia sua diabolus torqueretur.

Dicunt ergo exactores didragmae ad Petrum apostolum magister uester non soluit didragma; quo dicto, magistrum, ut pro omnibus discipulis solueret, conuenerunt. tunc saluator, cum pro se et Petro dari iubet, pro omnibus soluisse uidetur, quia, sicut omnes in saluatore erant causa magisterii, ita et post saluatorem in Petro continentur: ipsum enim post se reliquit pastorem. denique dicit illis ecce satanas expostulauit ut uos uentilet uelut triticum; ego autem rogaui pro te ne deficiat fides tua; et tu aliquando conuersus confirma fratres tuos. Manifestum est itaque omnes contineri: rogans enim pro Petro, pro omnibus rogasse dinoscitur: semper enim in praeposito populus aut corrumpitur (*conicio* corripitur[1]) aut laudatur.

LXXVIIII (LXXV).

semet ipsum semper machinari ostenderet, ad mare ire Petrum apostolum iubet, et capti piscis os aperire, et illic inuenire modum exactioni debitum, quo soluto, non solum scandalo non esset exactoribus, neque inclinaretur, requisito auxilio ad soluendum, uerum etiam signum uirtutis maximae demonstraret, per quod captos a diabolo ad se traheret, ut argumento et astutia sua diabolus torqueretur.

Dicunt ergo exactores didragmae ad Petrum apostolum magister uester non soluit didragmam; quo dicto, magistrum, ut pro omnibus discipulis solueret, conuenerunt. saluator autem cum pro se et Petro dari iubet, pro omnibus soluisse uidetur, quia, sicut in saluatore erant omnes causa magisterii, ita et post saluatorem in Petro omnes continentur. ipsum enim constituit esse caput eorum, ut pastor esset gregis dominici. nam inter cetera dicit discipulis uigilate et orate ne intretis in temptationem; et Petro dicit ecce satanas expostulauit ut uos uentilet uelut triticum; ego autem rogaui pro te ne deficiat fides tua; et tu tandem conuersus confirma fratres tuos. quid ambigitur? pro Petro rogabat, et pro Iacobo et Iohanne non rogabat, ut de ceteris taceam? manifestum est in Petro omnes contineri, quia et alio loco dicit ego pro his rogo quos mihi dedisti, et uolo ut, ubi ego sum, et ipsi sint mecum.

Nunc uideamus quid sit didragma, hoc est, qui modus sit ponderis, uel quantitatis, aut in qua substantia [*the rest is lost*].

[1] I have since found this obvious correction to be the reading of the Padua MS.

In spite of the incompleteness of the later form, which may have been given entire by the Padua manuscript before its mutilation, this is a good example of the author's method in revision.

I must now give a conspectus of the contents of the three editions of the *Quaestiones*. The first column in Arabic numerals gives the Questions in the order in which they appear in the manuscripts of the 'second' class, which in my opinion represent the first edition of the book. The second column gives in Roman numerals the numbers which these Questions bear in the MSS of the 'first' class, which in my opinion represent the second edition of the work. This second edition has alone of all three survived in manuscripts of the ninth and tenth centuries, and forms the main part of the forthcoming Vienna edition. The third column in thick Arabic numerals and thick Roman numerals represents the contents of MSS of the third class. This class consists of three sections, Questions from the Old Testament numbering **1–38**, Questions from the New Testament numbering **39–94** (or, separately numbered, **1–56**), and a 'liber questionum' numbering **I—XXI**. I am disposed to regard the third class as belonging to a later period than the author, and as the compilation of some one who selected from the first and second editions; but I have been unable as yet to enter into the problem thoroughly. The conspectus, which now for the first time appears in print, has been made through the kind help of Drs Brewer, Burn, Engelbrecht and Günther, and shows at a glance the contents of each edition, and the number of editions in which each Question occurs.

QVAESTIONES VETERIS TESTAMENTI.

1	I	**1**	11	X	**10**
2			12	XI	**11**
3	II	**2**	13	XXXV	**29**
4	III	**3**	14	XII	**12**
5	IIII	**4**	15	XIII	**13**
6	V	**5**	16	XIIII	**14**
7	VI	**6**	17	XV	**15**
8	VII	**7**	18	XVI	**16**
9	VIII	**8**	19	XVII	**I**
10	VIIII	**9**	20	XVIII	**17**

21	XVIIII	18
22	XX	19
23	XXI	20
24	XXII	21
25	XXIII	22
26	XXIIII	23
27	XXV	24
28	XXVI	25
29	XXVII	26
30	XXVIII	**II**
31	XXVIIII	31
32	XXX	**III**
33	XXXI	27
34	XXXII	28
35	XXXIII	**IIII**
36	XXXIIII	30
37		
38		
39	XLII	35
40		
41		
42		
43	XXXVI	32
44	XXXVII	**V**
45		
46		
47		
48		
49		
50		
51		
52	XXXVIII	**VI**
53	XXXVIIII	33
54		
55	XL	34
56	XLI	**VII**
	XLIII	36
	XLIIII	**VIII**
	XLV	37
	XLVI	**VIIII**
	XLVII	38

QVAESTIONES NOVI TESTAMENTI.

1	XLVIII	39 (N.T. 1)
2	LXXXVII	78 („ 40)
3		77 („ 39)
4		76 („ 38)
5		75 („ 37)
6		74 („ 36)
7		73 („ 35)
8	LXXXV	72 („ 34)
9	XLVIIII	40 („ 2)
10	L	41 („ 3)
11	LIIII	45 („ 7)
12	LII	43 („ 5)
13	LI	42 („ 4)
14	LIII	44 („ 6)
15	LV	46 („ 8)
16	LVI	47 („ 9)
17		
18		
19		
20	LXVIIII	60 („ 22)
21	LX	51 („ 13)
22		
23		
24	LVIIII	50 (N.T. 12)
25	LXI	52 („ 14)
26	LXIII	54 („ 16)
27	LXII	53 („ 15)
28		
29		
30	LVII	48 („ 10)
31	LVIII	49 („ 11)
32		
33		
34	LXIIII	55 („ 17)
35	LXV	56 („ 18)
36	LXVII	58 („ 20)
37	LXVI	57 („ 19)
38	LXVIII	59 („ 21)
39		
40	LXXII	63 („ 25)
41	LXXIII	64 („ 26)
42		

43		
44		
45		
46	LXXXVI	**XIIII**
47	LXXV	**X**
48		
49	LXXVI	**XI**
50		
51		
52		
53		
54	LXXVII	**66 (N.T. 28)**
55		
56	LXXVIII	**67 („ 29)**
57		
58		
59	LXXVIIII	**68 („ 30)**
60		
61		
62		
63	LXXX	**69 („ 31)**
64	LXXXI	**XII**
65		
66		
67		
68	LXXXII	**70 („ 32)**
69		
70		
71		
72		
73		
74	XCVIIII	**XVIII**
75		
76		
77		
78		
79	LXXXIII	**XIII**
80		
81		
82		
83		
84	XCV	**85 („ 47)**
85	LXXI	**62 („ 24)**

86	LXXXIIII	**71 (N.T. 33)**
87	LXXXVIIII	**79 („ 41)**
88	XC	**80 („ 42)**
89	XCII	**82 („ 44)**
90	XCIII	**83 („ 45)**
91	XCVI	**86 („ 48)**
92		
93	XCI	**81 („ 43)**
94	XCVII	**XVI**
95		
	LXX	**61 („ 23)**
	LXXIIII	**65 („ 27)**
	LXXXVIII	**XV**
	XCIIII	**84 („ 46)**
	XCVIII	**87 („ 49)**
	C	**88 („ 50)**
	CI	**XVII**
	CII	**XVIIII**
	CIII	**XX**
	CIIII	**89 („ 51)**
	CV	**90 („ 52)**
	CVI	**XXI**
	CVII	
	CVIII	
	CVIIII	
	CX	
	CXI	
	CXII	
	CXIII	**91 („ 53)**
	CXIV	
	CXV	
	CXVI	**93 („ 55)**
	CXVII	
	CXVIII	
	CXVIIII	
	CXX	**92 („ 54)**
	CXXI	**94 („ 56)**
	CXXII	
	CXXIII	
	CXXIIII	
	CXXV	
	CXXVI	
	CXXVII	

CHAPTER VI.

HIS BIBLICAL TEXT.

§ 1. *General Remarks.* The importance of the biblical text employed by Ambrosiaster is due first to its date, and secondly to the locality in which it was employed. It must be at least as old as 370, that is, thirteen years older than the Vulgate Gospels: how much older still, is a question for students of the history of biblical texts to determine. At any rate, it is at least coeval with our oldest complete manuscripts of the Greek Bible, and thus presupposes a Greek text anterior to them.

It is specially fortunate for our purposes that this text was in use in Rome, and that it was in use among Catholics. We have seen that the author was of high social position, a member of the Catholic Church, and a supporter of Damasus. This being so, the text employed by him was presumably that commonly employed in Rome at the time, and identical with that form of the Old Latin, of which Jerome speaks as the 'vulgata editio.' Are we not, then, justified in concluding that this text was continually before Jerome's eyes in his revision of the New Testament? May we not even go further, and suggest as a great probability that this was the only Latin text of the New Testament to which Jerome paid any regard at all? If these suggestions be right, then it is of the highest importance to find out what that text was, as we can then estimate with certainty, where it is quoted, the extent of Jerome's revision.

While the author has been bountiful with his right hand in giving us a complete text of St Paul's epistles, he has been niggardly with his left: for the quotations from the rest of the Bible are very short, with the exception of three complete psalms which I have edited and put together in this chapter, a fairly long quotation from Luke, and a really long quotation from the Apocalypse. The other quotations are often accurate, as far as they go; but many are mere paraphrases, and do not help us much.

The value of Ambrosiaster's text of the Pauline epistles could not be exaggerated. Properly edited, they are equivalent to a complete fourth century pre-Vulgate Latin codex of these epistles, such a treasure, in fact, as does not exist outside this author. The reports of Tischendorf in his eighth edition are practically valueless, as they are based on uncritical editions. Many a time the real evidence is exactly the opposite of that which he gives, and Ambrosiaster's witness has to be placed in the other scale. I have, on Mr Burkitt's suggestion, drawn up a double set of collations, which include all the quotations from these epistles made by Cyprian and Lucifer, and ought to be of value to students of the Vulgate and Codex Claromontanus (d_2) as well. If this be the text which Jerome altered to make the Vulgate, then, when the Bishop of Salisbury and Mr White have given us the Vulgate Epistles, and Father Brewer the commentaries of Ambrosiaster, we shall have a comprehensive view of Jerome's methods, such as has never been possible before.

§ 2. *Notes on the Books in Ambrosiaster's Canon.* Of Old Testament Books Ambrosiaster quotes all, except Ruth, Nahum, Susanna and perhaps one or two others. We have no reason to doubt that he regarded these books as canonical. The reason why he did not quote them is that he did not recollect or require passages from them.

As to the New Testament, a more detailed examination is necessary, especially as wrong statements have been made about the contents of his New Testament[1]. The truth is: *Every book in the New Testament is quoted by him, except Jude.* It is unnecessary to give references for all the other books, but, in view of prevailing error, the references to 2 Peter, James and 3 John must be given. 2 Peter is quoted on Philippians i 3–5 *sicut Petrus apostolus inter cetera dicens,* ut sitis, *inquit,* consortes diuinae

[1] The latest book on the Canon, Zahn's *Grundriss der Geschichte des Neutestamentlichen Kanons* (2. Aufl.), p. 69, is wrong on this point. He states that of the Epistles, 2 Peter, James, Jude, 2 and 3 John, *Ambrosiaster cites only* 2 *John.*

naturae (2 Pet. i 4), and again on 1 Timothy ii 1–4 *unde dicit Petrus apostolus* omnis scriptura indiget interpretatione (2 Pet. i 20). The epistle is alluded to at least twice in the *Quaestiones. Quaest.* 111 § 3 reads: *ut doceret omnem omnino terram domini esse, et quae sunt in ea, ut nihil esset exceptum, quod non eius sit; sicut putant quidam heretici, qui secundum dictum apostoli Petri* dominium deo abnegant (2 Pet. ii 1 or 10): so § 6 *ne, quia puniendos ostendit,* qui, *sicut dixi,* dominium deo abnegant. The Epistle of James is quoted on Gal. v 10 *dicente Iacobo in epistula sua* qui conuerti fecerit peccatorem, saluabit animam eius, et operiet multitudinem peccatorum (Iac. v 20)[1]. On Romans xvi 23, Gaius is identified with the Gaius, *ad quem scripsit Iohannes apostolus.*

The Gospels ought to be arranged, says the author, in the order Matthew, Luke, Mark, John (2 qu. N. T. 2). No Old Latin authority known to me, and no MS mentioned by Berger in his *Histoire de la Vulgate,* gives this order, but Dr Sanday informs me that it is advocated in Clement of Alexandria. The titles of the gospels have already been given[2]. The title of Acts was ACTA APOSTOLORVM. The prevailing order of the Pauline epistles in manuscripts of Ambrosiaster is Rom., 1 Cor., 2 Cor., Gal., Eph., Phil., 1 Thess., 2 Thess., Col., Tit., 1 Tim., 2 Tim., Philem. It would be hazardous to affirm that this was the order in which the Epistles occurred in Ambrosiaster's copy of the Apostle. The Benedictines tell us that this is the order of the epistles in Primasius and Sedulius (presumably, Sedulius Scottus), but it is not found in any MS of the Vulgate examined by Berger. It differs markedly also from that in the Roman Canon of 382 and other ancient canons[3]. As we have seen, the Epistle to the Hebrews is not regarded as Pauline[4].

§ 3. *References to Biblical Manuscripts and Various Readings.* I will now give those passages in the author's works which make reference to manuscripts of the Bible which differ from one another in text.

[1] Iac. ii 23 is wrongly given by the editors at *quaest.* 115 § 11.

[2] Page 171.

[3] 1 and 2 Thess. stand before Col. in x_2 (Bodl. Laud. 108 E. 67) of the Pauline epistles; see Gregory *Textkritik des N.T.* (II) p. 613. See Addenda.

[4] Page 171 ff.

The most interesting of all is that which comes earliest (in Rom. v 14). The verse reads: 'sed regnauit mors ab Adam usque ad Moysen, et in eos qui peccauerunt in similitudinem praeuaricationis Adae.' After expounding the text in this form, he says that the interpretation stands, 'even if the law be said not to be laid down thus in the Greek. For it said that the Greek reads that death reigned even over those who did *not* sin after the fashion of Adam's sin.' His Latin MS (or MSS) was, then, without the negative. Some cursives, as well as Origen sometimes, MSS known to Augustine, and d_2 (Claromontanus), agree with Ambrst in omitting the negative. But what follows in Ambrosiaster is of even greater interest. He has a strong feeling against those, whose cry is 'back to the Greek manuscripts.' His standpoint is, therefore, quite different from Jerome's, though at the time his words were written Jerome had not yet begun to write. The words are these:—*et tamen sic praescribere nobis uolunt de Graecis codicibus, quasi non ipsi ab inuicem discrepent; quod fecit studium contentionis. Quia enim propria quis auctoritate uti non potest ad uictoriam, uerba legis adulterat, ut sensum suum quasi uerbis legis adserat, uti non ratio sed auctoritas praescribere uideatur. Constat autem quosdam Latinos porro olim de ueteribus Graecis translatos codicibus, quos incorruptos simplicitas temporum seruauit et probat: post quam autem a concordia animis dissidentibus et hereticis perturbantibus torqueri quaestiones coeperunt, multa inmutata sunt ad sensum humanum, ut hoc contineretur litteris, quod homini uideretur. Unde et ipsi Graeci diuersos codices habent. Hoc autem uerum arbitror, quando et ratio et historia et auctoritas conseruatur: nam hodie quae*[1] *in Latinis reprehenduntur codicibus, sic inueniuntur a ueteribus posita, Tertulliano et Victorino et Cypriano.* The author's point of view is briefly this. Those readings which appear both in the Latin bible of his day and in the old authors, Tertullian, Victorinus and Cyprian, are correct. They are so, because the Latin translations used by these authors were made from Greek manuscripts which had not been corrupted,

[1] Tischendorf, who could not make the easy emendation *hodie quae* for *hodieque* of the printed editions, misunderstood the meaning of the passage. Haussleiter (Zahn's *Forschungen* IV 32) made the emendation, which is confirmed by at least three MSS.

as the later Greek manuscripts were, for doctrinal or other purposes. There is of course much that is true in this view, and the labour which Rönsch spent on the study of Tertullian's Bible and Dr Sanday and Mr Turner are spending on that of Cyprian, is of the highest value for the attainment of the original text.

At Romans ix 17, the text with comment runs thus: dicit enim scriptura ad Pharaonem quia ad hoc te ipsum reseruaui (*v. l.* seruaui), ut ostendam in te uirtutem meam, et ut nuntietur nomen meum in uniuersa terra. *Alii codices sic habent:* quia ad hoc te suscitaui, ut ostendam in te uirtutem meam. *Siue* reseruaui (*v. l.* seruaui) *siue* suscitaui *unus est sensus etc.* The reading *reseruaui*, if we may judge from Tischendorf's silence, is unique in the N. T.; it corresponds to the διετηρήθης of Ex. ix 16. The next instance is at Rom. xii 11: tempori seruientes: *in Graeco dicitur sic habere,* deo (*should be* domino) seruientes, *quod nec loco (ipsi) conpetit. Quid enim opus erat summam hanc ponere totius deuotionis, cum quando singula membra, quae ad obsequia et seruitia dei pertinent, memoret. In omnibus enim his quae enumerat plenum deo seruitium exhibetur. 'seruire tempori' quid sit, alibi soluit, etc.* With regard to this variant Tischendorf's admirable note should be consulted. Ambrosiaster has here the whole weight of modern criticism against him. On chapter xvi 11: salutate eos qui sunt ex Narcissi domo (qui sunt) in domino, we find *Narcissus hic illo tempore presbyter dicitur fuisse, sicut legitur in aliis codicibus...Hic ergo Narcissus presbyter peregrini officio fungebatur.* This variant is also unique. At 2 Cor. v 5 the text first commented on is: siquidem induti non nudi inueniamur...; then comes *Alii codices sic habent:* siquidem expoliati non nudi inueniamur, which is in its turn explained. He betrays no preference for the one over the other. The first is the reading of the great uncials (ἐνδυσάμενοι); the second is 'Western' (ἐκδυσάμενοι). The comment on Gal. ii 1–2 contains the following: *praeterea, cum legem dedissent non molestari eos qui ex gentibus credebant, sed ut ab his tantum obseruarent, id est, a sanguine et fornicatione et idolatria, nunc dicant sofistae Graecorum, qui sibi peritiam uindicant, naturaliter subtilitate ingenii se uigere, quae tradita sunt gentibus obseruanda? quae ignorabant, an quae sciebant? sed quo modo fieri potest ut aliquis discat ea quae nouit? ergo haec inlicita esse ostensa sunt gentibus, quae putabant licere: ac per hoc non utique ab homicidio prohibiti sunt, cum iubentur a sanguine obseruare . sed hoc acceperunt quod Noe a deo didicerat, ut obseruarent a sanguine edendo cum carne . nam quo modo fieri poterat ut Romanis legibus imbuti, quorum tanta auctoritas in seruandis mandatis est, nescirent homicidium non esse faciendum, quippe cum adulteros et homicidas et falsos testes et fures et maleficos et ceterorum malorum admissores puniant leges Romanae? denique tria haec mandata ab apostolis et senioribus data repperiuntur, quae ignorant leges Romanae, id est ut obseruent se ab idolatria et sanguine, sicut Noe, et a fornicatione . quae sofistae Grecorum non intellegentes, scientes tamen a sanguine abstinendum, adulterarunt scripturam, quartum mandatum addentes 'et a suffocato obseruandum* (*v. l.* abstinendum)*; quod, puto, nunc dei nutu intellecturi sunt, quia iam supra dictum erat, quod addiderunt.* In other words, the true text of Act. xv 29 contains only three prohibitions, from blood, fornication and idolatry. The learned Greeks through want of understanding have added a fourth, a prohibition from things strangled. The author takes a mistaken view as to the meaning of this extra clause, but he is quite right in attributing it to Greek authorities, as Codex Bezae alone among them wants it, while the bulk of Latin authorities are without it[1]. The text of Gal. ii 5 reads: *ad horam cessimus subiectioni,* without the negative. In a long argument he defends this reading, which is found in nearly all the Latin authorities, against the *nec ad horam cessimus* of the Greeks.

Ambrosiaster, who had evidently little or no knowledge of Greek, holds firmly to his Latin text, and has no respect for the original languages. He is an entire contrast to Jerome, who always keeps the Hebrew or the Greek in view. Jerome's custom, in commenting on Old Testament passages, is to consult the Hexapla, place before us the various readings therein given, and then offer his decision. Our author had probably never seen the Hexapla, and would not have known very well how to use it, if he had. Yet his very conservatism makes him a more important witness to the Latin text as he knew it.

[1] See either Tischendorf's or Wordsworth and White's note on the passage.

§ 4. *His Method of Quotation.* Ambrosiaster's knowledge of Holy Scripture is extensive: as we have seen, he quotes from nearly every book of the Bible. But it is remarkable that he rarely chooses a long passage for quotation, and in his short quotations, unless I am doing him an unintentional injustice through inability to confront him with his Bible, is not always particular about exactness. In this he shares a general characteristic of ancient writers, who were satisfied if they gave the substance of a passage. We may safely assume in him, as in other writers, that, if the quotation go beyond one verse, it is copied from the open Bible. If he had written half-a-dozen pages after the manner of Cyprian's *Testimonia* or Lucifer's works we should be able to tell much more about the text of his Bible outside Acts and the Pauline epistles than we at present can.

To illustrate his general method, I have chosen at random some quotations from Question 102, 'Against Novatian.' On page 2305 Matth. xvi 19 is quoted thus: *hic aut ligantur aut soluuntur peccata* (cf. xviii 18): the Vulgate reads: *quodcumque ligaueris super terram erit ligatum in caelis, et quodcumque solueris super terram erit solutum in caelis.* On the next page Prou. xx 9 is quoted: *nemo gloriabitur mundum se habere cor,* but the LXX have τίς καυχήσεται ἁγνὴν ἔχειν (τὴν) καρδίαν; On the same page occurs Hiob xiv 4, 5 *nemo sine sorde, nec infans unius diei*; but the Greek is τίς γὰρ καθαρὸς ἔσται ἀπὸ ῥύπου; ἀλλ' οὐθείς, ἐὰν καὶ μία ἡμέρα ὁ βίος αὐτοῦ ἐπὶ τῆς γῆς. On the following page we find Luc. xi 52 thus: *uos habetis clauem scientiae, et neque uos intratis neque alios sinitis introire,* which is very different from any known form of the verse. My last example shall be Matth. xiii 47–49 from page 2309, where we read it thus: *simile est regnum caelorum retiae missae in mari, quae ex omni genere piscium colligit . cum autem uenissent ad litus, bonos segregauerunt in uasa sua, malos uero foras miserunt . sic erit in consummatione saeculi: exibunt angeli, et segregabunt de regno dei omnia scandala, et eos qui iniquitatem faciunt.* At the beginning, this text is almost identical with *a* (Vercellensis) and *b* (Veronensis); in the middle it is rather a paraphrase; at the end it is contaminated with verse 41.

The specimens here given are not encouraging to the investigator, but an extensive examination of quotations from all parts of the Bible has shown me that quotations as inaccurate as these form in reality a small proportion of the whole. There is plenty of material in the author for the formation of an opinion as to the character of his Biblical text.

§ 5. *Old Testament Quotations.* I have spent much time in the examination of the quotations from the Old Testament, in the hope that I might reach some results that would be of use to the editors of the larger Cambridge Septuagint. I have to confess failure to attain this end, and have come to realise that after all their simplest course will be to consult the indexes of Scripture quotations which will be provided by the editions of the Vienna Academy. Having an authoritative standard in the valuable collations of Greek MSS in their possession, they will be able without trouble to estimate the character and value of our author's quotations. Here I propose to give briefly the results of the comparison of a few passages with the material provided by Dr Swete in his *Old Testament in Greek*, and to offer to the student of the Septuagint the text of three psalms, critically edited. It will be observed that their text is almost identical with that of the *Codex Sangermanensis* given by Sabatier.

Ex. xx 11 (qu. 106 § 16)	agrees	with	AF	against	B.
Deut. xxxii 8, 9 (qu. 109)	,,	,,	B	,,	F.
Ios. v 15 (qu. 111)	,,	,,	A	,,	BF.
Title of Ps. xxiii (qu. 111)	,,	,,	A	,,	BℵU.
Ps. xxiii 3 (qu. 111)	,,	,,	Bℵ	,,	RU.
Ps. xxiii 6 (qu. 111)	,,	,,	B	,,	others.

Ps. xxiii has the DIAPSALMA where Bℵ have it : A has none.

Ps. l 8 (qu. 112) has *cordis*, where all the Greek authorities have σοφίας: but the St Germain MS, and quotations in Ambrose agree with Ambrosiaster.

Ps. l 16 (qu. 112) *sanguine*, which presupposes αἵματος, for which there is no authority. Is *sanguine* merely an attempt to smooth the Latinity? In the same verse *domine* is contained as in Bℵ, against RT.

Ps. lxxxviii 34 (qu. 112) has αὐτῶν RT against BAℵ.

Ps. cxx 6 (qu. 107) agrees with ℵ against ART.

Ps. cxxxv 6 (quu. 107, 111) agrees with ART against ℵ.

Prou. iv 19 (qu. 110) has *omnes*, which is unrepresented in Greek.

The title of Canticles is CANTICA CANTICORVM, agreeing with A against BℵC.

Os. vi 6 (qu. 103) agrees with B against AQ.

Mal. i 8 (qu. 103) differs from all Greek authorities. It reads :—*Si adducatis ad uictimam caecum aut claudum aut aegrum, non est bonum. Offers* (this is imperative) *autem ea duci aut praeposito tuo, si suscipiet te, dicit dominus omnipotens*[1]. In qu. 5 it is different.

Esai. xiv 13 (qu. 113) agrees with א against BAQT.
Esai. xxx 25 (qu. 105) agrees with B against AOQΓ.
Esai. xliii 26 (qu. 112) „ „ BA „ א.
Hier. vii 22 (qu. 103) „ „ AQ „ B.

Texts of Psalms I, XXIII and L.

PSALMUS I (quaest. 110).

(1) Beatus uir qui non abiit in consilio impiorum,
et in uia peccatorum non stat,
et in catedra pestilentiae non sedit :
(2) sed in lege domini uoluntas eius,
et in lege eius meditabitur die ac nocte.
(3) et erit tamquam lignum quod plantatum est iuxta decursus aquarum,
quod fructum suum dabit in tempore suo,
et folium eius non defluet :
et omnia quaecumque fecit prosperabuntur.
(4) non sic impii, non sic,
sed tamquam puluis quem proicit uentus a facie terrae.
(5) ideo non resurgent impii in iudicio,
neque peccatores in consilio iustorum :
(6) quoniam scit dominus uiam iustorum,
et iter impiorum peribit.

PSALMUS XXIII (quaest. 111).

(1) Domini est terra et plenitudo eius,
orbis terrarum et omnes qui habitant in eo.
(2) ipse super maria fundauit eam,
et super flumina praeparauit illam.
(3) quis ascendet in montem domini,
aut quis stabit in loco sancto eius ?
(4) innocens manibus et mundus corde,
qui non accepit in uano animam suam,
nec iurauit proximo suo in dolum.
(5) hic accipiet benedictionem a domino,
et misericordiam a deo salutari suo.

[1] In the rare instances where comparison is possible, the text of the prophets is practically identical with *Weingartensis*. Ambrosiaster has not been used by Mr Oesterley (in *The Journal of Theological Studies*) for passages from the Minor Prophets.

(6) haec est generatio requirentium illum,
quaerentium faciem dei Iacob. DIAPSALMA.
(7) Tollite portas principis uestri,
et eleuamini, portae aeternales,
et introibit rex gloriae.
(8) quis est iste rex gloriae?
dominus fortis et potens,
dominus potens in proelio.
(9) tollite portas principis uestri,
et eleuamini, portae aeternales,
et introibit rex gloriae.
(10) quis est iste rex gloriae?
dominus uirtutum, ipse est
rex gloriae.

PSALMUS L (quaest. 112).

(3) Miserere mei, deus, secundum magnam misericordiam tuam,
et secundum multitudinem miserationum tuarum dele iniquitatem meam:
(4) usque quaque laua me ab iniustitia mea,
et a delicto meo munda me.
(5) quoniam iniquitatem meam ego agnosco,
et delictum meum contra me est semper.
(6) tibi soli peccaui, et malum coram te feci:
ut iustificeris in sermonibus tuis,
et uincas cum iudicaris.
(7) ecce enim in iniquitatibus conceptus sum,
et in delictis concepit me mater mea.
(8) ecce enim ueritatem dilexisti,
incerta et occulta cordis manifestasti mihi.
(9) asparges me hysopo et mundabor,
lauabis me et super niuem dealbabor.
(10) auditui meo dabis gaudium et laetitiam:
[1]exultabunt ossa humiliata.
(11) auerte faciem tuam a peccatis meis,
et omnes iniquitates meas dele.
(12) cor mundum crea in me, deus,
et spiritum iustum dedica in uisceribus meis.
(13) ne proicias me a facie tua,
et spiritum sanctum tuum ne auferas a me.
(14) redde mihi laetitiam salutaris tui,
et spiritu principali confirma me.
(15) doceam iniquos uias tuas,
et impii ad te conuertentur.

[1] Perhaps *propterea exultabunt.*

(16) libera me de sanguine, deus deus salutis meae :
exultabit lingua mea iustitiam tuam, (17) domine.
labia mea aperies, et os meum adnuntiabit laudem tuam.
(18) quoniam si uoluisses sacrificium, dedissem utique :
holocaustis non delectaberis.
(19) sacrificium deo spiritus contribulatus,
cor contritum et humiliatum deus non spernet.
(20) benigne fac, domine, in bona uoluntate tua Sion,
et aedificentur muri Hierusalem.
(21) tunc acceptabis sacrificium iustitiae,
oblationes et holocausta:
tunc inponent super altare tuum uitulos.

§ 6. *Gospel Quotations.* The statements made here are the result of an examination of almost all the gospel quotations in the commentaries and *Quaestiones.* To give the quotations in full would demand far too much space. They are for the most part short, and require to be critically edited, before they can be used. It is possible that it will be found necessary to present them in full elsewhere, but here I must content myself with a few examples, and with a statement of the results at which I have arrived.

The general conclusion is that the quotations harmonise to a considerable extent with the text given by *Codex Veronensis* (*b*), of the early years of the fifth century, which is generally regarded as the best specimen of the European recension. If the gospel quotations given in the second chapter be examined, this will be found to be the case. When they do not agree with *b*, they usually agree with some other representative of the European recension. There are at times distinct agreements with ff_2, if we can trust the published reports of the readings of that MS. In Luc. xxiv 13 *b* alone gives the order *cleofas et ammaus,* the same order as that of Ambrosiaster[1]. John xiv 27 agrees with *b* and *q*; John xvii 3 with *b e q* Cyprian, Novatian and Victorinus Afer.

But there is a large element in Ambrosiaster's text which is individual to him, and cannot be paralleled from Tischendorf's apparatus, such as the insertion of *ambulantes* in Luc. ii 48. The

[1] The only other Church Father known to me, who refers to Emmaus as a person, is Ambrose, e.g. *exp. euang. Luc.* x 173 (see Migne's note). The Ambrosiaster passages are in Rom. i 4; in 1 Cor. xv 5; quaest. 77 (73).

author undoubtedly had *proprium sibi* in John v 18, but there is nothing exactly like this elsewhere except the *proprium* in the margin of one of Wordsworth and White's MSS.

I will take one or two of the few long quotations, and illustrate them by comparison with other Old Latin texts and the vulgate.

Matth. xv 3—6 (quaest. 16).

quare et uos praeteritis mandatum dei, ut traditionem uestram statuatis? nam dixit deus: Honora patrem et matrem, et Qui maledixerit patri aut matri, morte moriatur: uos autem dicitis: Quicumque dixerit patri aut matri: omne munus quodcumque fuerit ex me, tibi proderit, et non honorabit patrem aut matrem suam

om. et *q* transgredimini *a b d ff*¹ *g vg* sine intellectu estis in *q* propter traditionem uestram *a b d g q vg* propter uestram traditionem *ff*¹ deus dixit *a b ff*¹ *g vg* deus enim dixit *d q* aut *d* patrem tuum *a b g q vg* matrem tuam *a b q* quicumque *a* maledicit *a d* *om.* aut matri *a* *habent* uel matri *b ff*¹ *q vg* morietur *a d ff*¹ maledixerit *ff*¹ uel *a b ff*¹ *g q vg* matri] + corbam quod est *b* †reus erit gehennae ignis quod *ff*¹ (*et tunc* non *etc.*) quodcumque...proderit] quod a me melioratus fueris *q* quod ex me tibi prodest *d* omne *om. a b d g q vg* fuerit *om. a g*, *habent* est *b vg* et *om. a b d g* honorificauit *a b ff*¹ honorificabit *g q vg* honorauit *d* patrem suum *a b d ff*¹ *g q vg* aut matrem suam] *om. a d* et matrem *b* uel matrem suam *ff*¹ aut matrem *g vg* et matrem suam *q*

Luc. i 68—72 (quaest. 105).

Benedictus est deus Israhel, quia uisitauit et fecit redemtionem plebi suae; et erexit cornu salutis nostrae in domo Dauid pueri sui, sicut locutus est per os sanctorum prophetarum suorum, qui a saeculo sunt: et liberauit nos ab inimicis nostris, et de manibus omnium qui oderunt nos, ad faciendam misericordiam cum patribus nostris

(*a* is somewhat mutilated here) benedictus deus *a b etc.* benedictus dominus deus *d vg* salutem *d* populo *a d* plebis *b c etc.* suo *d* eleuauit *d* nobis *a b d vg* suorum prophetarum q. ab aeuo s. *b* q. a. s. s. prophetarum eius *vg* suorum] eius *d* sunt *om. d* et l. n. ab inim. nos. et de manibus] salutem de manu inimicorum nostrorum et *d* salutem ex i. n. et de manu *vg* manu *b d vg* nos oderunt *a b* ad faciendam] facere *a d*

Ioh. viii 44 (quaest. 90).

uos de patre diabolo estis, et concupiscentias patris uestri uultis facere. Ille homicida fuit ab initio, et in ueritate non stetit, quia ueritas non est in eo; cum loquitur mendacium, ex suis propriis loquitur, quia mendax est, sicut et pater eius

ex *b f q vg* concupiscentias *d Cyp* desideria *a f q vg* concupiscentiam *b* erat *a q vg* ueritatem *a* stat *d* quoniam *a d* ueritas non est in eo *d m q* non est ueritas in illo *a* ueritas in eo non est *b l r* non est ueritas in eo *f vg* quando *b* de suo *a d e* de suis *b* ex suis propriis *c ff₂ l q aur* ex propriis *f vg* de suo proprio *r* quoniam *a b d* *om.* sicut *d f q vg* *om.* et *ff*¹ (?)[1]

Ioh. xiv 15—17 (quaest. 93; 97).

si diligitis me, praecepta mea seruate; et ego rogabo patrem, et alium paracletum dabit uobis, ut uobiscum sit in aeternum; spiritum ueritatis, quem mundus non potest accipere, quia non uidet nec cognoscit eum; uos uidetis eum et cognoscitis, quia apud uos manet et uobiscum est

mandata *a d vg* custodite *c ff*² *r* aduocatum *a c e m q* qui *m q* maneat uobiscum i. a. *vg* u. in aeternum sit *b* maneat in aeternum uobiscum *d* hic mundus *a b etc.* quoniam *a* non uidet illum nec agnoscit *a* non uidet eum nec cognoscit eum *b* non uidet eum nec scit eum *vg* non uidet eum nec adnoscit eum *d* uos autem *d* uidetis eum et cognoscitis] agnoscitis eum *a* cognoscitis eum *vg* scitis eum *d* quoniam *d* uobiscum manet et in uobis est *a* apud uos manebit et in uobis erit *vg* apud uos manet et in uobis est *d*

The readings of the Old Latin codices in John vi 71 explain why in quaest. 104 Judas Iscariot is called simply *Simon Scarioth*.

§ 7. *Quotations from Acts.* The text of *Acts* employed can be identified without difficulty. It was almost to a letter identical with that of the celebrated MS *gigas* (*Holmiensis*), of the thirteenth century. A comparison of Ambrosiaster's quotations, edited from the manuscripts, with the text of *gigas*, as collated for the Oxford Vulgate by Dr Henrik Karlsson[3], shows this quite clearly. The same text was employed by Lucifer of Cagliari, and it is of interest to know that *gigas* represents also a text employed in Rome anterior to the publication of the Vulgate. There can be

[1] I have borrowed largely from Wordsworth and White here.

[2] For further variants, see Wordsworth and White.

[3] Rev. H. J. White kindly favoured me with the proof-sheets of the Vulgate *Acts*, before it appeared.

little doubt, then, that the ultimate original of *gigas* contained, instead of *Elymas*, the form *etoemas* (or *etoemus*) in Acts xiii 8. Codex Bezae (*d*) has *etoemas*, Lucifer has *etoemus*, and Ambrosiaster (quaest. 102) has *etimas*[1]. Instead of the form *Silas*, the manuscripts of Ambrosiaster are consistent in offering the form *sileas* (*syleas*), which seems to have been the prevailing form in Old Latin bibles, and is found in some Vulgate manuscripts, in spite of the scant courtesy dealt out to it in the *Encyclopaedia Biblica*. It was the form in the bibles used by Cyprian, Lucifer, Irenaeus, Jerome, Auctor Itineris Burdigalensis, *gigas*, etc. While it is easy to believe that *Silas* is the pet form of *Siluanus*, it is rather difficult to explain the form *Sileas*. From the character of the comments on the three passages of St Paul's Epistles where *Siluanus* is mentioned, we are justified in inferring that our author did not connect him in any way with the *Sileas* of the Acts.

§ 8. *Apocalypse Quotations*. The Apocalypse was a favourite book of the author, who had imbibed an interest in Chiliasm, perhaps from Victorinus. He quotes it with fair frequency, and the longest New Testament quotation he makes, apart from the Epistles of St Paul, is from the second chapter of the Apocalypse, verses 12—26, 29. The possession of this quotation at once makes it unnecessary to collect the others, and reveals to us the character of his text. For purposes of comparison I have chosen the Old African text as preserved by Primasius of Hadrumetum, and the Vulgate as it appears in Amiatinus and Fuldensis. It is unfortunate that the text used by Victorinus is not available, as there is no doubt that our author used the works of Victorinus, without, however, adhering to the Biblical text employed by him. In the first column I place the text of Primasius, and those of Ambrosiaster and the Vulgate follow, the seniority being from left to right.

[1] The printed text has *Elymas*, but the evidence of the MSS is as follows: *ethimas* (corr. m. 2 *elymas*) *P*, *etymas* (corr. m. rec. *elemas*) *M*, *atrmas C*, *tymas N*, *thimas FEGAB*. The form had naturally a very precarious existence, and in quaest. 69 (a) (of first edition) it no longer survives.

Primasius (ed. Haussl. p. 87 ff.).	Quaest. 102 § 8.	Vulgate (*Amiatinus*).
Et angelo ecclesiae Pergami scribe: Haec dicit qui habet rumpheam ex utraque parte acutam: Scio ubi habitas, ubi thronus satanae est: et tenes nomen meum et non denegasti fidem meam: in illis diebus Antiphas testis meus et fidelis, qui occisus est apud uos, ubi satanas inhabitat. sed habeo pauca aduersus te dicere: habes ibi doctrinam tenentes Balaam, qui docebat Balaac mittere scandalum sub oculis filiorum Israhel, edere de sacrificiis et fornicari. similiter habes et tu tenentes doctrinam Nicolaitum. similiter age paenitentiam . . . . . qui habet aures audiendi audiat, quid spiritus dicat ecclesiis: Qui uicerit, dabo ei de manna illa absconsa (*etc.*)	Et angelo Pergami ecclesiae scribe: Haec dicit qui habet gladium ex utraque parte acutum: Scio ubi habitas, ubi sedes est satanae: et tenes nomen meum et non negasti fidem meam: in diebus quibus Antiphas testis meus fidelissimus, qui occisus est apud uos, ubi satanas habitat. sed habeo aduersus te pauca, quia habes illic tenentes doctrinam Balaam, qui docebat Balaac mittere scandalum sub oculis filiorum Israhel, manducare delibata et fornicari. ita et tu habes tenentes doctrinam Nicolaitarum. similiter age paenitentiam . . . . . haec dicit spiritus ecclesiis: Vincenti dabo manducare manna, quod est absconditum	Et angelo Pergami ecclesiae scribe: Haec dicit qui habet romphaeam utraque parte acutam: Scio ubi habitas, ubi sedes est satanae: et tenes nomen meum et non negasti fidem meam: et in diebus Antipas testis meus fidelis qui occisus est apud uos, ubi satanas habitat. sed habeo aduersus te pauca; habes illic tenentes doctrinam Balaam, qui docebat Balac mittere scandalum coram filiis Israhel edere et fornicari. ita habes et tu tenentes doctrinam Nicolaitarum similiter. paenitentiam age . . . . . qui habet aurem audiat, quid spiritus dicat ecclesiis: Vincenti dabo ei manna absconditum (*etc.*)
Et angelo ecclesiae qui est Tyatirae scribe: Haec dicit dei filius, qui habet oculos ut flamma ignis, et pedes eius similes auricalco: Scio opera tua et caritatem et fidem et ministerium et patientiam et nouissima opera tua plura quam priora. sed habeo aduer-	Et angelo Thyatirae ecclesiae scribe: Haec dicit filius dei, qui habet oculos suos sicut flamma ignis, et pedes eius similes aeramento Tyrino: Scio opera tua et dilectionem et fidem et ministerium et patientiam et opera tua nouissima meliora priorum. sed habeo	Et angelo Thyatirae ecclesiae scribe: Haec dicit filius dei, qui habet oculos tamquam flammam ignis, et pedes eius similes orichalco: Noui opera tua et caritatem et fidem et ministerium et patientiam tuam et opera tua nouissima plura prioribus. sed habeo aduersus

3 inhabitas *fuld* 6 mei *fuld* 13 nicolaitarum. Similiter *fuld* 16 abscondita *fuld* 21 ut flamma *fuld* 22 aericalco *fuld* 24 *om.* et opera tua *fuld*

Primasius (ed. Haussl. p. 87 ff.).

sum te multa, quod (sinis) uxorem tuam Zezabel quae se dicit propheten sinis (eam) docere et seducere seruos meos, fornicari et manducare de sacrificiis. dedi ei tempus ut paenitentiam ageret, et paenitere noluit a fornicatione sua. ecce mitto illam in lectum et eos qui cum illa moechati sunt in maximam tribulationem, nisi paenitentiam egerit ab operibus suis. et filios eius interficiam morte, et scient omnes ecclesiae quia ego sum scrutator renis et cordis, et dabo uni cuique uestrum secundum opera uestra. uobis autem dico reliquis qui estis Tyatirae: Quotquot non habent doctrinam hanc, qui non scierunt altitudinem satanae, quemadmodum dicunt, non mittam super uos aliud pondus, sed quod habetis tenete usque dum uenio. et qui uicerit et qui seruauerit usque in finem opera mea, dabo ei potestatem super gentes (*v.* 29 *periit*)

Quaest. 102 § 8.

aduersum te quod sinis mulierem Zezabel quae se dicit prophetam et docet et seducit seruos meos, fornicari et manducare inmolata idolis. et dedi ei tempus ad paenitendum, et noluit agere paenitentiam a fornicatione sua. ecce mittam illam in lectum et adulteros eius cum illa in tribulationem magnam, nisi egerint paenitentiam factorum suorum. et natos eius occidam morte, et scient omnes ecclesiae quia ego sum qui scrutor renes et corda, et dabo uni cuique uestrum secundum opera sua. uobis autem dico ceteris qui Thyatirae estis: Qui hanc doctrinam non habetis, et ignoratis altitudinem satanae, sicut dicunt, non mitto in uos aliud pondus, uerum tamen tenete quod habetis donec ueniam. uincenti autem et seruanti opera mea usque ad finem, dabo ei potestatem super gentes . . . . qui habet aures, audiat quid dicat spiritus ecclesiis.

Vulgate (*Amiatinus*).

te, quia permittis mulierem Hiezabel quae se dicit propheten docere et seducere seruos meos fornicari et manducare de idolothytis. et dedi illi tempus ut paenitentiam ageret, et non uult paeniteri a fornicatione sua. ecce mitto eam in lectum et qui moechantur cum ea in tribulationem maximam, nisi paenitentiam egerint ab operibus suis. et filios eius interficiam in morte, et scient omnes ecclesiae quia ego sum scrutans renes et corda, et dabo uni cuique uestrum secundum opera uestra. uobis autem dico ceteris qui Thyatirae estis: Quicumque non habent doctrinam hanc, qui non cognouerunt altitudines satanae, quemadmodum dicunt, non mittam super uos aliud pondus, tamen id quod habetis tenete donec ueniam. et qui uicerit et qui custodierit usque in finem opera mea, dabo ei potestatem super gentes . . . . qui habet aurem, audiat quid spiritus dicat ecclesiis [*transcriptional errors have been corrected*].

29 illis *fuld* 30 agerent *fuld* 33 tribulatione maxima *fuld* 35 suis] eius *fuld* 47 illi *fuld*

From this comparison we can gather that both the earlier texts were before Jerome in his revision of the Apocalypse, and that he followed now one, now the other, deserting both at times in favour of a translation more nearly representing the Greek. The alteration *et in diebus* (l. 5) brings the text into conformity with AC and other Greek authorities. The only Greek authority for the omission of *quia* (l. 9) is C. *Coram* (l. 11) is an improvement of the Latinity and closer to the Greek: Jerome was always anxious to give good Latin renderings, and again and again in his writings criticises harsh renderings of the Old Latin. The Vulgate is alone in omitting an object to *edere* (l. 11). In l. 13 Jerome agrees with the great uncials in connecting *similiter* with what precedes. *Aurem* (l. 14) is literal: the Greek is οὖς (so l. 48). The only Greek uncial which omits *suos* in l. 21 is A. In the same line Jerome deserts literalness for smoothness. In l. 22 the change from *scio* to *noui* is one which Jerome has made elsewhere, perhaps from a desire to keep the old distinction in meaning between the two words. In l. 24 the only uncial without the *tuam* is ℵ. In l. 25 *meliora* is unique, and *priorum* is an interesting survival of the genitive after the comparative, borrowed by the early translators from the Greek. In l. 26 the only Greek uncial authority for *multa* (πολύ) is ℵ. In l. 27 the Old Latin *Zezabel*, of which Tischendorf has nothing to say, is removed by Jerome. Here also the Greek authorities are reversed, the authorities for *tuam* being AB, while those who omit are ℵCP. It is as difficult to answer why Jerome kept the Greek word *idolothytis* in l. 29, as to say why he retained *dyscolis* in 1 Pet. ii 18. In l. 35 *in morte* is an example of more literal adherence to the Greek, as are *scrutans* in l. 37, and *altitudines* (l. 42). In l. 38 Ambrosiaster follows B, the others ACP; ℵ omits the word. In l. 43 the future is read by Bℵ, the present by ACP.

It has been noted that the text of the Apocalypse in the *Liber Comicus*, a seventh century service-book of Toledo, printed by Dom Morin as the first part of his *Anecdota Maredsolana*[1], has analogies with that of our author. But this text has also analogies with that of Primasius, and has also obviously been contaminated with the Vulgate. It is possible that in its original form it may

[1] Maredsoli: 1893, pp. xiv + 463, 4to.

have been identical with that of Ambrosiaster, but, if that be so, few similarities are now left.

§ 9. *The Text of S. Paul's Epistles*[1]. It is proposed in the present section to examine the character of the text of the Pauline Epistles, which Ambrosiaster used and incorporated complete in the commentaries which he wrote on these epistles. Two sets of collations are provided. The first tests the text for 'Africanisms'; the purpose of the second is to examine the character of its 'Europeanism.' The two sets are also linked together in a way presently to be described.

For the first set, all quotations from S. Paul's epistles in Cyprian's *Testimonia* are, in company with the same verses as quoted by Ambrosiaster, collated with the Latin side of Codex Claromontanus, the celebrated bilingual manuscript of the epistles, which is generally known as D^{paul} or D_2, to distinguish it from Codex Bezae (D). For the second, all quotations found in the works of Lucifer of Cagliari are, in company with the same verses as quoted by Ambrosiaster, collated with the Clementine Vulgate. Both Cyprian and Lucifer quote with exactness and are preserved in good manuscripts; they are therefore admirable witnesses for our purpose.

The value of the collations has been increased by the cross references which have been added throughout. Every reading in the first apparatus, which is found in the Vulgate, has added to it the letters *vg*; every reading in the second, which is found in d_2, has similarly added to it the symbol d_2.

It is hoped that the great trouble which has been taken to make these collations perfectly accurate will result in their usefulness to students of the biblical texts of Cyprian, Lucifer, the Vulgate and Claromontanus, as well as that of Ambrosiaster. I have been enabled to purify the text of Ambrosiaster in the second set by the kindness of Father Brewer, who lent me many valuable collations in his possession, and in both sets by the use of the Bodleian manuscripts, which are, for the most part, almost as good as any of the older MSS.

[1] The plan of the present section is due to Mr F. Crawford Burkitt, University Lecturer in Palaeography, Cambridge, who very kindly gave me the benefit of his advice.

The Migne text of Ambrosiaster is far from satisfactory. It would have saved me much trouble, if I had allowed myself to edit the quotations first, and then presented them edited. But I have preferred to be honest with the reader, and let him see for himself wherein the differences from the printed text exactly consist. There need be no hesitation in regarding as the genuine text of Ambrosiaster such readings as are common to the MSS of Ambrosiaster and Cyprian on the one hand, and the MSS of Ambrosiaster and Lucifer on the other. In such cases the printed text is absolutely valueless. Its errors are due to three causes, harmonisation with the Vulgate in MSS and in editions, errors of manuscripts, and the adoption of readings from the Roman edition of Ambrose (1579).

The Roman edition of our commentaries is probably the best in existence. It was based on good manuscripts and on the whole resists the seductions of the Vulgate. But for two reasons it cannot always be relied on. As the title-page naively confesses[1], the text of the Epistles has often been brought into harmony with quotations found in 'the other works of Ambrose.' Further, I cannot divorce from myself the suspicion that at times the worthy editors wrote the text for themselves. When all deductions are made, however, there remains enough to give the edition as great distinction as its paper and typographical arrangement promise.

Different persons will draw different conclusions from the facts here presented. The collations are intended to be much more useful than any deductions I draw from them. It must be remembered that the study of the Latin texts of the Pauline epistles is as yet in its infancy. Few except Ziegler and Corssen have faced the subject seriously. If, then, my conclusions seem either puerile or wrong, that does not affect the value of the evidence on which they are based.

The texts of Cyprian and Ambrosiaster are obviously far apart from one another. Take a long passage like 1 Cor. i 17—24, for example, and see how often *Cyp* stands alone; or, again, such as Rom. iii 8, 1 Cor. xv 47—49, 2 Cor. ix 12, 2 Tim. ii 23 f. Yet, there is some sort of a connexion between them; else, how could

[1] '*Textus sacrae scripturae tum ex commentariis ipsis, tum ex aliis auctoris locis conquisitus, ad germanam sancti Ambrosii lectionem fideliter est restitutus.*'

both have the renderings *legis constitutio* (Rom. ix 4), *festa* (1 Cor. v 8), *expono* (Eph. iv 22)? If Cyprian's be the earliest Latin text of the epistles, as seems possible, it underwent a single or double revision to become Ambrosiaster's.

The texts of Lucifer and Ambrosiaster, who were contemporaries, are, on the contrary, closely related. Their relationship may be either that of brothers, the latter being the more cultivated of the two, or that of father and son. If the second view be correct, then I see nothing to prevent us regarding Cyprian's version as the earliest Latin version of the epistles, Lucifer's as a thorough revision of that, and Ambrosiaster's as Lucifer's text polished. We do not know when the text employed by Lucifer was introduced into Sardinia. This may have happened some generations before his day, and it was probably brought from Rome.

One thing seems to be clear, namely that Claromontanus is Lucifer's text, contaminated with the Vulgate in the longer epistles. The agreements seem too close for any other explanation.

The differences between Ambrosiaster's text and the Vulgate are such as Jerome might have made, according to his usual plan in revision. The Latinity of both is about equally good, and Ambrosiaster's text must have been known to Jerome, whether it was the basis of his revision or not. It will be seen that the differences between them are due sometimes to Greek authorities, sometimes to improvements, as Jerome would regard them, of the language. In Eph. iv 16, for example, Jerome adds the words *secundum operationem* from good Greek authorities like BℵA.

Our author's text is a good 'Western' text, from which editing eliminates many errors. It will readily be observed from the collations provided that it was not possible for Tischendorf to represent the text properly. Sometimes 'Ambrst' has to be struck out of his apparatus, sometimes the weight of his evidence has to be transferred to the other side. I hope it may be possible, after the appearance of Father Brewer's edition, to publish a recension of Ambrosiaster's Pauline text apart from the commentary.

Collations of Pauline Quotations in Cyprian's *Testimonia*[1] and Ambrosiaster with the Latin of *Codex Claromontanvs*.[2]

Ambrst = Ambrosiaster Commentaries as in Migne.

B = Codex Bodleianus 756 (s. xi) } quoted only when they give a different
Bo = Codex Bodleianus 689 (s. xii) } text from *Ambrst*.

vg = Clementine Vulgate of the New Testament, except in *Galatians*, where it is Dr P. Corssen's text (Berol. 1885).

rom = The Roman edition of Ambrose (1579), seldom cited.

Rom. i 25 f. = *Cyp* 122.

et coluerunt et seruierunt creaturae potius quam creatori qui est benedictus in saecula amen. Propterea tradidit illos deus in passionis ignominiae

relicto creatore *Cyp* *om.* qui......amen *Cyp*
propter quod *Cyp* passiones *Cyp Ambrst vg*

Rom. ii 1 = *Cyp* 139.

Propterea inexcusabilis es o homo omnes qui iudicas In quo enim alterum iudicas te ipsum condemnas eadem enim agis qui iudicas

quare *Cyp* quapropter *Ambrst* sine causatione (*corr.* 2 *m.* excusatione) *Cyp*
om. omnes qui iudicas *Cyp* omnis *Ambrst vg* In quo—*alt.* iudicas *om.* *B*
iudicas alium *Cyp* iudicas alterum *Ambrst vg* quae *Cyp Ambrst vg*

[1] By Cyprian's *Testimonia* I mean the text offered by L (*codex Vindobonensis* 962, s. IX), of which Dr Sanday very kindly lent me a complete photograph. This has enabled me to give occasionally a more accurate report of its readings than that of Hartel, whose pages I add.

[2] I use Tischendorf's superb apograph (Lips. 1852), the use of which was granted to me by the Editor of this series, and later by Dr Sanday.

Rom. ii 3, 4, 5, 6 = *Cyp* 139, 147.

Existimas autem hoc o homo qui iudicas eos qui talia agunt et facies ea quia tu effugies iudicium dei an diuitias bonitatis eius et patientiae et longanimitatis contemnis ignorans quoniam benignitas dei ad paenitentiam te adducit secundum autem duritiam tuam et sine paenitentiam cor thensaurizasti tibi iram in die irae et reuelationis iusti iudicii dei qui reddet unicuique secundum opera eius

speras *Cyp* ergo *B* *om.* hoc *B* hoc o homo] tu *Cyp* eos] de iis (his *B Bo*) *Ambrst* talia] mala *Cyp* facies ea] eadem facis *Cyp* facis ea *Ambrst vg* facies ea (*corr.*) *B* quoniam *B* tu] ipse *Cyp* an *add* numquid *Cyp* opulentiam *Cyp* patientiae et longanimitatis] sustinentiam et patientiam *Cyp* et longanimitatis] *om.* *B* contemnis] contestinis *errore Cyp* ignoras *B Bo vg* quoniam] quia *Cyp* bonitas *Cyp Ambrst* ad] in *Cyp* adducit *B vg* prouocat *Ambrst* secundum autem] tu autem secundum *Cyp* autem dur. *B*] dur. autem *Ambrst* sine paenitentiam cor] cor inpatiens (*errore pro* inpaenitens) *Cyp* inpaenitens cor *Ambrst vg* cor inpaenitens *B* thesaurizas *Cyp Ambrst vg* diem *Cyp* eius *B vg*] sua *Cyp Ambrst*

Rom. ii 12, 13 = *Cyp* 178, 177.

quicumque enim sine lege peccauerunt sine lege peribunt et quicumque in lege peccauerunt per lege iudicabuntur. Non (enim) auditores legis iusti sunt aput deum sed factores legis iustificabuntur

quicumque *bis*] quodquod *Cyp* *om.* enim *Cyp* sine lege *bis*] inique *Cyp* et *ante* peribunt *Ambrst*, *om.* *B Bo vg* peccauerint *B* lege] legem et *Cyp* legem *Ambrst vg* *om.* enim *Cyp* *om.* sunt *Cyp*

Rom. iii 8 = *Cyp* 178.

faciamus mala ut ueniant bona quorum damnatio iusta est

ut ueniant] dum ueniunt *Cyp* condemnatio *Cyp*

Rom. iii 23—4 = *Cyp* 94.

omnes enim peccauerunt et egent gloriam dei iustificati gratis per ipsius gratiam per redemptionem quae est in Christo Iesu

gloriam *B* claritate *Cyp* gloria *Ambrst vg* iustificantur autem dono ipsius et gratia *Cyp* iustificatis (*corr.*) *B* ip. gr.] gr. ip. *Ambrst vg* redemptione *Cyp*

Rom. v 2—5 = *Cyp* 119.

gloriamur in spe gloriae dei Non solum autem sed et gloriamur in tribulationibus scientes quod tribulatio patientiam operatur patientia autem probationem probatio autem spem spes autem non confundit quia caritas dei diffusa est in cordibus nostris per spiritum sanctum qui datus est nobis

claritatis *Cyp*   filiorum *add. Ambrst* (*non B*) *vg*   *om.* autem *B*   pressuris *Cyp*   *add.* nostris *Ambrst*   quoniam *Cyp*   quod (d *in ras.*) *B*   pressura *Cyp*   tolerantiam *Cyp*   tolerantia *Cyp*   prob. autem] prob. uero *Bo*   dilectio *Cyp*   infusa *Cyp*   *om.* in *Cyp*   uestris *B*

Rom. viii 16 f. = *Cyp* 132.

(quod) simus fili dei si autem fili et heredes haeredes autem dei coheredes autem Christi si ita conpatimur ut et simul glorificemus

(quod) simus] sumus *Cyp Ambrst vg*   filii *Cyp bis Ambrst bis vg bis*   *om.* haeredes autem *Cyp*   autem *alt.*] quidem *Ambrst vg*   si ita] siquidem *Cyp* si tamen *Ambrst vg*   conpatimur *Bo* conpatiamur *Cyp Ambrst*   simul glorificemus] commagnificemur *Cyp* simul glorificemur *Ambrst*

Rom. viii 18 = *Cyp* 132.

indignae sunt passiones huius temporis ad futuram gloriam que reuelabitur in nobis

non sunt condignae *Cyp Bo vg* non sint condignae *Ambrst*   passionis *Cyp*   superuenturam *Cyp*   claritatem *Cyp*   uobis *Cyp*

Rom. viii 24 f. = *Cyp* 151.

spe enim salui facti sumus spes autem que uidetur non est spes nam quod uidet quis quid sperat si autem quod non uidemus speramus per patientiam expectamus

enim *om. Cyp*   salui facti] saluati (*ex* saluti) *Cyp* saluati *Ambrst*   autem] enim *B Bo*   quod enim *Cyp*   si autem] sed si (si *in ras. Bo*) *Ambrst*   patientiam expectamus] exspectationem speramus *Cyp*

Rom. viii 35—37 = *Cyp* 133.

Quis ergo nos separauit a caritate Christi tribulatio an angustia persecutio an famis an nuditas an periculum an gladium sicuti scriptum est quia propter te morti adficimur tota die extimati sumus quasi oues occisionis. Sed in his omnibus superamus propter eo qui dilexit nos

qui (*corr.*) *Cyp Bo*   qui *B*   *om.* ergo *Cyp Ambrst*   separabit *Cyp Ambrst vg* ab agape *Cyp* (2*m. s. l.* dilectione)   pressura *Cyp*   *om.* an *pr. B*   angustiae *Cyp*   an *ante* persec. *Cyp Ambrst*   fames *Cyp Ambrst vg*   gladius *Cyp Ambrst vg*   sicut *Cyp Ambrst vg*   quoniam *Cyp*   causa tui *Cyp*   mor. adf.] occidimur *Cyp*   morte (*om. Bo*) adf. (adficiuntur *B* afficiamur (*corr.*) *Bo*) *Ambrst*   deputati *Cyp*   aestimati *Ambrst vg*   ut *Cyp* uelut *Ambrst*   uictimae *Cyp*   superuincimus *Cyp*   pro *Cyp*   eum *Ambrst vg*   qui] quod *Cyp*

Rom. ix 3—5 = *Cyp* 70.

optabam enim anathema esse ipse ego a Christo pro fratribus meis qui sunt cognati secundum carnem qui sunt Israhelitae quorum adoptio est filiorum et gloria et testamenta et legislatio et obsequium et promissa quorum patres et ex quibus Christus secundum carnem qui est super omnia deus benedictus in saecula amen

ego (*pro* enim) *Cyp* ego ipse a. esse *Ambrst vg* a. esse ego ipse *B* ipse ego a. esse *Bo* *om.* ego *Cyp* a *om.* (*add*) *Bo* *om.* meis *Cyp* cognatis meis qui sunt *Cyp* cognatis *Ambrst* *om.* est filiorum *Cyp* claritas *Cyp* testamentum *Cyp vg* legis latio et testamenta *Bo* legislatio] legis constitutio *Cyp B* famulatus *Cyp* promissiones *Cyp* saecula saeculorum *B* *om.* amen *Cyp*

Rom. xi 20 f. = *Cyp* 117.

noli altum sapere sed time si enim deus naturalibus ramis non pepercit ne forte nec tibi parcat

Rom. xi 33—36 = *Cyp* 155.

O altitudo diuitiarum en sapientiae scientiae dei quam inconprehensibilia iudicia eius et inuestigabilis uiae eius quis enim cognouit sensum dei aut quis consiliarius eius fuit aut quis prior dedit illi et retribuetur illi quoniam ex ipso et per ipsum et in ipsum omnia ipsi gloria in saecula amen

en sap. sci.] et sap. et sci. *Cyp* sap. et sci. *Ambrst vg* inexscrutabilia *Cyp* inscrutabilia *Ambrst* (*non Bo*) sunt *post* inexscr. *Cyp post* inscr. *Ambrst post* inconpreh. *Bo vg* et inuestig. uiae eius] et cetera *Bo* et quam *Cyp* inuestigabiles *Cyp Ambrst vg* ipsius *Ambrst* eius *B vg* domini *Ambrst vg* (*pro* aut *post* fuit) uel *Cyp* eius] illi *Ambrst* eius *B Bo vg* fuit] *add.* et ostendit illi *Bo* illi *pr.*] ei *Cyp* reddetur *B Bo* illi] ei *Ambrst vg* ipsum *alt.*] ipso *Cyp Ambrst vg* sunt omnia *Cyp Ambrst vg* claritas *Cyp* in s. am.] *om.* *Ambrst* amen] saeculorum *Cyp*

Rom. xii 14 = *Cyp* 126.

benedicite et nolite maledicere

benedicentes et non maledicentes *Cyp*

Rom. xii 17 = *Cyp* 140.

nulli malum pro malo reddentes

nulli] non enim *Bo* nemini *Cyp Ambrst*

Rom. xii 19 = *Cyp* 180.

mihi uindictam ego retribuam dicit dominus

et *ante* ego *Ambrst* *sine* et *B Bo vg*

Rom. xii 21 = *Cyp* 140.

noli uinci a malo sed uince in bono malum

non *Cyp*

Rom. xiii 3 = *Cyp* 149.

uis autem non timere potestatem bonum fac et habebis laudem ex illa

om. autem *Cyp* bona *B* facito *Ambrst* ex] ab *Cyp* illa] ea *Cyp*

Rom. xiii 7—8 = *Cyp* 118.

reddite ergo omnibus deuita cui tributum tributum cui uectigal uectigal cui timorem timorem cui honorem honorem nemini quidquam debeatis nisi ut inuicem diligatis

om. ergo *Cyp* quae debentur *Cyp* debita *Ambrst vg*

Rom. xiv 4 = *Cyp* 139.

tu quis es qui iudices alienum seruum suo domino stat aut cadet stabit autem potens est enim deus statuere eum

qui *Cyp* iudicas *Cyp Ambrst vg* domino suo *Cyp vg* stat *Cyp B vg* aut stat *Ambrst* cadit *Cyp Ambrst vg* enim] autem *Bo* deus *om. B* eum] illum *Ambrst vg*

Rom. xiv 17 = *Cyp* 164.

non est enim regnum dei esca eet potus sed iustitia et pax et gaudium in spiritu sancto

om. est *Bo* *om.* enim *Cyp* dei regnum *Bo* et *Cyp Ambrst vg*

1 Cor. i 10 = *Cyp* 174.

Obsecro autem uos fratres per nomen Iesu Christi domini nostri ut id ipsum dicatis omnes et non sint in uobis scissurae sitis autem perfecti in eodem sensu et in eadem scientia

domini nostri Iesu Christi *Cyp Ambrst vg* dicatis] iudicatis *Cyp* scismata *Cyp Ambrst vg* perfecti] compositi *Cyp* scientia] sententia *Cyp vg*

1 Cor. i 17—24 = *Cyp* 169, 63.

non enim misit me Christus baptizare sed euangelizare non in sapientia uerbi ut non euacuetur crux Christi Verbum enim crucis pereuntibus stultitia

om. non enim *Cyp* *om.* baptizare sed *Cyp* adnuntiare *Cyp* sermonis sapientia *Cyp* ne inanis fiat *Cyp* pereuntibus] *add.* quidem *Ambrst vg* stultitia est his qui pereunt *Cyp* est his autem qui salui fiunt uirtus dei est scriptum est enim perdam sapientiam sapientium et prudentiam prudentium reprobabo Ubi sapiens ubi scriba ubi conquisitor huius saeculi nonne stulta fecit deus sapientiam huius mundi nam quia in sapientia dei non cognouit mundum per sapientiam domini placuit deo per stultitiam praedicationis saluos facere credentes quoniam quidem Iudaei signa petunt et Graeci sapientiam quaerunt nos autem praedicamus Christum crucifixum Iudaeis quidem scandalum gentibus autem stultitiam ipsis autem uocatis Iudaeis et Graecis Christum dei uirtutem et dei sapientiam

saluantur *Cyp* scr. est enim *add.* in Esaia *Ambrst* et (*eras.*) *ante* prudentiam *Cyp* intellectum *Ambrst* saeculi huius *Cyp* infatuauit *Cyp* stultam fecit *Ambrst vg* nam quia] quoniam quidem *Cyp* nam quoniam *Ambrst* in (*eras.*) sapientiam *Cyp* mundus *Cyp Ambrst vg* domini] deum *Ambrst vg* conplacuit *Cyp* saluare *Cyp* quidem] *om. Cyp Ambrst* et *vg* petunt] desiderant *Cyp* prudentiam *Cyp* autem] uero *Ambrst* et Gr.] atque gr. *Ambrst vg*

1 Cor. iii 1—3 = *Cyp* 115.

et ego fratres non potui loqui uobis quasi spiritalibus sed quasi carnalibus quasi paruolis in Christo lac uobis potum dedi et non escam nondum enim poteratis sed neque adhuc potestis adhuc enim estis carnales Cum enim sit inter uos aemulatio et contentio et dissensiones nonne carnalis estis et secundum hominem ambulatis

quidem *post* ego *Cyp* uobis loqui *Cyp Ambrst vg* infantibus *Cyp* lacte uos potaui *Cyp* *om.* et *Ambrst vg* cibo *Cyp* adhuc *pr.*] nunc *Cyp Ambrst vg* estis carnales *Cyp B Bo* carnales estis *Ambrst vg* ubi enim *Cyp* nam cum *B Bo* *om.* sit *Cyp Ambrst* in uobis *Cyp Ambrst* (aem. in uobis *Bo*) aemulatio *Cyp B Bo* aemulationes *Ambrst* contentio et dissensiones] contentiones sint *Ambrst* non *Cyp* (*m.* 1) carnales *Cyp Ambrst vg*

1 Cor. iii 16 f. = *Cyp* 142.

Nescitis quia templum dei estis et spiritus dei habitat in uobis si quis templum dei uiolauerit disperdet illum deus

quis] qui *Cyp* uiolabit *Cyp* illum *Cyp B Bo vg* eum *Ambrst*

1 Cor. iii 18 f. = *Cyp* 170.

Nemo uos seducat banis uerbis si quis uidetur sapiens esse inter uos in hoc saeculo stultus fiat ut sit sapiens sapientia enim huius saeculi stultitia est aput deum scriptum est enim adpraehendam sapientes in astutia eorum

uos seducat] se decipiat *Cyp* se seducat *Ambrst vg* *om.* uanis uerbis *Cyp Ambrst vg* quis uidetur] qui putat *Cyp* sapiens] sapientem se *Cyp* in uobis *Cyp* in hoc saeculo] saeculo huic *Cyp* sit] fiat *Cyp* saeculi] mundi *Cyp Ambrst vg* adpraehendam] reprehendes *Cyp* reprehendens *Ambrst* ipsorum *Cyp B Bo*

1 Cor. iv 7 = *Cyp* 116.

quid autem habes quod non accepisti quod si accepisti quid gloriaris quasi non acceperis

autem *B Bo vg* enim *Cyp Ambrst* acceperis *Cyp* si autem *Cyp Ambrst vg* accepisti∗ *Bo*

1 Cor. iv 20 = *Cyp* 177.

non enim in sermone est regnum dei sed in uirtute

nec *Ambrst* *om.* enim *Cyp*

1 Cor. v 7 f. = *Cyp* 125.

expurgate uetus fermentum ut sitis noua consparsio sicut estis azymi Etenim pascha nostrum immolatus est Christus itaque diem festum celebremus non in fermento uetere neque in fermento malitiae et nequitiae sed in azymis sinceritatis et ueritatis

nam et *Cyp* etenim *Cyp B Bo vg* *om. Ambrst* diem festum] festa *Cyp Ambrst* ueteri *Cyp Ambrst vg* nec *Ambrst*

1 Cor. vi 1 f. = *Cyp* 151.

Autdet aliquis uestrum aduersus alterum negotium habent iudicari aput iniustos et non aput sanctos aut nescitis quia sancti de hoc mundo iudicabunt

audet *Cyp Ambrst vg* quisquam *Cyp* habens neg. *Ambrst vg* (*sed* h. n. a. a. *vg*) neg. habens *Cyp* disceptare *Cyp* iniquos *Ambrst vg* omnes (*exp. m.* 2) sanctos *Bo* *om.* aut *Cyp* ignoratis *Ambrst* quoniam *Ambrst vg* de hoc mundo *B Bo vg*] mundum *Cyp* hunc mundum *Ambrst*

1 Cor. vi 7—9 = *Cyp* 151.

quidem omnino delictum est uobis quia iudicia habetis inter uos quare non magis iniuriam patimini quare non magis fraudamini sed uos fraudatis et iniuriam facitis et hoc fratribus aut nescitis quoniam iniqui regnum dei non possidebunt

quidem] iam q. *Cyp Ambrst vg* omnino] in totum *Cyp* est uobis] in uobis est *Cyp Ambrst* (i. u. o. d. *B*) quod *Ambrst vg* inter uos] aduersus inuicem *Cyp* patimini *Cyp B* accipitis *Ambrst vg* fraudem patimini *Cyp Bo vg* fraudamini *B* fraudem *Ambrst* fr. et ini. fac.] ini. fac. et fr. *Cyp Ambrst vg* fratres *Cyp* an *Ambrst vg* quia *Ambrst vg* iniusti *Cyp* consequuntur *Cyp*

1 Cor. vi 9—11 = *Cyp* 167.

neque inpudici neque idoliseruientes neque adulteri neque molles neque masculorum concubitores neque fures neque auari neque ebriosi neque maledici neque rapaces regnum dei possidebunt Sed haec aliquando fuistis sed abluti estis sed sanctificati estis sed iustificati estis in nomine domini Iesu Christi et in spiritu dei nostri

fornicarii *Cyp Ambrst vg* idolis seruientes *Cyp Ambrst vg* neque masc. conc.] et neque idolis seruientes (n. i. s. *eras.*) neque masc. adpetitores *Cyp* n. a. n. f. *Bo* auari] fraudulenti *Cyp* raptores *Cyp* consequentur *Cyp* sed] et *Cyp Ambrst vg* haec *Cyp B Bo vg* hoc *Ambrst* aliquando] quidem (*corr.* quidam *et deinde rursus corr.* quidem) *Cyp* quidem *Ambrst* quidam *vg* domini *add.* nostri *Ambrst vg* *om.* in *Ambrst*

1 Cor. vi 15 ff. = *Cyp* 166.

nescitis quia corpora uestra menbra Christi sunt tollens ergo menbra Christi faciam membra meretricis absit Aut nescitis quia qui se iungit meretrici unum corpus est erunt enim inquid duo in carne una qui autem se iungit domino unus spiritus est

quia *Cyp B Bo* quoniam *Ambrst vg* Christi sunt *Cyp B Bo* sunt Christi *Ambrst vg* tollam *Ambrst* tollens *B Bo* auferens *Cyp* *om.* ergo *Cyp* et *ante* faciam *Ambrst* (*non B Bo*) fornicariae *Cyp* *om.* absit *Cyp* an *Ambrst vg* *om.* qui *Cyp* se iungit] conglutinantur *Cyp* adhaeret *Ambrst vg* fornicariae *Cyp* est] sunt *Cyp* sit *B* fit *Ambrst* *om.* enim *Ambrst* *om.* inquid *Cyp* coniunxerint *Cyp* adhaeret *Ambrst vg* deo *B* sunt *Cyp*

1 Cor. vi 18 = *Cyp* 167.

Omne peccatum quodcumque fecerit homo extra corpus est qui autem fornicatur in corpus suum peccat

delictum *Cyp*

1 Cor. vi 19 f. = *Cyp* 123.

non estis uestri empti enim estis praetio glorificate deum in corpore uestro

praetio] magno *Cyp* pretio magno *Ambrst vg* clarificate et portate *Cyp Ambrst* glorificate et portate *Bo vg* dominum *B*

1 Cor. vii 1—7 = *Cyp* 145.

bonum est homini mulierem non tangere propter fornicationes autem unusquisque suam uxorem habeat et unaqueque suum uirum habeat Uxori uir

tangere *Bo vg* contingere *Cyp B* p. fornicationes autem] tamen p. fornicationem *Ambrst* suam uxorem *B Bo vg* uxorem suam *Cyp Ambrst* uirum suum *Cyp* debitum reddat similiter autem et uxor uiro mulier sui corporis potestatem non habet sed uir similiter autem et uir sui corporis potestatem non habet sed mulier nolite fraudare inuicem nisi forte ex consensu ad tempus ut uacetis orationi et iterum ad id ipsum ne uos temptet satanas propter intemperantiam uestram hoc autem dico secundum consilium non secundum imperium uolo autem omnes homines esse sicut et me ipsum sed unusquisque proprium habet donum a domino alius sic alius autem sic

om. autem *Cyp B* mulier] uxor *Cyp* sui corporis] corporis sui *Cyp* habet (*bis*) *Cyp B Bo vg* habeat (*bis*) *Ambrst* *om.* autem *Cyp Ambrst* corporis sui *Cyp* mulier] uxor *Cyp* fraudari (*corr. m.* 2) *Bo* *om.* forte *Cyp Ambrst* conuentione *Cyp* et *ante* ad *Cyp* iterum] *add.* reuertimini *Ambrst vg* temptet uos *Cyp vg* incontinentiam *Cyp vg* uestram *om. Cyp* autem *om. Cyp* consilium] ueniam *Cyp* indulgentiam *Ambrst vg* iussum *Cyp* uolebam *Ambrst* *om.* et *Ambrst vg* *om.* ipsum *Cyp* donum habet *Ambrst vg* carissima *errore* (carisma) *Cyp* a *B* ex *Ambrst vg* domino] deo *Cyp Ambrst vg* alius *pr.*] *add.* quidem *Ambrst vg* autem] uero *Ambrst vg*

1 Cor. vii 10 f. = *Cyp* 175.

His autem qui matrimonio iuncti sunt praecipio non ego sed dominus uxorem a uiro non discedere quodsi discesserit manere innuptam aut uiro reconciliari et uir uxorem ne dimittat

his *Cyp B Bo* iis *Ambrst vg* qui m. i. sunt] quae nupserunt *Cyp* iuncti (*corr.* coniuncti) *B* uincti *Bo* denuntio *Ambrst* (praecipio *B Bo vg*) discedere] separari *Cyp* quodsi] si autem *Cyp* recesserit *Cyp* uiro reconc.] reconc. uiro *Cyp* uiro suo reconc. *Ambrst vg* uir] uirum *Cyp Ambrst* ne demittat] non dimittere *Cyp Ambrst*

1 Cor. vii 29—31 = *Cyp* 123.

tempus breuiatum est relicuum est ut et qui habent uxores tanquam non habentes sint et qui flentes tanquam non flentes et qui gaudent tanquam non gaudentes et qui emunt tanquam non possidentes et qui utuntur hunc mundum tanquam non utantur praeteriit enim habitus huius mundi

collectum *Cyp* et *ante* rel. (*om. B Bo*) *Ambrst* superest ergo *Cyp* ita sint ac si (quasi *Bo*) non habentes *Ambrst* tanquam *pr.*] quasi *Cyp Bo* flent *Cyp Ambrst vg* quasi *Cyp* quasi *Cyp* gaudentes] *add.* sint *Bo* quasi *Cyp* hoc mundo utuntur *Cyp* utuntur hoc saeculo *Ambrst* quasi *Cyp* non *om. B* praeterit *Cyp Ambrst vg* figura *Cyp Ambrst vg*

1 Cor. vii 32—34 = *Cyp* 145.

qui sine uxore est sollicitus est quae sunt domini quomodo placeat domino qui autem cum uxore est cogitat quae sunt huius mundi quomodo placeat

qui—est] caeleps *Cyp* soll. est] cogitat *Cyp Ambrst* ea *in ras. ante* quae *Cyp* domini sunt *Ambrst vg* quomodo placeat domino *om. Ambrst habent B Bo* deo *Cyp B Bo vg* cum uxore est] matrimonium contraxit *Cyp* sollicitus est *Ambrst vg* *post* cogitat ea *in ras. Cyp* mundi huius *Cyp*

uxori diuisa est et mulier et uiro quae innupta est cogitat quae sunt domini ut sit sancta et corpore et spiritu quae autem nupta est cogitat quae sunt mundi quomodo placeat uiro

diuisa—innupta est] sic et mulier et uirgo innupta *Cyp* *om.* et *ante* mulier *Ambrst* uirgo *Ambrst* nam quae non est nupta *Ambrst* quae autem n. e. n. *B* q. autem innupta e. *Bo* cogitat *add.* ea *in ras. Cyp* sollicita est de iis (his *B Bo*) *Ambrst* dom. sunt *Ambrst vg* et *ante* corp. *om. Bo* quae autem] nam quae *B Bo* quae uero *Ambrst* nupta est] nupsit *Cyp* cogitat *add.* ea de his (ea *s. l.*) *Cyp* mundi *add.* huius *Cyp Bo* huius mundi *Ambrst*

1 Cor. vii 39 f. = *Cyp* 166.

Mulier alligata est quanto tempore uiuit uir eius quodsi dormitionem uir eius acceperit liberata est cui uult nubat tantum in domino beatior autem est si sic permanserit

uxor *B Bo* uincta *Cyp Ambrst* *add.* lege *Ambrst* (*Bo* 2 *m.* legi *vg*) quanto tempore] quamdiu *Cyp Ambrst* quodsi] si autem *Cyp Ambrst* dormitionem] dormierit *Cyp rom vg* mortuus fuerit *Ambrst* *om.* uir eius *Cyp rom* *om.* acceperit *Cyp Ambrst vg* uult] uolet *Cyp* felicior *Cyp* est] erit *Cyp Ambrst vg* manserit *Cyp*

1 Cor. viii 2 = *Cyp* 139.

quodsi quis se existimat cognouisse aliquid nondum cognouit quemadmodum oporteat scire

quodsi] si *Cyp vg* se existimat] putat *Cyp* existimat se *Ambrst* cognouisse aliquid] scire aliquid *Cyp vg* aliquid scire *Ambrst* scire *B Bo* cognouit] scit *Cyp* scire *Cyp B Bo* eum scire *Ambrst vg*

1 Cor. viii 8 = *Cyp* 164.

esca autem nos non commendat deo neque enim si manducauerimus abundauimus neque enim si non manducauerimus egemus

esca] cibus *Cyp* *om.* autem *Cyp* *om.* enim *ambo Cyp* ederimus *Ambrst* abundabimus *Cyp Ambrst vg* *om. alt.* enim *Ambrst vg* mand. *alt.*] ederimus *Cyp Ambrst* egebimus *Cyp* deerit nobis *Ambrst*

1 Cor. ix 24 f. = *Cyp* 141.

Nescitis quoniam qui in stadio currunt omnes quidem currunt unus autem accipit brabium sic currite ut conprehendatis omnes autem qui in agone contendit ab omnibus se abstinet illi quidem ut corruptibilem coronam accipiant nos autem incorruptibilem

quia *Cyp* sed unus *Bo vg* autem] tamen *Cyp* palmam *Cyp Ambrst* occupetis *Cyp* omnes—abstinet] *om Cyp* omnis *Ambrst vg* et *ante* illi *Cyp Ambrst vg* incorruptibilem *B* incorruptam *Cyp Ambrst vg*

1 Cor. x 1 = *Cyp* 42.

Nolo enim uos ignorare fratres quod patres nostri omnes sub nube erant

quia *Cyp Ambrst* fuerunt *Cyp Ambrst vg*

1 Cor. x 12 f. = *Cyp* 139, 175.

Itaque qui te putant stare uideat ne cadat temptatio uos non adpraehendit nisi humana fidelis autem deus qui non patietur uos temptari super id quod non potestis sed faciet cum temptatione etiam prouentum ut possitis sustinere

itaque] et *Cyp* propterea et *Ambrst* putat se *Bo* te] se *Cyp Ambrst vg* putant] putat *Cyp Ambrst* adpraehendit] occupabit *Cyp* adprehendat *Ambrst vg* *om.* qui *Cyp* supra *Ambrst vg* super *B* *om.* id *Cyp Ambrst* quod *Bo vg* quam *Ambrst* *om.* non *Cyp Ambrst vg* sed] et *Cyp* prouentum] euadendi facultatem *Cyp* tolerare *Cyp Ambrst* subtinere *B* sustinere *Bo vg*

1 Cor. x 23 = *Cyp* 176.

Omnia licent sed non omnia expediunt omnia licent sed non omnia aedificant

licent (*bis*) *Cyp B Bo* mihi licent (*bis*) *Ambrst vg* non omnia *pr.*] omnia non *Bo*

1 Cor. xi 19 = *Cyp* 176.

oportet enim et haeresesse ut et probati manifesti fiant inter uos

om. enim *Cyp* haereses esse *Cyp Ambrst vg* ut et] ut ut *Cyp* probati] qui probati sunt *Ambrst vg* fiant] sint *Cyp* inter uos] in uobis *Cyp vg*

1 Cor. xi 27 = *Cyp* 176.

Itaque quicumque manducauerit panem aut biberit calicem domini indigne reus erit corporis et sanguinis domini

om. itaque *Cyp* ederit *Cyp Ambrst* panem *add.* hunc *Ambrst vg* indigne *Cyp B Bo vg* indigne domino *Ambrst*

1 Cor. xi 33 f. = *Cyp* 164.

conuenientes ad manducandum inuicem expectate si quis esurit domi manducet ut non ad iudicium conueniatis

cum conuenitis *Cyp Ambrst vg* ad *alt.*] *om.* *Cyp* in *Ambrst vg*

1 Cor. xiii 2—8 = *Cyp* 115.

et si habeam omnem fidem ita ut montes transferam caritatem autem non habeam nihil sum Et si in cibos diuisero omnem substantiam meam et tradidero corpus meum ut ardeam caritatem autem non habeam nihil prodest mihi Caritas patiens est benigna est caritas non aemulatur caritas non est perpera non inflatur non ambitiosa est non quaerit quae sua sunt non inritatur non cogitat malum non gaudet super iniquitatem congaudet autem ueritati omnia sufferit omnia credit omnia sperat omnia sustenet caritas numquam excidet

habuero *Cyp Ambrst vg* caritatem—sum *om. Ambrst* agapen *Cyp m*1 (dilectionem *Cyp m* 2) haberem *Cyp m*1 in cibos diuisero] erogauero *Ambrst* *om.* in *Cyp m* 2 *add.* pauperum *post* cibos *Cyp m*2 *vg* distribuero *Cyp vg* (*sed* d. i. c. *vg*) omnia mea *Cyp* *add.* si *post* et *Cyp Ambrst vg* caritatem—habeam *om. Ambrst* agapem *Cyp* prodest mihi] proficio *Cyp* mihi prodest *Ambrst vg* agape *Cyp et sic constanter* magna anima *corr.* magnanima *Cyp* magnanima *Ambrst* agape *ante* benigna *Cyp* benigna] iucunda *Ambrst* est *om. Bo* 1*m* *om.* caritas *ante* non est perp. *Ambrst vg* n. infl. n. perperam agit *Ambrst* agit perperam *Cyp vg* perperam agit *Ambrst* non ambitiosa—sua sunt *om. Cyp* est ambitiosa *B vg* super iniquitatem *Bo vg* in iniquitate *Ambrst* iniquitate *B* super iniustitiam *Cyp* conlaetatur *Cyp* in ueritate *Cyp* sufferit] diligit *Cyp* tolerat *Ambrst* o. sp. o. sust.] omnia suffert omnia sperat *B Bo* sustinet *Cyp Ambrst vg* cadīt *Ambrst sed B Bo* excidit *vg*

1 Cor. xiii 12 = *Cyp* 155.

Videmus nunc per speculum in aenigmate tunc autem faciem ad faciem nunc scio ex parte tunc autem cognoscam sicut ego cognotus sum

uero *Ambrst* faciem *pr.*] faciem (m *exp. et eras.*) *Cyp* facie *Ambrst vg* modo *Ambrst* uero *Ambrst* (*om. B*) cognosco *B* sicut ego] sicuti ego *Cyp* sicut et *Ambrst vg* cognitus *Cyp Ambrst vg*

1 Cor. xiv 34 f. = *Cyp* 152.

(missing in Claromontanus) but there is no gap between 33 and 36

1 Cor. xv 33 = *Cyp* 177.

corrumpunt mores bonos conloquia mala

mores bonos] ingenia bona *Cyp* conloquia mala] confabulationes pessime *Cyp*

1 Cor. xv 36 = *Cyp* 159.

insipiens tu quod seminas non uiuificatur nisi prius moriatur

stulte *Cyp Ambrst* quod tu *Bo* si non *Cyp* *om.* prius *Cyp B* mortuum fuerit *Cyp*

1 Cor. xv 41—44 = *Cyp* 159.

stella enim stellae differet in caritate Ita et resurrectio mortuorum seminatur in corruptionem surgit in incorruptionem seminatur in contumeliam surgit in gloria seminatur in infirmitate surgit in uirtute seminatur corpus animale surgit corpus spiritale

om. enim *Cyp* differt a stella *Bo* stellae] a (ab) stella *Cyp Ambrst vg* differt *Cyp Ambrst vg* claritate *Cyp Ambrst vg* sic *Cyp vg* erit et *Ambrst* *post* seminatur *pr. add.* corpus *Cyp* corruptione *Cyp vg* corruptela *Ambrst* surgit *pr.*] resurget *ex* resurgit *Cyp* surget *Ambrst vg* in incorruptionem] sine corruptela *Cyp* in incorruptelam *B* (-a *Ambrst*) contumeliam] ignominia *Cyp Ambrst* surgit *alt.*] resurget *ex* resurgit *Cyp* resurget *vg Ambrst* gloriam *B Bo* surgit *tert.*] resurgit *Cyp* surget *Ambrst vg* seminatur *ult.*] semina (*corr. m* 2) *Bo* surgit *ult.*] resurget *ex* resurgit *Cyp* surget *Ambrst vg* corpus *ult.*] *om. Cyp*

1 Cor. xv 47—49 = *Cyp* 75, 123.

Primus homo de terra terrenus secundus homo de caelo qualis terrenus talis et terreni et qualis caelestis talis et caelestis sicut portauimus imaginem terrestris portemus et imaginem caelestis

terrae limo *Cyp* *om.* terrenus *Cyp* *post* caelo *add.* caelestis *Ambrst vg* ille e limo *Cyp* tales *Ambrst vg* qui de limo *Cyp* tales *Cyp Ambrst vg* caelestes *Cyp Ambrst vg* quo modo *Cyp* igitur sicut *Ambrst vg* portamus *B* eius qui de limo est *Cyp* illius terreni (t. i. *Bo*) *Ambrst* eius qui de caelo est *Cyp* huius caelestis *Ambrst*

1 Cor. xv 53—55 = *Cyp* 159.

oportet enim corruptibile hoc induere incorruptionem et mortale hoc induere inmortalitatem [Cum autem corruptibile hoc induerit incorruptalitatem et mortale hoc induere inmortalitatem] tunc fiet sermo qui scriptus est absorta est mors in uictoria ubi est mors stimulus tuus ubi est mors uictoria tua

corruptiuum istud *Cyp* incorruptibile *B* *om.* (?) hoc *B* incorruptelam *B Bo* cum autem—inmortalitatem *om. Cyp* corruptibile—et *om. Ambrst vg* induerit *Ambrst vg* sermo qui scriptus] uerbum quod scriptum *Cyp* absumpta *Cyp* uictoria] contentionem *Cyp* uictoriam *B* stimulus tuus *B Bo* aculeus tuus *Cyp* uictoria tua *Ambrst vg* uictoria tua *B Bo* contentio tua *Cyp* stimulus tuus *Ambrst vg*

2 Cor. iii 14—16 = *Cyp* 42.

obtunsi sunt sensus eorum usque in hodiernum diem id ipsum uelamen in lectione ueteris testamenti manet dum non rebelatur quoniam in Christo

hunc *Cyp* hoc eodem uelamento *Cyp* hoc (id *B Bo vg*) i. u. *Ambrst vg* manente *Cyp* quod non *Cyp* et nondum *B* reuelatur *Cyp Ambrst* quia *Cyp Ambrst* aboletur Sed usque in hodiernum cum legitur Moyses uelamen est positum super cor eorum cum autem conuersus fuerit ad deum auferetur uelamen

euacuatur *Cyp Ambrst vg* et *Cyp* *add.* diem *Ambrst vg* si quando *Cyp* Moses *Cyp* uelamentum *Cyp* *om.* positum *Cyp B Bo* supra *Ambrst* mox *Cyp* es *Cyp* dominum *Cyp Ambrst* (*B ex* deum) *vg* aufertur *Cyp* uelamentum *Cyp*

2 Cor. v 10 = *Cyp* 96, 157.

(nam) omnes uos manifestari oportet ante tribuna Christi ut ferat unusquisque propria corporis secundum quod gessit siue bonum siue malum

o. enim *Ambrst vg* nos *Cyp Ambrst vg* tribunal *Cyp Ambrst vg* ut unusq. (*ex* unusq. ut) recipiat *B* reportet *Cyp* recipiat *Ambrst* sui corporis propria *Cyp* secundum quod] secundum quae *Cyp* prout *Ambrst vg* egit *Cyp* bona *Cyp Ambrst* mala *Cyp Ambrst*

2 Cor. vi 14 = *Cyp* 166.

nolite iugum ducere cum infidelibus Quae enim participatio iustitiae cum iniquitate aut quae societas lucis ad tenebras

iugum ducere] coniungi *Cyp* enim] autem *Cyp* partic. *add.* est *Cyp* cum iniquitate] et iniquitati *Cyp B Bo* societas] communio est *Cyp* lucis] lumini *Cyp Ambrst* luminis *B* luci *Bo* ad tenebras *Bo vg* cum tenebris *Ambrst*

2 Cor. viii 12 f. = *Cyp* 114.

(Nam) si promptus animus est secundum quod habet acceptus est non secundum quod non habet non enim ut aliis sit remissio uobis tribulatio

si enim *Ambrst vg* uoluntas prompta *Cyp Ambrst vg* quod habet] quodcumque habuerit *Cyp* facultatem (uoluntatem *B Bo*) *Ambrst* acceptabile *Cyp* acceptabilis *Ambrst* habuerit *Cyp* habeat *Bo* non enim] neque *Cyp* sit remissio] refrigerium *Cyp* refrigerium (refugium *Bo*) sit *Ambrst* tribulatio] pressura sit *Cyp* autem angustia *Ambrst*

2 Cor. viii 14 f. = *Cyp* 113.

uestra abundantia ad illorum inopia ut et illorum abundantia sit ad uestram inopiam ut fiat aequalitas sicut scriptum est qui multum non abundauit et qui modicum non minorauit

om. ad *Cyp vg* inopiam suppleat *Cyp vg* inopiam *Ambrst* *om.* ut *Ambrst* s. a. u. i. u. f.] uestrae inopiae sit supplementum (*vg*) et sit *Cyp* fiat ad uestram inopiam ut fiat *Ambrst* ut fiat *vg* aequitas *B Bo* (*B* a. f.) *add.* habuit multum *post* multum (*alt.* multum *eras.*) *Cyp* *add.* habuit *post* multum *Ambrst* indiguit *Cyp*

2 Cor. ix 6—7 = *Cyp* 113.

qui seminat parce parce et metet et qui seminat in benedictione de benedictione et metet unusquisque sicut proposuit corde non ex tristitia aut necessitate hilarem enim datorem dicit deus

parce seminat *Cyp Ambrst vg* et q. s. i. b.] q. autem i. b. s. *Ambrst* benedictione *pr.*] benedictionem *Cyp* *om.* de *Cyp* in *habent B Bo* et *ante* metet *om. Bo* autem *add. post* unusquisque *Cyp* sicut corde proposuit *Cyp* secundum propositum cordis (cor *Bo*) *Ambrst* *add.* quasi *post* non *Cyp* aut] uel ex *Cyp* aut ex *B Bo vg* diligit *Cyp Ambrst vg*

2 Cor. ix 10—11 = *Cyp* 113.

Qui autem subministrat semen seminanti et panem in escam subministrauit et multiplicabit semen uestrum et augebit nascentia iustitiae uestrae in omnibus locupletati

om. autem *Cyp* administrat *Cyp vg* semen * * * (m *in ras.*) *Bo* seminanti (*ex* seminantis) *Cyp* ad edendum *Cyp Ambrst* ad manducandum *Bo vg* praestabit *Cyp Bo vg* ministrabit *Ambrst* seminationem uestram *Cyp* amplificabit *Ambrst* nascentia] incrementa frugum *Cyp Bo vg* fructum *Ambrst* ut i. o. locupletemini *Cyp Ambrst*

2 Cor. ix 12 = *Cyp* 113.

ministratio officii huius non solum replens ea quae desunt sanctis sed et abundat per multarum gratiarum actionem deo

administratio *Cyp* ministerium *Ambrst*[1] *rom vg* huius officii *Cyp vg* solum *om. Bo* tantum *Cyp* suppleuit *Cyp* subplet *Ambrst vg* sanctis desunt *Cyp* habundauit *Cyp* abundabit *Ambrst* multam *Cyp* multorum *Ambrst* multarum *B Bo* actiones *Ambrst* (*non B Bo*) *vg* in deum *Cyp* in deo *Ambrst*

2 Cor. xii 7—9 = *Cyp* 119.

datus est mihi stimulus carnis angelus satanae ut me colaphizet propter hoc dominum ter rogaui ut discederet a me et dixit mihi sufficit tibi gratia mea nam uirtus in infirmitate perficitur

add. meae *post* carnis *Cyp Bo vg* qui *Cyp B vg* *add.* ut non extollar *Cyp* ne extollar *Ambrst post* colaphizet quod *Cyp Bo vg* ter dominum *Cyp Ambrst vg* ait *Ambrst* dixit *B Bo vg*

Gal. i 10 = *Cyp* 156.

si adhuc hominibus placere Christi seruus non essem

om. adhuc *Cyp* *add.* uellem *post* placere *Cyp* placerem *Ambrst vg* seruus Christi *Ambrst* Christi seruus *B Bo vg*

[1] Printed text *mysterium*. The two words are very often confused in MSS (*misterium* and *miisterium*).

Gal. iii 6—9 = *Cyp* 43.

Abraham credidit deo et reputatum est ei ad iustitiam cognoscite ergo quia qui ex fide sunt hi sunt fili Abrahae prouidens autem scriptura quia ex fide iustificat gentes deus pronuntiauit Abrahae quia benedicuntur omnes gentes igitur qui ex fide sunt benedicentur cum fideli Abraham

credidit Abraham *Ambrst* reputatum *Bo vg* deputatum *Cyp* aestimatum *Ambrst* in *ex* ad *Cyp* cognoscitis *Cyp Ambrst* *om. pr.* sunt *B Bo* hii *Cyp Bo* ii *vg* filii *Cyp Ambrst vg* praenuntiauit *Cyp Ambrst vg* benedicentur *Cyp Ambrst vg* *et post* in illo *Cyp* in te *Ambrst vg* ergo *Ambrst* *om.* sunt *Bo* benedicti sunt *Cyp* benedicuntur *Ambrst* benedicentur *B Bo vg* ex *Ambrst* cum *B Bo rom vg*

Gal. iv 4 = *Cyp* 73.

postquam uero uero uenit plenitudo temporum misit deus filium suum factum ex muliere

at ubi *Cyp Ambrst vg* adubi (at ubi) autem *B Bo*[1] *om.* uero uero *Cyp Ambrst vg* adinpletio *Cyp* temporis *Cyp Ambrst* (s *in ras. Bo*) *vg* factum *Ambrst vg* natum *Cyp* natum (na *m2 in ras, quae add. s. l.* factum) *B* de *Cyp*

Gal. v 14 f. = *Cyp* 115.

diges proximum tuum sicut te ipsum quodsim mordetis et inaccusatis inuicem uidete ne consummamini[2] ab inuicem

diliges *Cyp Ambrst vg* tamquam *Cyp* *om.* ipsum *Cyp* si autem *Cyp* quod (quod * *Bo*) si *Ambrst vg* m. inuicem *Ambrst* inuicem m. *vg* incusatis *Cyp* criminatis *Ambrst* *om.* inuicem *Ambrst vg* ab inu. cons. *Ambrst vg* consumamini *Cyp Ambrst* (*exc. B*) *vg* inuice *Cyp*

Gal. v 17 = *Cyp* 167.

nam caro concupiscit aduersus spiritum spiritus autem aduersus carnem haec enim inuicem aduersantur ut non quaecumque uultis ista faciatis

om. nam *Cyp* nam caro] caro uero *B* spiritus autem *Bo vg*] et spiritus *Cyp* spiritus uero *Ambrst* inuicem *Bo* inuicem sibi *B* sibi inuicem *Ambrst vg* aduersantur *add.* sibi *Cyp* quaecumque] quae *Cyp* ea quae *Ambrst* ista] ipsa *Cyp* *om. Ambrst*

Gal. v 19—24 = *Cyp* 167.

Manifesta autem sunt opera carnis quae sunt adulteria fornicationis immunditia inpudicitia idololatrocinia beneficia inimicitiae contentiones aemulationis

autem sunt *Bo* sunt autem *Ambrst vg* *om.* autem *B* opera] facta *Cyp* adulterium *Ambrst* fornicationes *Cyp* fornicatio *Ambrst vg* inmunditiae *Cyp* impuritas *Ambrst* inpud.] spurcitiae *Cyp* obscenitas *Ambrst* idolatria *Cyp Ambrst* ueneficia *Cyp et add.* homicidia *Cyp* ueneficia *Ambrst vg* aemulationes *Cyp vg* simulationes *Ambrst*

[1] See above, chap. III, p. 71.

[2] This confusion with *consumo* is frequent in MSS.

irae inritationes dissensiones haeresis inuidiae homicidiae ebrietatis comisationes et similia his quae praedico uobis sicut et praedixi quia qui talia agunt regnum dei non possidebunt. Fructus autem spiritus est caritas gaudium pax patientia bonitas mansuetudo fides lenitas continentia castitatis aduersus huiusmodi non est lex qui autem Christi carnem crucifixerunt cum passionibus et concupiscentiis

irae] animositas *Cyp* inrit.] prouocationes simultates *Cyp* simultates *Ambrst* haereses *Ambrst* *om.* homicidiae *Cyp B Bo* *habet* homicidia *Ambrst vg* ebrietates *Cyp Ambrst vg* ebrietas *B* commemorationes *B* et] *add.* quae sunt *Ambrst* his similia *Cyp Ambrst vg* quae—quia *om. Cyp* et *om. Bo vg* quia] quod hi (hii *Bo*) *Ambrst* *ut supra sed* consequentur *vg* regni dei *Ambrst* hereditatem non consequentur *Ambrst* uero *Ambrst* caritas] agape *Cyp* patientia] magnanimitas *Cyp* longanimitas *Ambrst vg* benignitas *Ambrst vg* mans. fid.] fid. mans. *Cyp* spes *Ambrst* *om.* lenitas *Cyp* castitatis] castitas *Cyp* castitas bonitas *Ambrst* aduersus—lex *om. Cyp* autem] enim *Cyp* Christi] sunt Christi *Cyp Ambrst vg* Christi sunt *B* carnem] *add.* suam *Ambrst vg* passionibus] uitiis *Cyp Ambrst vg*

Gal. vi 1 f. = *Cyp* 120.

considerans unusquisque seipsum ne et ipse temptetur Alter alterius honera portate et sic impleuitis legem Christi

in contemplatione habentes *Cyp* *om.* unusquisque *Ambrst vg* *om.* seipsum *Cyp* temet (te *Bo vg*) ipsum *Ambrst* ipse temptetur] uos temptemini *Cyp* tu tempteris *Ambrst vg* alter alterius] alterutrum *Cyp* inuicem *Ambrst* honera *Bo* onera *Cyp*, *Ambrst* (*add.* uestra), *vg* sustinete *Cyp* adimplebitis *Cyp vg* implebitis *Ambrst*

Gal. vi 14 = *Cyp* 124.

mihi autem absit gloriari nisi in cruce domini nostri Iesu Christi per quem mihi mundus crucifixus est et ego mundo.

autem *Bo vg* uero *Ambrst* crucem *Cyp* *om.* nostri Iesu Christi *B*

Eph. ii 17 f. = *Cyp* 94.

et ueniens euangelizaui pacem uobis qui longe et pacem his qui iuxta quia per ipsum habemus accessum ambo in uno spiritu ad patrem

cum uenisset *Cyp* adnuntiauit *Cyp* euangelizauit *Ambrst vg* uobis pacem *Cyp* his *B Bo* hiis *Cyp* iis *Ambrst vg* *om.* qui *Cyp* prope *Cyp vg* *om.* accessum *Cyp* utrique *Ambrst*

Eph. iv 22—24 = *Cyp* 124.

deponere uos secundum priorem conuersationem ueterem hominem eum qui corrumpitur secundum concupiscentiam seductionis renouamini autem spiritu

exponite prioris conuersationis ueterem hominem *Cyp* ut exponatis (deponatis *Ambrst*) s. p. c. u. h. *B Bo* *om.* eum *Cyp Ambrst vg* concupiscentias *Cyp* desideria *Ambrst vg* deceptionis *Cyp* erroris *Ambrst vg* innouamini *Cyp* sensus uestri et induite nouum hominem qui secundum deum creatus est in iustitia et sanctitate et ueritate

sensu (spiritu *rom vg*) mentis uestrae *Ambrst vg* induimini *Ambrst* hominem] *add.* eum *Cyp* constitutus *Cyp* *om.* est *Bo* in iust. et sanct. et uer.] in uer. et iust. *Ambrst* in iust. et uer. *Bo* et (*ante* sanct.) *om. Cyp*

Eph. iv 26 = *Cyp* 120.

irascimini et nolite peccare sol[1] non occidat super iracundiam uestram

delinquere *Cyp*

Eph. iv 29—31 = *Cyp* 126, 120.

omnis sermo malus ex ore uestro non procedat sed si quis bonus ad aedificationem fidei ut det gratiam audientibus et nolite contristare sanctum spiritum dei in quo signati estis in diem redemptionis omnis amaritudo et ira et indignatio et clamor et blasphemia tollatur a uobis

de *Cyp Ambrst* prodeat *Cyp* *om.* si quis *Cyp* et *non citat Cyp* contristari *B Bo*[2] spiritum sanctum *Cyp Ambrst vg* auferantur *Cyp* auferatur *Ambrst*

Eph. v 3 f. = *Cyp* 150.

nec nominetur in uobis sicut decet sanctos aut turpitudo aut stultiloquium aut scurrilitas quae ad rem non pertinet

stultiloquium (*corr. ex* stultol.) et scurilitas (*sic B*) quae ad rem non pertinent ne nominentur quidem in uobis *Cyp* *ut supra exc.* inter uos (in uobis *Bo vg*) *et* pertinent (pertinet *B Bo vg*) *Ambrst* turpitudo] turpido *B*

Eph. vi 1—6 = *Cyp* 170, 171.

Fili obaudite parentibus uestris hoc enim est iustum honora patrem tuum et matrem Quod est mandatum primum in promissione et bene tibi sit et eris longae uitae super terram Et patres nolite ad iracundiam prouocare filios uestros sed et nutrite eos in disciplinam et correptionem domini Serui

filii *Cyp Ambrst vg* obsequentes estote *Cyp* obedite *Bo vg* uestris] *add.* in domino *Ambrst* (*non B Bo*) *vg* iustum est *Ambrst vg* promissionis *Ambrst* et *ante* bene] ut *Cyp B Bo vg* ut et *Ambrst* sit tibi *Cyp Ambrst vg* eris] sis *Cyp Ambrst vg* longae uitae] longaeuus *Cyp Ambrst vg* uos *ante* patres *Ambrst* (*non B Bo*) *vg* ad] in *Cyp* prouocare] mittere *Cyp* *om.* et *ante* nutrite *Cyp Ambrst vg* educate *Ambrst vg* illos *Ambrst vg* disciplina *Cyp Ambrst vg* correctione *Cyp* correptione *Ambrst vg*

[1] My copy of Migne XVII (1879) has *sed.* There must be over a thousand misprints in this reprint. What is said of the three preceding volumes (see Jülicher in *Theologische Literaturzeitung* XXVIII (1903) 102 f.) is equally true of this.

[2] *Contristari* (depon.) is hitherto unexampled.

obaudite dominis carnalibus cum timore et tremore in simplicitate cordis uestris sicut Christo non ad oculum seruientes quasi hominibus placentes sed ut serui Christi

oboedite *Cyp Ambrst vg* timore] metu *Cyp* uestri *Cyp Ambrst vg* homini *Cyp* sicut] sicut et *Bo* sed *om. Bo* ut serui Christi *om. B Bo* ut] quasi *Cyp*

Eph. vi 9 = *Cyp* 171.

Et domini eadem facite ad illos remittentes minas scientes quia et uestrum ipsorum dominus est in caelis et personarum acceptio non est aput deum

nos *post* et *Cyp Ambrst vg* eos *Cyp* laxantes *Cyp* dimittentes *B Bo* iracundiam *Cyp* quod *Ambrst* uester *Ambrst* et *ante* ipsorum *Cyp B Bo* (illorum *Ambrst*) exceptio personarum *Cyp* non est acceptio *Ambrst* aput deum] in illo *Cyp* apud eum *Ambrst* (apud deum *B Bo*) *vg*

Eph. vi 12—17 = *Cyp* 183.

quia non est uobis colluctatio (*sic*) aduersus sanguinem et carnem sed contra potestates contra huius mundi rectores tenebrarum harum contra spiritalia nequitiae in caelestibus Propterea accipite arma dei ut possitis resistere in die malo et omnibus operis stetis praecincti lumbos uestros in ueritate induentes loricam iustitiae et calciati pedes in praeparationem euangelii pacis in omnibus adsumentes scutum fidei in quo possitis omnia iacula nequissimi candentia extinguere et galeam salutaris et gladium spiritus quod est uerbum dei

om. quia *Cyp* quoniam *Ambrst vg* nobis *Cyp vg* conluctatio *Cyp Bo* (inluctatio *B* lucta *Ambrst rom, unde nescio*) *vg* carnem et sanguinem *Cyp Ambrst vg* contra] aduersus *Cyp Ambrst vg* potestates] principatus *Ambrst* principes *Bo vg* contra (*alt.*)—contra] et principes h. m. et har. t. ad *Cyp* et potestates h. m. aduersus (*om. B Bo* aduersus) t. h. rectores aduersus *Ambrst* spiritalis *Cyp* *ante* in *hab.* quae sunt *Ambrst* (*om. B Bo*) propterea] propter hoc *Cyp* ideo *Ambrst* accipite] induite *Cyp* tota *ante* arma *Cyp* uniuersitatem armorum *Ambrst* *om.* dei *Cyp Ambrst* *om.* in die *B Bo* malo] nequissimo *Cyp* et omn. op. st.] ut cum omnia perfeceritis *Cyp* et in omnibus perfecti stare *Ambrst vg* p. l. u. i. u. *om. Cyp* succincti *Ambrst vg* ueritate *Cyp B Bo rom vg* caritate *Ambrst* et induti *Ambrst vg* iustitiae] fidei *B* praeparationem *B Bo* praeparatione *Cyp Ambrst vg* in] super his *Ambrst* poteritis *Ambrst* i. n. candentia] ignita i. n. *Cyp* tela maligni (nequissimi *Bo*) ignita *Ambrst* saluationis *Cyp* salutis *Ambrst vg* *post* salutis *Ambrst* accipite (*non B Bo*) spiritus] sp̄s (s. *alt. in ras.*) *Cyp* quod] qui *Cyp B* sermo *Cyp*

[Col. follows Eph. in Claromontanus, then Phil. follows Col.]

Phil. ii 6—11 = *Cyp* 79, 149.

qui cum in forma dei constitutus non rapinam arbitratus est esse se aequalem deo sed semetipsum exinaniuit formam serui accipiens in similitudine hominum factus et habitu adinuentus ut homo humiliauit se ipsum factus obaudiens usque ad mortem mortem autem crucis propter quod et deus illum exaltauit et donauit illi nomen super omne nomen ut in nomine Iesu omne genu flectat celestium (*sic*) et terrestrium et infernorum et omnis lingua confiteatur quoniam dominus Iesus Christus in gloriam dei patris

om. cum *Cyp* figura *Cyp* constitutus] esset *Ambrst vg* aequalem *Bo vg* parem *Ambrst* semetipsum] se *Cyp* (149) inaniuit *Cyp* (149) similitudinem *Ambrst vg* hominis *Cyp* inuentus *Cyp B Bo vg* repertus *Ambrst* *om.* ut (*s. l. add.* 79) *Cyp* semet *Ambrst* *om.* ipsum *Cyp* oboediens *Ambrst vg* et *om. Cyp* (149) ill. exal.] exal. ill. *Cyp vg* superexal. ill. *B* ill. superexal. *Bo* superexal. eum *Ambrst* illi *Cyp B Bo vg* ei *Ambrst* ut sit ..*ante* super (..*fuit* au, *et* su *sunt in ras.* 79) *Cyp* quod est super *Ambrst vg* omne genu flectat] omnes genu curuent *Cyp* omne g. flectatur *Ambrst vg* *om.* et *ante* terr. *Ambrst vg* quia *Cyp Ambrst vg* *om.* Christus *Cyp B* gloriam] gloria est *Cyp Ambrst vg*

Phil. ii 14 f. = *Cyp* 127.

(v. 13 prout placet) Omnia facite sine murmurationibus et detractationibus et sitis sine crimine et sinceres fili dei inmaculati

pro bona uoluntate *Ambrst vg* omnia] *add.* autem pro delectatione *Cyp* detract.] reputationibus *Cyp* haesitationibus *Ambrst vg* ut *Cyp Ambrst vg* sine quaerella *Cyp vg* inreprehensibiles *Ambrst* *om.* sinceres *Cyp* simplices *Ambrst vg* inmaculati filii dei *Cyp* sicut filii d. inm. *Ambrst*

Phil. ii 15 = *Cyp* 141.

lucetis sicut luminaria in hoc mundo

lucete *Cyp* *om.* hoc *Cyp Ambrst vg*

Phil. ii 21 = *Cyp* 124.

omnes enim sua querunt non quae Iesu Christi

nam omnes *Ambrst* *om.* enim *Cyp* quae sua sunt *Ambrst vg* *add.* et *ante* non *Cyp* *post* quae *add.* sunt *Cyp vg* *om.* Iesu *Cyp*

Phil. iii 19—21 = *Cyp* 124.

quorum finis est interitus quorum deus uenter est et gloria in confessione

est *pr. om. Bo* est uenter *Cyp* gloria eorum *Bo* confusionem *Cyp* pudendis[1] *Ambrst* confusione *B Bo vg*

[1] So the Roman edition rightly, as is shown by the comment, and also by the fact that the text is twice elsewhere quoted with *pudendis* (in Rom. ii 29; in Tit. i 11); *Migne* has *confusione* here.

ipsorum qui terrena sapiunt nostra enim conuersatio in caelis constituta est unde et saluatorem expectamus dominum Iesum Christum qui transfigurauit corpus humilitatis nostrae conformatum corporis gloriae suae

ipsorum *om. Bo* eorum *Cyp Ambrst* (in Rom. ii 29, Tit. i 11) illorum *Ambrst* autem *Cyp Ambrst vg* *om.* constituta *Cyp Ambrst vg* *om.* et *B Bo* dominum *add.* nostrum *Ambrst vg* transformauit *Cyp* transfigurabit *Ambrst* conforme *Ambrst* corpori *Cyp Ambrst vg* claritatis *Cyp vg*

Col. i 15 = *Cyp* 63.

qui est imago dei inuisibilis primogenitus omnis creaturae

dei inu. *Cyp B Bo vg* inu. dei *Ambrst* et *post* inuis. *Cyp* totius *Cyp* uniuersae *Ambrst*

Col. i 18 = *Cyp* 63.

primogenitus ex mortuis ut sit in omnibus ipse primatum tenens

a *Cyp* fieret *Cyp* fiat *Ambrst*

Col. ii 11 = *Cyp* 45.

circumcisi estis circumcisione non manu facta in expoliatione corporis carnis in circumcisione Christi

expoliationem *Cyp Ambrst* spolatione *B Bo* *om.* corporis *Cyp* *add.* sed *post* carnis *Cyp vg*

Col. ii 20 = *Cyp* 124.

Si mortui estis cum Christo ab elementis mundi quare tanquam uiuentes in hoc mundo decernitis

si ergo *Ambrst* (*non B Bo*) *vg* essetis *Bo* elementis] *add.* huius *Cyp Ambrst vg* quid *Cyp B Bo* quid adhuc *Ambrst vg* tamquam *Cyp B Bo vg* uelut *Ambrst* *om.* hoc *Cyp vg* decernitis] uana sectamini *Cyp*

Col. iii 1—4 = *Cyp* 124.

Si ergo consurrexistis cum Christo quae susum sunt quaerite ubi Christus est ad dextram di(*sic*) sedens quae susu sunt sapite non quae in terram mortui enim estis et uita uestra absconsa est cum Christo in deo cum Christus apparuerit uita uestra tunc et uos cum illo apparebitis in gloria

om. ergo *Cyp* enim *Ambrst* conresurrexistis *B Bo* *om.* cum *Cyp* in dextera *Cyp vg* ad dexteram *Ambrst* dei *Cyp Ambrst vg* sursum s. *Cyp Bo vg* s. sursum *Ambrst* ea *ante* quae *Ambrst* in terram] terrena sunt *Cyp* super terram *Ambrst vg* abscondita *Cyp Ambrst vg* cum Christus] cum autem Christus *Cyp* apparebitis cum illo (ipso *B Bo vg*) *Ambrst vg* *om.* cum illo *Cyp*

Col. iv 2 = *Cyp* 184.

Orationi instate uigilantes in ea

instate orationi *Cyp* illa *Ambrst*

1 Th. iv 6 = *Cyp* 175.

ut ne quis supergrediatur et circumueniat in negotio fratrem suum quia uindex est dominus de omnibus his

ut *om. Cyp* ne quis] non *Cyp* *om.* supergrediatur et *Cyp* et] neque *Ambrst vg* circumuenire *Cyp* quoniam *Ambrst vg* uindex] ultor *Cyp* dominus] deus *Cyp* omnibus his] his omnibus *Cyp Ambrst vg*

1 Th. iv 12 f. = *Cyp* 159.

Nolumus autem uos ignorare fratres de dormientibus ut non contristemini sicut et ceteri qui non habent spem Si enim credimus quia Iesus mortuus est et surrexit sic et deus eos qui dormierunt per Iesum adducet cum eo

ignorare uos *Cyp* iis (his *B Bo*) qui dormiunt *Ambrst* ut non] ne *Cyp Ambrst* spem non habent *Ambrst vg* Nam si *Ambrst* quod *Ambrst vg* resurrexit *Cyp Ambrst vg* illos *Ambrst* per Iesum] in Iesu *Cyp*

1 Th. v 2 f. = *Cyp* 175.

dies domini sicut fur in nocte ita ueniet cum dixerint pax et munitio tunc subitaneus illis apparebit interitus

ut *Ambrst* *om.* in *Cyp Ambrst* noctu *Ambrst* sic *Ambrst* adueniet *Cyp* cum enim *Ambrst* (*non B Bo*) *vg* dicit *B* munitio] firmitas *Cyp B Bo rom* securitas *Ambrst vg* sub. ill.] ill. repentinus *Cyp* repentinus eis (illis *B Bo*) *Ambrst vg* adueniet *Cyp* superueniet *Ambrst vg*

2 Th. iii 6 = *Cyp* 169.

Praecipimus autem uobis fratres in nomine domini Iesu Christi ut subtrahatis uos ab omni fratre inquiete ambulante et non secundum rationem quam acceperunt a nobis

denuntiamus *Ambrst vg* *om.* fratres *Cyp* domini *add.* nostri *Ambrst vg* ut *om. Ambrst* subtr. uos] discedatis *Cyp* secerni (secernere *Bo*) uos *Ambrst* omnibus fratribus *Cyp* inquiete ambulante] ambulantibus inordinate *Cyp* intemperanter ambulante *Ambrst* traditionem *Cyp Ambrst vg* acceperunt *Cyp B Bo vg* accepistis *Ambrst*

1 Tim. ii 9—14 = *Cyp* 148, 152.

similiter et mulieres in habitu ornatu cum pudore et sobrietate ornantes se non ornaturis capillorum et auro aut margaritas (*sic*) aut uestitu praetioso sed

similiter et] sint *Cyp* mulieres *add.* uestrae *Cyp* *om.* in habitu ornatu *Cyp* ordinato (di *exp. Bo*) *Ambrst* ornato *vg* pudore] uerecundia *Cyp Ambrst vg* sobrietate] pudicitia *Cyp Ambrst* * * pudicitia *B* ornantes] componentes *Cyp* semet ipsas *Ambrst* ornaturis capillorum] in tortis (*sic Hartelius sed fortasse* intortis) crinibus *Cyp vg* tortis crinibus *Ambrst* et...aut] neque...neque *Cyp* aut...aut *Ambrst vg* margaritis *Cyp Ambrst vg* ueste *Cyp Ambrst vg* pretiosa *Cyp Ambrst vg* quod decet mulieres promittentes pietatem per opera bona Mulier in silentio discat cum omni obsequio docere autem mulierem non permitto neque dominari supra uirum sed esse in silentio Adam enim primus formatus est deinde Eua et Adam non est seductus sed mulier seducta in praeuaricatione fuit

quod] ut *Cyp* profitentes *Ambrst* pietatem] castitatem *Cyp* opera bona] bonam conuersationem *Cyp* bona opera *Bo* in] cum *Cyp* cum *Ambrst vg*] in *Cyp B Bo* obsequio] summissione *Cyp* subiectione *Ambrst vg* d. autem *B Bo vg* nam d. *Ambrst* mulieri *Cyp Ambrst vg* permittitur *Ambrst* dominari supra uirum] praeposita esse uiro *Cyp* dominari uiro (uiro *ex* uiri *B*) *Bo* d. in uirum *Ambrst vg* sed—silentio *om. Cyp* creatus *Ambrst* seductus non est *Cyp* sed mulier] mulier autem *Cyp Ambrst* (*B om.* autem) *vg* seducta] seducta est *Cyp* seducta facta est *Ambrst* in praeuaricatione fuit *om. Cyp* praeuaricationem *B* fuit *om. Ambrst*

1 Tim. v 3 = *Cyp* 171.

Viduas honora quae uere uiduae sunt

honora * * *Bo* uere uiduae sunt] reuera sunt uiduae *Cyp*

1 Tim. v 6 = *Cyp* 171.

quae autem in deliciis agit uiuens mortua est

quae autem] nam quae *Ambrst vg* in deliciis agit] delicata est *Cyp* in deliciis est *B vg* (*add.* uidua *post* est *Ambrst*) uiuens] uiua *Cyp*

1 Tim. v 8 = *Cyp* 171.

si quis autem suorum ex maxime domesticorum curat non habet fidem denegauit et est infidele deterior

ex] et *Cyp Ambrst vg* curat non habet] non agit curam *Cyp* curam non habet *Ambrst vg* denegat *Cyp* negauit *Ambrst vg* deterior infideli *Cyp* infideli deterior *Ambrst vg*

1 Tim. v 11 f. = *Cyp* 171.

Adulescentiores autem uiduas deuita cum enim in deliciis egerint in Christo nubere uolunt habentes damnationem Quia primam fidem inritam fecerunt

iuniores *Cyp B Bo* adulescentulas *Ambrst* autem *Cyp B Bo vg* uero *Ambrst* praeteri *Cyp* in deliciis egerint *B Bo*] indeliciatae fuerint *Cyp* uitam in deliciis egerint *Ambrst* damnationem] iudicium *Cyp* quia] quoniam *Cyp* inr. fecerunt] reprobauerunt *Cyp*

1 Tim. v 19 = *Cyp* 172.

Aduersus praesbyterum accusationem noli recipere

aduersum *Ambrst* praesbyterum] maiorem natu *Cyp* noli recipere] ne receperis *Cyp Ambrst* (*B* n̄ (*i.e.* non) rec.)

1 Tim. v 20 = *Cyp* 172.

peccantes autem coram omnibus argue ut et ceteri timore habeant

delinquentes *Ambrst* *om.* autem *Cyp vg* hominibus *Bo* corripe *Cyp* *om.* et *Ambrst* timore] metum *Cyp Ambrst*

1 Tim. vi 7—10 = *Cyp* 165.

nihil enim intulimus in hunc mundum uerum quoniam nec effere (*sic*) possumus habentes autem uictum et uestitum his contenti sumus nam qui uolunt diuites fieri incident in temptationem et laqueum diaboli et desideria multa inutilia et nociua quae mergunt homines in interitum et perditionem radix enim omnium malorum est cupiditas quam quidam adpetentes errauerunt a fide et se inseruerunt doloribus multis

om. enim *Cyp* hunc *Cyp B Bo om. Ambrst* *om.* quoniam *Cyp* quia *Ambrst* auferre *Cyp Ambrst vg* possumus] *add.* quicquam *Ambrst* autem] itaque *Cyp* uictum] exhibitionem *Cyp* alimentum *Ambrst* alimenta *vg* uestitum] tegumentum *Cyp* quibus tegamur *Ambrst vg* (*B om.* et quibus tegamur *ob homoeoteleuton, puto, et habere debet* tegumentum *uel* uestimentum) sumus *B vg*] simus *Cyp Ambrst* nam qui] qui autem *Cyp* incidunt *Cyp Ambrst vg* laqueum diaboli *Bo vg*] muscipula *Cyp* laqueum *Ambrst* *om.* inutilia *Cyp* et *ante* inutilia *B Bo* nocentia *Cyp* demergunt *Ambrst* hominem *Cyp* inter. et perd.] perd. et inter. *Cyp* exitium (exitum *B*) et inter. *Ambrst* *om.* enim *Bo* auaritia *Ambrst* cupiditas *B Bo vg* errauerunt] naufragauerunt *Cyp Bo* se inser.] inser. se *Cyp Ambrst vg*

2 Tim. ii 4 f. = *Cyp* 124.

nemo militans inplicat sae negotiis secularibus et ei qui se probauit placeam si autem et certet quis non coronatur nisi legitime certauerit

nemo *add.* enim *Ambrst* militans] *add.* deo *Cyp Ambrst vg* obligat *Cyp Ambrst* negotiis ac mysteriis (2*m* ministeriis) *Bo* molestiis *Cyp* et ei—placeam] ut possit placere ei qui se probauit *Cyp* ut placeat ei cui se probauit *Ambrst* ut ei pl. c. s. p. *Bo vg* si—certet] sed et si certabit *Cyp* et si (*B* nisi) certet (certe *Bo*) *Ambrst* coronabitur *Cyp Bo* pugnauerit *Cyp*

2 Tim. ii 17 = *Cyp* 172.

sermo eorum et (*sic*) cancer serpit

sermo *add.* enim *Ambrst* et] ut *Cyp vg* sicut *Ambrst*

2 Tim. ii 23 f. = *Cyp* 156.

Stultas autem et sine disciplina quaestiones deuita sciens quod generant lites seruum autem domini non oportet litigare sed mitem esse ad omnes

sine disciplina] ineruditas *Cyp Ambrst* euita *Cyp* quia *Cyp Ambrst vg* lites generant *Cyp* dei *Cyp*

2 Tim. iv 3 f. = *Cyp* 169.

erit tempus cum sanam doctrinam non sustinebunt sed ad sua desideria sibi coaceruabunt magistros prurientes aures et quidem a ueritate auditum auertent ut fabulas autem conuertentur

enim *post* erit *Ambrst vg* quando *Cyp* ad] secundum *Cyp* sibi coac. mag.] coac. sibi mag. *Cyp vg* mag. sibi aggerent (*B s. l.* uel coaceruabunt) *Ambrst* aures] in audiendo scalpentes aures *Cyp* auribus *Ambrst vg* q. a u.] a u. q. *Cyp Ambrst vg* ut] ad *Cyp Ambrst vg* d fabulas uero coni *periit in B* uero *Ambrst*

2 Tim. iv 6—8 = *Cyp* 131.

ego enim delibor et tenpus meae solutionis instat Certamen bonum certaui cursum consummaui fidem seruaui de cetero reposita est mihi iustitiae corona quam reddet mihi dominus in illa die iustus iudex non solum autem mihi sed et his qui diligunt aduentum eius

enim] iam *Cyp* enim iam *Ambrst vg* libor *Cyp* meae solutionis i.] i. adsumptionis *Cyp* s. m. i. *Ambrst* resolutionis meae i. *Bo vg* certamen b.] b. agonem *Cyp* certaui *B Bo vg* decertaui *Ambrst* perfeci *Cyp* de cetero reposita est] iam superest *Cyp* quod reliquum est r. e. *Ambrst* in reliquo r. e. *vg* iust. cor. *B*] cor. iust. *Cyp Ambrst vg* reddet mihi] mihi reddet *Cyp* illa] illo *Cyp* die] *add.* ille *Cyp* iustus iudex] iudex iustus *Cyp* autem *om. Bo* et *om.* (*add. s. l. m2*) *Bo* his] omnibus *Cyp* iis (his *B Bo*) *Ambrst vg* dilexerint *Cyp*

Tit. iii 2 = *Cyp* 180.

neminem blasphemare non litigeos esse

de nullo mali loqui (*i.e.* maliloqui[1]) nec litigiosos esse *Cyp* n. b. non litigiosos esse *Ambrst vg*

Tit. iii 10 f. = *Cyp* 172.

Haereticum hominem post unam correptionem et duo deuita sciens quoniam peruersus est huiusmodi et peccat cum sit a semetipso damnatus

hereticum *Cyp Ambrst* primam *Ambrst* *om.* et duo *Cyp Ambrst* *euita *Cyp* quod *Ambrst* delinquit (derelinquitur *Bo*) *Ambrst vg* cum sit] et est *Cyp* *om. Ambrst*

[1] Cf. *maliuolus, maliuolentia* quae formae fere semper in codicibus apparent, non *maleuolus, maleuolentia*.

Cf. ben*i*uolus Matt. v 25 *k d* vg $^{\text{cod M}}$; Terence, *Hec.* 761; uen*i*uoli Lc. xxii 25 *d*; mal*i*uoli Plautus *Stich.* 385 (not 208 A) (? *Poen.* 393). [F. C. B.]

Collations of Pauline Quotations in Lucifer and Ambrosiaster with the Vulgate.

Symbols.

Lucif = Hartel's edition of Lucifer Calaritanus (in Vienna *Corpus*).

Vulgate. The edition mainly used was published at Venice, 1697; for the Epistle to the Galatians, the edition of P. Corssen (Berol. 1885) has been compared.

d_2 = the Latin side of D (Claromontanus s. VI) of the Pauline epistles (ed. Tischendorf Lips. 1852)[1]

Cass = codex Casinensis, p. 14 (n. 1).
Sang (pr) = Sangallensis prior, p. 15 (n. 2)
Colon = Coloniensis, p. 15 (n. 3)
Bo = Bodleianus, p. 15 (n. 9)
B = Bodleianus, p. 15 (n. 10)
Par = Parisiacus, p. 15 (n. 13)
Treuer = Treuericus, p. 15 (n. 14)
Corb = Corbeiensis, p. 15 (n. 15)
Colon alt = Coloniensis, p. 15 (n. 17)
Vat = Vaticanus, p. 15 (n. 18)
Pal = Palatinus, p. 16 (n. 27)
Harl = Harleianus, p. 16 (n. 28)
Gent = Gandauensis, p. 16 (n. 29)
Troy = Troyes, p. 16 (n. 30)
Sang alt = Sangallensis, p. 16 (n. 33)
Ashb = Ashburnhamensis, p. 16 (n. 34)

These MSS of Ambrosiaster's Commentaries are referred to only when they disagree with the printed text (*Ambrst*), and I do not profess to give the readings of each in full.

Rom. i 28—32 = *Lucif* p. 158 Hartel.

Et sicut non probauerunt deum habere in notitia, tradidit illos deus in reprobum sensum, ut faciant ea quae non conueniunt, repletos omni iniquitate

et quoniam estimauerunt deum non habere horum noticiam *B*   notitiam *Lucif* (*alio loco* notitia) *Corb Treuer Bo*   *om.* ea *B*   conueniant *Lucif alio loco*

[1] p. 105 Tischendorf for XIII read III.

malitia fornicatione auaritia nequitia, plenos inuidia homicidio contentione dolo malignitate, susurrones, detractores, deo odibiles, contumeliosos, superbos, elatos, inuentores malorum, parentibus non oboedientes[1], insipientes, inconpositos, sine adfectione, absque foedere, sine misericordia, qui, cum iustitiam dei cognouissent, non intellexerunt quoniam qui talia agunt digni sunt morte, et non solum qui ea faciunt, sed etiam qui consentiunt facientibus

fornicatione *B* inpudicitia *Lucif Ambrst* cupiditate *Lucif* homicidiis *Lucif Ambrst* (= d_2) malis moribus *Lucif* susurrones *Bo* (= d_2) susurratores *Lucif Ambrst* elat. contum. superbos *Bo* superbos sibi placentes gloriantes inu. *Lucif* inoboedientes *Bo* non obsequentes *Lucif Sang pr B* affectu *Lucif* sine misericordia (*om. B*) *Lucif* cognouerint *Lucif* (-unt d_2) talia *B* haec *Ambrst* et *om. Lucif Ambrst* (= d_2) qui *om. Ambrst* (= d_2) faciunt ea (*B om. add. s. l.*) *Ambrst* illa *Lucif* (= d_2) ea *add. post* facientibus *Lucif*

Rom. ii 4—6 = *Lucif* 64.

An diuitias bonitatis eius et patientiae et longanimitatis contemnis, ignoras quoniam benignitas dei ad paenitentiam te adducit? Secundum autem duritiam tuam et inpaenitens cor thesaurizas tibi iram in die irae et reuelationis iusti iudicii dei, qui reddet uni cuique secundum opera eius

numquid sustinentiam *Lucif* patientiam contemnis, ignorans *Lucif* patientiam *Colon* *om.* et longanimitatis *B* ignorans *Ambrst* (= d_2) Ignoras *B Bo* bonitas *Lucif Ambrst* prouocat *Ambrst* adducit *B Bo* tu autem secundum dur. *Lucif* duritiam autem *Ambrst* (*non B*) cor inpaenitens *Lucif Corb B* operam *Lucif* sua *Ambrst* (*non B*)

Rom. viii 16—18 = *Lucif* 289, 314.

Sumus filii dei: si autem filii, et heredes: heredes quidem dei coheredes autem Christi, si tamen conpatimur, ut et conglorificemur. Existimo enim quod non sunt condignae passiones huius temporis ad futuram gloriam, quae reuelabitur in nobis

Simus d_2 dei *post* filii *Lucif* dei *post* heredes *Lucif* her. quid. dei *om. Lucif* si quidem *Lucif* compatiamur *Ambrst* (*non Bo*) simul glorificemur *Lucif Ambrst* (= d_2) existimo non esse condignas *Lucif alio loco* enim *B Bo* ergo *Ambrst* sint *Lucif Ambrst* (*non Bo*) superuenturam *Lucif* futuram *Lucif alio loco*

Rom. viii 28—29 = *Lucif* 146.

Scimus autem quoniam diligentibus deum omnia cooperantur in bonum, iis, qui secundum propositum uocati sunt sancti. Nam quos praesciuit, et praedestinauit conformes fieri imaginis filii sui

dominum *Lucif* procedunt *Lucif Ambrst* (= d_2) (*non Bo*) his *Lucif* (= d_2) *B Bo* sancti *om. Lucif* (= d_2) *om.* nam *Lucif B Bo* et praedest. *errore om. Ambrst* (*legitur in septem saltem codd. et rom*) imagini *Lucif* eius *Lucif* (= d_2)

[1] *Ambrst et Bo* hic textum corruptissimum exhibent, ab *insipientes* usque ad *misericordia*: itaque cod. *B* solum cito.

Rom. viii 35—37 = *Lucif* 72, 299.

Quis ergo nos separabit a caritate Christi? tribulatio? an angustia? an fames? an nuditas? an periculum? an persecutio? an gladius? sicut scriptum est: quia propter te mortificamur tota die: aestimati sumus sicut oues occisionis. Sed in his omnibus superamus propter eum qui dilexit nos

qui *B* ergo *om. Lucif Ambrst* *om.* an *ante* angustia *B* an persecutio *ante* an fames *hoc ordine Lucif Ambrst* (= d_2, *sine* an) morte adficiemur *Lucif* occidemur *Lucif alio loco* morte afficimur (adficiuntur *B*) *Ambrst* (= d_2) afficimur *ex* afficiamur (*sine* morte) *Bo* ut *Lucif* uelut *Ambrst*

Rom. x 10 = *Lucif* 113.

same in all three.

Rom. xii 17—18 = *Lucif* 159.

Nulli malum pro malo reddentes, prouidentes bona non tantum coram deo, sed etiam coram omnibus hominibus: si fieri potest, quod ex uobis est, cum omnibus hominibus pacem habentes

nemini *Ambrst* non enim *Bo* non tantum—etiam *om.* d_2 solum *Lucif* *pr.* omnibus *om. Lucif* (= d_2) *B* *post* uobis *add.* ipsis *Lucif*

Rom. xiii 8 *b* = *Lucif* 176.

same in all three.

1 Cor. ii 9 = *Lucif* 316.

oculus non uidit, nec auris audiuit, nec in cor hominis ascendit, quae praeparauit deus iis, qui diligunt illum

nec oculus uidit *Lucif* dominus diligentibus se *Lucif* deus diligentibus eum (se *Paris Bo*) *Ambrst* (= d_2)

1 Cor. iv 4 *a* = *Lucif* 324.

Nihil enim mihi conscius sum

in nullo mihi mali *Lucif* quidem *Ambrst* (*mult codd* enim (= d_2))

1 Cor. v 1—7 = *Lucif* 23, 169.

Omnino auditur inter uos fornicatio et talis fornicatio, qualis nec inter gentes, ita ut uxorem patris sui aliquis habeat. Et uos inflati estis, et non magis luctum habuistis, ut tollatur de medio uestrum qui hoc opus fecit.

'sic' which Hartel reads before 'omnino' as part of the quotation, really belongs to Lucifer's own 'dixit,' see H.'s index *s. v.* sic in uobis *SG Par Cass Vat B* in nobis *Bo* et talis fornicatio *om. Lucif* (23) *add.* est *post* gentes *B* ita ut quis uxorem *Ambrst* sui *om. Lucif* (23) *Ambrst* (= d_2) potius *Lucif Corb Gent* (= d_2) tolleretur *Lucif Ambrst* (= d_2) e *Lucif*

Ego quidem absens corpore praesens autem spiritu iam iudicaui ut praesens eum qui sic operatus est, in nomine domini nostri Iesu Christi, congregatis uobis, et meo spiritu, cum uirtute domini nostri Iesu, tradere huius modi satanae in interitum carnis, ut spiritus saluus sit in die domini nostri Iesu Christi. Non est bona gloriatio uestra. Nescitis quia modicum fermentum totam massam corrumpit? expurgate uetus fermentum, ut sitis noua conspersio, sicut estis azymi

sicut *inser. Lucif SG Par Pal B Bo ante* absens (*cf* enim ut d_2) hoc admisit *Ambrst* sic operatus est *Par* ita o. e. *Gent Corb* *pr.* nostri *om. Lucif Cass Gent Corb* *pr.* Christi *om. Lucif* (= d_2) *B* spiritu meo *Lucif* (= d_2) nostri *om. B Bo* *post* Iesu *habet* Christi *Lucif*: *ut Vulg Lucif bis alias* hunc *pro* huiusm. *Ambrst* (*non Bo*) *post* huiusmodi *ins.* hominem *Lucif* fiat *Gent Corb* *ult.* nostri *om. Ambrst* (= d_2) (*non Bo*) non est *om. Lucif B Bo* *om.* est d_2 bona est (*sine* non) ? *Ambrst* ut *Lucif*

1 Cor. v 9—11 = *Lucif* 23.

Scripsi uobis in epistula: ne commisceamini fornicariis, non utique fornicariis huius mundi, aut auaris, aut rapacibus, aut idolis seruientibus: alioquin debueratis de hoc mundo exisse. Nunc autem scripsi uobis non commisceri: si is, qui frater nominatur, est fornicator, aut auarus, aut idolis seruiens, aut maledicus, aut ebriosus, aut rapax, cum eius modi nec cibum sumere

non misceri *Lucif* non commisceri *Corb Gent* (= d_2) raptoribus *Lucif* idololatris[1] *Lucif* idolatris *Corb Gent* (= d_2) exire *Gent Vat Bo B* (= d_2) ne commisceamini *Ambrst* si quis f. n. fornicator *Lucif* (*cf.* d_2) si quis f. n. et est fornicator *Bo B* inter uos *post* nominatur *ins. Ambrst* (*om. Corb Gent Vat Bo*) idolorum cultor *Lucif* (= d_2) idolorum seruiens *Par* huiusmodi ne c. quidem s. *Ambrst* huiusmodi nec c. s. *Bo* huiusmodi nec c. quidem s. *B*

1 Cor. vi 15—20 = *Lucif* 24.

Nescitis quoniam corpora uestra membra sunt Christi? Tollens ergo membra Christi, faciam membra meretricis? Absit. An nescitis quoniam qui adhaeret meretrici unum corpus efficitur? 'Erunt' enim, inquit 'duo in carne una.' Qui autem adhaeret domino unus spiritus est. Fugite fornicationem. Omne peccatum quodcumque fecerit homo extra corpus est: qui

quia *Lucif Sang pr Par Gent Corb Vat Bo B* (= d_2) Christi sunt *Lucif* (= d_2) *B Bo* tollam *Ambrst* (tollens *B Bo*) et *ins. post alt.* Christi *Ambrst* (*non Bo*) aut *Lucif Gent Corb* (= d_2) quia *Lucif Ambrst* (= d_2) se iungit *Lucif* (= d_2) coniungit se *Corb Gent* est *Lucif Corb Gent* (= d_2) fit *Ambrst* sit *B* enim *om. Ambrst* iungit se *Lucif* (*cf.* se iungit d_2) deo *B* fugite fornicationem *om. B Bo* quod *Lucif*

[1] It is very possible that we ought to read the short form in Lucifer, but I have seen the long form in excellent MSS of authors as late as Hier. and Aug.

autem fornicatur in corpus suum peccat. An nescitis quoniam membra uestra templum sunt spiritus sancti, qui in uobis est, quem habetis a deo, et non estis uestri? Empti enim estis pretio magno. Glorificate et portate deum in corpore uestro

corpus uestrum *Corb Gent* $(=d_2)$ [v. 19 An nescitis...deo et *non citat Lucif*] quia *Ambrst* $(=d_2)$ corpora *Ambrst* est *Ambrst* *om.* qui—est *B Bo* magno *om. Lucif Sang pr Corb Gent Vat* $(=d_2)$ clarificate *Ambrst* (*non Bo*) dominum *Lucif B*

1 Cor. vii 23 = *Lucif* 170.

same in all three.

1 Cor. xv 33 = *Lucif* 25.

enim inserted after *corrumpunt*. It perhaps belongs to Lucif. himself. *Ambrst* and *Vulg* agree.

2 Cor. iv 16 = *Lucif* 296.

licet is qui foris est noster homo corrumpatur, tamen is qui intus est renouatur

cum uetus homo noster *Lucif* licet si exterior h. n. *Ambrst* et si qui foris est h. n. d_2 corrumpitur *Lucif Ambrst* $(=d_2)$ tamen is *om. Lucif* sed *Ambrst* d_2 interior *Ambrst* innouetur *Lucif* (*fort. ob orat. obliq. pro* innouatur)

2 Cor. v 1 = *Lucif* 297.

si terrestris domus nostra huius habitationis dissoluatur

d. nostri corporis dissoluitur *Lucif* nostrae *Corb Gent*

2 Cor. v 6—10 = *Lucif* 191, 297.

dum sumus in corpore, peregrinamur a domino: per fidem enim ambulamus, et non per speciem: audemus autem et bonam uoluntatem habemus magis peregrinari a corpore, et praesentes esse ad dominum: et ideo contendimus, siue absentes, siue praesentes, placere illi. Omnes enim nos manifestari oportet ante tribunal Christi, ut referat unus quisque propria corporis, prout gessit, siue bonum, siue malum

d. s. i. c.] positi i. c. *Lucif alio loco* inhabitantes in hoc (*om.* hoc *Bo B*) c. *Ambrst* ex fide *Lucif* et *om. Lucif Ambrst* $(=d_2)$ aud. etiam b. *Lucif* aud. etiam d_2 aud. ergo et consentimus *Ambrst* habentes *Lucif* $(=d_2)$ deum *Ambrst* et ideo] ideo enim *Bo B* ideo *om. Lucif* $(=d_2)$ enitamur *Cass* (*Vat*) conamur *Gent* imitamur *Corb* siue p. siue peregrinantes *Ambrst* siue p. siue a. d_2 nam omnes *Lucif* $(=d_2)$ oportet manifestari *Lucif* ut unusq. recipiat *B* ferat *Lucif* $(=d_2)$ recipiat *Ambrst* secundum quod *Lucif* $(=d_2)$ bona *Ambrst* mala *Ambrst*

2 Cor. vi 14—18 = *Lucif* 28, 285.

Nolite iugum ducere cum infidelibus. Quae enim participatio iustitiae cum iniquitate? Aut quae societas lucis ad tenebras? Quae autem conuentio Christi ad Belial? Aut quae pars fideli cum infideli? Qui autem consensus templo dei cum idolis? Vos enim estis templum dei uiui, sicut dicit deus quoniam 'inhabitabo in illis, et inambulabo inter eos et ero illorum deus et ipsi erunt mihi populus.' Propter quod 'exite de medio eorum et separamini, dicit dominus,' et 'inmundum ne tetigeritis: et ego recipiam uos' et 'ero' uobis 'in patrem, et' uos eritis 'mihi in filios et filias, dicit dominus omnipotens'

ad iniquitatem *Harl* et iniquitati *Sang Par B Bo* et iniquitate *Corb* lumini (luminis *B Harl Sang Gent Vat*) cum tenebris *Ambrst* luci ad tenebras *Bo* quaeue (*om.* ue *B*) consensio C. cum B. *Ambrst* quae confessio C. cum B. *Bo* participatio *Harl Sang Par Vat Gent Corb B Bo* infidele *Lucif Ambrst aliq codd* $(=d_2)$ uel (*om. B*) quae conuentio *Ambrst* enim] autem *Bo* templum estis d. u. *Ambrst* (d. e. u. *Harl Sang*) t. d. e. u. *B Bo* (*om.* uiui *Bo*) scriptum est enim *Lucif* dixit *Ambrst* quia *Corb* habitabo *B* inter illos ambulabo *Lucif* i. eos a. *Lucif bis alias*, *Ambrst* $(=d_2)$ inter eos inambulabo *Bo* illi *B* (*sed infra* ipsi) quapropter *Ambrst* (*ut supra codd*) illorum *Gent Corb B* nolite tangere *Ambrst* suscipiam *Ambrst* mihi eritis *Lucif*

2 Cor. xi 1—3 = *Lucif* 267.

Utinam sustineretis modicum quid insipientiae meae, sed et supportate me: aemulor enim uos dei aemulatione. Despondi enim uos uni uiro uirginem castam exhibere Christo. Timeo autem ne sicut serpens Heuam seduxit astutia sua, ita corrumpantur sensus uestri et excidant a simplicitate quae est in Christo.

s. pusillum i. m. *Lucif* s. pusillum insipientiam meam *Bo* s. pusillum imprudentiam meam *Ambrst* portaretis pusillum insipientiam meam d_2 patimini *Ambrst* aemulans enim uos Deo aemulor *Lucif* $(=d_2)$ zelans e. u. D. zelo *Ambrst* Statui *Lucif* $(=d_2)$ paraui *Ambrst* enim *om. Sang Par Bo B* assignare (*non Bo*) *Ambrst* enim *Sang B* ita *om. Lucif* $(=d_2)$ sic *Ambrst* s. u. c. (*hoc ordine*) *Ambrst* et excidant *om. Lucif Ambrst* $(=d_2)$ castitate *Lucif Ambrst* c. dei *Harl Gent Vat Bo B* c. et simplicitate d_2 *post* Christo *habent* Iesu *Lucif Ambrst*

2 Cor. xi 13—15 = *Lucif* 267.

Nam eius modi pseudoapostoli sunt operarii subdoli transfigurantes se in apostolos Christi. Et non mirum; ipse enim satanas transfigurat se in angelum lucis. Non est ergo magnum, si ministri eius transfigurentur uelut ministri iustitiae, quorum finis erit secundum opera ipsorum

huiusmodi enim p. *Ambrst* operarii sunt *B* dolosi *Lucif* $(=d_2)$ nec mirum *Lucif* nec mirandum d_2 nec utique mirum *Ambrst* transfiguratur *Ambrst* sicut angelus lucis *Lucif* $(=d_2)$ uelut angelus luminis *Ambrst* non magnum *Lucif* $(=d_2)$ non ergo magnum *Ambrst* non magnum ergo *Bo Sang Par Corb Gent Vat* et ministri *Ambrst* transfigurantur sicut *Lucif Ambrst* (*codd* uelut) $(=d_2)$ est *Lucif* $(=d_2)$ operationem *Lucif* eorum *Ambrst*

Gal. i 6—9 = *Lucif* 279.

Miror quod sic tam cito transferimini [*Corssen* transferemini] ab eo qui uos uocauit in gratiam Christi in aliud euangelium ; quod non est aliud, nisi sunt aliqui, qui uos conturbant, et uolunt conuertere euangelium Christi. Sed licet nos aut angelus de caelo euangelizet uobis praeter quam quod euangelizauimus uobis, anathema sit. Sicut praediximus, et nunc iterum dico : si quis uobis euangelizauerit praeter id quod accepistis, anathema sit

transferemini d_2 ab eo *om. Lucif* uocauit uos *Ambrst* (= d_2) gratia *Lucif* (= d_2) per gratiam *Ambrst* Christi *om. Lucif Bo B* quod—aliud *om. pleriq. codd-Ambrst* aliqui sunt *Ambrst* conturbant uos *Ambrst* (= d_2) inuertere *rom* euertere *Bo*[1] et si *Ambrst* uos *Ambrst* nos *B Bo* euangelizauerit *Lucif Ambrst* (= d_2) euangelizat *B Bo* uobis *pr. om. Lucif B Bo* quod *om. Lucif* (= d_2) *err. Bo* uobis *alt. om. Ambrst* adnuntiauerit *Ashb* (= d_2) adnuntiauerit quam quod *Lucif* praeterquam quod *Ambrst* (= d_2)

Gal. iii 1 = *Lucif* 280.

O insensati Galatae

stulti *Lucif Ashb*

Gal. v 7—9 = *Lucif* 30, 31.

Currebatis bene : quis uos inpediuit ueritati non oboedire ? Persuasio haec [*om. Corssen*] non est ex eo qui uocat uos. Modicum fermentum totam massam corrumpit

uobis *Lucif* nemini consensistis *Ashb* nemini consenseritis, suasio uestra ex deo est q. u. u. *Lucif* suasio uestra non est a Deo q. u. u. *Ambrst* suasio ex eo est qui uos uocat d_2 nescitis quia *ante* modicum *habet Lucif*

Gal. v 19—21 = *Lucif* 158.

Manifesta sunt autem [autem sunt *Corssen*] opera carnis, quae sunt fornicatio, inmunditia, inpudicitia [*om. Corssen*], luxuria, idolorum seruitus, ueneficia, inimicitiae, contentiones, aemulationes, irae, rixae, dissensiones, sectae, inuidiae, homicidia, ebrietates, comessationes, et his similia; quae praedico uobis, sicut praedixi, quoniam qui talia agunt, regnum dei non consequentur.

autem sunt *Lucif Sang duo Ashb Cass* (= d_2) *Bo om.* autem *B* adulteria fornicationes *Lucif* (= d_2) adulterium f. impuritas obscenitas *Ambrst* *om.* luxuria *Ambrst* idololatria *Lucif Ambrst* (= d_2) idololatrocinia d_2 simulationes[2] *Ambrst* (*om. Sang alt*) *sed* c. a. i. *rom* simultates *Ambrst* (*pro* rixae) haereses *Lucif Ambrst* (= d_2) *om.* homicidia *Bo B* ebrietas *B* et quae sunt h. s. *Ambrst* et *ins. ante* praedixi *Ambrst* (= d_2) (*non Bo*) quia *Lucif* (= d_2) quod hi (hii *Bo*) *Ambrst* regni dei hereditatem *Ambrst*

[1] This is an error as the comment shows, and is due to the contraction.

[2] This error is due to dittography of the final *s* of *contentiones* and the thought of the word *simultas*.

Eph. ii 1—3 = *Lucif* 31.

Et uos, cum essetis mortui delictis et peccatis uestris, in quibus aliquando ambulastis secundum saeculum mundi huius, secundum principem potestatis aeris huius, spiritus qui nunc operatur in filios diffidentiae: in quibus et nos omnes aliquando conuersati sumus in desideriis carnis nostrae, facientes uoluntatem carnis et cogitationum, et eramus natura filii irae, sicut et ceteri

cum uos *Bo* sec. saec. m. h. *om. Lucif* huius mundi *Ambrst* spiritum *Ambrst* filiis *Lucif Ambrst* (= d_2) omnes *om. Ambrst* conuersati sumus aliq. *Lucif* (= d_2) concupiscentia *Lucif* (= d_2) uoluntates *Lucif Sang alt* uolumptates d_2 uoluptates *aliq. ut Cass Sang pr Bo B* *om.* carnis *B* consiliorum *Lucif* (= d_2) consiliorum eius *Ambrst* naturales *Lucif*

Eph. iv 7—18 = *Lucif* 200 ff.

Uni cuique autem nostrum data est gratia secundum mensuram donationis Christi. Propter quod dicit 'ascendens in altum captiuam duxit captiuitatem, dedit dona hominibus.' Quod autem ascendit quid est nisi quia et descendit primum in inferiores partes terrae? Qui descendit ipse est et qui 'ascendit' super omnes caelos ut impleret omnia. Et ipse dedit quosdam quidem apostolos, quosdam autem prophetas, alios uero euangelistas, alios autem pastores et doctores; ad consummationem sanctorum in opus ministerii, in aedificationem corporis Christi, donec occurramus omnes in unitatem fidei et agnitionis filii dei, in uirum perfectum, in mensuram aetatis plenitudinis Christi; ut iam non simus paruuli fluctuantes, et circumferamur omni uento doctrinae in nequitia hominum, in astutia ad circumuentionem erroris. Veritatem autem facientes in caritate crescamus in illo per omnia, qui est caput Christus, ex quo totum corpus conpactum et conexum per omnem iuncturam subministrationis secundum operationem in mensuram unius cuiusque membri, augmentum corporis facit in aedificationem sui in caritate. Hoc igitur dico et testificor in domino ut iam non ambuletis, sicut et gentes ambulant, in

dignationis *Lucif* domini nostri (n. *om. Cass Sang ambo B*) Iesu *ins. ante* Christi *Ambrst* (*eras. Bo*) ascendit *Cass Sang ambo B Bo* altitudinem *Ashb* etiam *Ambrst* et descendit etiam *Bo* primum *om. Lucif* (= d_2) prius *Ambrst* (*om. Sang ambo Bo B*) inferiora terrae *Lucif Ambrst* (= d_2) et qui desc. *Lucif* ipse est qui et *Ambrst* (et *om. Ashb Sang ambo B*) adimpleret *Lucif* (= d_2) quosdam u. eu. *Lucif* quosdam autem eu. d_2 quosdam a. past. *Lucif* (= d_2) quosdam uero past. *Ambrst* magistros *Ambrst* (*non Bo*) unitate *Lucif Cass Sang duo* agnitione (*Sang duo*) dei *Lucif* agnitionem f. d. *Ambrst* ultra *Ambrst* p. neque fl. *Ambrst* remedium err. *Lucif Ambrst* (= d_2) crescamus in c. *Lucif semel, suis prob. uerbis usus* (*bis ut supra*) augeamur in ipso *Ambrst* augeamus in ipsum omnia *Sang ambo Bo B* omnem *om. Lucif* secundum op. *om. Lucif Sang ambo B Bo* (= d_2) partis *Lucif Ambrst* (= d_2) incrementum *Lucif Ambrst* (= d_2) ad *Ambrst* itaque *Lucif* (= d_2) ergo *Ambrst* testor *Ambrst* non amplius *Lucif* iam *om. Ambrst*

uanitate sensus sui, tenebris obscuratum habentes intellectum, alienati a uita dei, per ignorantiam quae est in illis propter caecitatem cordis ipsorum

mentis suae *Lucif Ambrst* $(=d_2)$ tenebris *om. Lucif Ambrst* $(=d_2)$ obscurati in intellectu *Lucif* insensati *Lucif, alio loco, suo prob. uerbo usus* obscurati intellectu *Ambrst* $(=d_2)$ *om.* a *B* fide *Ambrst* ign. q. e. i. i. p. *om. Lucif alio loco, breuiter sententiam perstringens* per ignorantiam quae est in ipsis. Propter ignorantiam quae est in illis *Bo B* propter ign. *Ambrst* ipsis *Ambrst* propter caecitatem] et duritiam *Bo B* et caec. *Ambrst* illorum *Ambrst*

Eph. iv 21—25 = *Lucif* 203.

sicut est ueritas in Iesu, deponere uos secundum pristinam conuersationem ueterem hominem qui corrumpitur secundum desideria erroris. Renouamini autem spiritu mentis uestrae, et induite nouum hominem, qui secundum deum creatus est in iustitia et sanctitate ueritatis. Propter quod deponentes mendacium, loquimini ueritatem unus quisque cum proximo suo

deponentes s. p. *Lucif* ut deponatis (exponatis *Cass Sang ambo B Bo*[1]) s. *Ambrst* priorem *Ambrst* $(=d_2)$ h. eum q. *Lucif* $(=d_2)$ concupiscentiam *Lucif* $(=d_2)$ sensu (*rom* spiritu) m. u. *Ambrst* sensus uestri *Lucif* $(=d_2)$ induimini *Ambrst* *om.* est *Bo* iustitiam et sanctitatem et ueritatem *Lucif* iustitia et sanctitate et ueritate d_2 in ueritate et iustitia *Ambrst* in iustitia et ueritate *Bo* propter quod *om. Lucif* deposito mendacio *Ambrst* ad proximum suum *Lucif*

Eph. v 6—11 = *Lucif* 31.

Nemo uos seducat inanibus uerbis : propter haec enim uenit ira dei in filios diffidentiae. Nolite ergo effici participes eorum. Eratis enim aliquando tenebrae, nunc autem lux in domino. Ut filii lucis ambulate : fructus enim lucis est in omni bonitate, et iustitia, et ueritate, probantes quid sit beneplacitum deo, et nolite communicare operibus infructuosis tenebrarum, magis autem redarguite

decipiat (*a 2m*) *Ashb* p. hoc $(=d_2)$ u. (*sine* enim) *Lucif* propterea *Ambrst* itaque fieri *Lucif* $(=d_2)$ fuistis *Ambrst* *om.* enim *Cass B Bo* sicut *Lucif* $(=d_2)$ nam fr. luc. in *Ambrst* luminis (*pro alt.* lucis) *Lucif* $(=d_2)$ est *post* ueritate *Ambrst* probate quid sit quid (quod *Cass Sang ambo Bo B*) placet deo *Ambrst* acceptum *Lucif* (*aliter* d_2) autem et obiurgate *Ambrst* autem et redarguite d_2

Eph. v 15—17 = *Lucif* 199.

Videte itaque, fratres, quomodo caute ambuletis, non quasi insipientes, sed ut sapientes, redimentes tempus, quoniam dies mali sunt. Propterea nolite fieri imprudentes, sed intellegentes, quae sit uoluntas dei

ergo *Ambrst* igitur *Ashb* fratres *om. Lucif Ambrst* $(=d_2)$ ut ins. *Ambrst* quia *Lucif* $(=d_2)$ Ideo *Ambrst* effici *Lucif Ambrst* $(=d_2)$ est *Cass Sang ambo B* dei *Bo* d_2 domini *Lucif Ambrst*

[1] See above, p. 231.

Eph. vi 10—18 = *Lucif* 296, 301.

De cetero, fratres, confortamini in domino et in potentia uirtutis eius. Induite uos armaturam dei, ut possitis stare aduersus insidias diaboli, quoniam non est nobis colluctatio aduersus carnem et sanguinem, sed aduersus principes et potestates, aduersus mundi rectores tenebrarum harum, contra spiritualia nequitiae in caelestibus. Propterea accipite armaturam dei, ut possitis resistere in die malo et in omnibus perfecti stare. State ergo succincti lumbos uestros in ueritate, et induti loricam iustitiae, et calceati pedes in praeparatione euangelii pacis, in omnibus sumentes scutum fidei, in quo possitis omnia tela nequissimi ignea extinguere; et galeam salutis assumite et gladium spiritus (quod est uerbum dei), per omnem orationem et obsecrationem orantes omni tempore in spiritu et in ipso uigilantes

om. fratres *Lucif Cass Sang ambo B Bo* (= d_2)   confirmamini *Lucif* confortamini *Lucif alio loco* (= d_2)   et *ante* induite *Lucif*   induti *Lucif al. loc. sine* et   induimini *Ambrst*   uos *om. Lucif* (= d_2)   arma *Lucif Ambrst* (= d_2)   armis *Cass Sang ambo B rom*   aduersum *Cass Sang alt B*   remedia *Lucif*   remedium d_2 nationes *Ambrst*   damnationes (dam *eras.*) *Cass*   *om.* diaboli *Ambrst*   *Anne* <machi>-nationes?   uersutias diaboli *rom*   quia *Lucif* (= d_2)   uobis *Lucif Ambrst* (= d_2)   lucta *Ambrst rom*   conluctatio *codd*   sed contra potestates contra huius mundi r. t. h. *Lucif* (= d_2)   principatus *Ambrst* (*non Bo*)   pot. huius mundi adu. (*om.* adu. *Cass Sang ambo Bo B*) tenebrarum h. rectores aduersus s. n. quae sunt (*om.* quae sunt *B Bo*) i. c. *Ambrst*   ideo *Ambrst*   arma *Lucif* (= d_2)   uniuersitatem armorum (*sine* dei) *Ambrst*   in die *om. Cass Sang ambo B Bo*   state ergo *om. Lucif Ambrst* (= d_2)   praecincti *Lucif* (= d_2)   caritate *Ambrst err. typ.?* (ueritate *codd rom*)   et *om. Lucif* (= d_2)   induentes *Lucif* (= d_2)   lorica(m) fidei *Sang ambo B*   praeparationem *Bo B* (= d_2)   super his omnibus *Ambrst*   adsumentes *Lucif Ambrst* (= d_2)   poteritis *Ambrst*   iacula *Lucif* (= d_2)   maligni *Ambrst* (*non Bo*)   candentia *Lucif* (= d_2)   ignita *Ambrst*   galea *Cass*   assumite *om. Lucif* (= d_2)   accipite *Ambrst* (*om. Cass Sang ambo B Bo*)   qui *Cass Sang ambo B*   orat. et precem *Ambrst*   in omni temp. *Ambrst*   illum *Lucif*   illo d_2 ipsum *Ambrst* (ipso *Bo B*)

Phil. ii 6—8 = *Lucif* 125, 304, 311.

qui cum in forma dei esset, non rapinam arbitratus est esse se aequalem deo, sed semetipsum exinaniuit, formam serui accipiens, in similitudinem hominum factus, et habitu inuentus ut homo. Humiliauit semetipsum factus obediens usque ad mortem, mortem autem crucis

non est rapinam arb. *Lucif*   parem *Ambrst* (*non Bo*)   accipiens serui *Lucif semel* (*errore librarii prob*)   similitudinem—et *om. Lucif*   factus hominis *Sang alt*   repertus *Ambrst* (inuentus *B Bo*)   s.] se *Lucif*   se ipsum d_2 factus obediens *om. Lucif*   autem *om. Cass*

Phil. iii 2 = *Lucif* 32.

Down to *operarios*: same in all three.

Phil. iii 4—11 = *Lucif* 207.

Si quis alius uidetur confidere in carne, ego magis, circumcisus octauo die, ex genere Israel, de tribu Beniamin, Hebraeus ex Hebraeis, secundum legem Pharisaeus, secundum aemulationem persequens ecclesiam dei, secundum iustitiam quae in lege est conuersatus sine querela. Sed quae mihi fuerint lucra, haec arbitratus sum propter Christum detrimenta. Verum tamen existimo omnia detrimentum esse propter eminentem scientiam Iesu Christi domini mei, propter quem omnia detrimentum feci et arbitror ut stercora, ut Christum lucri faciam, et inueniar in illo non habens meam iustitiam quae ex lege est, sed illam quae ex fide est Christi Iesu, quae ex deo est iustitia in fide, ad cognoscendum illum et uirtutem resurrectionis eius et societatem passionum illius, configuratus morti eius, si quo modo occurram ad resurrectionem quae est ex mortuis

si quis autem (alter d_2) putat se fiduciam habere *Lucif* (= d_2) *om.* alius *Ambrst* (*habet rom*) carnem *Sang alt* circumcisione octaua *Lucif* (= d_2) circumcisus octaua *Ambrst* circumcisione octaui diei *Cass Sang alt rom* de *Lucif* (= d_2) de *om. Lucif Bo* (*add.* 2*m*) *B Sang ambo* (= d_2) de tribu *om. Cass* zelum *Lucif* (= d_2) dei *om. Lucif B Cass Sang ambo* (= d_2) ex *Ambrst* (in *B*) cum essem *ante* sine *Lucif* (= d_2) sed *om. Lucif* (= d_2) *B Bo* fuerunt lucra *Lucif* (= d_2) lucra fuerant (fuerunt *B Bo Sang ambo*) *Ambrst* existimaui *Lucif* (= d_2) damna *Ambrst* tamen] quidem *Ambrst* omnia arbitror *Lucif Ambrst* et omnia arbitror *B Bo* et arbitror omnia d_2 damna *Ambrst* detrimenta d_2 eminentiam scientiae Christi Iesu *Lucif* (= d_2) *Ambrst* (*om.* sci. *Cass Sang ambo B Bo*) nostri *Lucif* damna *Ambrst* damnum d_2 passus sum *Lucif* duxi *Ambrst* arbitro *Cass* ut *om. Lucif Ambrst* (= d_2) (*habet Bo*) lucrificiam *Lucif* ut *ante* inueniar *Ambrst* (*om. B Bo*) est ex lege *Lucif* (= d_2) eam *Ambrst* (*non B Bo*) per fidem Iesu Christi (*om.* est) *Lucif* est (*om. Cass Bo B* = d_2) per fidem Christi (*sine* Iesu) *Ambrst* (= d_2) quae ex deo—fide *om. Bo* iustitiam super fidem *Ambrst* agnoscendum *Lucif* eum *Ambrst* et *om. Bo* in uirtute *Bo* et soc. pass. ill. *om. Cass* communicationem *Lucif Ambrst* (= d_2) eius *Lucif Ambrst* (= d_2) cooneratus morte (morti (d_2)) ipsius *Lucif* (= d_2) conformatus morti (*Latinius*) conformans me morti ipsius *Ambrst* in resurrectionem eius *Lucif* in resurrectionem d_2 a *Lucif* (= d_2)

Phil. iii 14 = *Lucif* 286.

Ad brauium supernae uocationis

palmam supernae dei (*om.* dei *Sang alt B*) uocationis *Ambrst* sursum uocationis *Lucif*

Phil. iii 17—19 = *Lucif* 199, 305.

Imitatores mei estote, fratres, et obseruate eos qui ita ambulant, sicut habetis formam nostram. Multi enim ambulant, quos saepe dicebam uobis (nunc

coimitatores *Lucif* (= d_2) mihi *Ambrst* (mei *B Bo*) considerate *Ambrst* sic *Lucif Ambrst* (= d_2) quod *Lucif semel* autem et flens dico), inimicos crucis Christi, quorum finis interitus, quorum deus uenter est et gloria in confusione ipsorum, qui terrena sapiunt

uero *Ambrst* (*non Bo*) est *post* finis *Lucif Ambrst* ($=d_2$) (*non Bo*) *ante* finis *habet* et *Sang alt* est *post* uenter *om. Sang ambo* pudendis[1] *Ambrst* gl. eorum in confusione *Bo* illorum *Ambrst* (*om. Bo*)

Col. ii 4 = *Lucif* 19.

Hoc autem dico, ut nemo uos decipiat in sublimitate sermonum

itaque *Lucif* autem *om. Ambrst* (ergo *habet Ashb* enim *Bo*) circumueniat *Ambrst* ($=d_2$) subtilitate *Ambrst* ($=d_2$) uerborum *Lucif* sermonis *Ambrst* ($=d_2$)

Col. ii 8—9 = *Lucif* 19.

Videte ne quis uos decipiat per philosophiam et inanem fallaciam secundum traditionem hominum, secundum elementa mundi, et non secundum Christum; quia in ipso inhabitat omnis plenitudo diuinitatis corporaliter

depraedetur *Ambrst* seducat *Ashb* seductionem *Lucif rom* ($=d_2$) elementum *B ante* mundi *habet* huius *Ambrst* habitat *B Bo Sang alt* ($=d_2$) deitatis *Sang alt*

Col. ii 18—19 = *Lucif* 20.

Nemo uos seducat uolens in humilitate et religione angelorum quae non uidit ambulans frustra, inflatus sensu carnis suae, et non tenens caput, ex quo totum corpus, per nexus et coniunctiones subministratum et constructum, crescit in augmentum dei

conuincat *Lucif* ($=d_2$) decipiat *Ambrst* deuincat *Bo B Cass Sang pr* sensus *post* humilitate *Lucif* animi *post* humilitate *Ambrst* superstitione *Ambrst* quae uidetur (uidit d_2) ambulans sine causa *Lucif* ($=d_2$) ea quae uidet (in his quae non uidet *rom*) extollens se frustra *Ambrst* mente *Ambrst* illud *post* caput *Ambrst* omne *Lucif Ambrst* ($=d_2$) conexum et coniunctionem productum crescit *Lucif* conexum et conductione subministratum et prouectum crescit d_2 compagines (compages *Bo*) et coniunctiones *Ambrst* compaginationes et colligationes *rom* compaginatum *Ambrst* compactum *rom* conputatum (?) *Cass* fidei *Lucif*

1 Thess. v 21—22 = *Lucif* 200.

Omnia autem probate; quod bonum est tenete; ab omni specie mala abstinete uos.

Examinate, bonum continete *Lucif* ($=d_2$) autem *om. Ambrst* (*habent B Bo*) tene *Cass* uos abstinete *Ashb* continete *Lucif*

2 Thess. iii 6 = *Lucif* 18.

Denuntiamus autem uobis, fratres, in nomine domini nostri Iesu Christi, ut subtrahatis uos ab omni fratre ambulante inordinate, et non secundum traditionem quam acceperunt a nobis

praecipimus *Lucif* ($=d_2$) secerni *Ambrst* secernere *Cass Sang ambo Bo* inquiete ambulante *Lucif* ($=d_2$) intemperanter ambulante *Ambrst* accepistis *Ambrst* (acceperunt *B Bo*)

[1] See above, p. 234.

1 Tim. i 8—14 = *Lucif* 171, 207.

Scimus autem quia bona est lex, si quis ea legitime utatur: sciens hoc quia lex iusto non est posita, sed iniustis, et non subditis, impiis, et peccatoribus, sceleratis, et contaminatis, parricidis, et matricidis, homicidis, fornicariis, masculorum concubitoribus, plagiariis, mendacibus, et periuris, et si quid aliud sanae doctrinae aduersatur, quae est secundum euangelium gloriae beati dei, quod creditum est mihi. Gratias ago ei qui me confortauit, Christo Iesu domino nostro, quia fidelem me existimauit ponens in ministerio, qui prius blasphemus fui et persecutor et contumeliosus, sed misericordiam dei consecutus sum, quia ignorans feci in incredulitate. Superabundauit autem gratia domini nostri cum fide et dilectione quae est in Christo Iesu.

quoniam *Lucif* (= d_2) lex bona est *Bo* certum habens *Ambrst* quod *Ambrst* iusto lex *Lucif Ambrst* (= d_2) iniustis autem (uero *Cass Sang ambo B Bo*) *Lucif* (= d_2) inoboedientibus et *Lucif* non oboedientibus et *Lucif al loc* (= d_2) inobsequentibus *Ambrst* et scelestis (sceleratis *al loc*) et profanis *Lucif* (= d_2)[1] *Ambrst* (*sine pr* et) patricidis *Bo B Cass Sang ambo Lucif* (= d_2) patricidiis (parr- *al loc*) homicidis *om. Lucif al loc* d_2 *ord. turbat hic in latina*, *Ambrst add.* et *ante* forn. *B Bo* inpudicis *Lucif* (= d_2) fornicatoribus (fornicationibus *Cass*) homicidis (homicidiis *Cass* = d_2) *Ambrst* et *ante* periuris *om. Lucif Ambrst* (= d_2) sec. euang. est *Lucif al loc* (= d_2) et *ante* gratias *Lucif Ambrst* (= d_2) confortauit me *Lucif* in *ante* Christo *Ambrst* (= d_2) nostro *om. Lucif* quod *Lucif Bo B Sang ambo* (= d_2) aestimauit *Lucif Ambrst* (= d_2) (existimauit *B Bo*) me *post* ponens *Ambrst* (*om. B Bo*) ministerium *Lucif Ambrst* (= d_2) quia (*err. typogr.*) *Ambrst* (qui *B Bo*) fueram blas. *Lucif* (= d_2) eram (fui *Bo*) blas. *Ambrst* iniuriosus *Lucif* (= d_2) m. sum consec. *Lucif* m. consec. sum *Ambrst* (= d_2) quod *Lucif* (= d_2) qui *B* nondum credens *Ambrst* sunt *Ashb*

1 Tim. ii 1—4 = *Lucif* 250.

Obsecro igitur primum omnium fieri obsecrationes, orationes, postulationes, gratiarum actiones pro omnibus hominibus, pro regibus et omnibus qui in sublimitate sunt, ut quietam et tranquillam uitam agamus in omni pietate et castitate. Hoc enim bonum est et acceptum coram saluatore nostro deo, qui omnes homines uult saluos fieri et ad agnitionem ueritatis uenire.

obsecra d_2 exhortare *Ambrst* exhortor *rom* ergo *Ambrst* primo *Lucif Ashb* f. deprecationes *Ambrst* post. deprec. orat. *Bo* pro *ante* omnibus *Ambrst* (*non Bo*) sublimiori loco positi sunt *Ambrst* tranquillam et quietam *Lucif rom* placidam (placitam *B Bo*) et quietam *Ambrst* degamus *Ambrst* cum pietate et grauitate *Lucif* cum pietatem et castitatem d_2 est *om. Lucif* (= d_2) *B Bo* salutari *Lucif Ambrst* (= d_2) saluatore *B Bo* deo nostro *B* in *Ambrst* (= d_2)

[1] d_2 really has *est caelestis*.

1 Tim. iv 1—2 = *Lucif* 305.

Spiritus autem manifeste dicit, quia in nouissimis temporibus discedent quidam a fide attendentes spiritibus erroris et doctrinis daemoniorum, in hypocrisi loquentium mendacium et cauteriatam habentium suam conscientiam

manifesto *Ambrst* (*err. typ.?*)[1] recedent *Lucif Ambrst* (= d_2) recedant *B Bo* sp. seductoribus *Lucif* (= d_2) spiritus fallaces ac doctrinas *Ambrst* et *om. Lucif Bo B Sang ambo* (= d_2) simulatione *Ambrst* dissimulatione d_2 mendaciloquentium *Lucif* mendaciloquorum d_2 falsiloquorum *Ambrst* et *om. Lucif Ambrst* (= d_2) conscientiam suam *Lucif B Cass Sang ambo* mentem et conscientiam suam d_2 (*non in graeca* D_2) suam *om. Ambrst*

1 Tim. v 20—22 = *Lucif* 25, 250, 251.

Peccantes coram omnibus argue, ut et ceteri timorem habeant. Testor coram deo et Christo Iesu et electis angelis, ut haec custodias sine praeiudicio, nihil faciens in alteram partem declinando. Manus cito nemini imposueris, neque communicaueris peccatis alienis. Te ipsum castum custodi

delinquentem *Cass* delinquentes autem *Ambrst* peccantes autem d_2 et *om. Ambrst* metum *Ambrst* discrimine *Lucif* partem aliam declinans *Ambrst* aliam *Lucif* (= d_2) *post* partem *semel* sed aequitatem custodire *sine* declinando *Lucif* te commaculaueris *Ambrst rom* temet i. *Ambrst* serua *Lucif* (= d_2)

1 Tim. vi 2—5 = *Lucif* 25 f.

Haec doce et exhortare. Si quis aliter docet et non acquiescit sanis sermonibus domini nostri Iesu Christi, et ei, quae secundum pietatem est, doctrinae, superbus est, nihil sciens, sed languens circa quaestiones et pugnas uerborum, ex quibus oriuntur inuidiae, contentiones, blasphemiae, suspiciones malae, conflictationes hominum mente corruptorum et qui ueritate priuati sunt, existimantium quaestum esse pietatem

et (*ante* non) *om. Sang ambo B* adquiescet *Cass* huic *Cass Sang ambo B Bo* inflatus est autem *Lucif* (= d_2) superbit autem *Ambrst* superbus autem *Cass* superbit autem et *Sang ambo B Bo* aegrotat *Lucif* (= d_2) uerborum rixas *Lucif* (= d_2) fit inuidia *Cass Sang ambo B* nascuntur *Lucif* (= d_2) fiunt *Ambrst* malae *post, non ante* confl. *habet Lucif* conflictiones *Sang ambo B Bo* qui corrupti sunt mente *Ambrst* a ueritate destitutorum *Lucif* destitutorum a ueritate d_2 q. (*om. Cass Sang ambo B Bo*) u. caruerunt *Ambrst* (caruerant *B*) existimantes *Ambrst* *post* pietatem *add.* discede ab huiusmodi *Lucif* (*non* d_2) *add.* et dei culturam: discede ab huiusmodi *Ambrst*

[1] *manifesto* is the classical form of the adverb, but it was probably extinct at this time.

1 Tim. vi 20—21 = *Lucif* 26.

O Timothee, depositum custodi, deuitans profanas uocum nouitates et oppositiones falsi nominis scientiae, quam quidam promittentes circa fidem exciderunt

o *om. Ambrst* (*habent B Bo*) Thimothee *Lucif* (= d_2) commendatum *Ambrst* depositum commendatum *Bo* deuita *Cass* scientiae falsi nominis *Lucif* (= d_2) fallacis (fallaces *Sang ambo B Bo*) n. s. *Ambrst*

2 Tim. ii 16—17 = *Lucif* 28.

Profana autem et uaniloquia deuita : multum enim proficiunt ad impietatem, et sermo eorum ut cancer serpit

profanas (autem *add.* d_2) nouitates uocum deuita *Lucif* (= d_2) profanas autem uocum nouitates (inanitates *Ashb*) deuita *Ambrst* plurimum *Ambrst* proficient *Lucif Cass Bo B Sang ambo* (= d_2) inanitatem *Ambrst* (*at Cas. et rom, ut supra,* imp.) sermo enim (*sine* et) *Cass Sang ambo B Bo* sicut *Ambrst*

2 Tim. iii 1—5 = *Lucif* 305.

in nouissimis diebus instabunt tempora periculosa : erunt homines se ipsos amantes cupidi elati superbi blasphemi parentibus non obedientes ingrati scelesti sine affectione sine pace criminatores incontinentes immites, sine benignitate proditores proterui tumidi et uoluptatum amatores magis quam dei, habentes speciem quidem pietatis, uirtutem autem eius abnegantes ; et hos deuita

aduenient *Lucif* (= d_2) periculosa tempora *B* enim *post* erunt *add. Ambrst* et erunt (*sine* enim) *Bo Cass Sang ambo* erunt (*sine* enim) *B* sui tantum amatores *Ambrst* auari insolentes superbi *Ambrst* cupidi superbi fastidiosi *Lucif* auari fastidiosi superbi d_2 obsequentes *Ambrst* scelesti] impii *Ambrst* sine aff. sine pace] sine fide (foedere *Cass*) sine dilectione *Ambrst* fide (*ubi supra* pace) *Lucif* (= d_2) detractores *Lucif* (= d_2) bonorum inimici *Ambrst* (*ubi supra* sine benig.) inflati *Lucif* (= d_2) et *om. Lucif Ambrst* (= d_2) amatores uoluptatum *Ambrst* formam *Ambrst* quidem *om. Lucif Ambrst* (= d_2) autem *om. Sang ambo B Bo* ipsius negantes *Lucif* (= d_2)

2 Tim. iii 8—9 = *Lucif* 305.

quemadmodum autem Iannes et Mambres restiterunt Moysi, ita et hi resistunt ueritati, homines corrupti mente, reprobi circa fidem ; sed ultra non proficient ; insipientia enim eorum manifesta erit omnibus, sicut et illorum fuit

Iamnes *Lucif* (*ed. princ.*) *Cass Sang ambo Ashb m* 2 *B Bo* sic *Lucif* (= d_2) isti *Bo* resistent *Lucif* resisterunt d_2 mente* *Lucif* (mentem *an* mentes ?) et *ante* reprobi *Lucif* non prof. amplius *Ambrst* (proficiunt *B*) ignorantia *Ambrst* enim *om. Lucif* euidens *Ambrst*

2 Tim. iv 3—4 = *Lucif* 306.

Erit enim tempus cum sanam doctrinam non sustinebunt, sed ad sua desideria coaceruabunt sibi magistros prurientes auribus, et a ueritate quidem auditum auertent, ad fabulas autem conuertentur

enim *om. Lucif* (= d_2) propria *Cass* magistros sibi aggerent (aggregabunt *rom*) *Ambrst* aures *Lucif* (= d_2) auersabunt *Cass* uero *Ambrst*

Tit. i 5—14 = *Lucif* 196, 277.

Huius rei gratia reliqui te Cretae, ut ea quae desunt corrigas et constituas per ciuitates presbyteros, sicut et ego disposui tibi. Si quis sine crimine est, unius uxoris uir, filios habens fideles non in accusatione luxuriae aut non subditos. Oportet enim episcopum sine crimine esse sicut dei dispensatorem non superbum non iracundum non uinolentum non percussorem non turpis lucri cupidum, sed hospitalem, benignum, sobrium, iustum, sanctum, continentem, amplectentem eum qui secundum doctrinam est fidelem sermonem, ut potens sit exhortari in doctrina sana et eos qui contradicunt arguere. Sunt enim multi etiam inobedientes, uaniloqui, et seductores, maxime qui de circumcisione sunt, quos oportet redargui, qui uniuersas domos subuertunt docentes quae non oportet turpis lucri gratia [Dixit quidam ex illis proprius ipsorum propheta]: Cretenses semper mendaces, malae bestiae, uentres pigri. [Testimonium hoc uerum est.] Quam ob causam increpa illos dure, ut sani sint in fide, non intendentes Iudaicis fabulis et mandatis hominum auersantium se a ueritate

deerant *Lucif* (= d_2) presbyterium *Lucif* (= d_2) sicut ego tibi disposui *Lucif* (= d_2) tibi disposui *Ambrst* est sine crimine *Lucif Ambrst* (= d_2) mulieris *Ambrst* accusationem *Lucif* (= d_2) non subiectum *Lucif* non subiectos d_2 inobsequentes *Ambrst* disp. dei *Lucif* proteruum *Lucif Ambrst* (= d_2) uino deditum *Ambrst* turpilucrum *Lucif* (= d_2) turpia lucra appetentem *Ambrst* sobrium] prudentem *Ambrst* tenacem eius sermonis q. s. d. fidelis est *Ambrst* id quod *Lucif* (= d_2) fidem uerbi *Lucif* fidelis uerbi d_2 sana *om. Lucif* et contradicentes reuincere *Lucif Ambrst* (= d_2) (euincere *Troy Sang ambo* se uincere *B*) etiam *om. Ambrst* non subditi *Lucif* (= d_2) non obedientes *Ambrst* et n. o. *Cass Troy Sang ambo B*, (et *exp.*) *Bo* deceptores *Lucif* ii (hi *Cass Troy B* hii *Bo*) *ante* qui *Ambrst* ex *Lucif* (= d_2) sunt ex circumcisione *Ambrst* ex circ. sunt d_2 euertunt *Lucif* (= d_2) dixit—propheta *non sunt ap Lucif citata* ipsis *Ambrst* eorum *Ambrst* (= d_2) testimonium—est *non sunt ap Lucif citata* rem *Lucif* argue *Ambrst* acriter *Lucif* (= d_2) attendentes *rom* auertentium *rom* (= d_2) aduersantium *Bo*[1]

Tit. ii 6—8 = *Lucif* 197.

Iuuenes similiter hortare ut sobrii sint. In omnibus te ipsum praebe exem-

iuniores *Ambrst* continentes esse *Ambrst* in omnibus *cum anterioribus iungit, et* per omnia *ante* te *ponit Lucif* per omnia temet (te *B Bo* et *Troy*) ipsum *Ambrst* formam praebens *Lucif* praebens formam d_2 praebens exemplum *Ambrst*

[1] This error is one of the most frequent in MSS.

plum bonorum operum, in doctrina in integritate in grauitate, uerbum sanum irreprehensibile, ut is qui ex aduerso est uereatur nihil habens malum dicere de nobis

in sermone sanum inreprehensibilem *Lucif* sermonem sanum inrepraehensibilem d_2 ut aduersarius reuereatur *Lucif* $(=d_2)$ is] his *B fort. recte* e (ex *Bo*) diuerso *Ambrst* reuereatur *Ambrst* ut *ante* nihil *ins. Sang pr m.* d. d. n.] quod dicere malum de nobis *Lucif* quod dicere de nobis malum d_2 dicere de nobis (bonis *B* uobis *Bo*) dignum reprehensione *Ambrst*

Tit. ii 11—15 = *Lucif* 198, 277 f.

Apparuit enim gratia dei saluatoris nostri omnibus hominibus erudiens nos ut abnegantes impietatem et saecularia desideria sobrie et iuste et pie uiuamus in hoc saeculo, expectantes beatam spem et aduentum gloriae magni dei et saluatoris nostri Iesu Christi qui dedit semet ipsum pro nobis ut nos redimeret ab omni iniquitate et mundaret sibi populum acceptabilem sectatorem bonorum operum. Haec loquere et exhortare et argue cum omni imperio. Nemo te contemnat

inluxit *Lucif Ambrst* $(=d_2)$ corripiens *Lucif* $(=d_2)$ abnegata impietate et saecularibus desideriis *Ambrst* (*non Bo*) ac des. saec. *Lucif semel* sobrie] temperanter *Ambrst* et pie et iuste *Lucif* (*at semel ut Vulg*) in *Lucif* beati *Ambrst* (*at Bo rom ut supra*) pro nobis se ipsum *Lucif* $(=d_2)$ liberaret nos *Lucif* $(=d_2)$ redimeret nos *Ambrst* (*non Bo*) mundet *Lucif* $(=d_2)$ emundaret *Ambrst* (mundaret *B*) accept.] abundantem *Lucif Ambrst* $(=d_2)$ peculiarem *rom* aemulatorem *Lucif Ambrst* $(=d_2)$ sectatorem (sectatorem *eras.*) et emulatorem *Bo*

Tit. iii 1—7 = *Lucif* 278.

Admone illos principibus et potestatibus subditos esse dicto obedire ad omne opus bonum paratos esse neminem blasphemare non litigiosos esse sed modestos omnem ostendentes mansuetudinem ad omnes homines. Eramus enim aliquando et nos insipientes increduli errantes seruientes desideriis et uoluptatibus uariis in malitia et inuidia agentes odibiles odientes inuicem. Cum autem benignitas et humanitas apparuit saluatoris nostri dei non ex operibus iustitiae quae fecimus nos sed secundum suam misericordiam saluos

principatibus *Ambrst* magistratibus *Lucif* dicto *om. Lucif* $(=d_2)$ *Cass Sang alt B Bo Troy* oboedientes *Lucif* $(=d_2)$ ostendentes omnem mans. *Ambrst* E. e. a.] Nam eramus (e. enim *Cass Troy Sang ambo Ashb B Bo*) quondam *Ambrst* fuimus *Lucif* $(=d_2)$ aliquando et nos] et nos quondam *B Bo* et nos aliquando *Lucif* stulti et incredibiles *Lucif* $(=d_2)$ inconsulti inobsequentes *Ambrst* (non sequentes *Troy Sang alt*) odio nos i. habentes *Ambrst* alterutrum *Lucif* sed cum *Lucif* $(=d_2)$ cum uero *Ambrst* bonitas *Ambrst* inluxit *Lucif* $(=d_2)$ *Ambrst* salutaris dei nostri *Ambrst* (*B Bo ut supra*) nos fecimus *Lucif Ambrst* (f. n. *Bo*) misericordiam suam *Ambrst* (*non Bo*) nos fecit per lauacrum regenerationis et renouationis spiritus sancti quem effundit in nos abunde per Iesum Christum saluatorem nostrum ut iustificati gratia ipsius heredes secundum spem uitae aeternae

per spiritum sanctum *Lucif* $(=d_2)$ effudit *Lucif Ambrst* (vg[dem] d_2 etc.) nobis *Lucif* honeste *Lucif* $(=d_2)$ Christum Iesum *B Sang ambo* illius *Ambrst* efficiamur (simus *Bo*) *add. post* heredes *Lucif Ambrst* $(=d_2)$ aeternae *om. Lucif*

Tit. iii 9—11 = *Lucif* 30.

Stultas autem quaestiones et genealogias et contentiones et pugnas legis deuita: sunt enim inutiles et uanae. Hereticum hominem post unam et secundam correptionem deuita, sciens quia subuersus est qui eiusmodi est et delinquit cum sit proprio iudicio condemnatus

autem] *om. Lucif* ergo *B* originum enumerationes *Ambrst* contentionem *Cass Troy Sang ambo B Bo* lites *Lucif* $(=d_2)$ primam *Ambrst* et secundam *om. Lucif Ambrst* $(=d_2)$ correptionem] *add.* et duo d_2 quoniam *Lucif* $(=d_2)$ quod *Ambrst* peruersus *Lucif Ambrst* $(=d_2)$ qui eiusmodi est *om. Lucif* huiusmodi (*pro* q. e. e.) *Ambrst* $(=d_2)$ peccat *Lucif* $(=d_2)$ derelinquitur *Bo* cum sit *om. Ambrst* propr. iud.] a semet ipso *Lucif Ambrst* $(=d_2)$ damnatus *Lucif Ambrst* $(=d_2)$

INDEXES.

I. LATIN WORDS.

II. BIBLICAL QUOTATIONS.